Fiscal Systems and Practices in Asian Countries

PRAEGER SPECIAL STUDIES IN
INTERNATIONAL ECONOMICS AND DEVELOPMENT

Fiscal Systems and Practices in Asian Countries

Angel Q. Yoingco
Ruben F. Trinidad

FREDERICK A. PRAEGER, Publishers
New York · Washington · London

The purpose of the Praeger Special Studies is to make specialized research monographs in U.S. and international economics and politics available to the academic, business, and government communities. For further information, write to the Special Projects Division, Frederick A. Praeger, Publishers, 111 Fourth Avenue, New York, N.Y. 10003.

FREDERICK A. PRAEGER, PUBLISHERS
111 Fourth Avenue, New York, N.Y. 10003, U.S.A.
77-79 Charlotte Street, London, W.1, England

Published in the United States of America in 1968
by Frederick A. Praeger, Inc., Publishers

To

Fé and Lilia

PREFACE

This work is a comparative study of the fiscal systems of twelve selected Asian countries: Ceylon, the Republic of China, India, Indonesia, Japan, South Korea, Malaysia, Philippines, Singapore, Thailand, South Vietnam, and Cambodia.* It deals with the revenue, expenditure, and public debt patterns and policies of these countries, with emphasis on taxation.

The study was undertaken in response to the long-felt need expressed by the delegates from various Asian countries at the Japan Tax Association Special Meeting in Tokyo, April 6-16, 1963, for exchanging ideas on fiscal matters, such as tax policy and tax system, taxation for foreign corporations and aliens, special measures for industrial development, tax administration, and various problems relating to the avoidance of double taxation. The authors acknowledge with appreciation their designation by the late Secretary of Finance of the Philippines, Rodrigo Perez, as representatives of the Philippines to this tax meeting.

Among the important sources of information are the papers presented by members of the various delegations who attended the meeting and interviews with them. Those interviewed were: Chen Shao-shu, Director of Taxation Bureau, and Shao Horng-biau, Chief of Direct Tax Division, both of the Ministry of Finance, Republic of China; Shri V. T. Dehejia, former Secretary, Department of Revenue and Expenditure, Ministry of Finance, India; R. Santoso Brotodihardjo,

---

*Certain aspects of Cambodia's fiscal patterns are discussed only in Chapters 4, 5, and 11.

former Chief of Tax Directorate, Department of Revenue, Expenditure and Control, Indonesia; Kim Dong Soo, Director of Taxation Bureau, Ministry of Finance, South Korea; H. W. T. Pepper, Adviser on Federal Taxation, Malaysia and Lim Leong Seng, Deputy Comptroller-General, Inland Revenue, Malaysia; Leong Hong Toh, Acting Deputy Commissioner, Inland Revenue, State of Singapore; Luang Akranitniyom, former Deputy Director-General, Revenue Department, and Nai Paichitr Rojanavanich, Chief of Foreign Corporation Income Tax, Thailand; Vu Thien Vinh, Director-General of Taxation, Ministry of Finance, South Vietnam; Phan Thul, Director General des Impots from the Kingdom of Cambodia; A. J. van den Tempel, Chairman, Fiscal Committee of O.E.C.D.; Robert L. Chandler, former Representative in Manila, U.S. Internal Revenue Service; Taizo Hayashi, Chief of the International Tax Affairs Section; and Naoyuki Matsui, Vice-Director of the Tax Bureau, both from the Ministry of Finance, Japan.

After the meeting, further information was obtained by correspondence with these Asian tax officials. The exchange of fiscal materials, such as Internal and Customs Revenue Codes, tax publications, and other printed materials, with some of the Asian tax officials proved quite useful. The helpful suggestions and clarifications made by H. W. T. Pepper during one of his visits to the Philippines should also be mentioned. Assistance of the different diplomatic and consular offices in the Philippines was solicited. Finally, the libraries of various government and educational institutions were utilized in an attempt to provide a thorough background of the fiscal systems.

In spite of all these efforts, not all twelve countries are discussed in each chapter. Nevertheless, the authors sincerely hope that the study can contribute to the expansion of the meager information about these countries' fiscal systems.

The authors wish to express their sincere appreciation to the Japan Tax Association, particularly its General Manager, Hideyasu Iwasaki, for the use of its materials, including those relating to the proceedings of the Special Meeting of 1963.

Our gratitude also goes to Dr. Amando M. Dalisay, Andres Soriano Professor of Economics in the Graduate School of the University of the East, for his abiding interest in the study. We thank Professor Jesse Burkhead of Syracuse University for reviewing the manuscript, and we appreciate the encouragement for publication given by Professor Oliver Oldman of Harvard University and Dr. Harvey S. Perloff of Resources for the Future, Inc.

Appreciation is due to the National Research Council of the Philippines for financing this research project.

Finally, for their assistance in the research work, the authors are indebted to Victor C. Macalincag, Rolando P. Mendoza, and Mrs. Beatriz Uy Cura, members of the faculty, Department of Economics, Philippine College of Commerce; Miss Nilda D. Vasquez, Amelito B. Cura, Danilo R. Cueto and Mrs. Julia R. London, members of the faculty, School of Business and Economics, Lyceum of the Philippines; Reynaldo P. Palmiery, Victor Borromeo, Benjamin Santos, and Miss Minda Caoile, researchers, Joint Legislative-Executive Tax Commission. The authors are also grateful to Antonio O. Casem, Jr., Chief, Fiscal Policy Staff, Joint Legislative-Executive Tax Commission, and to Dr. Avelino B. Lim, Associate Lecturer of the Graduate School of Public Administration, University of the Philippines, for assistance given in editing the final manuscript. Acknowledgments are also due to Augurio Collantes, Librarian of the Tax Commission, for checking the footnotes.

Notwithstanding the immeasurable help given by all these, the statements made and views expressed are solely the responsibilities of the authors.

A.Q.Y.

R.F.T.

CONTENTS

Appendixes

Appendixes   Page

LIST OF TABLES

LIST OF CHARTS

Fiscal Systems and Practices in Asian Countries

CHAPTER **1** INTRODUCTION

In order to gain insights into the problems
with which developing nations have to contend with
respect to their socio-economic growth, it is necessary to explore their fiscal and economic policies,
systems, and practices, as well as the forces which
made exigent their integration in a country's fiscal and economic pattern.

The countries covered in this study are Cambodia, Ceylon, the Republic of China, India, Indonesia,
Japan, South Korea, the Federation of Malaya (now
Malaysia), the Philippines, Singapore,* Thailand,
and South Vietnam.

To concentrate on one particular country would
not be too arduous, since virtually all aspects of
its fiscal system could be explored. But the task
acquires new dimensions when the investigations are
widened to encompass the amalgam of policies, techniques, and practices in these twelve Asian countries, each with its own cultural milieu, its unique
political setting, and its own particular stages of

---

*Together with Malaya, Sabah (North Borneo),
and Sarawak, Singapore formed the Federation of
Malaysia on September 16, 1963. With the enactment
of Malaysia's Finance Act of 1965 which took effect
on January 1, 1965, Singapore's income tax system
became identical with that of the States of Malaya,
although Singapore remained responsible for the collection of income tax within its territorial jurisdiction. Considering that this study discusses the
tax system of Singapore prior to the enactment of
the Finance Act of 1965, Singapore's withdrawal from
the Federation on August 9, 1965, does not affect
the discussion.

1

economic development. To investigate all twelve, it
is possible to focus only on specific fiscal and economic areas by describing their outstanding features,
and from them, to try to derive meaningful comparisons and extract data which will yield salient clues
concerning fiscal and economic make-up.

Consequently, this work is not an exhaustive
compendium of all the policies, practices, and techniques which permeate the fiscal and economic structures of the countries studied. It is not appropriate to apply one's own standards to a particular
country because fiscal systems are not to be treated
as mere replicas of others, and the countries encompassed in the study are not cast in a common mold.
Still, any similarities that can be found will be
helpful in understanding the economic approaches
they adopt. This study attempts to portray these
similarities. More important, however, than the
particular fiscal and economic tools and techniques
of the countries are the features of their economic
and fiscal policies that are unique. In evaluating
these features, it must be kept in mind that a suitable technique adopted by one country may be wholly
unsuitable for another.

There are other basic limitations to this study.

First, the use of the exchange rate would be a
sound gauge for comparing tax rates if standard of
living, purchasing power, earning capacity of the
people and wage rates existing in all the countries
were relatively the same. But since these conditions
vary from country to country, the use of the exchange
rate is apt to be unreliable and would only lead to
distortions of the comparative effects of their respective tax systems.

Second, in comparing the tax structures of the
various Asian countries, a number of technical difficulties arise which hamper precise comparison.
Among these are the differences in the conceptions
of types of taxes, the coverage and scope of these
taxes, classification schemes, and the publication

and availability of data. However, by adjusting the
coverage of the types of taxes and, in some instances,
reclassifying some items, data can be compared.

Third, the paucity of materials poses another
stumbling block to a thorough, incisive study. Some
of the source materials are tax codes of the countries studied, annual reports, books, conference proceedings, brochures, studies, and technical publications. But other data, that would have facilitated
a more thorough study, were unavailable.

Basic research was conducted in order to bring
into focus the different types of taxes and their
relative importance. To show the different emphasis
that each country places on the disbursement of public funds, an analysis of the expenditure pattern of
each country was undertaken. A comparative assessment of the role of public debt in financing government requirements was also made, as well as an analysis
of tax-incentive measures to promote economic growth
and stability in the selected Asian countries. Among
the incentives discussed are those dealing with the
promotion of new industries and of export industries.

The subject matter covered in the study is discussed in relation to the Philippine setting. Because the Philippines is a developing country experiencing drastic changes in its pursuit of an accelerated pace of economic development, the fruitful features of the fiscal systems of other Asian countries
which are not found in the Philippines are outlined
and evaluated to determine their adaptability and ap-
plicability in the Philippines.

CHAPTER **2** PERSONAL

INCOME TAX

   Income brackets, tax rates, and exemptions re-
flect significant features of an individual income
tax system, including the level of exemptions, progressivity, flexibility, and the level of personal
income taxation in general.

   Since, as will be seen, some of the countries
studied have different tax rates for various types
of income, certain assumptions must be made to facilitate comparison and analysis. For instance, South
Korea levies different tax rates on five classes of
income: (1) real estate income, (2) dividend and
interest income, (3) business income, (4) wages and
salaries, and (5) other income. As a basis of analysis, it is assumed that income from salaries and
wages and other incomes represent income of the majority of the taxpayers in South Korea. Similarly,
South Vietnam imposes three sets of tax rates on two
classes of income: profits realized by individuals
and salaries and wages. In addition to the two sets
of tax rates imposed exclusively on each type, a
general income tax is also applied. Again, it is
assumed that the income arising from salaries and
wages constitutes the income of the majority of the
taxpayers.

   Comparison is difficult because of the absence
of a common denominator. Ostensibly, the foreign
exchange rate proffers a good basis for reducing all
currencies to a common factor. However, its use is
apt to introduce some distortions, considering the
varied political, social, cultural, and economic conditions in these countries. For instance, if the
U.S. dollar were to be used as a common factor, the

4

equivalent of 360 yen in Japan might not buy the same
amount of goods as ₱4 in the Philippines.[1] This variance in purchasing power of the two currencies needs
to be assessed in considering the tax burden or sacrifice; thus the tax burden of the Filipino taxpayer may
not be the same as that of his Japanese counterpart,
given the same amount of income expressed in U.S.
dollars.

Furthermore, because of the differences in standards of living in various countries, it would be quite
erroneous to conclude that a married taxpayer with
three dependents in the United States with a gross income of $4,000 is taxed less in spite of the tax rate
of 20 per cent on the first taxable bracket. With
such an income, a Filipino taxpayer will pay 880
pesos or U.S. $220 while a taxpayer in Japan will pay
203,000 yen or U.S. $564; both amounts are compara-
tively higher than the U.S. $120 tax the American has
to pay.

Even if the taxpayers in these selected countries pay more in terms of dollars, it is probable
that the rate of income tax will not be as heavy as
it is in the United States because of the different
conditions mentioned earlier. All other things remaining the same, if the extent of taxation were to be
determined by converting all currencies into a single
currency, then taxpayers in countries with higher con-
version rates in relation to the U.S. dollar would
have a heavier tax burden than the American taxpayer.

Furthermore, using the exchange rate would not
take into account such factors as comparative living
standards, production costs, taxable capacities, and
stages of economic development.

Since the use of the exchange rate in determining the relative burden of income taxation is not
feasible, percentages or ratios have to be used in a
comparative study of this nature in order to consider
the variables of the different countries.

Table 2 gives an idea of the U.S. dollar equivalent of each country's currency.

TABLE 1

Tax Liability on Equivalent Incomes of a Family of Three
Dependents for United States, Philippines, and Japan

	U. S.		Philippines		Japan
Gross income	$4,000		₱16,000		¥1,440,000
Less personal exemptions and standard deduction:					
For the taxpayer	$ 600	)₱3,000		¥110,000	
For the wife	600	)		105,000	
For 3 child dependents	1,800	3,000		105,000	
Standard deduction	400	1,000	7,000	—	320,000
	3,400				
Taxable income	$ 600		₱ 9,000		¥1,120,000
Tax due in respective currencies	$ 120		₱ 880		¥ 203,000
Tax due in U.S. dollars	$ 120		$ 220		$ 564

Note: Gross incomes for the Philippines and Japan were derived by multiplying
U.S. $4,000 by the exchange rates of the two countries, i.e., by ₱4 and
¥360, respectively.

TABLE 2

Dollar-Exchange Rate of Currencies
of Selected Asian Countries

Country	Currency	Equivalent of U.S. $1*
Cambodia	Riel (J)	35
Republic of China	NT Dollar (NT$)	NT$ 40.03
India	Rupee (Rs)	Rs 4.7619
Indonesia	Rupiah (Rp)	Rp 45
Japan	Yen (¥)	¥360
Federation of Malaysia	Malaysian Dollar (M$)	M$3
Philippines	Peso (₱)	₱3.89
Singapore	Malaysian Dollar (M$)	M$3
South Korea**	Won (Won)	Won 130
South Vietnam	Piastre (VN$)	VN$ 60
Thailand	Baht (Baht)	Baht 20.50

Sources of basic data: Reports of Consulates of the above Asian countries in the Philippines.

*As of April, 1963. Since 1963, however, the following countries have devaluated their currencies: India ($1 to Rs 7.50), effective June 6, 1966; Indonesia ($1 to 10 new Rp or 10,000 old Rp), effective January, 1966; Philippines ($1 to ₱3.90), effective November, 1965; Singapore ($1 to M$3.06), August 9, 1965; and South Vietnam ($1 to VN$ 118), effective June, 1966.

**The currency of South Korea was changed from hwan (HW) to won in 1962. (See n. 11 to Chapter 5, p. 85.)

INDIVIDUAL INCOME TAXATION

Republic of China (Taiwan)[2]

The tax rates in China rise progressively from 3 per cent to 40 per cent. The taxable income is divided into eleven brackets, the lowest tax rate applying to the first NT$ 50,000, and the highest applying to income in excess of NT$ 1,000,000.

A basic personal exemption of NT$ 6,000 is allowed to the taxpayer. If he is married, an additional amount of NT$ 6,000 is allowed for his spouse. Furthermore, an exemption of NT$ 6,000 is given to each of the following:

(1) Any ancestor of the taxpayer or his spouse more than sixty years of age who is dependent on the taxpayer for support;
(2) Any brother or sister of the taxpayer who is either less than twenty years of age, or more than twenty years of age if in school or disabled and unable to support himself; or
(3) All other dependents who are regarded as relatives pursuant to Article 1114 or 1123 of the Civil Code and are less than twenty or more than sixty years of age and are unable to support themselves.[3]

From the above exemptions, it will be observed that the clannish nature of the Chinese family is recognized by tax statutes.

India

In addition to the ordinary income tax, India imposes a supertax on the same income. However, the latter is levied only on the upper-income brackets. In addition, a fixed surcharge of 5 per cent is imposed on both the income tax and the supertax, after a certain level of income is reached.

The rationale of the supertax is to inject the element of progressivity in the higher-income levels. Specifically, the supertax attaches when the ordinary income tax imposed becomes a flat rate. As outlined in Appendix I, all income in excess of Rs 20,000 is subject to a flat rate of 25 per cent ordinary income tax. There is one basic difference between ordinary income tax and supertax: Certain deductions or exemptions allowed in computing the ordinary income tax are not available in determining the supertax. Taxable income is divided into fifteen brackets, starting at the income bracket of Rs 3,000 to Rs 5,000 at a rate of 3 per cent and ending at an income bracket of above Rs 70,000 at the highest tax rate of 25 per cent. The supertax starts at a level of taxable income above Rs 20,000 and ranges from 8 per cent to 47.5 per cent. Thus, the effective tax rate for the taxable bracket of Rs 20,000-Rs 25,000 is 33 per cent, assuming that the tax base for determining both the ordinary income tax and the supertax is the same. On the other hand, the surcharge of 5 per cent is uniformly applied on all brackets above Rs 7,500.

Limitations are set on exemptions. The exemption of Rs 3,000 is allowed only to a married individual whose taxable income does not exceed Rs 20,000. If it exceeds that amount, his basic exemption amounts to only Rs 1,000, the same amount allowed to an unmarried taxpayer.

Thus the coverage of the first taxable bracket subject to 3 per cent is expanded from Rs 3,000-Rs 5,000 bracket to Rs 1,000-Rs 5,000 bracket.

The taxpayer is allowed only Rs 300 for each of the first two child dependents, or a maximum exemption of Rs 600.

The computation of the surcharge is based on both earned and unearned income.[4] In addition to the 5 per cent surcharge normally levied on total income, a surcharge of 15 per cent is levied on the tax due on unearned income.

If the spouse of a taxpayer has an income, the
filing of a joint return is not required unless
(1) the spouse's income is derived from membership
in a firm carrying on a business in which the taxpayer is also a partner, or (2) the spouse's income
is derived from assets transferred by the taxpayer
(other than those connected with an agreement to
live apart).

Japan

The individual income tax of Japan is highly
progressive. The tax rates range from 8 per cent on
taxable income not exceeding ¥100,000 to 75 per cent
on taxable income above ¥60,000,000. There are fifteen taxable income brackets.

A basic exemption of ¥110,000 is allowed the
taxpayer. An additional ¥105,000 exemption is allowed for the taxpayer's wife provided that she
lives with the taxpayer and that her income for the
taxable year does not exceed ¥50,000. The amount of
exemptions allowed for dependents depends on the
wife's income. If it does not exceed ¥50,000, the
taxpayer is entitled to ¥50,000 for each dependent
fifteen years old and over and ¥35,000 for those
under fifteen years. If no exemption for the wife
is allowed because her income is above ¥50,000, the
taxpayer is allowed ¥70,000 for the first dependent
who is fifteen years or more, ¥50,000 for subsequent
dependents fifteen years or more, and ¥35,000 for
those younger than fifteen.

"Dependent" is defined as "any relative (excluding a spouse) supported by a taxpayer in one household and having an income of not more than ¥50,000."
With this definition, the term includes all blood
relatives of the taxpayer, no matter how distantly
related they are.

Another unusual feature of the individual income
tax system of Japan is its provision for numerous
tax credits.[5] The amount of the tax can be greatly
reduced if the total tax credit is significant. In
addition to credit for foreign taxes, ¥6,000 each is

allowed for the physically handicapped, the aged,
widows, and working students, subject to certain conditions. Moreover, certain percentages of contributions made and dividends received by the taxpayer
are also allowed as tax credit.

Malaysia

The taxable income is divided into thirteen
brackets ranging from M$2,500 to income in excess of
M$55,000. The tax rates applied on the brackets
rise from 6 per cent to 45 per cent.[6]

A personal exemption of M$2,000 is given to the
taxpayer. Likewise, his spouse is entitled to an exemption allowance of M$1,000 in addition to the re-
liefs given to child dependents which amount to M$750
for the first child, M$500 for each of the next two,
and M$300 each for the fourth and fifth child.

If the child is being educated and maintained
outside of Malaysia, the taxpayer is entitled to an
exemption equal to the amount he actually spends for
the child, but this amount must not exceed twice the
corresponding legal deduction.

Furthermore, the taxpayer is granted earned income relief equal to 10 per cent of the earned income but this amount should not exceed M$1,000.
This benefit is allowed only on income derived from
employment or pension, or from a trade, business,
profession, or vocation in which the taxpayer is engaged either as owner or working partner. This is
in addition to the other deductions which the taxpayer in Malaysia can claim.

Philippines

The Philippine income tax structure is relatively progressive. It has twenty-three income brackets,
ranging from ₱2,000 to over ₱500,000. The tax rates
range from a low 3 per cent to 60 per cent.

The basic exemption of the taxpayer depends upon
his civil status. If he is single, he is entitled to

₱1,800, whereas if he is either married or head of
the family, his exemption is ₱3,000. One is considered to be head of a family, even if he is not married, if he has dependents.

The taxpayer is also allowed an additional personal exemption of ₱1,000 for each child dependent,
with no limits placed on the number. Under the
Philippine Income Tax Law, child dependents are those
who are under twenty-three years of age, unmarried,
and not gainfully employed, or incapable of self-
support due to mental or physical defects.

A taxpayer in the Philippines can either use
itemized deductions (which he is required to support
with receipts and proofs) to arrive at the taxable
income, or use the standard deduction of 10 per cent
of the gross income, the amount not to exceed ₱1,000.

Singapore[7]

In Singapore there are thirteen brackets, the
lowest bracket not exceeding M$1,500 and the highest
amounting to more than M$100,000. Tax rates range
from 5 per cent to 55 per cent.

The taxpayer is allowed a basic exemption of
M$2,000 and an additional M$1,000 for his wife. An
exemption of M$750 is given for the first child,
M$500 each for the second and third children, M$300
each for the fourth and fifth children, and M$200
each for the sixth, seventh, eighth, and ninth children. If the child is being educated and maintained
outside of Singapore, the taxpayer is entitled to an
exemption equal to the amount he actually spends for
the child, but this amount may not exceed twice the
corresponding legal deduction.

There is also allowed as a deduction 20 per
cent of the earned income up to a maximum of M$1,000.

South Korea

Different tax rates apply to various classes of
income. The tax on real estate income rises progres-

sively from a minimum of 15 per cent on income not
exceeding 60,000 won to a maximum of 45 per cent on
income exceeding 540,000 won. Net income realized
from business is subject to tax rates ranging from
15 per cent to 45 per cent. Gross wages and salaries
are subject to two tax rates: (1) a flat 7 per cent
on daily or hourly wages of persons who have no definite employer, and (2) progressive tax rates of 7
per cent to 35 per cent on wages and salaries earned
by persons other than those mentioned in (1). Gross
income from sources other than wages and salaries is
subject to graduated tax rates of 7-35 per cent.

Personal exemptions are not computed with respect to the total income. Rather, the tax exemption is based on the computed tax for each type of
income. In other words, no tax liability attaches
to any type of income unless it exceeds the statutory limit. For example, if the computed tax on
real estate income does not exceed 1,500 won, no tax
has to be paid. Specific exemptions have also been
set for other types of income.

South Vietnam

Different income tax rates are applied to various classes of income. Income from salaries and
wages is subject to both the income tax and the general income tax. Individual income arising from
profit is subject to a profit tax of 16 per cent and
the general income tax.

Appendix I shows that, if the general income
tax rates are added to both the profit tax rates and
the tax rates on salaries and wages, the effective
tax rates for profits will still be greater than
those for income arising from salaries and wages.

The income tax on salaries and wages, which
starts at 1 per cent and ends at 16 per cent, is applied progressively on five taxable income brackets
ranging from the first VN$ 50,000, up to more than
1 million VN$. The general income tax, on the other
hand, ranges from 1 per cent to 50 per cent and is
levied on eighteen income brackets starting from the

first VN$ 10,000 and ending at a level in excess of
VN$ 800,000.

Personal deductions include abatements (the
equivalent of personal exemptions in the Philippines
and other countries) and family allowances. The following abatements are provided by law: (1) VN$
30,000 for single persons and the head of a household; (2) VN$ 15,000 for taxpayer's spouse, provided
that her income or salary does not exceed VN$ 15,000;
(3) VN$ 5,000 each for child dependents under age
twenty-one who do not earn income and are supported
by the taxpayer, or child dependents under age twenty-
five who are either studying in universities or physically handicapped; and (4) VN$ 3,000 for each parent
or grandparent who is either more than the age of
sixty and supported by the taxpayer or less than
sixty years but who is incapable of self-support.

Family allowances are granted, the amount depending upon whether the taxpayer is employed privately or by the government. Even if the taxpayer derives his income from a private firm, the amount of
family allowance varies depending upon his national-
ity. European and other foreign resident taxpayers
who are married are entitled to a maximum allowance
of VN$ 8,604 with additional allowances for children
which increase up to the fifth child and decrease
thereafter. By contrast, privately employed Vietnamese and Asian resident taxpayers who are married are
allowed only a maximum of VN$ 5,544 and additional
allowances for child dependents.

Government employees are entitled to larger family allowances. Married individuals are given
VN$ 8,400. For child dependents, the taxpayer is
entitled to an amount more than twice that allowed
to Vietnamese and Asian resident taxpayers and more
than one and a half times that accorded European and
foreign resident taxpayers.

Thailand

There are ten taxable income brackets on which
tax rates ranging from 10 per cent to 50 per cent are

levied. The lowest tax rate is imposed on income
not exceeding 10,000 baht, and the highest on income
over 400,000 baht.

A taxpayer is given a basic personal exemption
of 4,000 baht and an additional 2,000 baht for his
wife. He is allowed 900 baht for each legitimate or
adopted child under twenty-five years old who is
studying in a university. The same amount of exemption is given for minor children and those regarded
as incompetent. Exemption is not allowed for a child
dependent who earns an income of at least 1,000 baht.

Instead of itemized deductions, the individual
taxpayers are provided with standard deductions as
offset against gross income. A 20 per cent deduction on income derived from employment is allowed,
but the amount may not exceed 20,000 baht. With respect to rental income, the rates of standard deduction vary from 10 per cent to 30 per cent, depending
upon the type of the property leased. A 30 per cent
deduction is allowed on income from the practice of
a profession specified by royal decrees, such as law,
medicine, engineering, architecture, accountancy,
and fine arts; 80 per cent on the income of contractors; and 75-90 per cent on income from business, industry, or any other occupation.

Thailand does not allow any form of tax credit.

Other Countries

Cambodia

Cambodia levies three types of income tax:
(a) tax on profit, (b) general income tax, and (c)
tax on pay, salary, pension, and life annuity.

Income from profit is divided into fifteen taxable brackets, the lowest bracket not exceeding ₫30,000
and the highest over ₫700,000. The tax rates range
from 13-62 per cent. Similarly, income subject to
the general income tax has fifteen taxable brackets
with tax rates ranging from 1-50 per cent. The lowest and the highest taxable incomes are the same as

those of income arising from profit. On the other
hand, incomes from pay, salary, pension, and life
annuity are subject to rates ranging from 1-40 per
cent, imposed on taxable income consisting of nine-
teen brackets that range from Ɉ 18,000 to over
Ɉ600,000.

Taxpayers with income subject to either the
profit tax or the general income tax are allowed the
same exemptions. Personal deduction varies according to the type of income. The taxpayer is allowed
Ɉ14,000 for himself and Ɉ7,000 for each of the following: (a) his wife, provided that she is not
divorced from the taxpayer and not subject to a separate tax; (b) any child dependent who is either a
minor or disabled, and (c) any ascendent who is dependent, over sixty years of age, or disabled. Personal
exemptions are allowed for the wife or for children
separated from the head of the family and living outside of Cambodia.

A taxpayer subject to the tax on pay, salary,
pension, and life annuity is allowed a personal exemption of Ɉ9,600 for himself and Ɉ7,200 for his
wife; Ɉ7,200 may be allowed for each child dependent, depending on the child's age and educational
attainment.

Indonesia

Indonesia imposes three sets of tax rates.
There are eleven categories on which progressive
taxes are paid, ranging from Rp 20 to Rp 830. One
tax table consists of amounts of tax imposed on the
different income categories which are based on outward signs of prosperity.

The second table permits the taxable income to
be subject to the ordinary tax rates. This table
does not provide the tax in terms of rates, but in
absolute amounts. There are twenty-one taxable income levels starting from 0 to Rp 1,800,000, with
the tax ranging from 0 to Rp 1,063,050. An additional tax is imposed on each full Rp 100 in all taxable
income levels.

Income arising from salaries and wages is subject to graduated tax rates levied on gross income
above Rp 3,000. Graduated tax rates from 2-5 per
cent are levied on gross income of Rp 3,000 and over,
but such taxable income may not exceed Rp 24,000.

A basic exemption of Rp 3,000 is allowed for the
taxpayer. In addition, he is allowed a family deduction of Rp 600. The same amount is provided for the
taxpayer's legitimate wife, for each member of his
family, and for immediate relatives whom he fully
supports, including adopted children. This family
deduction is, however, limited to a maximum of twelve
persons.

TAX STRUCTURES

Extent of Income Subject to
the Minimum Tax Rate

To insure comparability, the following assumptions will be made: (1) that the income considered
is that of a family consisting of five members, (2)
that the term "income" shall mean the income of five
persons arrived at by multiplying by 5 the per capita
income[8] in each country, and (3) that the amount of
personal exemptions allowed in each country is that
which conforms to the maintenance of a certain standard of living. This analysis will determine how much
income must be earned by a taxpayer for him to be
subject to the minimum tax rate. To achieve this objective, the ratio of the total exemption of a family
of five members to total income of the same family
will be established.

All the countries except Japan and Thailand
have lower incomes compared to what is considered
the amount necessary to maintain a certain living
standard. As for Japan and Thailand, Japan has the
highest per capita income in southeast Asia, while
Thailand has one of the lowest levels of personal
exemption.

Table 3 shows that in most of the countries under study, the taxpayers would have to raise their incomes by 37 to 209 per cent to be subject to the lowest income tax rate. In the Philippines,[9] a family would have to earn more than three times its total income to be taxed. In South Vietnam, the income must be raised by more than 175 per cent to fall under the first taxable income bracket; in India, more than 126 per cent; and in the Republic of China, more than 37 per cent.

Extent of Burden of Personal
Income Taxation

The personal income tax lends itself more readily to the analysis of tax burden than other kinds of taxes because of its direct bearing to income and because no other form of taxation can adhere more closely to the "ability-to-pay" principle.

The principal factors necessary for a fair evaluation of the income tax structures are the levels of personal exemption, flexibility, and progressivity.[10]   An examination of these factors may indicate the impact of the personal income tax on the taxpayer.

Level of Personal Exemption

To measure and compare the level of personal exemptions, it would be proper to compute that portion of income that goes to exemption per unit of currency earned. Inasmuch as the amount of personal exemption allowed in each country is calculated to permit a certain level of living standard to be maintained by the taxpayer, a ratio which relates the exemption to the gross income earned will reveal different levels of personal exemption. This is shown in Table 4. Since high ratios would indicate high exemption levels, the tax structure is less onerous as compared to those which indicate low exemption levels.

Table 4 shows that South Vietnam has the highest level of personal exemption while the Republic of China registers the lowest. The exemption ratio in South Vietnam for a married individual rises from

TABLE 3

Ratio of Personal Exemptions Allowed to Married Taxpayers
with Three Children to Per Capita Income

	Per Capita Income (unit currency)	Income of 5 Persons (unit currency)	Exemptions for Married Taxpayer with 3 Dependents (unit currency)	Ratio of Exemptions to Income of 5 Persons
Republic of China (NT Dollars)	4,364 (1960)	21,820	30,000	1.37
India (Rupees)	318 (1959)	1,590	3,600	2.26
Japan (Yen)	122,650 (1960)	613,250	320,000	.52
Philippines (Pesos)	388 (1960)	1,940	6,000	3.09
South Korea (Won)	71,400 (1960)	357,000	-	not applicable
South Vietnam (Piastre)	5,174 (1956)	25,870	71,197	2.75
Thailand (Baht)	1,971 (1960)	9,855	8,700	.88

Sources: Reports submitted by the Delegates to the Tax Seminars held in Tokyo, Japan, April, 1963; Statistical Reporter; Civic Education Service, Inc., 733 R Street, N.W., Washington 6, D.C.; U.N. Demographic Yearbook of 1959; U.N. Statistical Yearbook of 1961.

Notes: 1. The figures enclosed in parentheses indicate year.
2. No figures are available for Singapore and Malaysia.

TABLE 4

Percentage of Personal Exemptions of Married Taxpayers
to Gross Income, by Number of Dependents[1]

No. of Child Dependents	Republic of China	India	Japan[2]	Malaysia	Philippines	Singapore	South Vietnam[3]	Thailand
None	19.35	60.00	68.25	54.54	60.00	66.67	83.20	37.50
1	26.47	62.26	71.43	60.00	66.67	71.43	85.02	40.83
2	32.43	64.28	74.02	62.96	71.43	73.91	86.48	43.82
3	37.50	64.28	76.19	65.52	75.0	76.0	87.68	46.52
4	41.86	64.28	78.02	66.89	77.78	77.10	88.69	48.98
5	45.65	64.28	79.59	68.15	80.00	78.10	89.54	51.22
6	48.98	64.28	80.95	68.15	81.82	78.72	90.17	53.27

[1] All ratios are based on the first taxable income bracket.

[2] Only exemptions for child dependents less than fifteen years of age are considered.

[3] In determining the ratio for Vietnam, the family allowances for a Vietnamese taxpayer employed in the private sector are considered.

83.20 per cent to 90.17 per cent as the number of
his child dependents increases to six. This may be
attributed to the fact that, aside from allowing personal exemptions, South Vietnam also grants family
allowances as concessions to married taxpayers.

In Japan the rate goes up to 80.95 per cent
from 68.25 per cent. While the exemption ratio in
Japan increases in proportion to the number of dependents, that of the Philippines indicates a much faster rate of increase. At the point where the number
of child dependents is six, the ratio for the Philippines is 81.82 per cent, which is higher than that
of Japan at the same level. This trend is brought
about by the fact that the ratio of additional exemptions to the first taxable bracket ($\frac{P1,000}{2,000}$ or 50 per
cent) in the Philippines is greater than that in
Japan ($\frac{¥ 35,000}{100,000}$ or 35 per cent). All countries showing a higher ratio for the same variables, compared
to others, register a higher rate of increase of personal exemptions in relation to total gross income
as the number of dependents increases.

Singapore also registers a high exemption level.
From 66.67 per cent for a married taxpayer, the ratio
is 78.72 per cent at the level of six dependents.

India and Malaysia show an almost identical
trend. Starting from 60 per cent, India's ratio
stops increasing in excess of the two-dependent
level (which gives 64.28 per cent) because the maximum number of child dependents given exemption in
that country is only two. In Malaysia, after the
five-dependent level, the rate does not increase any
more for the same reason: After the fifth child dependent, no additional allowance is given.

The ratio for Thailand is 37.50 per cent at a
level where the exemption claimed is for the taxpayer as a married individual, and 53.27 per cent at
a six-dependent level.

The Republic of China registers the lowest rate
of exemption. From 19.35 per cent, it rises gradually
to 48.98 per cent.

However, it is important to keep in mind that
the term "dependents" here refers only to child dependents. Thus in reality the ratio for the Republic of China and Japan may be actually greater, because persons who are not even related to the taxpayer may be considered dependents.

Flexibility

Built-in flexibility is usually measured by the
extent to which the amount of the tax will respond
to a change in income. Using this definition, the
economist Joseph A. Pechman has devised a formula
whereby built-in flexibility is computed as a ratio
between a change in tax liability and change in gross
income.[11] The use of this formula requires data on
tax liability and gross income based on income tax
returns covering a series of years. However, for
lack of data on income tax liability and gross income for all the countries under study, a deviation
from the above formula has to be resorted to in determining built-in flexibility. For purposes of
this study, built-in flexibility in the income tax
structure is measured by the degree to which income
is taxed at various rates as it moves from one bracket to another. In other words, flexibility is gauged
by the rate at which income becomes subject to varying tax rates as its level changes, either upward or
downward. Flexibility takes into account the rate
of change in income that will subject it to new tax
rates at different income levels. From this standpoint, it follows that flexibility depends upon the
number of income brackets subject to different tax
rates and the size of each bracket (marginal gap between brackets) in relation to the maximum taxable
income.

Table 5 shows the relation of each bracket to
total taxable income. To ascertain the degree of
change in income that makes a new tax rate applicable,
one must determine the ratio of the difference between the upper and the lower limits of each bracket
to the upper limit of the maximum taxable income
bracket. As shown in the table, lower ratios indicate greater flexibility, whereas higher ratios show

TABLE 5

Percentage of Taxable Income to Maximum Taxable Income

Taxable Income Bracket	Republic of China	India	Japan	Malaysia	Philip- pines	Singapore	South Korea	South Vietnam	Thailand
1st	5.00	2.98	.17	4.55	.40	1.50	33.33	1.25	2.50
2nd	5.00	3.73	.17	4.55	.40	.50	50.00	1.25	10.00
3rd	5.00	3.73	.50	4.55	.40	1.00	16.67	1.25	12.50
4th	5.00	3.73	.50	4.55	.40	1.00		1.25	12.50
5th	5.00	3.73	.67	9.09	.40	1.00		1.25	12.50
6th	5.00	3.73	1.00	9.09	2.00	2.00		1.25	12.50
7th	10.00	3.73	1.17	9.09	2.00	3.00		1.25	12.50
8th	10.00	7.46	2.50	9.09	2.00	5.00		1.25	12.50
9th	15.00	7.46	3.33	9.09	2.00	10.00		1.25	12.50
10th	15.00	14.93	6.67	9.09	2.00	10.00		1.25	12.50
11th	20.00	14.93	16.67	18.18	2.00	15.00		12.5	
12th		14.93	16.67		2.00	50.00		12.5	
13th		14.93	25.00		2.00			12.5	
14th			25.00		2.00			12.5	
15th					4.00			12.5	
16th					4.00			12.5	
17th					4.00			12.5	
18th					8.00				
19th					10.00				
20th					10.00				
21st					20.00				
22nd					20.00				

relatively less flexibility. Thus, the Philippine
income tax structure shows the greatest flexibility
while that of South Korea shows the least. The
Philippines has the most income brackets (twenty-
two),[12] and the range of each bracket in relation to
the maximum taxable income is relatively small. On
the other hand, South Korea has only three brackets
subject to different tax rates.

In the Philippines, a relatively slight change
in income, especially in the first eighteen income
brackets, will subject the income to a different tax
rate. As the income earner experiences a .4 per
cent change in income for the first five taxable
brackets, a new tax rate becomes applicable. This
rate of change rises gradually with ratios of 2 per
cent from the sixth to the fourteenth bracket, and 4
per cent from the fifteenth to the seventeenth bracket. Beyond this, the ratios become larger, ranging
from 8-20 per cent.

In the case of Japan, the proportions which
range from .17 per cent to 1.17 per cent are relatively less for the first seven brackets compared to
those of the Philippines. But above this level, the
magnitudes show a wider proportion, thus requiring a
greater amount of increase in income in order that a
taxpayer in Japan be subject to a higher tax rate.

A 1.25 per cent change in income for the first
ten brackets in Vietnam will subject a taxpayer to a
different tax rate. Beyond the tenth income bracket,
a 12.5 per cent change in income is required before
a different tax rate applies. In effect, there are
only two ratios in all income levels which will subject to various tax rates the income as it changes.
It will be noted that for the first five taxable
brackets, the rate of change is greater, that is,
less flexible compared to that of the Philippines.
For the succeeding brackets up to the tenth, however,
the required rate of change in income is smaller, in-
dicating more flexibility in South Vietnam. The succeeding brackets beyond the tenth register a higher
ratio, denoting that a taxpayer in Vietnam may receive a larger increase in income before a higher
tax rate applies.

Compared to the Philippines, India shows less flexibility in the low-income levels and a wider gap in the bracketing in the upper-income classes. Thus the first nine income brackets in India show that a greater change in income may occur before the tax-payer is subject to different tax rates. The same pattern holds true with respect to the succeeding income brackets.

The first six income brackets in Singapore reveal a certain degree of flexibility. But this flexibility is relatively less than that in the Philippines. Beyond the sixth taxable bracket, a greater change in income is required to enable the taxpayer to fall under a different tax rate. With respect to the last income bracket, a 50 per cent change in income must occur for the taxpayer to be taxed under the next tax rate.

The income schedules of the Republic of China and Malaysia show almost the same degree of flexibility. In the initial brackets, a 5 per cent and 4.55 per cent change, respectively, is required for a taxpayer to be subject to a new tax rate. The succeeding brackets show greater ratios.

While Thailand registers a 2.5 per cent change in the first income bracket for its taxpayer to fall under a different tax rate, the succeeding brackets indicate ratios ranging from 10-12.5 per cent.

Effective Tax Rates[13]

The determination of the effective tax rate at different income levels will more or less show the extent of graduation and progressivity in the tax structure. Similarly, it will show the burden of taxation on the different taxpayers falling under the various categories of taxable income. It is assumed that taxpayers who are in the highest taxable income bracket in the different countries under study are on the same level of satisfaction. It follows that taxpayers in different countries who earn the same fraction or percentage of the maximum taxable income in their respective countries are on equal levels of satisfaction.

With these assumptions, it can be stated that a certain level of taxable income in any one country yielding a high effective tax rate is more burdensome than a low effective tax rate for the same level of taxable income obtaining in another country.

Table 6 reveals that Japan and the Philippines have the highest effective tax rates at all levels of taxable income. At a level of 28.26 per cent effective tax rate for its 5 per cent of taxable income, Japan registers an effective tax rate of 59.83 per cent at 100 per cent of taxable income. For the same levels of taxable income, the Philippines shows effective tax rates of 19.92 per cent and 52.88 per cent, respectively. This may be accounted for by the highly progressive income tax rates and the existence of a great number of taxable income brackets subject to different tax rates, as shown in Table 7. This table shows the number of taxable income brackets and the lowest and the highest tax rates imposed in each country. It is presented because of its significance in analyzing the extent of variation in the effective tax rates shown in Table 6 and in determining the degree of progressivity and graduation in the tax rates.

India also registers a relatively progressive tax structure which, however, is less progressive than that of the Philippines. From a level of 4.61 per cent effective tax rate at 5 per cent of taxable income, it rises to 44.67 per cent effective tax rate at 100 per cent of taxable income. Table 7, however, will show that both the Philippines and India have 3 per cent as the minimum tax rates but India has a higher maximum tax rate of 72 per cent compared to the Philippines' 60 per cent. The less progressive tax structure of India may be attributed to fewer taxable income brackets and the steepness of the tax rates at high income brackets. (See Appendix I.)

South Vietnam, which levies minimum and maximum tax rates almost identical to those of the Philippines and which has a great number of taxable income brackets, registers a low effective tax rate.

TABLE 6

Effective Income Tax Rates (Per Cent)

Per Cent Maximum Taxable Income	Republic of China	India[1]	Japan	Malaysia	Philippines	Singapore	South Korea	South Vietnam[2]	Thailand
5%	3.00	4.61	28.26	6.18	19.92	7.10	7.00	3.50	11.50
10	4.00	6.79	35.80	7.27	28.16	10.45	7.00	5.25	12.25
15	5.00	8.63	40.53	8.36	33.31	12.96	7.00	9.16	13.00
20	6.00	10.74	43.73	9.54	37.08	15.97	7.00	11.87	13.75
25	7.20	13.00	45.98	10.63	40.10	17.78	7.00	13.50	14.20
30	8.50	16.20	47.48	11.63	42.32	19.81	7.00	15.41	15.16
35	9.57	19.22	48.80	12.54	44.07	21.27	7.38	16.78	15.85
40	10.37	22.19	50.20	13.40	45.44	23.61	8.33	18.12	16.68
45	11.66	24.92	51.28	14.14	46.61	25.43	9.07	19.44	17.61
50	12.70	27.13	52.16	14.90	47.55	26.89	9.66	20.50	18.35
55	13.90	28.94	53.32	15.57	48.41	28.99	10.15	21.81	19.40
60	14.91	31.24	54.30	16.86	49.13	30.74	10.55	22.91	20.29
65	15.76	33.22	55.12	17.13	49.81	32.22	10.89	24.23	21.23
70	16.18	34.92	55.82	18.05	50.39	33.49	11.19	25.71	22.21
75	17.66	36.91	56.44	18.99	50.90	34.59	11.44	27.00	23.06
80	18.43	38.66	57.28	20.00	51.34	35.55	11.66	28.43	24.12
85	19.41	40.21	58.03	21.06	51.80	36.40	12.05	29.70	25.05
90	20.27	41.86	58.70	22.12	52.20	37.16	12.77	30.97	26.02
95	21.05	43.34	59.29	23.06	52.55	37.83	13.42	32.23	27.02
100	21.75	44.67	59.83	23.90	52.88	38.44	14.00	33.37	29.92

[1] The income tax and the supertax were consolidated.

[2] The general income tax and the income tax on salaries and wages were consolidated.

27

TABLE 7

Minimum and Maximum Tax Rates and Number
of Taxable Income Brackets

Country	No. of Taxable Brackets	Tax Rates	
		Lowest	Highest
Republic of China	12	3	40
India	14	3	72.5
Japan	15	8	75
Malaysia	13	6	45
Philippines	23	3	60
Singapore	13	5	55
South Korea	4	7	35
South Vietnam	18	2	60
Thailand	10	10	50

Notes: 1. Tax rates for South Korea represent only
those for wages and salaries.

2. The income tax and the supertax for
India were consolidated.

Again, this situation is accounted for by the steepness of the tax rates on the higher-income brackets
and the gradually rising tax rates on the lower-and
middle-income brackets.

South Korea registers the least progressivity,
as revealed by the effective tax rates for 5 per
cent and 100 per cent of taxable income. This is expected since this country has only four taxable income brackets on which various tax rates are levied.

Thailand's effective tax rates range from a minimum of 11.5 per cent to a maximum of 27.92 per cent. The range between the two effective tax rates is narrow because there are only ten taxable brackets and the maximum tax rate is only 50 per cent.

The Republic of China's effective tax rates are quite low. Starting from 3 per cent for 5 per cent of its taxable income, the highest rate is 21.75 per cent for 100 per cent of its taxable income. This can be attributed to low tax rates (which range from 3 per cent to 40 per cent) and the rather steep rates for the high-income brackets.

Malaysia shows a pattern almost similar to that of the Republic of China. On the other hand, Singapore has more progressive tax rates compared to those of Malaysia because of the high tax rates (which range from 5 per cent to 55 per cent).

CONCLUDING COMMENTS AND OBSERVATIONS

General Observations

In most developing economies, the direct tax, of which the income tax is the major item, accounts for a small portion of total tax collection. The opposite trend is characteristic of highly developed economies where the average ratio of personal income tax collection to total tax collection is 35 per cent. In developing countries, the average ratio is 18 per cent. In spite of the fact that Japan is considered to be the most advanced country in Asia, its ratio is only 28.8 per cent. This is due to a number of factors, foremost of which are the low levels of income, relatively low tax rates, greater personal exemption, and a relatively low level of efficiency in the collection machinery compared to those found in advanced economies.

Almost all the countries under study show a small percentage of total personal income tax yield to national income. Except for Japan, which has an average of 3.42 per cent, all the others have less than 1 per cent. The above ratio confirms the observation that the higher the per capita income, the greater is the tax capacity and consequently the tax collection, given the same collection efficiency.

Since data on income distribution in each country is not available, it is necessary to assume that the pattern of income distribution is the same. Inasmuch as the measure of taxable capacity is best gauged by the level of national income, this alternative is used.

The Level of Personal Exemptions

South Vietnam, Japan, and the Philippines have the highest levels of personal exemption. This is so in South Vietnam because of the existence of the family allowances granted to a married taxpayer and his family dependents, in addition to personal exemptions. In the case of Japan and the Philippines, the exemptions are high, especially for the low-income brackets. On the basis of such considerations as these, it can be seen that a hard and fast rule cannot be adopted as to how much personal exemptions should be allowed in a particular country. The determination of exemptions would have to depend on the standard of living and the tax-exempt income which a government would allow its populace. However, one factor cannot be overlooked: Japan and China allow personal exemptions for dependents who are not even related to the taxpayer; but if such a practice were adopted in the Philippines or in any other Asian country where strong family ties exist and extended families are typical, the already narrow income tax base would only be eroded further. For the same reason, the granting of family allowance, as is done in South Vietnam, is not applicable to Asian countries with already liberal exemptions.

The granting of personal exemptions for children who are pursuing university studies in South Vietnam, Thailand, and Singapore is commendable because it serves as an incentive for parents to send their children to higher schools of learning. This is wholesome not only from the social but also from

the economic standpoint, by aiding in the development of a sound technical base necessary for economic growth.

Another factor that deserves attention is the
practice (in Singapore, Malaysia, and India) of diminishing the amount of exemption for children as
their number increases. Because of the high level
of personal exemptions and the problem of population
explosion, its adoption could be fruitful in other
Asian countries.

The Tax Rates

The study reveals that out of the nine countries being studied, five (Thailand, Japan, South
Korea, Malaysia, and Singapore) have initial tax
rates higher than 3 per cent. Except for Japan and
Malaysia, which have the highest per capita income,
the other three have a lower per capita income than
the Philippines.

Per capita income is one of the measures of a
country's taxable capacity. This being so, countries with higher per capita income can absorb higher taxes. Viewed from this perspective, some of the
countries under study with higher per capita income
but lower initial tax rates can afford an upward tax
rate adjustment.

Some Striking Features

1. In South Vietnam a greater amount of family
allowance is extended to European and foreign residents (other than Asians) than to Vietnamese and
Asian resident taxpayers. This is also true with respect to family allowances granted to Vietnamese government employees, which are higher than those allowed for taxpayers employed in the private sector.

Lower tax rates apply to income received for
labor in the form of salaries and wages than to
other income such as returns on investment and capital. This seems to be an application of the "earned-
income-credit" principle which postulates that those

who derive their income from sources which the tax
law considers unearned, such as rent, dividend, and
interest, should be taxed higher.

2.   India appears to have the most complicated
method of arriving at the total tax liability; but at
the same time, India's is the only system that adheres closely to some economic considerations. For
instance, earned income is subject to a surcharge
different from that imposed on unearned income. The
method of computation involves determination of
total income; computation of surcharges on total income, earned, and unearned income; and adjustments
of the income tax and the supertax on the basis of
certain exclusions, deductions, and exemptions.

3.   The amount of personal exemption allowed to
a married taxpayer in India depends on his taxable
income. If his income does not exceed Rs 20,000,
the exemption allowable is Rs 3,000, in excess of
Rs 20,000, the exemption is only Rs 1,000. The
ability-to-pay principle is manifested by allowing
a taxpayer with high income only a relatively small
exemption.

4.   In Japan a larger exemption is given for
children above the age of fifteen, presumably on the
grounds that more expenses are required to maintain
older dependents.

5.   In Indonesia a taxpayer who shows some outward sign of prosperity is subject to additional income tax. The tax is determined by the income category under which the taxpayer falls.

6.   Two different sets of tax rates are imposed
on salaries and wages in South Korea. Daily and
hourly wages of taxpayers who have no definite employer are taxed at a flat rate of 7 per cent.
Other income from wages and salaries is subject to
progressive tax rates, ranging from 7-35 per cent.

7.   In addition to other deductions, a 10 per
cent earned-income exemption is allowed on income derived from employment or pension, or from a trade,

business, profession, or vocation in which the taxpayer is engaged, either as owner or working partner.

8. In Thailand no itemized deductions from
gross income are allowed. Instead, standard rates
of deduction are authorized as offset against gross
income for each type of income.

The foregoing comparison and analysis should be
considered in the light of the limitations and assumptions set forth, for they are intended only to provide a perspective of the various personal income
tax structures of selected southeast Asian countries. This study does not attempt to show which
practices and policies adopted by various countries
are effective and easy to administer and which are
not.

The tax structure of a certain country hinges
on the socio-economic goals of that country. It
should be geared to the requirements of the economy,
by taking into consideration economic, social, and
political factors.

Notes to Chapter 2

1. Rounded to the nearest peso to facilitate
computation. Legal rate before the 1960 decontrol
was ₱2 to $1.

2. For details, refer to Appendixes I and II.

3. Article 1114 of the Civil Code of the Republic of China defines relatives as:
      a. lineal relatives by blood;
      b. spouse and the parents of the other
           spouse living in the same household;
      c. brothers and sisters;
      d. the head and the members of a house.
Article 1123 provides that any persons living together in the same household are considered legal

members of the household, even if they are not relatives, provided that they intend to live together
permanently.

4. Earned income includes: (a) income from
salaries or in payment of past services of the taxpayer or any deceased person, (b) income from profits
and gains of a business, profession, or vocation
carried on by the taxpayer, (c) income from profits
and gains of a business, profession, or vocation on
account of a share in a registered partnership or an
unregistered partnership assessed as a registered
partnership, if the taxpayer is actively engaged in
the conduct of the partnership business, and (d) income from other sources if immediately derived from
personal exertion. Harvard Law School International
Program in Taxation, Taxation in India (Boston:
Little, Brown & Co., 1960), p. 322.

5. Tax credits are not deducted from the gross
income but are offset against the computed income
tax.

6. In 1965 the number of taxable income brackets was reduced to ten, ranging from M$2,500 to in-
come in excess of M$55,000. Likewise, the maximum
tax rate was changed to 50 per cent.

7. Before the formation of Malaysia. Effective
January 1, 1965, the income tax system of Singapore
is identical to that of the States of Malaysia.

8. Because of the lack of available data on
personal income of the countries under study, per
capita income will be used as the basis for determining income.

9. In terms of per capita income, the Philippines ranks third in southeast Asia, after Japan and
Malaysia.

10. For lack of available data on income distribution, the pattern of income distribution for all
countries is assumed to be the same.

11. The formula of Joseph A. Pechman was cited by Leo Cohen of Kansas State College in "An Empirical Measurement of the Built-in Flexibility of the Individual Income Tax," American Economic Review, XLIX, No. 2 (May, 1959), 532-41.

12. Reference to Appendix I and Table 7 will show that the number of taxable brackets in all countries in Table 5 is short by one. The last taxable bracket is eliminated because the amount involved is infinite.

13. Presented below is an illustration of the method by which the effective tax rate is computed. Taking the Philippine case as an example, the effective tax rate for 5 per cent of the maximum taxable income is derived. The method used in computing the effective tax rate for 5 per cent of the maximum taxable income is the same method employed in determining the effective tax rates for all levels of income in different countries.

```
Maximum taxable income . . . . . . .    ₱500,000
5% thereof . . . . . . . . . . . . .      25,000
Amount of income tax due on ₱25,000:
First ₱ 2,000 @  3%  ₱  60
next    2,000 @  6%    120
 "      2,000 @  9%    180
 "      2,000 @ 16%    320
 "      2,000 @ 20%    400
 "     10,000 @ 24%  2,400
Balance of
        5,000 @ 30%  1,500
```

Total income tax on ₱25,000 is ₱4,980

$$\text{Effective income tax rate} = \frac{\text{Total income tax}}{\text{Total taxable income}} = \frac{₱\ 4,980}{₱25,000} = 19.92\%$$

CHAPTER **3** CORPORATE INCOME TAX

INTRODUCTION

The corporate income tax has become one of the major sources of government revenue. Generally, developing economies collect less in taxes from income and property[1] than advanced countries, primarily because of the lower-income level, low tax rates, and the prevalence of noncompliance with tax obligations. Of total collections from income and property, however, the corporate income tax contributes a substantial share, as shown in Table 8.

Attempts have been made recently to emphasize taxes on income and property. The contention is that since these taxes, unlike taxes on production and sales, are not generally shifted to consumers, taxation becomes a more effective tool for redistributing income and wealth. The incidence of a tax on income is on the subject; shifting the tax will not place the taxpayer in an advantageous position, for the income tax is a tax on the residual. Because of market imperfections, however, there are indications that a portion of the corporate tax is being shifted, but not as much as that of a tax on production and sale.

GENERAL FEATURES OF THE CORPORATE TAX SYSTEMS[2]

Classification of Corporate Taxpayers and Their Taxable Income

Corporations are usually classified as domestic and foreign. A corporation is considered domestic by the state under whose laws it was organized, and

foreign if it is incorporated under the laws of another country. Tax treatment of a corporate entity
is usually based on citizenship. Some countries,
however, adopt residence as the basis, in which case
alien resident corporations are taxed in the same
manner as domestic corporations. In most cases, nonresident alien corporations are taxed differently
and, in some cases, a further distinction is made between those engaged in trade or business and those
that are not so engaged in the country having tax
jurisdiction.

TABLE 8

Ratio of Corporate Income Tax Collection
to Total Collections from Income
and Property Taxes--1962

	Tax on Income and Property	Corpo- rate Income Tax	Per Cent of Corporate In- come Tax to Tax on Income and Property
India (thousand million rupees)	3.7	1.9	51.35
Indonesia (thous- and million rupiah)	18.2	11.6	63.73
Japan (thousand million yen)	1.216	700.0	57.56
Philippines (million pesos)	259.6	174.4	67.18
South Vietnam (thousand piastres)	1,532.491	460.836	30.07

Source: Proceedings of the Special Meeting of Japan
         Tax Association on Tax System and Adminis-
         tration in Asian Countries, April 8-16,
         1963.

In the Republic of China, domestic corporations
are taxed on net income derived from sources within
and outside the country. However, foreign corporations, both resident and nonresident, which are engaged in trade or business in China are taxed only
on net income derived from sources within the country.
Nonresident foreign corporations not engaged in trade
or business are taxed on dividends, interest, salaries and wages, rents, and royalties received from
within the Republic of China. A foreign company is
considered to be engaged in business in China if it
is carrying on business in a fixed place (such as an
office, branch, management, factory, or farm) or if
it is carrying on business through an agency which
habitually exercises general authority to negotiate
and conclude contracts on its behalf or which has a
stock of merchandise from which it regularly fills
orders.

Ceylon, India, Malaysia, Singapore, South Korea,
and South Vietnam regard a corporation as resident
if its principal office or the control and management of its business is exercised in those countries.
Domestic and resident corporations are taxed on income derived from all sources, whereas nonresident
corporations are taxed only on income derived from
sources within those countries. The taxable base in
these countries (except India) is net income, determined in the same manner as that of an individual.
Total income consists of all income, which is classified into six categories[3] excluding exempt receipts,
such as income from domestic agriculture; certain
types of interest, such as interest on certain gov-
ernment-approved loans from foreign sources to industrial undertakings in India; certain allowances
granted to employees to meet expenses incurred in
the performance of business[4] and reduced by deductions representing expenditures incurred in earning
the income.

The amount computed by applying the income tax
and the supertax on the total income does not represent the amount of the tax due. From the total income, certain tax-exempt income and deductions are
excluded. The proportion of the latter to total

income is first determined; the resultant figure is
then deducted from the tax tentatively computed to
arrive at the amount of tax due. Total income,
therefore, is only used as a basis for determining
the applicable income tax and supertax rates; it
does not represent true taxable income.

In Indonesia domestic and resident corporations
are taxed on income derived from sources inside and
outside the country. Nonresident foreign corporations are taxed only on income derived in Indonesia.

The Philippines classifies corporations into
two broad categories, domestic and foreign. The latter is further subdivided into those engaged in
trade or business[5] and those that are not. Domestic
corporations are taxed on income from all sources
while foreign corporations engaged in business in
the Philippines are taxed on income derived in the
Philippines, subject to deduction of expenses actually incurred. Foreign corporations not engaged in
trade or business in the Philippines are taxed on
the amount received from all sources within the Philippines and may not deduct expenses.

Thailand has a similar classification of corporate taxpayers. The only difference is that foreign
corporations, even if they are not engaged in business, are entitled to the same deductions allowed to
domestic corporations, provided such expenses are incurred in Thailand.

Tax Rates

Usually, fewer tax rates are imposed on corporate income than on personal income. A corporation
possesses a personality distinct from those of its
stockholders by virtue of its legal existence. However, taxation of corporate entities is based more
on revenue considerations than on some economic justifications. A system of corporate taxation usually
takes account of incentives for operating corporate
entities. While corporate tax rates are usually
graduated, they are not imposed in a progressive
series like those applied to personal income.

Progression in tax rates implies an ability to pay,
and "the concept of ability to pay relates to bur-
dens borne by individuals and cannot appropriately
be applied to corporations."[6] If one of the objectives of income taxation is the redistribution of
income, this objective cannot be achieved by applying the progressive personal income tax rates on
corporate income because this "would result in serious discrimination against low-income owners of
stock of large high-total-profit corporations."[7]
Not all stockholders of one corporation belong to
the same income bracket. Taxing corporate income at
progressive rates would therefore prove disadvantageous to low-income stockholders. Dividends received are based on stockholdings and computed on a
"per-share" basis. This method places all stockholders on the same tax ladder with respect to the dividends which are taxed at the corporate level given
to their distribution.

     In view of these considerations, most countries
under consideration apply only one to three corporate
tax rates except India and Indonesia, which impose
four and six rates, respectively.

     Tax rates in the Republic of China range from 6
per cent to 18 per cent on taxable income brackets
ranging from NT$10,000 to over NT$100,000. The
first NT$10,000 is exempt from the corporate income
tax. Foreign corporations doing business in that
country are taxed at the same rates as domestic
corporations. Those not engaged in business in
China are subject to a 15 per cent tax on income in
the form of dividends, interest, salaries and wages,
rents, and royalties.

     In Ceylon resident corporations are taxed at a
flat rate of 57 per cent on net income derived from
all sources, whereas nonresident corporations are
taxed at the rate of 63 per cent on net income derived from sources within Ceylon.

     In India "foreign corporations, whether resi-
dent or nonresident, are subject to special rates of
supertax if they have not made prescribed arrange-

ments for the declaration and payment of dividends."[8]
Therefore, domestic corporations and resident foreign
corporations which have made such arrangements[9] are
taxed in the same manner. Nonresident corporations
which prescribe the same dividend payment arrangements in India are taxed in the same manner, but
only on income received or accruing in India.

The corporate income tax, applicable to all
classes of corporations, is set at 25 per cent. In
addition, supertax rates, varying from 5 to 25 per
cent, are imposed on different classes of dividend
income. Various rates of supertax apply to distributable income.

Foreign corporations that have not made the prescribed arrangements for declaration and distribution of dividends within India are taxed at 63 per
cent (income tax and supertax); certain intercorporate dividends are taxed at lower rates.

Both domestic and foreign corporations in Indonesia are subject to the same tax rates, which range
from 40 per cent to 52.5 per cent on six income
brackets, ranging from under Rp 50,000 to over Rp
2,500,000.

In Japan domestic and foreign corporations engaged in trade or business are levied the same tax
rates on their income. Foreign corporations not engaged in trade or business are subject to a flat rate
of 20 per cent on gross receipts derived from sources
within Japan. Domestic and foreign corporations not
engaged in trade or business are subject to two sets
of tax rates: (1) rates on ordinary income not intended for dividend distribution, and (2) rates on
income earmarked for dividends. The ordinary income
is subject to a higher set of tax rates than income
earmarked for dividends. The tax rates for the first
type of income are 33 per cent on less than 2 million
yen and 38 per cent on more than 2 million yen. On
the other hand, the rates for income earmarked for
dividends are 24 per cent on less than 2 million yen
and 28 per cent on more than 2 million yen. Before
applying the above rates, the two types of income are

first separated. The proportion the first income
bracket bears to the total taxable income is multi-
plied by the amount of either type of income. The
product obtained becomes the first taxable bracket on
which the first tax rate is applied.

To illustrate, assume that the total taxable income of a certain corporation for a given year was
earmarked for dividends. The corporate tax is computed as follows:

Tax on portion of income earmarked for dividends:

$$\frac{¥\ 2,000,000}{¥20,000,000} \times ¥5,000,000 = ¥\ \ 500,000 \ @24\% = ¥\ \ 120,00$$

$$¥\ 5,000,000 - ¥\ \ 500,000 = ¥4,500,000 \ @28\% = \underline{¥1,260,00}$$

Tax on income earmarked for dividend
   payments. ¥1,380,00

Tax on portion of undistributed incomes:

$$\frac{¥\ 2,000,000}{¥20,000,000} \times ¥15,000,000 = ¥\ 1,500,000 \ @33\% = ¥\ \ \ 495,$$

$$¥15,000,000 - ¥\ 1,500,000 = ¥13,500,000 \ @38\% = \underline{¥5,130,}$$

Tax on undistributed income ¥5,625,

Total corporate tax due ¥7,005,

The excess of total taxable income over the first taxable income base is subject to the second income tax
rate.

The Japanese corporate tax system also imposes
an additional tax on family corporations. It attaches
only on earnings retained in excess of 15 per cent of
the profits realized during the same period or over
1 million yen, whichever is greater.

Malaysia, Singapore, South Korea, South Vietnam,
and Thailand apply the same rates of corporate tax on
both domestic and foreign corporations or resident
and nonresident corporations. However, foreign or
nonresident corporations are taxed only on income derived from sources within these countries. Only one

corporate tax rate is applied in Malaysia and Singapore (40 per cent), and in South Vietnam (24 per cent). The corporate tax rates in Thailand are 15 per cent, 20 per cent, and 25 per cent, respectively, on taxable income of 500,000 baht, on the next 500,000 baht, and in excess of 1 million baht. In South Korea, the tax rates are 20 per cent on income not exceeding 1 million won and 25 per cent on that exceeding 1 million won.

The Philippines imposes the same tax rates (22 per cent on the first ₱100,000 taxable income, and 30 per cent on the excess over ₱100,000) on taxable income of domestic corporations and foreign corporations engaged in trade or business therein.[10] With respect to the latter, only income derived from the Philippines is taxable. Foreign corporations not engaged in trade or business, on the other hand, are subject to a flat rate of 30 per cent on the amount received from all sources within the Philippines.

OBSERVATIONS

Corporations in the selected Asian countries are generally classified as resident or nonresident. The first group usually includes domestic corporations and foreign corporations engaged in trade or business. The second category includes corporations not engaged in trade or business in the country concerned. No distinction is made between a domestic corporation and a foreign corporation engaged in trade or business. Nonresident corporations, on the other hand, are taxed at a higher rate on income derived from sources within the country. Some countries, including Indonesia and Thailand, do not distinguish between nonresident corporations that are engaged in trade and business within the jurisdiction of the taxing state and those that are not.

Only three countries tax corporate income of foreign corporations not engaged in trade or business on the basis of gross income: the Republic of China, Japan, and the Philippines. Others allow deductions of expenses incurred in the production of income.

(The allowance of deductible expenses is conducive
to tax evasion, for it is difficult to ascertain
such expenditures.)

While other countries tax nonresident foreign
corporations at par with their resident or domestic
corporations, the Republic of China, Japan, and the
Philippines tax them at source, usually at a higher
rate on gross income if these corporations are not
engaged in trade or business in the country concerned.

Some countries impose different sets of tax
rates on various classes of income. Others levy different tax rates on income depending upon the type
of the recipient corporation.

In India, for example, the supertax rate on
dividend income is lower than that on income derived
from other sources. This practice encourages corporate investment in stocks of other corporations.
From the standpoint of capital formation, a corporation is in a better position to provide the necessary funds for the establishment or expansion of
various lines of industry. This scheme has, however,
a double-edged effect: While it encourages corporations to utilize investible funds for the operation
of other corporations, it restricts the declaration
of dividends to stockholders, thus deferring the tax
that may be collected on the latter's income.

It will be observed further that the supertax
on dividends and other income of companies in which
the public is substantially interested and whose income does not exceed Rs 25,000 is lower compared to
that on dividends and other income received by other
corporations. This can be attributed to government
participation in the ownership of an enterprise.
The practice of providing a lower supertax for companies in which the public is substantially interested could inhibit private participation in stock
investments.

The supertax is higher for companies that have
not made proper arrangement for dividend payment.
The purpose of this is to place on more or less

equal footing the shareholders of resident corporations and stockholders of nonresident corporations, considering that the former pay income tax on dividends received in India while the latter do not.

As a whole, the method of computing corporate tax in India is as complicated as that of the individual income tax.

In Japan the tax rates on income distributed as dividends are lower than those imposed on income not intended for dividend distribution. Perhaps this practice is designed to avoid undue accumulation of corporate earnings and to encourage distribution of dividends. The policy of taxing unduly accumulated profits more heavily is also being followed in the Philippines. The only difference is that in the Philippines a surtax of 25 per cent is imposed instead of a higher rate of income tax.

Japan's additional tax on family corporations (on earnings retained in excess of 15 per cent of total earnings or in excess of 1 million yen, whichever is greater) appears to be designed to avoid the concentration of shareholdings among certain families, a policy which adheres to the concept of capital diffusion. The practice also restricts the avoidance of individual income tax payment by accumulating profits of the corporation.

The corporate income tax in Ceylon, Malaysia, Singapore, and South Vietnam is proportional. These countries do not adopt progression in corporate income taxation. Most countries, however, impose graduated rates on corporate income because they recognize the corporation's ability to pay as separate from that of the individual stockholders.

The Republic of China, Indonesia, Japan, South Korea, the Philippines, and Thailand do impose a progressive corporate income tax. India has a graduated scale of income tax because of the supertax.

Compared to tax rates in the Philippines, those in the Republic of China, South Korea, Thailand, and

South Vietnam are lower. The other countries, however, impose higher corporate income tax rates.
Even if the ordinary tax rate in India is only 25
per cent, the supertax makes the effective tax rate
quite high.

With the exception of Japan, all the countries
studied are developing economies, so that their goal
is industrialization. In the process, a network of
fiscal and monetary policies is conceived and laid
down to provide a favorable climate for private ini-
tiative. The encouragement of private enterprise
would bring about the release of resources to finance
investment requirements. Some lines of activity, however, demand tremendous amounts of capital, so the
need arises to pool the resources of several persons.
This can be accomplished most effectively through
the establishment of a corporate form of business.

In a free enterprise system, the need for more
private capital for investment in large business ventures grows as the economy develops. Since corporations are needed for large-scale production, they
have become one of the major sources of government
revenue, and their taxable capacity has not yet been
fully tapped in developing Asian countries.

Notes to Chapter 3

1. Instead of classifying taxes as direct and
indirect, this study groups taxes into two broad
categories: (1) tax on income and property, and
(2) tax on production and sale. The latter classification is not only more descriptive, but it is more
neutral in that it does not imply whether the tax is
shiftable or not.

2. See Appendix III. For an analysis of corporate taxation in underdeveloped countries, see also
The United Nations Finance Commission, "Special Features of Corporate Taxation in Underdeveloped Countries," Corporate Tax Problems (E/CN.8/66, November

25, 1952), Chap. 6, pp. 57-75. (Mimeographed.) Reprinted in Readings on Taxation in Developing Countries, Ed. Richard Bird and Oliver Oldman (Baltimore: The Johns Hopkins Press, 1964), pp. 199-214.

3.   Harvard Law School International Program in Taxation, Taxation in India (Boston: Little, Brown & Co., 1960), p. 158.   The six categories of income are: salaries, interest on securities, income from property, profits and gains of business, capital gains, and income from other sources.

4.   Ibid., pp. 159-60.

5.   The phrase "engaged in trade or business" conveys the notion of progression, continuity, or sustained activity.   Accordingly, the consummation of a few isolated transactions, the profits from which constitute a very small portion of the taxpayers' total gross income, does not constitute engaging in trade or business.

6.   John F. Due, Government Finance: An Economic Analysis (Homewood, Illinois: R. D. Irwin, Inc., 1963), p. 211.

7.   Ibid.

8.   A supertax is one imposed on total income of both individuals and corporations, in addition to the ordinary income tax.   Unlike the supertax on personal income, which is imposed only at higher income levels, the supertax on corporations is imposed at all income levels, the rates varying according to the type of income as well as the nature of the corporate taxpayer.

9.   In order for a resident foreign corporation to be taxed in the same manner as a domestic corporation, the following conditions must be met:
     1.   The register of all shareholders of the corporation must be regularly maintained from April of the base year at the corporation's principal place of business in India.
     2.   The general meeting for approving

accounts and declaring dividends of the base
year must be held in India.

    3.   Any dividends declared must be payable
only in India to all shareholders.

Taxation in India, op. cit., p. 158.

    10.   The following tax rates, however, apply:

    12 per cent on the total net income of
building and loan associations

    10 per cent on the total net income of private educational institutions

    6 1/2 per cent on the total investment income of life insurance companies organized under the laws of the Philippines or foreign life insurance companies authorized to carry on business in the Philippines.

CHAPTER **4** TAX TREATMENT OF DIVIDENDS,
DEPRECIATION, INTEREST,
CAPITAL GAINS, AND TAX CREDITS

TAX CREDITS

Tax credits are technically different from deductions and exemptions allowed for tax purposes. The latter consist of refinements of gross income to arrive at taxable income,[1] while tax credits are deductions permitted from the amount of tax payable.[2]

Some Asian countries make no distinction between these two types of tax-liberalization grant. A number of so-called tax credits are actually deductions or exemptions which reduce taxable income. The discussion of tax credits will be confined to only those items referred to in the technical definition above.

The rationale for a tax credit may involve equity, welfare, or incentive. The equity consideration furnishes the basis for tax credits for dividends or foreign income taxes. From the welfare viewpoint, credits may be given for a handicapped or aged person, for contributions to provident funds, or for premium payments on life insurance policies. Finally, as an incentive measure, a tax credit may likewise be granted for special types of investment.

In the Asian countries considered in this study, the most common types of tax credit are those granted for foreign taxes, dividends, and specified categories of contributions or donations.

Existing Tax Credits

A common type of tax credit is that granted for taxes paid abroad for income earned there. In India

49

the credit allowed against the tax payable on such
income is equivalent to either the amount of foreign
tax determined at average rates or the tax payable
in India at average rates with respect to such income, whichever is lower.[3] This general rule applies
to taxes paid in countries with which India has not
entered into any agreement for the avoidance of
double taxation. Otherwise, the credit is determined according to the terms of the existing treaty.

A citizen of the Philippines is entitled to
credit for income tax paid or accrued in a foreign
country. Any alien resident of the Philippines is
also entitled to the tax credit if the foreign country of which he is a citizen accords the same concession to citizens of the Philippines residing there.
One limitation on the amount of credit is that the
ratio of credit for taxes paid or accrued in any one
country to the tax against which such credit is
taken, should not exceed the ratio of the taxpayer's
net income from that country to his total net income
for the period. Similarly, the total amount of
credit cannot exceed the same proportion of the tax
against which such credit is taken that the taxpayer's total net income from abroad (and normally taxable under Philippine laws) bears to his total net
income for the period.

Japanese income tax laws allow credit for any
foreign income taxes, subject to statutory limitations. Credit for foreign income tax (or any counterpart of Japanese income tax for the taxable year during which it accrued) cannot exceed the following
limitation:

$$\text{Japanese income tax} \quad \times \quad \frac{\text{Total income from source outside Japan}}{\text{Entire income subject to Japanese income tax}}$$

Should the foreign tax be greater than this limitation, the balance of the foreign tax can be carried forward for the succeeding five-year period.
If, however, the allowable credit exceeds the accrued foreign tax, then the excess can be carried

forward so as to increase the limitation for the
next five years.[4]

In Indonesia only foreign taxes are allowed for
credit. The amount is equal to the total foreign
taxes paid. The basis for computation is rate B (ordinary rate) of the Indonesian tax system. Under
rate B, there are 21 levels of taxable income, ranging from 0 Rp to 1,800,000 Rp. The tax is expressed
in absolute amounts rather than as a percentage of
taxable income. The basic tax reaches the maximum
amount of 1,063,050 Rp. An additional tax is levied
over and above the basic tax for each full Rp 100 at
all levels of taxable income.[5]

A resident taxpayer in Singapore is entitled to
credit for tax paid on income from the United Kingdom or from Commonwealth countries which grant re-
ciprocal relief. The amount of the credit cannot exceed one-half of the foreign tax.

Credit for foreign tax may be claimed by a
Malaysian taxpayer if it is paid in a reciprocating
Commonwealth country or in a country with which
Malaysia has a double taxation convention.[6] In the
first instance, the amount of credit is the same as
in Singapore--a maximum of 50 per cent of the foreign
tax or less, depending on the taxpayer's effective
rate of Malaysian tax. Where the tax is paid in a
country with which Malaysia has a tax convention,
the amount of credit depends on the terms of the convention. In general, the foreign tax has as its
maximum the applicable Malaysian tax on the same income.

Certain categories of dividends provide the
basis for tax credit in some countries. Thus, in
India, it applies to dividends received from that
portion of a new industrial firm's profits which is
exempt from income tax and supertax under the tax-
holiday scheme.[7] The taxpayer is also entitled to
credit for dividends from a hotel establishment if
(a) the latter's paid-up capital is at least Rs 5
lakhs; (b) the hotel building is owned by the company; and (c) it meets certain prescribed conditions

regarding number and type of guest rooms. The amount
of credit is equivalent to the income tax, the supertax, and the surcharge applicable to the total income
at the average rates.

Japan grants credit of the same nature. (This
is discussed in connection with special treatment of
dividend income.)[8]

Credit is granted in Ceylon to a taxpayer other
than a company for dividends received from a resident
company; the credit is equivalent to 33 1/3 per cent
of the gross dividends received. Under Ceylonese
tax laws, the company withholds 33 1/3 per cent of
the dividend as part of the tax it has to pay, so
that the shareholder receives the net dividends
amounting to 66 2/3 per cent of the gross. The tax
withheld is the credit allowed to individuals.

A taxpayer in Malaysia or Singapore who receives
dividends from a resident company is entitled to
credit against tax liability amounting to 40 per cent
of gross dividends.[9]

Credit may likewise be granted for certain types
of contribution or donation. A credit existing in
India pertains to contributions to certain provident
funds, superannuation funds, and deposits under
small savings schemes approved by the government.
Taxes, however, are credited against the income tax
and the income tax surcharge on the payments made at
average rates. Donations to charity also provide a
basis for credit against Indian tax liability. The
charitable institutions or funds must meet prescribed
conditions regarding such matters as maintenance of
accounts. The donation for which credit is allowed
cannot exceed 10 per cent of the taxpayer's total income or Rs 25,000, whichever is lower. The credit
covers the applicable income tax, the supertax, and
the surcharge at the average rates, the entire amount
not to exceed 50 per cent of the donation.

In Japan a credit of 6,000 yen against income
tax is allowed for a resident taxpayer who is physically handicapped and for each physically handicapped

dependent. The same amount may be credited against income tax if the resident taxpayer is sixty-five years or over, a widow with dependents, or a working student with a total income not exceeding 200,700 yen. Finally, contributions by a resident to the government or to institutions for scientific experiment or research, such as schools and universities, provide another basis for credit. The creditable amount is 20 per cent of the contributions in excess of 3 per cent of the sum of ordinary income, retirement income, and timber income, or 300,000 yen, whichever is smaller. However, this cannot exceed 2 per cent of the total of ordinary income, retirement income, and timber income.[10]

In Ceylon credit may be claimed for premium payments on life insurance policies and annuities and employees' contributions to provident or pension funds. The credit is equal to the effective rate on the amount of the premiums or contributions with the ceiling fixed at Rs 1,000. Donations to the Ceylon Government or to a public charitable trust or to an institution declared by the Minister of Finance to be an approved charity provide another basis for tax credit. The permitted allowance is equivalent to the amount of the donation or one-tenth of the assessable income of the individual (in the case of a company, one-twentieth of its assessable income), or Rs 50,000, whichever is the least. As in the preceding case, the credit relates to the permitted allowance at the marginal rate or rates of tax applicable, but cannot exceed one-half of the permitted allowance.

A tax credit may also be granted as an investment incentive. Thus, in Ceylon, credit applies to investments in industrial projects adjudged essential in the economic development of Ceylon as well as to investments in government securities. The permitted allowance is the amount of the investment, or one-fifth of the assessable income, or Rs 50,000, whichever is the least. The credit is based on the permitted allowance at the marginal rate or rates of tax applicable to the particular taxpayer, and cannot exceed one-half of the permitted allowance.

Summary and Comments

The incorporation of tax credit in the tax system of various Asian countries is justified on the basis of equity and economic efficiency. But the circumstances which favor the grant of such credit and the specific method employed vary with the national setting, depending largely on government policies, especially where incentive aspects are involved. Some countries, like India, Japan, and Ceylon, grant various types of credit whereas Thailand, Cambodia, and Korea do not grant any.

A tax credit may be allowed on several counts. Apparently the most common basis for credit is the payment of foreign income tax by nationals for income earned in another country. In the Philippines and Indonesia, the taxpayer is entitled to credit against income tax solely for this reason. In the countries concerned--Japan, India, the Philippines, Indonesia, Malaysia, and Singapore--the maximum allowable amount is determined on the basis of the tax structure (i.e., the tax normally payable) in the taxpayer's country.

Credit for dividends also exists in India, Ceylon, Malaysia, and Singapore. In India, such credit is selective in nature, devised chiefly as an incentive scheme for preferred areas of investment.

Donations and contributions of taxpayers to approved charities and public funds also entitle them to credit against tax liability in India and Ceylon. Furthermore, these two countries grant the same tax concession for payments to pension or provident funds, and superannuation schemes, subject to a prescribed maximum and upon fulfillment of certain requirements. Incorporated to benefit employees and workers, this is a desirable feature of the tax systems of India and Ceylon. The welfare rationale is also evident in the Japanese tax system. Credit is granted under exceptional circumstances which affect the taxpayer's ability to pay and also for contributions to research institutions.

Finally, a tax credit in Ceylon may be allowed for investments in selected areas. The incentive effect, while similar to that of credit for dividends, may even be greater inasmuch as the act of investing per se is directly encouraged.

India, Japan, and Ceylon have the most liberal systems of tax credit of the countries under study.

CAPITAL GAINS

Capital gains are accorded special tax treatment in most Asian countries. Gains arising from the sale of capital assets are not taxable as ordinary income, but are usually subject to a smaller tax liability, for reasons of equity and economic incentive. Income from the transfer of assets is different from regular income in that it represents the total amount of income realized during the year of transfer. That is, the gains were accumulated over the entire period that the asset was held, not only in the year of realization. If such gains were included as ordinary taxable income for that year, the taxpayer would be pushed up to a much higher-income bracket, especially if the income tax structure is sufficiently progressive. The equity principle involved is the "avoidance of unfair progression in the taxation of bunched income."[11]

The other major argument for special treatment of capital gains involves economic considerations: Capital gains represent a reward for risk investment, an essential element in the growth process. They are part of income that is likely to enter into savings. Proceeds from the transfer of capital assets are usually reinvested through the purchase of new securities. Besides, favorable tax treatment encourages reinvestment in more productive ventures, rather than the freezing of successful investments into their existing forms.[12]

Capital gains taxation in India recently underwent two important changes with the passage of the

1962 budget.[13] First, a distinction was made between
short-term and long-term capital gains on the basis
of the length of time capital assets are held. For
tax purposes, short-term capital gains are defined
as those which arise from the disposal of assets
within one year of their acquisition; long-term
gains pertain to assets held for over a year. Short-
term capital gains are treated as ordinary income
and are therefore subject to both income tax and
supertax. Short-term gains of individuals are subject to tax if total income, including short-term
gains, exceeds Rs 3,000. On the other hand, long-
term gains are entitled to an exemption limit of Rs
5,000 and are taxable at a flat rate of 25 per cent
or at the rate of income tax applicable to the total
income including capital gains, whichever is less.
A flat-rate tax of 30 per cent is levied on a company's long-term capital gains.

The equity argument has been invoked to justify
this distinction. It is held that short-term capital gains are similar to profits realized in the ordinary course of business and should therefore be
placed on equal footing with them.

The Indian tax system also provides for the
setting off of capital losses.[14] Losses on short-
term capital assets may be set off against both
short-term gains and long-term gains of the same
year; any balance of loss can be carried forward and
set off against short-term capital gains for the
next eight years but not against any other income or
long-term capital gain. On the other hand, long-
term capital losses can be set off against long-term
capital gains of the same year, and may be carried
forward for four years.

Special treatment of capital gains in Japan[15]
consists of an exemption level of 150,000 yen after
which 50 per cent of the residue becomes subject to
tax at normal graduated rates. Aside from this,
there are specific types of capital gains that are
accorded a more favorable treatment, such as those
relating to the replacement or sale of residential
property, expropriation of property under the Land

Expropriation Law, replacement and/or exchange of property held for business use, and capital gains realized by emigrants. For example, if the gains arise from the sale of a principal residence, the tax-payer is entitled to a deductible amount of 500,000 yen instead of the usual 150,000 yen. Incentive pro-visions regarding capital gains taxation take the form of an increase in the amount deductible, post-ponement of assessment, or liberal assessment or valuation, depending on the nature of the gains, the circumstances surrounding the transfer, and the financial situation of the taxpayer.

A selective capital gains tax, such as that which exists in India and Japan, is the usual prac-tice in these Asian countries; the bases are the nature of the asset or the recipient, or the length of the holding period. For example, in Nationalist China, if gains arise from the sale or exchange of property or property rights, ordinary income tax rates apply. Those obtained from the sale of securi-ties held for over a year are totally exempt from tax, as a measure to encourage investment.

Similarly, in Thailand taxable capital gains of individuals are only those realized in the normal course of business. Gains accruing to corporations and partnerships are taxable as ordinary income.

The assessment of capital gains in the Philip-pines[16] is based on the nature of the recipient. In the case of individuals, gains are classified accord-ing to the length of time the assets have been held. Gains from assets held for not more than a year are included in the estimate of taxable income as com-pared to gains from long-term assets, of which only 50 per cent is included. No such classification ex-ists in the case of companies--100 per cent of the gains are regarded as taxable income. The deduction of capital losses incurred by individuals and compan-ies is allowed only to the extent of capital gains.

The tax on profits is applied to capital gains in a few cases. In Cambodia proceeds from the dis-position of capital assets are taxable at the same

rate as commercial, industrial, and agricultural
profits, as well as profits from land. These are
taxable at a flat rate of 25 per cent for companies.
In the case of individual taxpayers, progressive
rates, ranging from 13 per cent to 62 per cent, are
levied. These are the rates of tax on profits, which
differs from the general income tax.

Similarly, South Vietnam levies a 16 per cent
tax on profits, separate from the general income tax.
An added advantage is that only gains from tangible
fixed assets are taxable under existing law, and
even these gains become fully exempt if the realized
amount is reinvested within three years. Companies
avail of the same privileges with respect to their
capital gains, on which a 24 per cent tax on profits
is imposed. Profits from the disposal of tangible
fixed assets are exempt from the corporate income
tax if the realized amount is reinvested within
three years.

Three of the countries, South Korea, Malaysia,
and Singapore, provide an unusually favorable atmosphere for capital gains. No tax is imposed on
gains realized from the sale of capital assets.

On the other hand, in a few isolated instances,
the treatment of capital gains bears little or no
difference from that of ordinary income. Under
Indonesian tax laws capital gains of individuals are
taxable if the property is transferred within a two-
year period. The taxpayer is entitled to a basic
exemption of Rp 50,000. Company income from this
source is taxable as ordinary income. The only exception arises in the case of expropriation of property under the Land Expropriation (Reform) Law.

In Ceylon capital gains of individuals and
companies are subject to ordinary income tax up to
45 per cent.

Summary and Comments

The countries covered in the study distinguish
gains from the disposal of capital assets from

ordinary income. Although the particular methods employed differ, there are certain similarities in
treatment. Significant among these is the distinction between so-called short-term and long-term capital gains. In India and the Philippines long-term
gains relate to capital assets held for over a year.
Where such explicit distinction is not made, as in
China and Indonesia, the holding period of the asset
may still be a determinant of the amount of the capital gains tax.

Taxation of capital gains also involves selectivity as to the type of asset or the nature of the
enterprise, especially where preferential treatment
is given as an incentive measure. In Japan, the Republic of China, and South Vietnam this is a factor
in determining the extent of taxability. A unique
incentive provision in South Vietnam is the exemption on proceeds from the sale of the asset reinvested within three years.

Tax liability also differs for individuals and
corporate establishments. Tax laws in India, Japan,
the Philippines, Indonesia, Thailand, Cambodia, and
South Vietnam discriminate between capital gains of
individuals and those accruing to companies. In the
first four countries, the individual taxpayers receive a more favorable treatment than companies.
The reverse is true, however, in the latter two.

Of the eleven countries under study, South
Korea, Malaysia, and Singapore do not levy a tax on
capital gains. Ceylon is the only country that
treats capital gains as ordinary income.

Japan has an exhaustive list of those types of
assets and/or transactions that warrant exceptionally
liberal treatment of capital gains.

DIVIDENDS

Dividends received from corporations are also
accorded special tax treatment. As in the case of
capital gains, this is based on considerations of

equity and economic efficiency. The question of
fairness arises since dividend income becomes
"uniquely subject to double taxation"[17] barring a
forward shifting of the corporate income tax. Where
corporate income tax is levied on the corporation,
double taxation of investment income results because
distributed dividends become taxable in the hands of
shareholders. Since double taxation of dividends is
undesirable in that it tends to discourage or retard
growth, attempts are made to lighten such a tax burden and thus encourage investment. Several Asian
countries attempt it by means of partial or complete
exemption of dividends, grant of tax credit, or
rates lower than those levied on ordinary income.

Japan is one of the countries that provide
favorable treatment of dividend income.[18] An individual taxpayer is entitled to credit against income
tax up to 15 per cent of dividends received from a
domestic company. However, if the total taxable income (including dividends) is in excess of 10 million yen, 15 per cent of dividends can be credited
only up to the level at which the sum of ordinary
income and dividends equals 10 million yen. On the
remaining dividend income, a tax credit of 7.5 per
cent applies. Dividends received by companies from
domestic sources are not ordinarily included in taxable income. With regard to dividends received after January 1, 1962, the exemption is 75 per cent of
the amount by which dividends received exceed dividends paid by the recipient company.

In South Vietnam the only tax liability on dividends accruing to individuals from shareholdings in
a domestic company is the amount of the general income tax. Recipient companies are liable for only
a portion of dividends from domestic companies.
Thus, 40 per cent of dividends of banks and credit
institutions is tax exempt while the remaining 60
per cent is included in taxable income. Other companies may enjoy a more liberal treatment in that
the entire 90 per cent of dividends is deductible,
and only 10 per cent becomes taxable.

Under the Indian tax system, dividends received

by an individual are generally taxed. Otherwise,
credit is given to him for whatever amount of tax on
dividends has been withheld at source. However, a
lower tax or none at all may be levied on such income, depending on the source or nature of the paying company.[19]

In Malaysia 40 per cent of dividends is credited
against tax payable to avoid the possibility of taxing the same investment income twice. The 40 per
cent credit serves to make up for the company income
tax of 40 per cent paid by the declaring company.
The Malaysian tax law entitles the declaring company
to deduct 40 per cent from the shareholder's gross
dividends in payment of the company's income tax.[20]

Similarly in Ceylon dividends of individuals
are treated as ordinary income, but a credit equivalent to 33 1/3 per cent of the gross dividends received is granted. Under Ceylonese tax laws, the
company withholds 33 1/3 per cent of the shareholder's dividends as part of the corporate income tax
which the company has to pay, so that the shareholder
receives the net dividend amounting to 66 2/3 per
cent of the gross. The credit allowable is equal to
the amount of the tax withheld. In the case of a
corporate taxpayer, dividends received from resident
companies are not included in its taxable income.
Thus, credit is not allowed on the 33 1/3 per cent
tax withheld by the declaring companies. In effect,
a flat rate tax of 33 1/3 per cent is levied on
dividends received by companies.

A 5 per cent tax is withheld from dividends received by individuals and companies in Nationalist
China.[21] Where applicable, there exists a unique
method of taxing undistributed or accumulated profits
of individual stockholders: Profits accumulated over
a period of three consecutive years, and amounting to
25 per cent of a company's paid-in capital, become
taxable to its shareholders, depending on the shares
held by each.

The tax on income from marketable or negotiable
securities applies to dividends of individuals and

companies in Cambodia. A withholding tax of 20 per
cent is levied on dividends and other profits from
operations.

In the Republic of Korea individuals and companies pay a flat rate tax of 12 per cent on dividend income paid within the country or by a domestic
corporation.

In Indonesia a tax of 20 per cent is withheld
at source on dividends received by individuals from
domestic sources. In the case of recipient companies, 20 per cent of dividend income is withheld as
advance payment of their corporate income tax. In
effect, dividends are treated as ordinary corporate
income inasmuch as these are included in the computation of profits subject to corporate income tax.

Under Philippine laws, the total amount of dividends received by individuals are taxable. In the
case of domestic companies or resident foreign corporations, only 25 per cent of the dividends from a
domestic corporation is taxed.[22]

Dividends paid by a resident company in Singapore are treated as ordinary income, but credit
against tax payable is granted for tax withheld on
income from this source.

Summary and Comments

Dividend income is treated in a different way
than ordinary income. Here again, as in capital
gains taxation, there is no uniform method, although
similarities exist.

One type of liberal treatment is to exempt a
portion of dividends from the computation of taxable
income. This is practiced in Japan, South Vietnam,
and, to some degree, in Nationalist China and the
Philippines.

An alternative scheme is the imposition of a
lower rate of tax or a smaller tax liability on this
type of income. In Nationalist China a 5 per cent

tax is levied; in South Korea, 12 per cent; and in
Cambodia, 20 per cent. In South Vietnam the only
tax liability on dividends is the general income tax.

As an equity measure, a tax credit is sometimes
granted. Japan allows credit for dividends received
by individuals and companies. In Malaysia the credit
against income tax is 40 per cent of the gross dividends.

In Japan, India, Nationalist China, and South
Korea complete exemption from tax liability is granted on some types of dividends to encourage investments in preferred areas.

Different methods of taxing dividend income may
be employed simultaneously by any one country. The
usual practice is to employ several methods at the
same time and to adopt each according to the particular circumstances involved.

In Indonesia, Singapore, Malaysia, and Ceylon
dividends received by individuals are treated as ordinary income, but credit is granted for tax withheld as advance payment of income tax. Individual
taxpayers in the Philippines are also liable to the
ordinary income tax but there is no withholding tax
on dividends.

In both Malaysia and Ceylon the declaring company is allowed to withhold a portion of each shareholder's dividends in the same percentage as the corporate income tax. The incidence of the corporate
income tax is therefore on the stockholder, who in
turn obtains relief either through a credit against
income tax or exemption of dividends from taxable income. While double taxation of investment income is
eschewed, such income is nevertheless liable to ordinary income tax.

DEPRECIATION METHODS

Expenses for the wear and tear and the obsoles-
cence of fixed assets are normally reflected in the
firm's depreciation allowance. These represent

imputed costs, or estimates of the extent of normal depreciation incurred in the course of business.

Charges for depreciation are entered as a non-cash expense in the computation of taxable income. The allowable methods of depreciation are usually prescribed by the ministry of finance or any similar agency. The schedule of useful lives of various categories of depreciable assets may be similarly prescribed.

The standard practice is to spread the cost of the depreciable asset over its useful life. Several methods of spreading the total cost are used. The straight-line method is to distribute the cost equally over the life of the asset. The declining-balance method is to make larger deductions or allowances during the early years, so that the stated value of the asset declines rapidly during this period. Under the sinking-fund method, depreciation is relatively small during the early years, and increases yearly "by the interest imputed to a theoretical depreciation fund consisting of previous depreciation deductions and interest accrued."[23] Also commonly employed are the working-hours method and the production method, in which the useful life is estimated in terms of either the number of units to be produced or the hours to be worked, respectively, and depreciation is charged accordingly.[24]

Corporations in Japan can employ either the straight-line or the declining-balance method. However, only the first method is applied to intangible assets, deferred expenses, cattle, and fruit trees. Two additional methods may be used in a few cases-- the production method for mining assets and the replacement method for fixed assets subject to fixed replacement, such as rails and electric poles. The Ministry of Finance Ordinance prescribes the useful lives of fixed assets. The 1964 Tax Reform effected the shortening of useful lives by about 15 per cent.[25]

Corporations allowed to maintain their accounts under the blue return system (a system of taxpayers' accounting procedures devised to improve bookkeeping

techniques and promote honest self-assessment) may
make use of special depreciation methods which grant
more liberal wear-and-tear allowances for the various types of fixed assets. Corporations filing blue
returns enjoy an added privilege in that a depreciation allowance, which falls below the statutory limit
or the legally allowable amount, may be carried over
for three years.[26] Individual taxpayers write off
depreciation charges in a similar manner, except
that these charges must conform to the amounts set
by the statute.

Only two depreciation methods--the straight-line
and the production method--are employed by individuals as well as companies in the Philippines. The
basis for computation is the acquisition value of the
capital asset plus costs involving major repairs.
Under the production method, the depreciation charge
for any one period is estimated by multiplying the
acquisition value of the asset by the ratio of actual
production for that period to the total estimated
production which the asset is expected to yield during its lifetime.

In Nationalist China individuals and companies
may make use of either the straight-line, the dimin-
ishing-balance, or the working-hours method. The
annual depreciation charge is estimated according to
the table of service life of fixed assets prescribed
by the Ministry of Finance.[27] The actual service
life of each type of asset must not be shorter than
the minimum number of years prescribed in the table,
unless special permission to accelerate depreciation
has been granted to encourage reinvestment.

In Indonesia only the straight-line method is
employed in writing off depreciation charges for
fixed assets or assets whose useful lives exceed one
year. The schedule of useful lives is drawn up by
the Ministry of Finance. As an incentive scheme,
preferred types of capital expenditures are allowed
to be written off within a four-year period.

In Singapore the declining-balance method applies to plant and machinery at varying annual rates

based on the written value of the asset. Certain
types of industrial building or structure are granted
an initial allowance of 10 per cent and an annual
allowance of 2 per cent of the cost. Liberal provisions pertain to the deduction of capital expenditures
(other than those covered by the normal depreciation
allowance on plant and machinery) incurred by a mining
firm over the lifetime of the asset. Similarly, capital expenditures of a plantation may be depreciated
over a ten-year period.

Tax laws of South Vietnam give individuals and
companies the option to use "any of the usual methods
of depreciation." The rates of depreciation allowable differ according to the nature of the fixed
asset.

Steamship	2 to 5%
Building	2 to 5%
House built of light materials	10%
Furniture	10 to 15%
Automobile	20 to 33%
Rubber plantation	2.5 to 5%

Charges for the wear and tear of depreciable
assets under the Indian tax machinery are estimated
on the basis of prescribed rates. The declining-
balance method is usually employed to estimate depreciation. A major exception is the case of ships,
where the allowance may be computed through the
straight-line method at a percentage of the actual
cost. Furthermore, depreciation charges in the case
of new buildings, constructed for the purpose of
housing low-income employees or promoting labor welfare activities, may be allowed at 20 per cent of
cost.

In Cambodia annual amortizations are allowed
according to the local bookkeeping method. The allowance takes into consideration the useful life of
the asset and the working stock which affects the
operation of the enterprise. Some conventional
rates of depreciation are:

        Construction in masonry   5%
        Construction in wood and
            tile   7%
        Movable furniture   10%
        Machineries   10%
        Light machinery and equip-
            ment, tools, etc.   33%
        Vehicles for transport   20%
        Typewriters, calculating
            machines, etc.   20%

The method of writing off depreciation expenses in Ceylon differs according to the period of purchase of the asset. A unique depreciation procedure applies to fixed assets, such as plant, machinery, and fixtures purchased after March 31, 1959: The depreciation charge is a lump sum allowance given in the year of acquisition of the asset.[28]

The Republic of South Korea allows either the straight-line method, the declining-balance method, or the production method to be applied. The Ministry of Finance sets forth the schedule of useful lives of fixed assets, in accordance with which the depreciation charge is determined through the selected method.

Companies and individual enterprises in Thailand employ the declining-balance method. The allowable rates of depreciation are prescribed by Royal Decree.

Summary and Comments

Depreciation charges or capital consumption allowances are estimated by any of a number of methods: straight-line, sinking-fund, declining-balance, production, and working-hours. The government usually prescribes the specific method or methods to be used. Two or more methods are usually employed and the taxpayer is allowed to choose from these, as in Japan, the Philippines, South Vietnam, South Korea, and Nationalist China. At the same time, existing tax laws in some countries provide that a definite method be followed for a given type of asset.

The schedule of useful lives and annual depreciation rates of the different categories of assets may also be prescribed, usually by the Ministry of Finance or a similar agency, as in Nationalist China, Indonesia, South Vietnam, Cambodia, India, South Korea, and Thailand.

Aside from normal depreciation rates and allowances, some countries (Singapore, Indonesia, Ceylon, Japan, and India) permit liberal write-off charges against selected fixed assets as an incentive for investment and expansion in preferred lines of production. The depreciation charge, in the form of a lumpsum allowance, is granted in Ceylon with regard to assets acquired after March 31, 1959. In India welfare considerations are an overriding factor in allowing liberal charges against new buildings for housing low-income employees or for promoting labor welfare activities.

Notes to Chapter 4

1. James Maxwell, Tax Credits and Intergovernmental Fiscal Relations (Washington, D.C.: The Brookings Institution, 1962), p. 97.

2. John Due, Government Finance: An Economic Analysis (Homewood, Illinois: R. D. Irwin, Inc., 1959), p. 154.

3. Harvard Law School International Program in Taxation, Taxation in India (Boston: Little, Brown & Co., 1960), pp. 299-300.

4. Japan Tax Bureau, An Outline of Japanese Tax 1963, pp. 85-86.

5. See Appendix I of Chapter 2.

6. Malaysia Income Tax Ordinance, 1947, sec. 46.

7. See Chapter 9.

8. See section on dividends.

9. See section on dividends.

10. Japan Tax Bureau, op. cit., pp. 48-49.

11. Dan Throop Smith, Federal Tax Reform (New York: McGraw-Hill, 1961), p. 124.

12. Ibid.

13. I. S. Gulati, "A Note on the Capital Gains Tax in India," Public Finance, XVIII (1963), 103-4.

14. Ibid., pp. 105-6.

15. Japan Tax Bureau, op. cit., pp. 31-36.

16. A proposed amendment has been submitted to Congress to effect a more liberal treatment of capital gains. One measure proposes to extend the same preferential treatment of capital gains to corporations. Another aspect of the proposal is the suspension of capital gains tax for five years on gains from assets held for more than twelve months. This proposal is envisioned as an incentive for capital-asset holders to release their idle or unproductive properties and channel the funds into preferred areas of investment.

17. Smith, op. cit., p. 205.

18. Japan Tax Bureau, op. cit., pp. 47, 49.

19. See Chapter 10 on tax incentives.

20. Malaysia Income Tax Ordinance, 1947, Secs. 40 and 42.

21. See Chapter 9 on tax incentives for a discussion of concessions given to companies.

22. See Chapter 9 on tax incentives.

23. Smith, op. cit., p. 170.

24.   Dan Throop Smith and J. Keith Butters, <u>Taxable and Business Income</u> (New York: National Bureau of Economic Research, Inc., 1949), p. 59.

25.   Japan Tax Bureau, <u>op. cit</u>., p. 67.

26.   <u>Ibid</u>., p. 69.

27.   <u>Income Tax Law of the Republic of China</u>, Article 47.

28.   See Chapter 9.

CHAPTER **5** OTHER TAXES
ON INCOME
AND PROPERTY

DISCUSSION OF THE TAX STRUCTURE

Transfer Taxes

Transfer taxes (estate, inheritance, and gift taxes) are levied in most of the Asian countries studied. An estate tax, which is usually progressive, is one levied upon the gross estate of a deceased person previous to its division.[1] An inheritance tax is levied upon the property which individual beneficiaries receive from the estate of a deceased person.[2] The gift tax is a tax levied upon the value of a gift after certain specified exemptions; usually the rate of the tax increases in proportion to the value of the gift.[3]

Collections from transfer taxes in the selected Asian countries represent only a small percentage of total collections from all taxes on income and property.

Table 9 shows that collections from transfer taxes in Indonesia represent less than 1 per cent of total collections from all taxes on income and property. Singapore, on the other hand, registers the biggest collections in transfer taxes.

Estate Tax

Estate taxes are levied according to a graduated schedule of rates. Appendixes IV, V, VII, and VIII show the schedules of estate tax rates of India, Singapore, the Philippines, and the Republic of China.[4]

71

TABLE 9

Percentage of Transfer Taxes to Total
Taxes on Income and Property

Countries	1960	1961	1962 (Estimated)
India	14.0	15.0	13.0
Japan	12.0	13.0	14.0
Federation of Malaysia	23.0	16.0	16.0
Philippines	20.7	20.5	22.3
Singapore	50.6	28.3	34.4
South Korea	1.9	2.8	4.7
Indonesia	0.06	0.05	0.02
Ceylon	3.4	2.8	2.4

Source: Proceedings of the Special Meeting on Tax
System and Administration in Asian Countries, sponsored by the Japan Tax Association (Tokyo, 1963).

In India estates which exceed the exemption
level after the deduction of permissible allowances
are taxed at progressive rates. The rates range
from 7 1/2 per cent on the first bracket of Rs 5,000
of taxable property to 40 per cent on the bracket
above Rs 5 million.[5]

The estate tax rates in the Philippines range
from 1 per cent of the amount by which the net estate exceeds ₱5,000 and does not exceed ₱12,000 to
15 per cent of the amount by which the net estate
exceeds ₱ 1 million. Estate taxes are payable

within nine months after the decedent's death.[6]

In Singapore the exemption level for the estate tax is M$10,000. The rates of duty range from 5 per cent on M$15,000 to 60 per cent on the principal value exceeding M$4 million.[7]

Estate taxes in the Republic of China may be paid in either cash or kind. With the approval of the estate-tax collection agency,[8] taxes may be paid in two or five installments, depending upon the amount of the tax. The tax rates range from 2 per cent for taxable estates amounting to NT$ 20,000 but not exceeding NT$ 40,000 to 70 per cent for taxable estates in excess of NT$ 2 million.

In Ceylon the estate duty ranges from 5 per cent on amounts exceeding Rs 30,000 to 70 per cent on that exceeding Rs 600,000.[9]

Inheritance Tax

The inheritance taxes are also levied according to a graduated schedule of rates. Appendixes VI and VII show the inheritance tax rates of Japan and the Philippines, respectively.

In Japan the inheritance tax applies to the amount arrived at after deducting from the total value of all properties acquired the liabilities and funeral expenses incurred. The inheritance tax rates range from 10 per cent of the taxable amount which does not exceed ¥300,000 to ¥55,125,000 plus 70 per cent of the taxable amount over ¥ 100 million.[10]

The inheritance tax rates in the Philippines range from 2 per cent of the amount of the share not in excess of ₱12,000 to 22 per cent of the amount of the share which exceeds ₱ 1 million. The first ₱5,000 is exempt from the inheritance tax. Inheritance taxes are payable within twelve months after the decedent's death.

In South Korea the inheritance tax applies to estates of decedents which exceed 500,000 hwan.[11]

A Korean resident who inherits the estate of two decedents is given a basic deduction of 500,000 hwan.

The inheritance tax is assessed on a graduated
rate. There are ten applicable tax brackets. The
lowest rate, 5 per cent, is applicable to amounts below 1 million hwan. The highest is that levied on
estates valued over 100 million hwan.

Beneficiaries are held responsible for payment
of the taxes. When the tax is paid at the stipulated time, certain deductions are permissible.[12]

Gift Tax

The gift tax is imposed as a complement to the
estate and inheritance taxes.

In India the tax on gifts was first imposed in
1958 as a complement to the estate duty and the
wealth tax. All donors, except charitable institutions, government companies, and public companies
are liable for payment of the gift tax. Some gifts
are excluded from the tax, such as gifts of savings
certificates, wedding gifts (up to Rs 10,000), gifts
to the taxpayer's wife (up to Rs 100,000), and gifts
under a will.

The tax is levied on total gifts which exceed
Rs 10,000. It is assessed on the value of all gifts
made by a donor during a year. The tax rates range
from 4 per cent on the first bracket of Rs 50,000 to
40 per cent on gifts over Rs 5 million.[13] (See Appendix IV.)

The gift tax of Ceylon applies to all types of
taxpayers (individuals, Hindu undivided families,
firms, companies, and association of persons) but it
does not apply to gifts made by government companies,
by corporations established by Central, State, or
Provincial Acts, by charitable institutions and funds
that are exempt from income tax, by companies in
which the public is substantially interested, and by
subsidiaries that have more than 50 per cent of the
nominal value of the equity share capital held by
such public companies.

A gift of property other than cash is valued at the price it would yield in the open market at the time it was given. Gift tax rates range from 5 per cent on the first Rs 50,000 to 100 per cent on the balance of the taxable gifts in excess of Rs 450,000.[14]

In Japan the property gift tax is levied on the value of the properties in one year. The lowest tax rate is 15 per cent of amounts not exceeding ¥300,000. The highest tax rate is ¥17,950,000 plus 70 per cent of amounts over ¥30 million. (See Appendix VI.)

The gift tax is called a "donation tax" in South Korea. Donations from relatives are taxed at graduated rates on ten brackets, ranging from 6 per cent on donations below 1 million hwan to 25 per cent on donations exceeding 100 million hwan. Donations from persons other than relatives are also taxed at a graduated rate. The lowest rate for donations below 500,000 hwan is 15 per cent and the highest is 35 per cent for those over 10 million hwan.[15]

The gift tax in the Philippines differs from that of the other countries in that separate schedules of rates apply to the donor and to the donee. The donor is not taxed for gifts valued at less than ₱5,000. All other net gifts in excess of ₱5,000 are taxed at graduated rates ranging from 1-15 per cent. (See Appendix VII.)

The rates of tax payable by a recipient range from 2 per cent for net gifts whose value is less than ₱12,000 to 22 per cent for net gifts whose value exceeds ₱1 million. (See Appendix VII.)

The rates of the recipient's tax depend upon his relation to the donor: The closer the kinship, the lower the tax. Gifts to the taxpayer's spouse and children and the cumulative value of gifts made to or for the use of the government or its instrumentalities are exempt from the gift tax.[16]

Land and Buildings Tax

A land tax is levied in most of the twelve Asian countries, and they are generally paid in cash rather than in kind.

In South Vietnam the taxation of real property is governed by the following considerations:

(a) the tax is primarily a central government source of revenue, with other levels of government receiving income based on percentage additions to the central government tax;

(b) land is taxed a specific amount per square meter per hectare, according to locational value or productive capacity while buildings are taxed on the basis of actual or estimated rental value;

(c) four basic distinctions are made in the tax rates applicable to land, depending on whether it is located in an urban center, used for rice production, used for other agricultural production, or borders a rural highway or street.[17]

The local taxes on land and buildings in India are assessed on the "annual value" (normally the actual rent) or "ratable value." In some states "capital value" (fair market value) is sometimes used as the basis of the tax. These taxes are administered and collected by local officials.[18]

Local taxes on land and buildings are payable by the owners or occupiers of the land.

The Indian tax rates on land and buildings are relatively low; most of the rates fall between 10 per cent and 30 per cent of the annual value.

In the Philippines real property taxation is essentially a function of local governments. The provincial board of each province is authorized to fix a uniform tax rate which may not be less than one-eighth or more than four-eighths of 1 per cent of

the assessed valuation as the province's share in
the property tax. A municipality through its municipal council also fixes a uniform rate of tax of not
less than two-eighths nor more than four-eighths of
1 per cent. Thus, the combined provincial and municipal rate of tax on real property may vary from
three-eighths of 1 per cent to a maximum of 1 per
cent. In most provinces, the present combined rate
is 1 per cent.

City governments are also empowered to levy additional real property taxes at their option. The
maximum rate provided in almost all city charters is
2 per cent.[19]

In 1959 the Barrio Charter was enacted authorizing barrios to levy additional property taxes which
do not exceed one-fourth of 1 per cent.

The Republic of China has two types of land
taxes, both of them local: land value tax and land
increment tax. The land value tax, imposed annually
on the land, is based on the price declared by its
owner. The land value increment tax is levied on
the net increment on the price of land when ownership is transferred, or after the lapse of ten full
years if ownership has not been transferred. The
ten-year period begins when the land is first legally assessed.(See Appendix IX.)

The Land Law of the Republic of China makes provision for additional tax on private vacant land.
When private vacant land has not been used according
to law, a private vacant land tax, in addition to
the land value tax, is imposed of not less than
three times nor more than ten times the land value
tax assessable on the land.

The same law also provides for a tax on private
uncultivated land. Aside from the land value tax, a
tax is imposed on private uncultivated land after
the expiration of the time limit within which it is
required to be used. The tax on uncultivated land
is not less than the amount of or more than three
times the land value tax collectible on the land.

The Land Law has a further provision concerning absentee landlords. Land value taxes collectible on any kind of land owned by absentee landlords are double the amount of the regular land value taxes due.[20]

The ratio of collections from land taxes to total collections from all taxes on income and property varies considerably in the Asian countries studied, as shown in Table 10.

TABLE 10

Percentage of Taxes on Land and Buildings
to Total Taxes on Income and Property

Countries	1960	1961	1962 (estimated)
Republic of China	a/	a/	a/
India	.20	.17	.18
Philippines[1]	20.8	20.6	20.8
Singapore[2]	-	30.7	35.24
South Korea	11.9	21.3	-
South Vietnam	15	14.7	14.4
Thailand	5.6	3.4[b]	5.3
Cambodia[3]	2.9	1.9	1.7
Ceylon	2.7	3.7	4.2

[1]Reports of the Auditor General to the President and the Congress of the Philippines on Local Governments, 1960-62.

[2]Land tax collections are assumed to be collections from property tax.

[3]Land tax collections are assumed to be collections from Impot sur les terres o heveas.

[a]Data not available.

[b]Nine months only.

Source: Japan Tax Association, Proceedings of the Special Meeting on Tax System and Administration in Asian Countries (Tokyo, 1963).

It will be noted from Table 10 that collections
in Singapore are quite sizable. This may be attributed to the fact that the property taxes referred to
may include all other properties, movable or immovable. The Philippines, South Vietnam, and South
Korea collect considerable amounts from land taxes,
while collections from land taxes in India are less
than 1 per cent of the total collections from taxes
on income and property.

Education Tax

South Korea imposed an education tax in 1958 to
finance compulsory education. It is levied on individuals who have resided in South Korea for more
than one year and on corporations that have offices
in South Korea.

The education tax has two categories, national
and local. The national tax is equivalent to a progressive rate of 60 per cent less than the tax rate
applied to individual incomes. For the local education tax, a 3 per cent rate is levied on wage earners, while 5 per cent is imposed on other income
groups.[21]

Revenues from the education tax make up a large
portion of the total revenues from taxes on income
and property. Collections from this source amounted
to 1,459 million won in 1960, and 1,524 million won
in 1962, which represented about 11 per cent and 16
per cent of the total collections from all taxes on
income and property.[22]

In the Philippines a school tax has been proposed to help meet the demands of the increasing
school enrollment.

Residence Tax

In the Philippines every individual over
eighteen years of age is generally subject to payment of the annual basic residence tax of ₱0.50.
Moreover, he is subject to the additional residence
taxes of ₱2.00 for every ₱5,000 worth of real prop-

erty in excess of ₱10,000, ₱2.00 for every ₱5,000 of
gross receipts or earnings in excess of ₱10,000, and
₱1.00 for every ₱1,000 of salaries or gross receipts
from the exercise of any profession or occupation.

Every corporation is also subject to an annual
residence tax of ₱5.00 and an additional tax, not exceeding ₱2,000, according to the following schedule:

> 1) for every ₱5,000 worth of real prop-
> erty in the Philippines owned by it in the
> past year, two pesos;
> 2) for every ₱5,000 of gross receipts
> or earnings derived by it from business in
> the Philippines in the past year, two pesos.[23]

Collections from residence taxes amount to over
₱3 million yearly,[24] which represents about 1.5 per
cent of the total annual collections from all taxes
on income and property.

An immigration tax of ₱25.00 is likewise levied
on aliens over sixteen years of age admitted into
the country for more than sixty days.[25]

South Vietnam imposes an alien residence tax.
The percentage of collections from this tax to the
total collections from all taxes on income and property is only about .72 per cent.[26]

Expenditure Tax

Expenditure tax is a personal tax on consumption expenditures; it is levied in Ceylon and India.

In Ceylon the taxable unit is the family. The
tax rates range from 10-200 per cent. A married
couple with four dependents becomes liable to the
maximum rate of 200 per cent on expenditures in excess of Rs 115,000. For a single person, the maximum rate applies to expenditures in excess of Rs
47,000. Exempt expenditures include: the cost of
educating children abroad; medical expenses, funerals,
marriage, and birth expenses; legal expenses and
premiums on life, accident, health, and disability

insurance and annuity contracts.[27]

In India the tax is imposed annually on expenditures incurred by individuals and Hindu undivided families, but not on corporations. (A Hindu undivided or "joint" family consists of all male Hindus descended in the male line from a common ancestor, their wives, and their unmarried daughters.) The tax is based on world-wide expenditures, expenditures within India, or expenditures outside India from Indian sources. The residence and citizenship status of the taxpayer are also taken into consideration when the expenditures are assessed.

A standard deduction of Rs 30,000 is allowed. Expenditures in excess of this allowance are taxed at progressive rates. (See Appendix IV.) Some of the exempt items from the expenditure tax of India are expenses of business or employment, investments, and capital outlays for personal use and gifts.[28]

Collections in 1961 and 1962 amounted to Rs 9 million and Rs 8 million, respectively. Although this represents only about 3 per cent of the annual total collections from taxes on income and property,[29] the expenditure tax has succeeded in regulating excessive consumption.

Annual Tax on Wealth

India imposes an annual tax on net wealth, "the aggregate value of all assets owned by the taxpayer on the valuation date less his debts on that date."[30]

Certain properties are totally exempt from the tax. Notable among these are agricultural properties, properties belonging to charitable or religious trusts, works of art, personal effects (up to a maximum of Rs 25,000), and balances in provident funds and life insurance policies.

The exemption level is Rs 200,000 for individuals, Rs 400,000 for joint Hindu families, and Rs 500,000 for corporations. Corporations are taxed at a flat rate of 1/2 per cent. (Appendix IV shows the details of the tax rates.)   The liability for wealth tax is determined on the basis of residence and citizenship.[31]

Registration Tax

A registration tax is levied in South Vietnam, South Korea, and Malaysia.

South Vietnam levies the tax on most types of professional, commercial, and manufacturing activities.   Teachers, farmers, businesses engaged in the extraction of natural resources, and a few other kinds of businesses are exempt.

In addition to a basic tax which is a specific levy determined by the type of business, there is an ad valorem levy imposed on the rental value of the business property.   The tax rates on rental value are progressive, ranging from 3-10 per cent, depending on the assessment of the basic tax.   Thus, the tax rate applied to the annual rent plus the basic tax compose the total registration tax for the central government.[32]

Collections from business license taxes in South Vietnam constitute about 11 per cent of taxes on income and property.   In South Korea the registration tax comprises about 2-5 per cent of the annual total collections from income and property taxes.   Collections from the same sources are much less in Malaysia: Revenues from business registration taxes make up only about .2 per cent of the total collections from taxes on income and property.[33]

CONCLUDING COMMENTS AND OBSERVATIONS

Total revenues from the taxation of income and property in underdeveloped economies, including individual and corporate income taxes, are small in proportion to the total revenues from all tax sources. This is shown in Table 11.

TABLE 11

Percentage of Taxes on Income and
Property to Total Taxes

Countries	1960	1961	1962 (estimated)
Republic of China	a/	a/	a/
India	32	32	31
Japan	60	58	59
Malaysia	23	28	28
Philippines	20	21	19
Singapore	36	44	47
South Korea	51	42	28
South Vietnam	16	15	15
Thailand	13	13	9
Cambodia	16	24	24
Indonesia	32	37	41
Ceylon	19	19	18

[a] Data not available.

Source: Japan Tax Association, op. cit.

The small percentages can be ascribed to a number of factors. Foremost is the fact that most of
these countries have been having problems in tax administration and collection. In Thailand, for example, defects in the tax-collection machinery have

been cited as one of the causes of the poor yield
from taxation.[34] Furthermore, the rates of the different taxes on income and property, other than the
individual and corporate income taxes, are not high
enough to allow for substantial returns.

The examination of the structures of the different taxes on income and property, other than the individual and corporate income taxes, has disclosed
some unusual features, including:

1. The gift tax in the Philippines has separate schedules of rates applicable to the donor and
donee. The rates of the donee's tax are based upon
his relation to the donor: The closer the blood relationship, the lower the tax.

2. The Land Law in the Republic of China provides for separate taxes on private vacant land and
private uncultivated land, in addition to the land
value tax and the land value increment tax. Furthermore, the land value taxes collectible on land owned
by absentee landlords are double the amount of the
regular land value taxes.

3. In South Vietnam the real property tax is a
source of revenue for the central government. In
other countries, the Philippines, for example, collections from taxes on real property accrue to local
governments.

4. To finance compulsory education, South
Korea imposes a school tax on individuals having
residence in Korea and on corporations which have
offices in that country.

5. In India an expenditure tax and an annual
tax on net wealth are levied as direct personal taxes.
The expenditure tax is levied on consumption expenditures, while the annual tax on wealth is imposed on
the "aggregate value of all assets owned by the taxpayer on the valuation date less his debts on that
date."

Notes to Chapter 5

1. Harold S. Sloan and John A. Zurcher, _Dictionary of Economics_ (New York: Barnes & Noble, Inc., 1957), p. 13.

2. _Ibid._, p. 166.

3. _Ibid._, p. 141.

4. A new schedule of estate tax rates for Malaysia which took effect on January 1, 1965, is also shown in Appendix V-A.

5. Harvard Law School International Program in Taxation, _Taxation in India_ (Boston: Little, Brown & Co., 1960), pp. 111-16.

6. Philippines (Republic), _National Internal Revenue Code_, Sec. 85.

7. Singapore Estate Duty Office and Stamp Office, _Reports for the Year 1955-6_ (Singapore: Government Printing Office, 1957), p. 1.   (See Appendix V-A for the new rates which took effect on January 1, 1965.)

8. China (Republic), _Laws of the Republic of China_ (Taiwan: October, 1962), p. 558.

9. "World Tax Review," _Bulletin for International Fiscal Documentation_, XVIII (March, 1964), 113-15.

10. Japan Tax Bureau, _Outline of Japanese Tax, 1964_, pp. 88-90.

11. The currency of South Korea was changed from hwan to won in 1962. Figures expressed in hwan can be converted with the equivalence of 10 hwan to 1 won.

12. _A Guide to Investment in Korea--Basic Information for Foreign Businessmen_ (Seoul: Korean Reconstruction Bank, 1962), p. 124.

13. Taxation in India, op. cit., pp. 111-16.

14. Bulletin for International Fiscal Documentation, op. cit., pp. 113-15.

15. A Guide to Investment in Korea, loc. cit.

16. National Internal Revenue Code, Secs. 109-10.

17. Milton Taylor, Taxes of Vietnam (Michigan State University Vietnam Advisory Group, 1960), pp. 4-10.

18. Taxation in India, op. cit., pp. 93-95.

19. Commonwealth Act No. 470, June 16, 1939.

20. Laws of the Republic of China, op. cit., p. 257. In this connection, the Joint Legislative-Executive Tax Commission has proposed to tax idle lands in the Philippines.

21. A Guide to Investment in Korea, op. cit., p. 125.

22. Japan Tax Association, Proceedings of the Special Meeting on Tax System and Administration in Asian Countries (Japan: The Association, 1963), p. 187.

23. Commonwealth Act No. 465, Sec. 1.

24. Japan Tax Association, op. cit., p. 219.

25. Commonwealth Act No. 613, Sec. 13.

26. Japan Tax Association, op. cit., pp. 255-65.

27. Richard Goode, "New System for Direct Taxation in Ceylon," National Tax Journal, XIII (December, 1960), 334-35.

28. Taxation in India, op. cit., pp. 422-23.

29. Japan Tax Association, op. cit., pp. 142-43.

30. Taxation in India, op. cit., p. 405.

31. Indian Investment Center, Investing in India (New Delhi, 1962), pp. 92-98. The illustration below shows the operation of the net wealth tax of India.

Mr. X is not a citizen of India. He arrived in the country for the first time on April 1, 1958. As of March 31, 1962, he had acquired the following assets:

(1) Bank balances in India	Rs 150,000
(2) Bank balances outside India	Rs 100,000
(3) House property outside India	Rs 200,000
(4) Jewelry	Rs 100,000
(5) Household effects	Rs 50,000
(6) Balance to the credit of recognized provident funds	Rs 50,000
(7) Shares in foreign companies	Rs 500,000
(8) Shares in Indian companies	Rs 100,000

Since Mr. X is not an "ordinary resident" of India, he is liable for the payment of taxes on assets located only in India. Hence, items (2), (3), and (7) are excluded. Furthermore, items (5) and (6) are totally exempt. Item (4) is partially exempt. His taxable wealth is:

Bank balance in India	Rs 150,000
Jewelry (Rs 25,000 exempt)	Rs 75,000
Shares in Indian companies	Rs 100,000
TOTAL	Rs 325,000
Less: Exemption Limit	Rs 200,000
	Rs 125,000
Wealth Tax at 1 per cent	Rs 1,250

32. Taylor, loc. cit.

33. Japan Tax Association, op. cit., pp. 213-15.

34. International Bank for Reconstruction and Development, A Public Development Program for Thailand (Baltimore: Johns Hopkins University Press, 1959), p. 245.

6

INTRODUCTION

Taxes on production and sales, which are basically levies on consumption, include taxes on the production and sale of goods and services and those levied on the importation and exportation of commodities. Many of these taxes come under the conventional category of indirect taxes.[1] As such, they are generally wholly or partially shifted, either forward to the consumers or backward to the owners of the factors of production through the price mechanism.

The imposition of taxes on production and sales is usually defended on the ground of administrative feasibility: They are convenient to pay since they are hidden from the ultimate taxpayer in that they are included in the prices of goods or services purchased. A corollary justification for the imposition of production and sales taxes, especially in developing economies, is their high revenue productivity. The general sales tax, which is levied extensively, is particularly effective; in more developed countries, sales tax provides an effective tool for counteracting inflationary trends and serves to regulate and control particular items of consumption, such as liquor and tobacco.

On the other hand, the imposition of taxes on production and sales is usually opposed on the grounds that these taxes generally take a greater percentage of the earnings of those in the lower-income brackets than of those in the higher-income brackets. Furthermore, to the extent that a production tax or a sales tax is applied only to a few goods or consumption items, they are often criticized as not being neutral since they tend to disturb consumer preferences and the allocation of factor resources.

The various production and sales taxes in the Asian countries can be classified into four major categories:

(1) import and export duties
(2) special excises
(3) sales taxes[2]
(4) licenses and other business and occupation taxes.[3]

IMPORT AND EXPORT DUTIES

Import and export duties are levied on goods and commodities transacted in international trade. These levies are applied either to all imported or exported items, or only to selected items.[4] Except for Japan and Indonesia, collections from these sources constitute the bulk of total revenue. Thailand, Malaysia, and Ceylon rely heavily on export and import duties: Revenues from these sources comprise about 39.7 per cent, 63.9 per cent, and 52.9 per cent, respectively, of total revenue and about 89.1 per cent, 88.6 per cent, and 70.5 per cent of total tax collections from production and sales taxes in 1963. In South Korea, the Philippines, and India collections from these sources have comprised about 20-25 per cent of total revenue. The imposition of import duties in many of the countries also serves as a protective measure for local industries producing goods similar to the imported ones.

The rates of import duties vary in many countries according to whether the commodities are considered luxuries, semiessentials, or essentials, and whether such commodities are domestically produced or not. Essential goods and those not domestically produced are usually taxed at lower rates than luxuries, semiessentials, and commodities produced domestically. Export taxes, on the other hand,

are levied at low rates and are usually confined to
a few selected primary export products. There are
cases where export taxes are applied on all items of
exports. In some countries supplementary taxes and
fees are levied in addition to export and import
duties.

In South Vietnam[5] import duties are applied on
almost all imported products. Duties on exports are
also levied, but only on a few products. Additional
minor fees are also imposed on exports and imports.

Import duties are applied in terms of either
minimum rates or general rates. Minimum rates apply
on goods imported from countries that grant their
lowest tariff rates or commensurate advantages to
Vietnamese goods. Goods not subject to minimum rates
are subject to general rates.

The rates vary between 5 and 80 per cent. However, most goods are subject to rates between 30 and
40 per cent. Duties are usually applied on an ad
valorem basis, but a few are subject to specific
rates. The rates are generally low on industrial
equipment and necessities, but higher on nonessentials. Thus, trucks and industrial diesel motors
are levied a tax of 5 and 15 per cent, respectively,
and essentials, such as condensed milk and wheat
flour, 10 and 12 per cent, respectively. Liquor and
cosmetics are taxed 75 and 80 per cent, respectively.

The perequation tax is also levied on thirteen
selected products, primarily to provide revenue to
finance export subsidies. It is applied in three
different ways:

(1) at ad valorem rates where the base is the
C.I.F. price of the following goods: textiles made
of ramie or filament fibers, 40 per cent; products
made of rayon and cresol, 60 per cent; products made
of synthetic fibers, 80 per cent; products made of
silk, 100 per cent; cigarette leaf tobacco, 50 per
cent; skins and hides (leather), 20 per cent; news-
print, 10 per cent; and wood panel, 20 per cent;

(2) at specific rates, such as on kerosene and automotive diesel fuel, at the rate of 40.8 VN$ per hecto-liter;

(3) on wheat flour, jute bags, and sugar at a rate equal to the difference between the authorized selling price per metric ton, including profit margin, and the actual wholesale price per metric ton.

A stabilization surtax is also levied on foreign-exchange purchases by importers of certain products (fifty categories of products in 1960). It is levied at a flat rate of VN$ 50 per U.S. $1, so that the effective rate of exchange is VN$ 85 per U.S. $1. Revenues from this source are allocated for subsidizing exports and purchasing United States dollars at the official rate of exchange.

Export duties, on the other hand, are imposed on over forty commodities, including copper, poultry, fish, and lacquer ware, at the rate of 5 per cent. In addition, special export taxes are levied at the rate of 12 per cent on paddy, 10 per cent on rice, 8 per cent on rice breakings, 6 per cent on flour, 3 per cent on rubber, and 2 per cent on ores.

Among the miscellaneous taxes and fees imposed on certain imports and exports[6] are the following:

    (a) statistics fee levied on imports and exports of VN$ 2 per package for package goods, or per metric ton, per cubic meter, or per head for other goods and animals;

    (b) inspection taxes on agricultural commodities varying from .40 to 10.0 VN$ per 100 kilograms;

    (c) sanitation and inspection fees on the import and export of forest and vegetable products based either on weight or per unit which are levied at low rates;

    (d) medical inspection fees on the import and export of animals which vary between VN$ .01 per head on poultry to VN$ 2.0 per head for dogs and cats; and

    (e) an annual progressive tax based on tonnage of VN$ 10 for ships of less than one ton

to 40 VN$ per ton for vessels over 10 tons
is also imposed on ocean-going vessels.

In Indonesia[7] duties on imports and exports are
also levied. Import duties and charges are assessed
on the C.I.F. value, while those on exports are
assessed on F.O.B. value. The basic import tariff
rates are divided into three main categories: (1) raw
materials and semimanufactured goods, 6 per cent;
(2) ordinary consumer goods, 12 per cent ad valorem;
and (3) luxury goods, 20 per cent ad valorem. A 50
per cent surtax has been added to these basic rates,
raising these duties to 9 per cent, 18 per cent and
30 per cent, respectively. Duties have been set
also for a few items at ad valorem rates. Furthermore, specific duties for about twenty items are
levied.

Exemption from import duties is granted on certain categories of commodities.[8]

In India[9] to supplement the various instruments
of foreign trade policy and to generate revenue, import and export duties are levied by the Central Government.[10] The Indian Tariff Act prescribed three
types of import rates: the "Commonwealth preference"
at favored rates, preferential rates, and the standard
rate of duty. Commonwealth preference at favored
rates are granted to certain goods and commodities
imported from the United Kingdom and other Commonwealth countries. Preferential rates are applied on
certain goods imported from Burma. The standard
rates of duty are the ordinary rates, including duties levied on certain commodities imported from
GATT (General Agreement in Tariffs and Trade) member-
countries as well as all other duties which are non-
preferential.

Under the First Schedule of the Indian Tariff
Act of 1934, the commodities are classified into
twenty-two categories and each duty levied on a commodity is classified either as "protective," "revenue," or "preferential revenue." Although most of
the duties are applied on an ad valorem basis, some
are made specific by fixing the tariff values of the

commodities to which the ad valorem duties apply.
Specific duties are applied either solely or in addition to ad valorem duties. Where a commodity may
be subject to either ad valorem or specific duty, the
higher rate is imposed. On some commodities an additional rate, based on the excise tax imposed on similar goods produced or manufactured locally, is levied
together with the import duty.

Goods subject to ad valorem tariff rates are
generally taxed at 30-40 per cent. Goods considered
to be luxuries and "nonessentials" and those produced locally in sufficient quantity are taxed at
higher rates than those classified as essential.
Thus, on tobacco, wines and spirits, silk garments,
certain fabrics, spices, and motor vehicles, the
rates vary from 75-200 per cent; while certain food
products, raw materials for industry, agricultural
implements, specified types of machinery, and fuel
oils are either exempted from the duty or taxed at
lower rates.[11] As prescribed in the tariff schedule at rates recommended by the Tariff Commission,
protective tariffs may be imposed for a limited
period on certain goods, such as coal tar dies, certain forms of aluminum and zinc, and certain machineries and parts. Certain imports from the United
Kingdom or other Commonwealth countries are levied
duties which differ by 10 percentage points or less
from the normal ad valorem duty. On the other hand,
most imports from Burma are either exempt totally or
subject to lower rates not exceeding 20 per cent.[12]

Exemptions from import duty are granted on particular goods by the Central Government or in exceptional cases by special order of the Central Board
of Revenue with the approval of the Central Government. The fixing or revising of tariff rates is
also prescribed by the Central Government. Regulations relating to the re-importation of goods previously imported, the re-importation of goods imported
less than three years previously, and goods imported
by an individual on a change of address are also provided.

An interesting feature of the Indian tariff

system is the concepts of "real value" and "drawbacks." The concept of "real value" is the basis of
an ad valorem duty on goods whose value is not prescribed in the tariff schedule. "Real value" is the
wholesale cash price (including wholesaler's or importer's profit) for which goods of similar kind and
quality are sold or are capable of being sold at the
time and place of importation. If the wholesale cash
price can not be determined, real value is ascertained on the basis of the cost at which the goods
in question could be delivered at the place of importation. Normal trade discounts are deducted and the
amount of import duty is excluded from the wholesale
cash price. On the other hand, "drawback" refers to
the refunded portion (seven-eighths) of the duty
previously paid on imports that have been re-exported
or shipped as ships' stores within two years. A different regulation is prescribed relating to drawbacks
for goods used as raw materials for products manufactured in India, as in the case of silk fabrics, dry
cell batteries, and plastic wares during the period
between import and re-export.

Export duties are levied at either ad valorem
or specific rates on twenty-one commodities listed
under the Second Schedule of the Indian Tariff Act
of 1934.[13] The duty on tea, which yields a substantial portion of revenue from exports, is levied a
specific rate. The following commodities are also
subject to export duty: cotton and cotton waste, 50
per cent; cut cloth, 25 per cent; iron and steel, 45
per cent; manganese ore, 25 per cent; and wood, 30
per cent. Other commodities subject to import duty
include jute, rice, coffee, cigarettes, and certain
vegetable oils. On some commodities such as tea,
jute, certain unprocessed cotton, lac, coffee, bones,
bristle, fibers, skins, tobacco, and raw materials,
excise duties or "cesses" are levied in addition to
the export duty.

Exemptions are granted to such selected export
commodities as black pepper, iron and steel products,
manganese ores, and vegetable oils.

The Philippines has two types of customs duty on

imports:[14] the ordinary customs duties and the
special import duties. Merchandise to be exported
abroad is not subject to export duty. The ordinary
customs duties are imposed either at ad valorem or
specific rate. The former is based on the prevailing wholesale market price at the time of importation and cost of ordinary transportation, including
freight and insurance, while the latter is based on
the quantity or the weight of the commodity. Certain merchandise may be subject either to both ad
valorem and specific rates or to whichever is higher.
The rates vary according to the classification and
essentiality of the merchandise being imported.
Rates on essential consumer and producer goods are
lower than on semiessential and nonessential consumer or producer goods.[15] Under the Laurel-Langley
Agreement between the United States and the Philippines, preferential rates are applied on goods imported from the United States.

A special import tax designed primarily to generate revenue is currently being levied on all imports. The rate was initially levied at 17 per cent
on January 1, 1956, and was then lowered gradually
to 1.7 per cent to take effect until December 31,
1965.

As in other Asian countries, in addition to ordinary import duties, several special import duties
are levied to protect local industries: the dumping
duty, the countervailing duty, the marking duty, and
the retaliatory duty. The dumping duty is imposed
on imported articles that are sold at a price less
than their fair market value. The duty is the difference between the purchase price or exporter's
price and the fair market value of the articles in
the importing country. The countervailing duty is
imposed on articles whose production, manufacture,
or export is granted a bounty, subsidy, or subvention in the country of origin or exportation and the
importation of which will materially injure an established industry or retard the establishment of an industry in the Philippines. The tax is equal to the
amount of the bounty, subsidy, or subvention. Marking duty of 5 per cent is levied on C.I.F. value of

imported articles that do not indicate the country of
origin. On articles imported from any foreign country which discriminates against the commerce of the
Philippines, a retaliatory duty of not more than 50
per cent of the existing tariff rates is imposed.

Under Section 401 of the Tariff and Customs Code,
upon investigation by the Tariff Commission and upon
recommendation of the National Economic Council, the
President under certain circumstances is empowered
to reduce by not more than 50 per cent or to increase
by not more than five times the rates of import duty
fixed by the statute.

Several additional fees, dues, and charges are
imposed, such as harbor fees on owners, agents, operators or masters of vessels entering or leaving the
country; wharfage dues on owners, consignees, or
agents of cargos or vessels engaged in foreign trade;
berthing charges on owners, agents, operators or masters of vessels mooring or making fast in any port;
storage charges on owners or agents of articles
stored in customs premises and government warehouses;
arrastre charges for handling, receiving custody of
articles or baggages; tonnage dues on articles dis-
charged or laden or on net tonnage of vessels; and
other fees and charges for services and documents
issued by the Bureau of Customs.

In the Republic of China[16] import duty applies
on several commodities which are grouped into fifteen broad categories. As is the case with other
Asian countries, essential goods and raw materials
are taxed lower than those imposed on nonessentials
and finished products. The rates are ad valorem on
the basis of the wholesale market value of the goods
in terms of domestic currency. On cotton and manufactures, the rates range from 10-50 per cent; on
wool and manufactures thereof, 15-100 per cent; and
on natural silks, 25-100 per cent. Metals and metal
manufactures are taxed at lower rates, 5-100 per cent
The rates on chemicals, pharmaceuticals, and dyes
range from 5-80 per cent, while on paper pulp and
other paper products, from 10-80 per cent. Other imported articles are taxed at rates from 7 1/2 -120
per cent.

Less extensive but similarly structured are the
tariff and customs duties imposed in Thailand, South
Korea, and Singapore. In Thailand certain goods imported from abroad or exported to other countries
are levied duties which vary for each classification
or group of merchandise. The duties are either levied
at an ad valorem or specific rate. However, reduction in rates and exemption from import duties of
raw materials and other imported merchandise considered vital and necessary to the economy are automatically provided under the law. Special privileges with respect to importation are also accorded,
with the approval of the cabinet.[17] Some of the commodities which are levied export duties are the following: sheet rubber or other kinds of rubber derived from any part of the rubber tree; nonmetallic
minerals or ores, excluding all articles produced of
rubber; and metallic minerals or ores.

In South Korea[18] duties apply only to imports.
The rates which are levied either on ad valorem or
specific basis vary and are designed to protect domestic industry. The ad valorem duty is determined on
the C.I.F. prices. Generally, lower rates are imposed on machinery and industrial equipment than on
luxury goods and imported commodities which are produced domestically. However, goods which have been
exported for processing or repairs and are then re-
imported are either exempted or taxed at low rates.
A tonnage tax at the rate of 1 won per ton is levied
on ships arriving in any port. Although Singapore
is a free port, a few commodities such as tobacco
and tea are subject to import duty.

SPECIAL EXCISES

Special excises are levies applied at the place
of production or manufacture of selected commodities.
Two main justifications advanced to support such imposition are that special excises are a lucrative
source of revenue and that they are easy to administer. Special excises are also defended on sumptuary
grounds. The usual arguments against special excises
center on their being regressive, and not neutral, as

they discriminate against consumer preferences. In
some instances, as in liquor and cigarette taxation,
if stretched beyond a certain limit, special excises invite tax evasion and "bootlegging." There
is no clearcut basis for choosing which commodity
should be subject to a special excise. An author
has suggested that a suitable object of special excise should be a commodity which has one or more of
these characteristics: (a) large volume, (b) inelas-
tic demand, (c) nonessential character, (d) ready de-
finability, and (e) no close substitutes which are
untaxed.[19]

Based on the above discussion, the special excises covered are those imposed on gasoline, liquor
and distilled spirits, tobacco products such as
cigars and cigarettes, playing cards, and a few
other items. The special excises referred to are
those imposed upon the production or manufacture of
these commodities, and not on the subsequent levies
that may be imposed on the same commodities.[20] It
should also be mentioned that special excises are
levied on certain imported goods.

Most of the excise taxes levied by countries included in the study are specific in nature. There
are a few instances, however, where ad valorem rates
are resorted to. Excise taxes are prominent features
of production and sales taxes in many Asian countries.
Like import and export duties, they yield substantial
revenues. In 1963 total excise tax collections in
Singapore constituted 37.5 per cent of total revenues;
in India, 43.3 per cent; in the Philippines, 22.2 per
cent; in Japan, 21.3 per cent; and in Indonesia and
South Korea, 16.8 and 16.2 per cent, respectively.

In Japan manufacturers of liquor or those who
receive liquor from bonded areas are liable to the
liquor tax on liquor shipped[21] from the manufacturing or bonded area. The tax is levied either at ad
valorem rates or at specific rates which are now common. The specific rates of duty vary according to
the kind, class, and percentage of alcohol content.[22]

TABLE 12

Specific Liquor Tax Rates in Japan

Item	Alcohol Content (per cent)	Tax Rate (yen / kilo liter)
Refined sake		
Special class	16	252,100
First class	15.5	152,100
Second class	15	85,800
Synthetic sake	15	62,500
Shochu		
Group A	35, 25, 20	113,850; 48,600; and 35,000, respectively
Group B	35, 25, 20	85,000; 37,400; and 27,000, respectively
Mining		
Group A	13	67,700
Group B	22	55,300
Beer	–	95,000
Wine		
Group A	–	63,000
Group B	–	24,000
Sweet wine	12	48,000
Special class	43	845,100
Whiskey		
First class	40	390,600
Second class	37	148,000
Spirits	47	188,000
Liquor		
Group A	20	200,000
Group B	–	48,000
Malt liquors		
Group A	–	95,000
Group B	–	67,000
Group C	–	40,000
Other liquors	–	48,000

Certain kinds of expensive liquor, however, are subject to ad valorem rates on the ground that these have sufficient taxbearing ability. The base on which such tax is imposed is the manufacturer's selling price or the price as received from a bonded area plus customs duty. The ad valorem rates and the liquor subject to it are as shown in Table 13.[23]

TABLE 13

Ad Valorem Liquor Tax Rates in Japan

Item	Nontaxable Maximum of Ad Valorem duty (yen / liter)	Tax Rate (per cent)
Refined sake (special class)	250	150
Wine		
Sparkling	900	50
Others	700	50
Sweet wine		
Sparkling	900	50
Others	700	50
Whiskey (special class)	800	150
Brandy (special class)	1,200	150
Spirits	400	100
Liquor (alcohol content more than 15% and essence more than 21%)	800	100
Others		
Sparkling	900	50
Others	700	50

Liquor for export, however, is not subject to tax on the principle that the tax is designed only for liquor consumption within the country.

Japan also imposes an excise tax on gasoline manufacturers at the point of shipping from refineries or receipts from bonded areas. The tax is based on the quantity of gasoline shipped from refineries or received from bonded areas after deducting allowances for storage and loss in transit.[24] The rate is 24,300 yen per kiloliter.

The other types of commodity subject to excise tax are sugar and playing cards. The rates are as shown in Table 14.[25]

TABLE 14

Japan's Excise Tax Schedule

Item	Rate
Class 1 sugar	
Domestic, noncentrifugal sugar	¥ 1/kg.
Sugar (which contains molasses)	¥ 3/kg.
Class 2 sugar (not specified in Class 1 and 3)	¥16/kg.
Class 3 sugar	
Crystallized sugar and the like	¥20.50/kg.
Cube sugar, bar sugar, and the like	¥25.50/kg.
Molasses	
Beet molasses and those below 40 sugar degrees	¥ 3.50/kg.
Other molasses	¥ 8.50/kg.
Liquid sugar	
Liquid sugar below 15 sugar degrees	¥ 2/kg.
Other liquid sugar	¥12/kg.
Mahjong	
Made of ivory	¥8,000/set
Made of cattle bone	¥3,000/set
Made of other materials	¥ 500/set
Playing cards	¥ 40/set

Excise taxation is also a prominent feature of the tax systems in Indonesia, South Vietnam, and Thailand. In Indonesia, sugar produced by farmers by the traditional method and without the aid of mechanically driven apparatus is not subject to the excise tax. Except on tobacco and other tobacco products, which are subject to ad valorem rates of 40 and 30 per cent of the retail price, all the other commodities are subject to specific rates. In South Vietnam, aside from the basic rates, additional taxes, surtax, and other fees are imposed. In Thailand varying rates of specific taxes are levied on several commodities. Table 15 shows the corresponding rates of excise taxes imposed in the above-mentioned countries.

In India[26] there are about twenty-seven types of commodities subject to excise tax by the Central Government, or what is more commonly referred to as "Union excise duty." Excise taxation of liquor and narcotics is, however, the exclusive right of the States. Most of the excise taxes levied by the Central Government are at specific rates, although a few commodities are subject to ad valorem rates. In addition, certain miscellaneous excise taxes are also levied. The taxes are levied on and collected from the manufacturers, or in the case of unmanufactured goods on the curers and wholesale dealers.

The list of commodities and the tax rates set forth in the First Schedule of the Central Excises and Salt Act of 1964 are shown in Table 16.

In the Philippines[27] specific tax rates are levied per unit of output on the manufacture of certain articles for revenue as well as sumptuary purposes. Commodities which are covered by the specific excise tax are, however, exempted from the sales tax.

TABLE 15

Excise Tax Rates for Indonesia, South Vietnam, and Thailand

Indonesia[28]

Item	Rate
Alcohol (50 per cent alcohol strength)	750 rupiah/hectoliter
Beer (domestically produced)	82.50 rupiah/hectoliter
Petroleum or kerosene (ordinary lighting)	7 rupiah/hectoliter
Gasoline, benzine, and other petroleum derivatives	50 rupiah/hectoliter
Tobacco products (cigars, cigarettes, cut tobacco, and others) unpacked or domestically packed	40% retail price
Other tobacco products	30% retail price
Cane, beet, and other sugar	27 rupiah/100 kgs.

South Vietnam[29]

Item	Rate
Tobacco	
Pipe tobacco, cigarettes	40% of retail price; 10% (surtax)
Cigars	VN$ 76.5 per kilo; 10% (surtax) and VN$ 5 kilo (additional tax) for every VN$ 50
Cigarettes (domestic tobacco)	25% retail price not in excess of VN$ 4 per package of 20 cigarettes 50% of retail price in excess of VN$ 4 per package of 20 cigarettes

TABLE 15 (continued)

Tobacco (processed by traditional Vietnamese method)	VN$ 8.50 per kilo
Tobacco (imported)	25%
Beer	
Beer (domestically produced)	VN$ 450/100 liters VN$ 60,000 verification fee
Beer (imported)	VN$ 450/100 liters 25% of C.I.F. plus customs duty (production tax) VN$ 1/100 liters
Alcohol	
Vietnamese wine (made from rice)	VN$ 5/liter
Chinese wine (with Chinese herbs)	VN$ 3.5/liter (additional tax) VN$ 4 (surtax) VN$ 2/VN$ 20 retail price exceeding VN$ 50 (over estimated tax)
French-type liquor	VN$ 25.5/liter VN$ 12/liter (surtax) VN$ 5.0/VN$ 50 retail price exceeding VN$ 100 per liter (over estimated tax)
Methyl alcohol	VN$ 1.7/liter
Imported alcohol	same as French-type liquor 35% C.I.F. price plus customs duty (production tax)
Sugar	
Sugar (imported, refined, palm)	VN$ 85/100 kilos
Sugar (domestic, brown, artisan)	VN$ 50/100 kilos
Matches	VN$ .10/box
Gasoline	VN$ 108.80/100 kilos VN$ 93.5 (surtax) VN$ .08/100 kilos (verification fee) VN$ .06 and VN$ .03 (warehousing fee)

104

Kerosene   VN$ 147.9/100 kilos   VN$ 35.7 (surtax)
Flints   VN$ 2,550/kilo   VN$ 5/kilo (verification fee)

Radio tubes   VN$ 17/tube

Thailand[30]

Item	Rate
Alcohol	
Absolute alcohol	8 Baht per liter
Methylated spirits	1 Baht per liter
Spirits of 28 degrees	44.80 Baht per 20 liters
Not over 15%, in bottle of not over 20 ct. liters	20 stamps
In bottle of over 20 ct. liters but not over 40 ct. liters	40 stamps
In bottle over 40 ct. liters	40 stamps
Over 15 degrees but not over 30	40 stamps
Over 30 degrees but not over 80	80 stamps
Over 80 degrees	120 stamps
Beer	Baht/liter
Beverages	
440 c.m.³	10 stamps
Over 440 c.m.³	20 stamps
Matches	
Not over 60-stick box, 100 boxes	0.33 Baht
Over 60-stick box for over 30 boxes	0.165 Baht
Mechanical lighter	0.40 Baht

TABLE 15 (continued)

Cigarettes

15 gms., 20 cigarettes	3 stamps	
25 gms., 20 cigarettes	5 stamps	
30 gms., 20 cigarettes	6 stamps	
35 gms. or 5 cigars	7 stamps	
40 gms. or 20 cigars	8 stamps	
55 gms. or 50 cigarettes	11 stamps	
60 gms., 50 cigarettes	12 stamps	
70 gms., 50 cigarettes	14 stamps	

Pipe tobacco

226.8 gms.	23 stamps/tin
198.45 gms.	20 stamps/tin
56.7 gms.	6 stamps/tin

Cement   2 stamps/kg.

Snuffs

First 2 gms.	30 stamps
Exceeding 2 gms.	15 stamps/gram

TABLE 16

Excise Tax Rates for India

Item	Specific Rates (rupees)	Ad Valorem Rates
Kerosene (any inflammable hydro-carbon normally used for illumination)	0.25/imp. gal.	
Matches	0.80-4.90/gross of boxes	
Mechanical lighters	0.50	75%
Motor spirit (usable for motor power)	1.39/imp. gal.	
Silver	0.225/troy ounce	
Steel ingots	40.00/ton (2,240 lbs)	
Sugar (factory produced)	5.60-11.25/cwt. (112 lbs) (basic) 3.31 (additional)	
Tobacco (unmanufactured)	0.47-7.50/lb. (basic); 0.50 (additional)	
Manufactured cigars	0.25-7.50/100 cigars (basic) 0.50 (additional)	
Cigarettes	1.20-17.40/1,000 cigarettes (basic) 8.60 (additional)	
Biris	0.60/1,000 biris	
Tires (containing some rubber) For motor vehicles		40%
All other tires		15%
Vegetable product (any vegetable oil or fat hardened for human consumption)	8.50/cwt.	
Cotton fabrics	0.06/cwt.; 0.22/sq. yd. (basic) 0.03-0.13 (additional)	

TABLE 16 (continued)

Item	Specific Rates (rupees)	Ad Valorem Rates
Rayon or artificial silk fabrics	0.06/sq. yd.	
Woolen fabrics	0.015 (additional)/sq. yd.	6 1/4% (basic) 5% (additional)
Coffee	0.19/lb.	
Tea	0.06-0.25/lb.	
Cement	24.00/ton	
Soap	4.50-14.00 cwt.	
Footwear		10%
Electric fans (excluding those indispensable in an industrial system)	1.50-10.00/fan	
Electric lighting bulbs and fluorescent lighting tubes	0.06-0.50/bulb or ft. of tube	
Electric batteries and parts		10%
Paper (including pasteboard, millboard, cardboard, etc.)	0.05-0.30/lb.	
Pigments, colors, paints, enamels, varnishes, blacks, and cellulose lacquers	5.00-28.00/lb.	
Vegetable nonessential oils (e.g., linseed, cottonseed oils)	0.44-5.00/imp. gal. 112.00/ton	
Refined diesel oils and vaporizing oil	0.80/imp. gal.	
Industrial fuel oils	29.00-52.00/ton	
Rayon and synthetic fibers and yarn	0.12-0.50/lb.	
Motor cars, including taxicabs	3,000.00/car	

TABLE 17

Philippine Excise Tax Rates

Item	Rate
Distilled spirits	₱0.70; ₱15.00/proof liter
Wines	₱1.00; ₱2.00; ₱12.00/liter of volume capacity
Fermented liquors	₱0.25/liter of volume capacity
Manufactured tobacco	
Chewing tobacco	₱0.60/kilogram
Others, e.g., smoking tobacco	.75 kilogram
Cigars	2.30; 4.60; 7.00/1,000 pieces
Cigarettes	
from Virginia-type or flue-cured tobacco	₱8.00–₱52.80, depending on length/ 1,000 sticks
from other types of leaf tobacco	₱2.50–₱11.00, depending on length/ 1,000 sticks
Matches	₱0.50/gross of boxes of 80 sticks or less to a box. If more than 80 sticks to a box, a proportionate additional tax
Firecrackers	₱20.00/kilogram
Manufactured oils and other fuels	
Kerosene or petroleum	₱0.025/liter of volume capacity
Lubricating oil	₱0.07/liter of volume capacity
Naptha, gasoline and similar products of distillation	₱0.08/liter of volume capacity
Denatured alcohol for motive power	₱0.01/liter of volume capacity

TABLE 17 (continued)

Item	Rate
Coal and coke	₱0.25/metric ton
Bunker fuel oil and similar fuel oils	₱0.40/metric ton
Diesel fuel oil and similar fuel oils	₱1.00/metric ton
Cinematographic films	
more than 8 mm. but less than 16 mm. in width	₱0.15/linear meter
more than 16 mm. in width	₱0.20/linear meter
Playing cards	₱10.00/pack of 60 cards or less. If more than 60 cards to a pack, proportionate additional tax
Saccharine	₱75.00/kilogram

Excise taxation in South Korea, the Republic of China, and Singapore is confined to a few selected commodities. In South Korea,[31] liquor is subject to an excise tax applied at specific rates. Industrial alcohol for manufacturing explosives is exempted from the tax. Ad valorem rates are levied on the following commodities: gasoline, 300 per cent; kerosene and light oil, 30 per cent; and 10 per cent on both heavy oil and other petroleum products. Among the products subject to excise taxation in the Republic of China are tobacco, tobacco products, and alcoholic liquors. The tax is based on the wholesale price of the commodity. The tax on leaf tobacco is 60 per cent, on tobacco cuttings, 40 per cent, and on cured leaf tobacco, 30 per cent. On alcoholic liquors, the tax is 100 per cent.

In Singapore the special excise tax applies to certain intoxicating liquors, petroleum products, tobacco, and tobacco products.

SALES TAXES

Sales taxes are general taxes imposed on the sale of products.[32] Unlike special excise taxes, they are applied extensively and cover a wide range of goods and services. Sales taxes are also generally imposed at ad valorem rates on total sales.

Sales taxes are usually levied for revenue purposes. In 1963 collections from sales taxes constituted 12.1 per cent of total revenue in South Korea, 5.0 per cent in the Philippines, 5.9 per cent in Indonesia, and 4.9 per cent in Japan.

Application of the sales tax varies among the countries covered in this study. The most common form is a general turnover tax, where the rate is imposed every time the product undergoes a market transfer. Since the tax base includes the portions of the final product which have been previously taxed, the effective rate on the final product varies. Some countries, such as India, Indonesia, and South Korea, resort to the so-called single-stage levy, by

exempting intermediate products and imposing the tax
only on the total value of the final product. Thus
the single-stage levy is generally applied at the retail stage. A few countries, including the Philippines and South Vietnam, use the value-added procedure, where the tax is applied on every transfer
from intermediate to the final product, but is confined to the value added by each transfer.

In South Korea the number of commodities subject to sales tax was reduced from seventy-five
items to only twenty-two.[33] Those commodities still
subject to tax are mostly goods with high elasticity
of demand. Tax rates are generally higher on goods
primarily consumed by those in the higher income
brackets. Under the revised commodity tax law, taxation on retail goods and on specified commodities
has been abrogated, but retained on raw materials,
manufacture, and delivery. Some of the commodities
subject to tax and the corresponding rates are shown
in Table 18.

On the other hand, a general sales tax on gross
receipts of traders is levied in Thailand.[34] Generally, the tax rates on raw materials and semiprocessed
goods are lower than those imposed on finished goods
and luxury items. Sales of precious stones and metal
are taxed at all levels. Those goods affected and
the corresponding rates are as shown in Table 19.

In the Philippines[35] sales taxes are imposed on
imported and locally manufactured articles. The
rate of sales tax varies according to the classification of goods. On locally manufactured goods, the
tax is levied on the gross selling price of the finished product, including the cost of raw materials
previously taxed. The tax base on imported items,
on the other hand, is the landed cost plus varying
mark-ups of 25 per cent, 50 per cent, or 100 per
cent, depending on the classification of the goods.
The schedule of sales tax rates is as shown in
Table 20.

TABLE 18

South Korean Sales Tax Rates

Item	Rate
Commodity type	
Raw wool	46%
Wool top	50%
Imported woolen yarn	60%
Cotton yarn	10%
Hemp yarn	10%
Commodity	
Staple fiber	10%
Filament yarn	10%
Other fiber products	15%
Fire coil yarn	10%
Imported textiles	40%
Raw hides	10%
Resin	40%
Raw rubber	20%
Paper products	2%
Cellophane	10%
Sheepskin	5%
Aluminum	10%
Flat glass	10%
Plywood	5%
Molasses	10%
Raw sugar	HW 180/kg.
Resh drinks	HW 30/liter
Coffee and tea	20%
Chemical fiber	10%

TABLE 19

Sales Tax Rates in Thailand

Item	Rate
Type 1 goods	
A) Goods and by-products not specified in types 2 to 9	5%
B) Goods and by-products under "A" but the manufacturers of which are not taxed under "A"	2%
Type 2 goods (Includes household appliances, refrigerators, cameras, etc.)	12%
Type 3 goods (Includes electric lamps and shades, motorcycles, motor units)	10%
Type 4 goods (Includes passenger cars and buses with not more than 10-passenger capacity)	20%
Type 5 goods (Whiskey, brandy, gin, rum, etc.)	25%
Type 6 goods (Books, documents, and printed materials)	2.5%
Type 7 goods (Precious stones and metals, and imitations)	3%
Type 8 goods (Rubber, sheet rubber, and metallic minerals or ores)	4%
Type 9 goods	
A) Semiprocessed goods or raw materials which are sold to a factory to be used for purposes of production and sale	1.5%
B) Goods sold to persons other than those specified in "A"	5%
C) Those under "A" which are used for purposes other than materials for production and sale	5%

TABLE 20

Philippine Sales Tax Rates

Item	Rate
Imported articles (advance sales tax)	
Automobiles	50%, 75%, or 100% of landed cost plus 100% mark-up
Other luxury articles	50% of landed cost plus 100% mark-up
Semiluxury items	30% of landed cost plus 50% mark-up
Ordinary items	7% of landed cost plus 25% mark-up
Locally manufactured articles	
Automobiles	50%, 75%, or 100% of gross selling price minus that of raw materials previously taxed
Other luxury items	50% of same
Semiluxury items	30% of same
Refrigerators and other cooling appliances manufactured by integrated and nonintegrated firms	7% or 15% of same
Ordinary articles	7% of gross selling price less cost of raw materials previously taxed

On imports not intended for sale and barter but for the importer's personal use, a compensating tax is imposed. The rates vary according to the classification of the article and are based on the landed cost. On automobiles, ad valorem rates of 50 per cent, 75 per cent, or 100 per cent are levied; on other luxury items, 50 per cent; and on semiluxury items such as refrigerators and other cooling appliances, 30 per cent. Ordinary items are levied a compensating tax of 7 per cent.

In Japan[36] sales taxes extend to fifty-nine commodities which fall into three broad categories. The rates and base for each of the broad classes vary. On Class 1 commodities, such as jewels and precious metal products, the tax rate is either 10 or 20 per cent of the retail sales price. Class 2 includes ordinary taxable commodities, such as television sets, automobiles, and cameras, and the tax is either 5, 10, 30, or 40 per cent of the manufacturer's sales price, depending on the group to which the commodity belongs. Class 3 commodities consist of matches and soft drinks, which are levied specific rates. The bulk of sales taxes is collected from Class 2 commodities. The schedule of sales taxes is as shown in Table 21.

TABLE 21

Japan's Sales Tax Schedule

Class 1

Group 1 (20% of the retailer's sales price)
   Precious stones, semiprecious stones, and their
      products
   Pearls and their products
   Precious metal products and gold or platinum
      products, excluding those in Class 1, Group 2
      and Class 2
   Tortoise-shell, coral, amber, and ivory products
   Cloisonné products
   Fur products

TABLE 21 (continued)

Group 2 (10% of the retailer's sales price)
  Articles for decoration of room and Keshomawashis
  Utensils for tea-art, incense-art and flower
    arrangement-art
  Articles for ornaments and toys
  Articles for "GO," "Shogi," or chess

Class 2

Group 1 (40% of the manufacturer's sales price)
  High-class passenger automobiles
  Motorboats, sculls, yachts, and their hulls
  Goods for golf and accessories thereof
  Clocks and watches, and parts thereof, in which
    precious stones or precious metals are used

Group 2 (30% of the manufacturer's sales price)
  Passenger automobiles
  Electric, gas, or mineral-oil radiators and room-
    coolers
  Electric, gas, or mineral-oil refrigerators
  Television, Braun tubes, and chassis
  Goods for billiards
  Rifles and cartridges
  Feather quilts

Group 3 (20% of the manufacturer's sales price)
  Small passenger automobiles
  Air-conditioning machines and parts thereof for
    automobiles
  Photographic or cinematographic apparatuses, and
    parts
  Films, dry-plates, and sensitive paper for photo-
    graphs
  Musical instruments, and parts and accessories
    thereof
  Record-players, and parts and accessories thereof
  Phonograph records
  Electric, gas, and liquid fuel refrigerators of
    small size
  Televisions of small size and Braun tubes

TABLE 21 (continued)

Electric fans
Heaters
Electric, gas, and liquid fuel instruments, not
  otherwise provided for
Lighting equipment
Furniture
Clothes, quilts, and gloves of leather
Bags, trunks, pouches, etc.
Articles for smoking
Game requisites

Group 4 (10 % of the manufacturer's sales price)
  Motorboats and sculls less than 6 meters long, and
    yachts less than 7.5 meters, and their hulls
  Engines for ships
  Radio receivers and their chassis
  Tape recorders and reproducers
  Clocks and watches, their movements and cases
  Binoculars
  Film-slide apparatus
  Photographic flashlights
  Neon tubes
  Fireworks, etc.
  Cutlery and manicure sets
  Beverages
  Coffee, cocoa, and tea

Group 5 (5% of the manufacturer's sales price)
  Passenger motorcycles and motorbicycles
  Microphones, amplifiers, and loudspeakers
  Vacuum tubes for receivers
  Toilet preparations
  Condensed juice

Class 3

Matches (1 yen per 1,000 sticks)
Refreshing drinks (5,000 yen per kiloliter)

The imposition of sales taxes in India[37] used
to be an exclusive power of the states until the enactment of the Central Sales Tax Act, which vested
in the Central Government certain powers of sales
taxation. The single-point sales tax is adopted by
urban states which have a high level of industrial,
manufacturing, and trade activities. Although a
large number of essential goods and raw materials
are exempt from sales taxes in these states, the
rates for those which are not exempt are relatively
high. The multi-point sales taxes are generally
utilized in predominantly rural states. In many
states, however, on account of varied needs, both
multi-point and single-point sales taxes are applied.

Sales taxes are imposed on the gross receipts
of wholesalers, retailers, and registered dealers.
The rates range from less than 1 per cent to 14 per
cent, depending on the nature of the goods whether
the sales tax is applied on a single-point or a
multi-point basis. Although single-point sales tax
rates are generally higher than multi-point sales
tax rates, total taxes that can be collected from
the latter are at times as high as those from the
former.

Exemptions and concessions are granted on certain types of goods. In the case of a multi-point
sales taxation, concessions may be in terms of taxing goods at only one stage of transfer. Luxury
goods, such as automobiles and electric appliances,
are usually levied higher sales tax rates than other
goods.

The Central Sales Tax Act prescribes the rates
on interstate sales. A standard tax rate of 7 per
cent is applicable to sales of similar goods within
the state which has jurisdiction of the sale, and a
higher rate is applied on sales of goods of particular importance to interstate commerce or trade.
Sales to the government and certain sales made to
registered dealers are levied a special tax rate of
1 per cent of the sales price.

In Indonesia[38] the turnover tax has been

replaced by a sales tax levied on manufactured goods,
both imported and domestically produced. Essential
goods and primary foodstuffs are exempted from sales
taxes. Goods classified as necessities are levied a
tax rate of 5 per cent; other goods and services, 10
per cent; and luxury goods, 20 per cent.

In South Vietnam[39] the turnover tax was likewise replaced by a production tax levied both on
domestic producers of goods and on importers. A uniform rate of 6 per cent is levied on goods produced
domestically. Tax credit, however, may be granted
on goods previously levied a production tax and
those which are considered raw materials. Because
of this concession, the effective rate on these
goods is actually only 5 per cent. Exemptions are
also granted to certain producers. Service industries and commercial undertakings are exempted from
the tax. Small producers with not more than six employees, whose gross annual sales do not exceed
VN\$ 500,000 and where hard labor is substantially
utilized, are also exempted.

Exemptions have recently been given to producers
of natural silk and rayon products, insecticides,
agricultural equipment, certain spare parts for
machines, moving pictures, and school supplies, such
as pencils, inks, and chalks.

Sales of precious metals and relics over fifty
years old, such as statues, paintings, and antiques,
are levied a multi-level transaction tax at a uniform rate of 20 per cent. Pure gold is taxed at 10
per cent. Sale of ice at the producers' level is imposed a specific tax of VN\$ 100 per metric ton.

In the Republic of China[40] ad valorem rates are
applied on the sale of several commodities. The
schedule is as shown in Table 22.

The taxable value of a commodity subject to tax
is based on the monthly average wholesale price prevailing in the market, including cost of packing,
minus the amount of tax previously paid and the cost
of transportation.[41]

TABLE 22

Sales Tax Rates in the Republic of China

Item	Rate
Rolled tobaccos	120%
Imported liquors and beers	120%
Flue-cured leaf tobaccos	30%
Matches	20%
Sugar	60%
Brown sugar	60%*
Saccharine	60%
Cotton yarn	15%
Linen yarn	10%
Woolen yarn and woolen thread	30%
Artificial silk	20%
Artificial and synthetic fibers yarn	20%
Mixed yarn	25%
Furs and leathers	15%
Plastics	17%
Rubber tires	17%
Cement	24%
Beverages	36%
Fruit juice	30%
Cosmetics, Category A	100%
Cosmetics, Category B	80%
Cosmetics, Category C	20%
Lumber	15%
Electric bulbs and lamp tubes	20%
Paper	5%
Flavoring powder	29%
Flat glass	23%
Gasoline	48%
Diesel oil	28%
Kerosene	20%
Fuel oils	10%
Natural gas	10%
Refined natural gas	48%
Liquefied petroleum	15%

*but with 20% discount

In Singapore[42] no sales or turnover tax is
levied. A turnover tax is being proposed throughout
Malaysia,[43] to be applied at the rate of 1/2 per
cent on sales and gross earnings for services of all
trades, businesses, professions, and vocations, including interest on loans and other advances made by
those engaged in such businesses as banking, finance,
and pawnbroking. Exemptions, however, are provided
in certain cases; e.g., where turnover from sale of
goods does not exceed $36,000 per year, or where
gross receipts derived mainly from services do not
exceed $20,000 per year.

LICENSES AND OTHER TAXES ON BUSINESSES AND OCCUPATIONS

Licenses and taxes on businesses and occupations are levied on the "privilege of doing business"
and engaging in specified occupations. These imposts
are applied to individual establishments, corporations in the same line of activity, and the practitioners of various occupations and professions.[44]
One of the strongest justifications for imposing
these duties relates to costs and benefits: It has
been argued that in return for the guarantee and protection of the right to pursue specified businesses
and engage in certain occupations, the government is
justified in exacting the levy. It is further contended that this privilege is only enjoyed through
the many benefits which the government renders, such
as orderliness, security, and general enlightenment.[45]

Generally, licenses and taxes on business are
levied at a fixed ad valorem rate. An initial tax
is imposed before the operation of the business or
the practice of profession, after which an annual
(or varying period) fixed tax is exacted. The latter is generally applied on the gross receipts of
businesses or people engaging in particular occupations.

In the Philippines[46] two business taxes are imposed: an annual fixed tax and a graduated annual
fixed tax. The rate of the annual fixed tax varies.

It is levied on importers, manufacturers, restaura-
teurs, common carriers, and millers (except those
dealing with rice and corn) at the rate of ₱20.00
annually. Brewers, distillers, rectifiers, wholesalers, and retailers of distilled spirits, liquors,
and soft drinks, tobacco brokers, lending investors,
and rice and corn millers pay rates which vary from
₱16-₱4,800. The graduated annual fixed tax is
levied on persons or firms not included in the above-
mentioned grouping. It is applied on gross sales of
over ₱2,000, at a rate which ranges from ₱10-₱500.

In addition to the annual or graduated fixed
tax, certain businesses are levied percentage taxes.
Operators and proprietors of sawmills are levied a
tax of 33 1/3 per cent, and on the gross cost of
logs purchased for a given year at the rate of 7 per
cent. Millers are taxed on the gross value of manufactured or milled products at the rate of 2 per
cent, while contractors are taxed at 3 per cent.
Keepers of restaurants, bars, and other eating places
are taxed at 3, 7, 10, or 20 per cent on their gross
receipts, while keepers of garages and common carriers are taxed at 2 per cent. Brokers and cinematographic film owners, lessors, or distributors are
taxed at 6 and 2 per cent, respectively, on their
gross receipts.

Certain occupations, such as lawyers, medical
practitioners, architects, engineers, insurance
agents, and interior decorators, are levied a tax of
₱50.00 or ₱75.00.

In the Republic of China[47] businesses or trades
are classified into three broad groups, each of
which is levied a varying range of business taxes.
The first group includes businesses which deal with
buying and selling, manufacturing, contracting,
printing, mining, public utility, food and drink,
entertainment, photography, finishing, dyeing and
mending, and decoration. This group of businesses
is taxed ad valorem rates ranging from 0.6 to 1.5
per cent of proceeds, prices, charges, or receipts.
Classified under the second group are businesses engaged in transportation, repairing, processing,

service work, hotelkeeping, bath and barber service, storage, moneylending, and banking. The rate of tax on receipts of these businesses ranges from 1.5 to 3 per cent. A tax ranging from 3 to 6 per cent is applied on the income, proceeds, receipts, commissions, and remunerations for work done in the following categories: surveying, insurance, pawnshop, brokerage, and acting as an agent. The rates are doubled where the business operator is an itinerant merchant.

With respect to businesses dealing in food supplies, the minimum rates are levied.

Similar taxes are imposed on specified businesses and occupations in Thailand.[48] For milling any kind of rice, the operator conducting the business is levied a 3.5 per cent tax on gross receipts. For those engaged in sawing any kind of logs, the rate is 4 per cent of gross receipts. For those engaged in the sale of electric current or by-products of generating plants, or water from waterworks or wells, the tax on gross receipts is 1.5 per cent. Such persons are considered manufacturers. A 2 per cent tax is levied on contractors or those engaged in the hiring of work including sale of parts and by-products as follows:

(a) printing, bookbinding, photoengraving, filming and producing motion pictures,
(b) building and construction of all kinds,
(c) advertising, using any means of execution,
(d) hair curling, cutting or dressing, or beauty treatment, and
(e) other types of hire work.

Renting out movable properties is taxable at 2.5 per cent of gross receipts. Gross receipts from warehousing or cold storage services are taxable at 2.5 per cent, and the tax is imposed on the operator. Operators of nightclubs or cabarets are levied a tax of 10 per cent on gross receipts, and hotels, 7.5 per cent. The tax on restaurants varies; operators of ordinary restaurants and those which sell mainly native food, tea, coffee, and carbonated water are taxed 5 per cent of gross receipts. Operators of pawn brokerages under the Pawn Brokerage Law are taxed at 2.5

per cent of gross receipts. Brokers, agents, auc-
tioneers or those managing the affairs of others not
specified under other categories are taxed 5.5 per
cent on gross receipts. Sale of immovable properties as a business for profit is taxed 3.5 per cent
of the gross receipts of seller. For savings banks,
commercial banks, or persons carrying on transactions
similar to those of commercial banks (e.g., furnish-
ing loans, guarantees, exchange of currencies, insurance purchases, sales of negotiable instruments, or
transfer of money abroad by any means, including
business of poeytuan or huaytua), the tax rate is
2.5 per cent on interest, discount, fees, or service
charges (Type 3) received by the operator, and 10.5
per cent on gross profits from exchange of currencies, issuance, purchase or sale of negotiable instruments or transfer of money abroad (Type 2). The
tax on gross receipts from life insurance premiums
is 2.5 per cent, while for other types of insurance
the tax rate is 3 per cent.

In South Korea the number of specified businesses
subject to taxation was reduced from thirty-two to
eighteen types. The mining and fishing industries
were recently included in the taxable business
categories. The different types of businesses subject to tax and their rates are shown in Table 23.

In South Vietnam[49] a business license tax known
as the patente is levied on certain professions, commercial, and manufacturing activities. It comprises
two parts: the basic tax, which is applied at specific rates, and an ad valorem duty applied on the
rental value of the business property. The rates of
the basic tax depend on the classification of the
profession, business, or establishment. Some of the
basic tax rates are shown in Table 24. The rate of
rental value tax ranges from 3 to 10 per cent, depending on the amount of the basic tax. The patente
tax may be increased by several per cent for the
benefit of the local governments. Percentage increases vary from 100 to 200 per cent, depending on
the province and village. A 2 1/2 per cent increase
in the patente is also earmarked for the Chamber of
Commerce.

TABLE 23

Business Tax Rates in South Korea

Item	Rate (Won)
Fisheries	5/1,000
Mining	5/1,000
Electricity-gas	3/1,000
Mutual loans	5/1,000
Railway-cable car	5/1,000
Insurance	3/1,000
Manufacturing industry A	3/1,000
Manufacturing industry B	7/1,000
Wholesale business A	3/1,000
Wholesale business B	7/1,000
Banking	7/1,000
Transportation	7/1,000
Construction	10/1,000
Retail business A	5/1,000
Retail business B	10/1,000
Public bath, barber, and beauty parlor	10/1,000
Pawnshops	10/1,000
Eating-houses	15/1,000
Other services	15/1,000
Restaurants	20/1,000
Entertainment and playground service	20/1,000

TABLE 24

South Vietnam Business Tax Schedule

Item	Rate
Air travel agency	VN$ 1,600 to 30,000
Restaurant	VN$ 160 to 16,000
Commercial bank	VN$ 3,000 to 100,000
Manufacturer of bottles	VN$ 100 to 2,000
Sugar factory	VN$ 30 for each horsepower of equipment
Mechanical weaving	VN$ 100/loom
Large commercial enterprises	VN$ 8,000 to 100,000
Importers	VN$ 2,000 to 50,000

A registration tax is also levied on new companies.[50] The tax is applied on the value of the
corporation's capital at the rate of 1.2 per cent.

Motor Vehicle Tax

Taxes on motor vehicles, whether public convey-
ances or not, are levied in Singapore, South Vietnam,
and the Philippines. The tax generally takes the
form of an annual license fee for every motor vehicle.
In Singapore[51] a motor vehicle tax is levied equal
to twice the amount of the annual license fee according to Section 45 of the Road Traffic Ordinance of
1941. Hackney carriages pay a separate rate, according to the number of passengers that can be accommodated. For every hackney carriage in which twenty
passengers can be accommodated the rate is $36, plus
$24 for each additional passenger in excess of twenty.
On nonpassenger motor vehicles, the tax is levied according to "weight unladen." It ranges from M$360 on
motor vehicles with unladen weight not more than
thirty cylindrical capacity to M$1,580 on those with
unladen weight exceeding one hundred cylindrical
capacity but not more than 110 centimeters. On every
additional 10 cylindrical capacity in excess of 110
cylindrical capacity, the rate is M$240. The tax
on road rollers is one-half of the enumerated rates.

In South Vietnam[52] different rates are applied
on passenger and nonpassenger motor vehicles. Flat
rates of VN$ 300 and VN$ 500 are levied on light two-
or three-wheeled vehicles such as scooters and vehicles used for public passengers and freight, respectively. By contrast, high progressive rates range
from VN$ 1,000 on privately owned passenger vehicles
with cylinders of 1,200 cubic centimeters or less to
VN$ 4,000 on those with cylinders over 4,000 cubic
centimeters.

In the Philippines[53] motor vehicle taxes are
levied upon the registration of the vehicle. Although the initial fee is levied on the basis of the
date of registration, the annual registration fee depends on the type of fuel and tires used. On motor
vehicles for hire using motor fuel oil other than

diesel oil, the rates on registration are ₱104.00 to
₱136.00 on jeeps and jitneys, depending on passenger
capacity; ₱120.00 to ₱288.00 on automobiles with pneumatic rubber tires; ₱8.00 and ₱11.00 per kilogram of
allowable gross weight or fraction thereof on motor
trucks, passenger buses, and trailers with pneumatic
and solid rubber tires respectively, ₱24.00 per kilogram of allowable gross weight or fraction thereof,
both in motor vehicles with metallic tires and motorcycles and motorbicycles. The corresponding rates
for the same types of motor vehicles used for private
purposes are ₱75.00-₱180.00, ₱65.00-₱85.00, ₱5.00-
₱7.00 and for the last two types, ₱15.00. On motor
vehicles for hire or for private purposes which use
diesel oil, the rates are 50 per cent more than those
imposed on the abovementioned types of vehicles which
do not use diesel oil. Additional fees are also
levied, such as those for special permits to operate
certain types of motor vehicles, change or transfer
of ownership, number plates, dealers' number plates
for demonstrating and testing, drivers' license fees,
and student drivers' permits.

All transport operators and those engaged in the
hire of work performed by vehicles are taxed 0.5 per
cent on gross receipts. What may be considered an extension of the motor vehicle tax is the traveling tax
applied in South Korea on passengers of railroad cars,
buses, airplanes, steamships, streetcars, coaches,
taxis, and jitneys. The rates, which depend on the
type of vehicle, are scheduled as shown in Table 25.[54]

TABLE 25

South Korea's Motor Vehicle Tax Rates

Item	Rate (Won)
Railway and airline fares	10/100
Sleeping car or express fares	10/100
Jitney or taxi fares	10/100
Bus fares	5/100
Steamship fares	5/100
Streetcar or motor-coach fares	5/100
City bus fares	5/100

Exemptions from this tax are granted to military personnel, and discounts are given to children, students, and certain groups. A travel tax is similarly applied in Japan. Unlike that of South Korea, it is levied only on passengers on trains (including electric cars and motor buses), steamships, and airplanes. Second-class passengers on trains and steamships are exempted. The travel tax is applied at the rate of 10 per cent of first-class fares. The rate of the travel tax was, however, temporarily reduced to 5 per cent effective from April 1, 1962, to March 31, 1965. In the Philippines the travel tax corresponds to the tax on common carriers, which is levied at 2 per cent of the gross receipts.

Entertainment Duty

Another popular type of taxation in these countries is the tax on admission to places of entertainment, or what is sometimes referred to as the "entertainment tax." It is generally included in the prices paid as admission fees to these places. On this basis, it can be considered an indirect tax.

In Singapore[55] an entertainment duty is levied on a graduated basis, depending on the admission fee. The rate ranges from five cents on admission fees from ten to twenty cents, to forty cents on admission fees exceeding $1 but not more than $1.50. Beyond $1.50 an additional twenty cents is levied for every fifty-cent increase in admission fees. Admission fees under ten cents are exempted from the entertainment duty.

Live shows and musical performances are levied only one-half of these rates, while amateur sports and dramatic entertainments are exempted.

The admission tax applies to theaters and billiard halls in South Korea.[56] On theaters the rate varies according to the amount of admission fees being charged. It ranges from 15 per cent on admissions amounting to less than HW400 to 60 per cent on those amounting to over HW600. On billiard halls, the tax on admission is imposed at the rate of 20 per cent.

In South Vietnam[57] the entertainment duty consists of a basic tax and a surcharge. The basic tax
rate varies according to the classification of the
entertainment. Theatrical performances, shows, musical presentations, concerts, exhibitions, athletic
events, and circuses classified under Group 1 are
levied an entertainment tax of 5 per cent of their
gross receipts. A 20 per cent tax is imposed on
gross receipts from cafe and tea-room entertainment,
horse races, theaters, nightclubs, and other forms
of entertainment not included in the first group.
The rate of the surcharge varies in different parts
of South Vietnam. In the southern region, the surcharge is equal to 100 per cent of the basic tax,
while in central South Vietnam and the highlands,
the surcharge is 50 per cent of the basic tax.

In Japan[58] a basic admission-tax rate of 10 per
cent of admission fees is charged on theaters, performances, sports events, shows, cycling, and horse
races. However, in cases where admission is free or
there is no fixed admission fee, the tax base is calculated by dividing the necessary expenses by the
seating capacity.

Admission fees of 30 yen or below and those
charged for educational purposes amounting to 50 yen
or below are exempted from the admission tax. Also
exempted are proceeds from shows and other forms of
entertainment given by schools and civic groups for
educational and charitable purposes. Admission fees
for amateur sports events and exhibitions of cultural properties are also exempted.

In the Philippines the entertainment duties are
known as "amusement taxes." These are levied on admission fees in theaters, concert halls, and boxing
exhibitions; on gross receipts of cockpits, cabarets,
nightclubs, and race tracks; and on net winnings in
horse races and jai-alai. On admission fees to theaters and concert halls from ₱0.21 to ₱0.99, the tax
ranges from ₱0.04 to ₱0.18. On those amounting to
₱1.00 and over the tax rate is 30 per cent. The tax
on admission fees to boxing exhibitions is 50 per
cent of the above rates. On cockpits, cabarets, and

nightclubs, the amusement tax is 10 per cent of the
gross receipts, and on race tracks, 20 per cent. A
tax of 2 1/2 per cent of net winnings in horse races
and jai-alai is also levied.

In Thailand duties on admission fees to certain
forms of entertainment are levied. On motion pictures, the rate is 50 per cent of the admission fee,
while on other forms of entertainment, the tax is 20
per cent. The tax on admission fees to sports events
organized by the Ministry of Education is 10 per
cent, while on those specified in Ministerial Regulations, the tax is 15 per cent. A tax of 20 per cent
is applied on entertainments featuring varied forms
of shows. Admission fees not exceeding fifty satangs
and official complimentary tickets are exempted from
the tax.

In Indonesia amusement taxes are levied by some
municipalities.

Documentary Stamp Tax

The stamp tax on certain kinds of documents,
papers, and other materials is applied extensively
in many Asian countries. In the Philippines, the
stamp tax is imposed on bonds, debentures, certificates of indebtedness, instruments, and documents.
Prevailing rates of documentary stamp tax range from
₱0.04 to ₱12.00, paid by the person making, signing,
issuing, accepting, or transferring obligations,
rights, or properties.

In Japan[59] the stamp tax is applied on deeds relating to creation, transfer, extinction, confirma-
tion, and approval of property rights. The rates
vary according to the nature of the deed and the
value involved. On deeds relating to the transfer
of ownership of real estate, vessels, and railway
foundations, and those concerning loans and contracts, the rates range from ¥20 on deeds involving
¥30,000 and less, to ¥10,000 on those involving over
¥50,000. Gift certificates and deeds relating to
power of attorney are taxed at ¥10 to ¥1,000 on prom-
issory notes and bills of exchange, depending on the

amount involved. Passbooks and chitbooks are also taxed.

All documents executed within the territory of the Republic of China, as well as those executed in foreign countries but used in that country, are subject to the stamp duty.[60] The tax rates vary according to the nature of the document and the amount involved and are applied either at specific or ad valorem rates. For example, invoices or statements of account are taxed at 0.4 per cent of their value; receipts for cash or goods, 0.4 per cent; contracts of transfer of claims, liabilities, etc., 0.1 per cent; and contracts of sale of securities, 0.05 per cent. On contracts relating to transportation, the tax is 2 yuan apiece; agency, 4 yuan apiece; and stock certificates and receipts of stock subscriptions, 0.30 yuan apiece.

Stamp taxes are also levied in South Korea and Singapore. The rates vary according to the type of document and value involved in a transaction.

OBSERVATIONS AND CONCLUSIONS

The predominance of taxes on production and sales is a characteristic feature of the tax systems of many developing countries in Asia. A comparison of the ratios of collections from production and sales to total revenue shows that in 1963 it was 69.3 per cent in India, 68.6 per cent in the Philippines, 58.5 per cent in South Korea, 55.2 per cent in Singapore, 44.6 per cent in Thailand, and 34.4 per cent in Indonesia (Appendix XI). Even in Japan, which is comparatively in a more advanced economic stage, the ratio of 36.9 per cent is also quite high. These ratios, which point to the heavy reliance on production and sales taxes, can be attributed to both the extensive application of these taxes and their relatively high rates. Heavy reliance on these taxes may also be ascribed to the fact that they offer greater administrative feasibility than other kinds of taxes. Furthermore, assessment and collection techniques in wealth and property taxation have not

been developed sufficiently in many of these countries to permit a shift in emphasis.

Of the four major categories of production and
sales taxes, export and import duties yielded the
bulk of revenues in these countries. For the same
year, the ratio of collections from import and export duties to total collection from taxes on production and sales in Thailand was 89.1 per cent; in
India, 35.3 per cent; in South Korea, 34.9 per cent;
and in the Philippines, 26.8 per cent (Appendix X).
This is quite understandable, since many of these
countries have high import propensities. It should
also be noted that in almost all of these countries
the import duty is extensively applied, as it virtually encompasses all imports. Import duties in many
of these countries are basically oriented toward
protection of the home industries. In the Philippines, India, and South Korea imported goods which
are also produced domestically are levied much higher duties than other imports. Redirection of demand
is also evident in the fact that nonessential and
luxury articles are taxed at higher rates than essential goods. In many of the countries covered in
this study, importation of necessities and industrial
equipment are either exempted or taxed at minimum
rates. On the other hand, a number of countries,
notably South Vietnam, India, Indonesia, and Thailand, levy an export tax. Except for India, where
about forty commodities are subject, the export duty
is imposed on a few selected primary-export products
and applied at relatively low rates. Generally, proceeds from this source are earmarked for export subsidies and export-promotion activities. In some countries, such as South Vietnam and India, minor fees
and additional taxes are levied in addition to the
export and import duty. Singapore, as a free port,
does not have what may be considered an import and export tax structure.

Excise taxation is also a major feature of the
tax systems in Asian countries. Collections from
this source comprised 67.9 per cent of total production and sales tax collections in Singapore, 62.5
per cent in India, 57.7 per cent in Japan, 48.7 per
cent in Indonesia, 31.6 per cent in the Philippines,

and 27.7 per cent in South Korea. Special excise
taxes, which provide a major portion of the revenues
in these countries, are generally levied on production and importation of selected commodities, among
which are tobacco, alcohol, kerosene, gasoline, and
playing cards. They are either applied at specific
or ad valorem rates or both. The majority of the
commodities are levied specific rates which vary according to the type of commodities.

A significant development in sales taxation in
some countries covered in the study relates to the
abandonment of the "turnover taxes" in favor of
either the value-added or the single-stage levy.
This has been the recent experience in South Vietnam
and Indonesia. An entirely different view is planned
in Singapore, which at present does not impose any
sales or turnover tax. With its integration into
the newly established Malaysia, a turnover tax has
been proposed. Significant changes in the sales tax
structure are also being designed in South Korea.
In India sales taxes are applied on a single-stage,
multi-point stage, and turnover basis. In the
Philippines a value-added tax is imposed. Sales
taxes contribute a significant amount to government
revenues, particularly in South Korea, Indonesia,
and Japan, where collections from these sources comprise 20.8, 17.2, and 13.3 per cent, respectively,
of total collections from production and sales taxes.

To supplement government revenues and to attain
other equally worthwhile objectives of taxation, such
as equity and uniformity, several minor taxes,
licenses, and fees are also levied in these countries.
Among these are the business and occupation taxes,
admission fees, documentary stamp taxes, and motor
vehicle licenses.

While heavy reliance on production and sales
taxes offers major advantages to the developing countries in terms of greater administrative feasibility
and greater revenue collections, the equity consideration has too often been questioned. It has been
contended that the regressive nature of these taxes
may create widening income disparity and inequality

in distribution of goods which might prove harmful
to these countries' over-all development efforts.
It is indeed exigent that the structure of production and sales taxes, especially in economies operating in a democratic framework, be examined with a
view to initiating reform measures.

Notes to Chapter 6

1. Hugh Dalton, Principles of Public Finance
(4th ed.; London: Routledge & Kegan Paul, Ltd.,
1954), pp. 23-24.

2. For an introductory article on sales taxation, see Clara K. Sullivan, "Concepts of Sales Taxation," in Readings on Taxation in Developing Countries, edited by Richard Bird and Oliver Oldman (Baltimore: The Johns Hopkins Press, 1964), pp. 503-44.

3. Because of the paucity of relevant materials, an exhaustive exposition of some taxes in the
countries discussed cannot be given.

4. Harold M. Groves, Financing Government (4th
ed.; New York: Henry Holt & Company, 1955), pp.
258-59.

5. Taylor, op. cit., pp. 21-24.

6. Ibid., p. 24.

7. U.S. Department of Commerce, Investment in
Indonesia, Basic Information for United States Businessmen (Washington: Government Printing Office,
1956), p. 104.

8. Refer to Chapter 9 on tax incentives.

9. Harvard Law School International Program
in Taxation, Taxation in India (Boston: Little,
Brown & Co., 1960), pp. 128-31.

10. Customs laws are set forth in the Sea Customs Act of 1878 and Land Customs Act of 1924.   The

rates of duty are provided in the Indian Tariff Act of 1934. Exemptions and rate changes are also prescribed.

11. *Ibid.*, p. 129.

12. *Ibid.*

13. These are listed semiannually in the Indian Customs Tariff. *Ibid.*, p. 131.

14. *Republic Act 1937* (*Tariff and Customs Code*) July 1, 1957.

15. Tariff rates range from 5-25 per cent. The bulk of the goods is levied rates of from 10-30 per cent. On essential producer and consumer goods the average import tariff rate is 18.4 per cent and 25.5 per cent, respectively; on semiessential producer and consumer goods, 27 per cent and 31.6 per cent, respectively; and on nonessential producer and consumer goods, 41.4 per cent and 59.3 per cent, respectively. Around 87 commodities are exempted from import duties. Angel Q. Yoingco, "Some Policy Considerations in Tariff Revision," *Economic Research Journal*, IX (December, 1962), 150.

16. *Laws of the Republic of China*, *op. cit.*, pp. 693-98.

17. Japan Tax Association, *op. cit.*, p. 70.

18. *Trade and Investment Guide to Korea* (Economic Bureau, Ministry of Foreign Affairs, Republic of Korea, 1963), p. 82.

19. Groves, *op. cit.*, p. 252.

20. A series of taxes is imposed on a commodity from its production up to the final distribution to the consumer.

21. "Shipment" refers to the removal of liquor from the manufacturing or bonded area in a geographical sense.

22. Japan Tax Bureau, op. cit., p. 102.

23. Ibid., p. 103.

24. Ibid., p. 112.

25. Ibid., pp. 114, 116.

26. Taxation in India, op. cit., pp. 454-69.

27. Handbook on Philippine Taxes (Manila: Joint Legislative-Executive Tax Commission, 1963), pp. 9-10.

28. Investment in Indonesia, op. cit., pp. 106-7.

29. Taylor, op. cit., pp. 14-18.

30. Japan Tax Association, op. cit., pp. 65-67.

31. Yearbook of Tax Statistics, 1961, Bureau of Taxation, Ministry of Finance, Republic of Korea, pp. 50-52.

32. Sullivan, op. cit., p. 320.

33. Yearbook of Tax Statistics, 1961, op. cit., pp. 47-48.

34. The Revenue Code, compiled and translated by Sanan Kettudat and Vid Tantayakul (Bangkok, Thailand: Revenue Department, 1961), pp. 60b-60c.

35. Handbook on Philippine Taxes, op. cit., pp. 12-13.

36. Japan Tax Bureau, op. cit., pp. 105-10.

37. Taxation in India, op. cit., pp. 436-52.

38. Japan Tax Association, op. cit., p. 106.

39. Taylor, op. cit., pp. 10-11.

40. Laws of the Republic of China, op. cit., pp. 636-49.

41.   Ibid., p. 652.

42.   Japan Tax Association, op. cit., p. 56.

43.   Tax Changes Within Malaysia (Kuala Lumpur: Jabatan Chetak Kerajaan, 1964), pp. 5-6.

44.   Groves, op. cit., p. 319.

45.   M. Slade Kendrick, Public Finance: Principles and Problems (Boston: Houghton Mifflin Company, 1951), p. 342.

46.   Handbook on Philippine Taxes, op. cit., pp. 11-13.

47.   Laws of the Republic of China, op. cit., p. 319.

48.   The Revenue Code, op. cit., pp. 60f-60h.

49.   Taylor, op. cit., pp. 8-9.

50.   Ibid., p. 19.

51.   Annual Report of the Customs and Excise, op. cit., p. 24.

52.   Taylor, op. cit., p. 13.

53.   Handbook on Philippine Taxes, op. cit., pp. 27-28.

54.   Yearbook of Tax Statistics, 1961, op. cit., p. 49.

55.   Annual Report of the Customs and Excise, op. cit., p. 23.

56.   Yearbook of Tax Statistics, 1961, op. cit., pp. 47-48.

57.   Taylor, op. cit., p. 12.

58.   Japan Tax Bureau, *op. cit.*, p. 121.

59.   Japan Tax Bureau, *op. cit.*, pp. 119-20.

60.   *Laws of the Republic of China*, *op. cit.*, pp. 510-20.

CHAPTER 7 WITHHOLDING TAX SYSTEMS

The withholding tax system is a recent development in Asian tax administration. Traditionally income tax payment is made at the end of the taxable period in conformity with the common practice of calculating income on an annual basis. Under the withholding tax system, however, as income is earned, a certain sum, corresponding approximately to the tax the income earner is liable to at the end of the taxable period, is withheld.

The withholding tax scheme is usually applied on fixed and determinable income. Originally, as in the United States and several European countries,[1] only wages and salaries were covered by the system. Recently, however, withholding has been applied also to interest, dividends, profits, rents, and royalties. Some countries, such as the Republic of China, Thailand, and India, use the withholding tax system on almost all determinable income, whereas other countries, such as Indonesia, Malaysia, and Singapore, employ it on selected sources of income and on a relatively limited scale.

As a method of income tax collection, the withholding tax system offers major advantages. Since the income of the employee is already net of the tax, the system effectively conceals the tax and therefore lessens taxpayer resistance. Convenient compliance is further facilitated by the payment of the accumulated tax liability being spread throughout the year. The very nature of the system also militates against arrangements which defeat the claims of the government. Since collections are immediately realized, the impact of tax payments on national

income is almost immediately felt. Furthermore,
automatic response of tax payments to tax rate
changes is made possible. In this way, the effectiveness of fiscal policies is enhanced.

The withholding tax system is not without short-
comings. First, substantial compliance costs are involved in tax withholding. Also, it is difficult to
formulate a scale of exemptions and graduated rates
so as to withhold the proper amount of taxes. Finally, the fact that taxes are effectively hidden might
cause taxpayers to be indifferent to where tax payments are channeled or spent.

REPUBLIC OF CHINA

The withholding system in the Republic of China
covers all types of determinable income earned or received by individuals or corporations, whether they
are residents or not.[2] Distinctions are made by imposing different withholding rates on the various
categories of income and on the nature or status of
each income earner.

A flat rate of 5 per cent is withheld on dividends or distributed profits, rents, royalties, and
interest. However, a 10 per cent withholding rate
is applied to interest on government or corporate
bonds. Salaries and wages in excess of NT$ 900 are
subject to 2 per cent. A withholding rate of 15 per
cent is applied to dividends or distributed profits,
interest, salaries and wages, rents, and royalties
received by a nonresident individual or a foreign
enterprise that does not have a fixed place of business within the territory of China.

An individual filing a return is required to
make an advance payment of 50 per cent of the total
amount of tax due from his estimated income for that
taxable year at the end of the first half of the
year.

INDIA

Withholding tax provisions in India apply to income received by nonresident aliens and foreign corporations, all determinable income received by corporations engaged in business in that country, and certain categories of income received by citizens and residents.

The withholding tax rates on income of nonresident aliens and nonresident companies are tied up with the tax rates imposed on income. The tax payable by a nonresident individual is the amount equal either to the income tax calculated at 30 per cent plus a supertax calculated at 19 per cent or the supertax on his total income, whichever is greater. A nonresident is given the option of being taxed on his total income in India at the applicable rate, wherever it accrues or arises.

Foreign companies that have made the prescribed arrangements for declaration and distribution of dividends within India are treated at par with Indian companies, while those that have not done so are ordinarily taxed at 63 per cent. Income from royalties received from an Indian concern pursuant to a duly approved agreement made by a foreign company with an Indian concern is taxed at 50 per cent.

Certain intercorporate dividends are taxed at lower rates. An amount equal to 25 per cent income tax plus a supertax of 5 per cent is withheld on dividends received by a subsidiary Indian company formed and registered before April 1, 1959, while an amount equal to 25 per cent income tax and a 25 per cent supertax is imposed on an Indian company (which is not a subsidiary) formed and registered before April 1, 1959. However, an amount equal to 25 per cent income tax and 10 per cent supertax is levied on any other Indian company formed and registered on or after April 1, 1959.

All companies are subject to a 25 per cent tax on total income and to a supertax which varies according to the ownership of the company and the type and source (as in dividends) of income received. Specifically, the withholding tax on corporations engaged in business in India is levied according to the following schedule:

(a) 25 per cent on the whole income (excluding interest payable on any security of the central government issued or declared to be income tax free, and interest payable on any security of a State government issued income tax free);

(b) 5 per cent on the whole income (excluding dividends payable to a company by an Indian company which is engaged in certain basic industries specified in the Fifth Schedule of the Income Tax Act).

Income of companies which are neither Indian-owned nor which have made the prescribed arrangements for the declaration and payment of dividends within India is subject to the following schedule:

(a) Dividends (excluding dividends payable to a company by an Indian company which is engaged in certain basic industries specified in the Fifth Schedule of the Income Tax Act), which are payable by subsidiary Indian companies formed and registered before April 1, 1961, are exempted from the withholding scheme. However, a 20 per cent rate is imposed on those payable by an Indian company which is not a subsidiary company, formed and registered before April 1, 1959. For those payable by any other Indian company formed and registered on or after April 1, 1959, a withholding rate of 5 per cent is required.

(b) Income from royalties payable by an Indian concern in pursuance of an agreement which was made by a foreign company with an Indian concern on or after April 1, 1961, and which has been approved by the central government is subject to a 20 per cent withholding rate.

(c) On other forms of income, a 33 per cent withholding rate is imposed.

Salaries and wages received or earned by Indian citizens or residents are subject to withholding at the rate of tax in force on income from salary.[3]   Income from dividends and interest on securities is subject to a 30 per cent withholding tax rate.

Taxpayers whose income exceeds the exemption level by Rs 2,500 are required to pay in advance a tax on that portion of their income not subject to withholding at source. The amount of this advance tax is calculated on the basis of the last completed assessment and is generally payable within a year in four equal installments. The taxpayer is given the option to pay the advance tax on the basis of his own estimate if he considers that his income during the relevant accounting period would be less than the income computed in the last completed assessment.

INDONESIA

Indonesia's withholding scheme, which is integrated in the provision that imposes the tax on income, covers employment and retirement income of individuals and dividend incomes of both corporations and individuals.[4]

Employment and retirement incomes of individuals are subject to withholding at the same rates imposed under the provisions of the income tax law.[5]   Income from dividends received by individuals or corporations is subject to a 20 per cent withholding rate. Tax withheld may be considered either as advance payment of the tax due or as final payment. Taxpayers whose sole income is already subject to withholding at source are not required to file income tax returns unless a return is issued to them.

Income from dividends of nonresidents or foreign companies is ordinarily subject to a 20 per cent withholding tax. Salaries, leave pay, pensions, and similar incomes, charged to the public or private resources of Indonesia, are subject to withholding at the rates set in the regulations issued by the Minister of Finance.

JAPAN

The withholding tax system of Japan covers income from interest and dividends, employment and retirement, as well as from personal services and charges.[6] Income from interest, dividends, salaries, royalties, rents from immovable properties, etc., of a nonresident or foreign corporation engaged in business in Japan is subject to withholding provisions.

Interest and dividend incomes of individuals and domestic corporations are subject to a 5 per cent withholding rate, and those of nonresident or foreign corporations, 20 per cent.

Employment income includes ordinary salaries and bonuses. The amount of tax to be withheld from salaries, which is determined by the nature of salary, the date of payment, and the number of dependents, is calculated according to the formula provided in the "Tax Amount Table." The amount of tax withheld from bonuses is determined by using the formula prescribed in the "Rate Table." The formula varies with the amount of salary of the income earner in the preceding month prior to the granting of the bonus and the number of dependents. Employment income of nonresidents is levied a 20 per cent rate. Employers, except those who employ on a daily basis, are allowed to make adjustment at the end of the year when the last payment is made, irrespective of whether the last payment is in the form of ordinary salary or bonus.

Retirement income is subject to withholding rates provided in the "Simplified Tax Table on Retirement Income." A 10 per cent withholding rate is imposed on income from personal services.

Individuals required to file returns have to make prepayments of about two-thirds of the total amount of the tax due, in two equal installments, the first not later than July 31 and the second not later than November 30. The total amount of the tax is calculated on the basis of the income received during the preceding calendar year.

SOUTH KOREA

The withholding system of South Korea covers dividend and interest incomes realized within the country or those paid by domestic corporations, interest accrued from nonbusiness loans, income from real estate and business, and wages and salaries (Class A).[7] Only dividends and interest are subject to withholding on corporate income.

Dividends and interest paid within the country and those paid by domestic corporations are subject to a 12 per cent withholding rate while interest accruing from nonbusiness loans regardless of the recipient is subject to a flat rate of 15 per cent.

Incomes from real estate and business fall under two categories. Under the statutory tax withholding scheme, a 1 per cent withholding tax rate is levied while under occasional assessment a tax withholding rate of 15 per cent is imposed. Applicable rates for wages and salaries (Class A) vary according to source.[8]

The withholding system applies equally to income of nonresidents, foreign corporations, residents, and domestic taxpayers.

MALAYSIA

The withholding tax system in Malaysia is applied only to salaries, dividends, and to interest income of nonresident individual and nonresident foreign companies.[9]

The rates on interest income of nonresident individuals and nonresident companies differ: A 30 per cent withholding rate is imposed on the former, while 40 per cent is imposed on the latter. Companies are allowed to deduct the income tax they pay from the dividends they declare. No deductions are allowed for nonresident individuals but they can claim 10 per cent of the tax they pay on interest income.

SINGAPORE

Income from dividends and interest of nonresident individuals and nonresident corporations is subject to withholding. Both are subject to the same withholding rate of 40 per cent, but the Comptroller may prescribe a lower rate.[10]

The 40 per cent withholding tax rate applies to interest income of a nonresident individual, regardless of whether it comes from trade, from business, or from any other source.

THAILAND

In Thailand all assessable income of individuals, including income derived from government organizations, is subject to the withholding scheme.[11] It also applies to all assessable income of foreign corporations not engaged in business in Thailand.

Graduated withholding tax rates, from 10 per cent to 50 per cent, are applied on personal income, depending on the amount of net income of individuals. Assessable income derived from government organizations is subject to a much lower withholding tax rate of 1 per cent. Graduated tax rates, from 15 per cent to 25 per cent, are imposed on all assessable income of foreign corporations not engaged in business in Thailand.

SOUTH VIETNAM

The withholding tax scheme in South Vietnam is applied on a limited scale. It covers only income in the form of dividends, interest, or royalties received by individuals and corporations and salaries of members of the armed forces of South Vietnam.[12]

The withholding rates applied vary according to the form of income received. Dividends and interest income are subject to withholding tax rates ranging from 18-30 per cent. A 24 per cent withholding tax

rate is usually applied on royalties. Withholding
rates on salaries of members of the Armed Forces are
subject to the applicable income tax rates on salaries and wages and those prescribed in the general
income tax.[13]

PHILIPPINES

The withholding tax system in the Philippines
covers all remunerations and wages derived from personal services, all fixed or determinable annual or
periodical income payable to a nonresident alien individual and those of nonresident alien firms, co-
partnerships, corporations, associations, trust companies, trustees, and insurance companies not engaged
in trade or business in the Philippines.[14] The
scheme does not cover interest on bonds, obligations,
or securities issued by domestic or resident foreign
corporations containing a tax-free covenant clause.[15]

The tax withheld on fixed or determinable, annual or periodic income of a nonresident alien individual not engaged in trade or business in the Philippines is 20 per cent, while that on nonresident foreign corporations is 30 per cent. The tax withheld
on wages is determined in accordance with the withholding tax tables which consider the amount of income, the allowable exemptions, and the regularity
of the receipt of income during the taxable year.

SUMMARY AND CONCLUSION

Major tax reforms initiated in each of the Asian
countries to enhance efficiency in tax administration
have included systems for withholding taxes. The Republic of China, Thailand, and India are among those
countries that have used such a system widely. The
Republic of China, for example, applies it to all
types of determinable income earned or received by
both individuals and corporations. In Thailand the
system covers all assessable income of individuals,
including those from government organizations, and
all assessable income of foreign corporations not

engaged in business in Thailand. The Indian system
applies, among others, to all income received by nonresident aliens and nonresident foreign corporations,
and all determinable income received by corporations
engaged in business in India. The schemes employed
in Japan, the Philippines, and South Korea also have
wide coverage. In Malaysia and Singapore, on the
other hand, only interest income of nonresident individuals and nonresident companies is covered by the
system. A unique feature of South Vietnam's withholding tax system is that, aside from dividends, interest, and royalties, it covers only salaries of
the members of the armed forces.

The various systems differ also with respect to
the rates imposed on different types of income or on
similar types of income: Some withholding rates are
on a flat rate basis, some on a graduated scale, and
others on a combination of both. In Indonesia dividends are taxed at a flat rate of 20 per cent regardless of whether these are paid to resident or nonresident individuals or companies. The same is true
in Singapore where interest income, both of nonresident individuals and companies, is subject to a 40
per cent withholding rate. In South Vietnam graduated rates, ranging from 18 per cent to 30 per cent,
are imposed on interest and dividend income. The
South Korean scheme utilizes both the flat rate and
the graduated rates.

Income of residents and domestic companies is
generally subject to withholding rates lower than
those applicable to nonresidents and foreign companies. Some countries make distinctions with respect
to the source of income. In Thailand personal income from government organizations is subject to a
1 per cent rate in contrast to the graduated rates,
ranging from 10 to 50 per cent, imposed on personal
income derived from other sources. In South Korea
1 per cent is imposed on income from real estate
falling under the statutory tax-withholding scheme,
while occasional income is subject to 15 per cent.
Withholding rates imposed on salaries and wages are
calculated by withholding tables devised by tax
authorities in the Philippines, Japan, and South

Korea. In the Republic of China salaries and wages
of residents are subject to a flat rate of 2 per
cent, while 15 per cent is imposed on those of nonresidents. India's withholding tax scheme is complex in the sense that, aside from a portion of the
total income tax, a supertax which varies according
to the ownership of a country, and the type and
source of income received is also withheld.

The withholding tax systems of the more advanced
countries like the United States, United Kingdom,
Germany, Sweden, and Australia cover a relatively
greater area. The United States system covers almost all income paid to nonresidents, such as income
from interest, dividends, royalties, wages, and salaries. In Germany many forms of income are subject
to withholding: dividends and other profits; distributions on corporate shares and on membership rights
of commercial entities other than corporations; certain types of interest; profit distributions to a
"typical" silent partner; employment income; director's fees; income from literary, artistic, athletic,
and related activities performed in any capacity (as
an employee, independently, or in the exercise of a
business); royalties from the licensing of patents,
copyrights, plans, processes, designs, or other pro-
tected or unprotected intangible property rights;
and compensations for the communication of industrial
or commercial know-how, experience, or similar information.[16] In the United Kingdom, aside from dividends, rents under "short leases," interest on government securities, remuneration from offices or employment, annuities, and other annual payments, the
system covers payments for patents and patent rights
and payments of copyright royalties to nonresidents.[17]
In Australia it applies to salaries, wages, and certain interest payments on bearer securities to residents; payments made to nonresident insurers; payments of royalties and interest from nonresident de-
benture holders; and income paid to film businesses
controlled abroad.[18] The withholding rates imposed
in these countries are generally higher than those
on the same types of income in the selected Asian
countries. In Germany corporate dividends are subject to 25 per cent if the tax is borne by the

recipient and 33.33 per cent if borne by the payor.
Certain interest income is subject to 25 per cent if
the tax is borne by the recipient and 42.85 per cent
if borne by the payor. In Australia the withholding
rate on interest is currently 37.5 per cent, and in
Sweden the rate on interest paid to nonresidents is
a flat 30 per cent.[19]

The continuing growth of many developing countries hinges significantly on the continuity with
which funds for developmental and budgetary purposes
are made available. The completion of many infra-
structural projects and essential government operations is frequently interrupted due to the halting,
sporadic flow of revenue into the government treasury.
The prevalence of tax evasion and avoidance, coupled
with inadequate and sometimes inefficient tax machinery, accounts for the chronic revenue shortages that
these countries experience.

The withholding tax system, with its inherent
advantages, promises much to the solution of these
problems. The institution of this scheme on a more
extensive scale would bolster tax compliance and
thereby assure the continuous flow of much-needed
government revenues to finance development projects.

TABLE 26

Schedule of Withholding Tax Rates in Selected Asian Countries

Countries	Interest	Dividends	Royalties	Rents	Wages and Salaries
Republic of China					
Citizen and resident	5%	5%	5%	5%	2%[3]
Domestic corporation[1]	10%				
Nonresident individual	15%	15%	15%	15%	15%
Foreign corporation[2]	15%	15%	15%	15%	
India					
Citizen and resident	30%	30%			according to the rate of tax in force for salary
Domestic corporation		25% + 5% supertax[4] 25% + 25% supertax 25% + 10% supertax	20%		
Nonresident individual	30% + no less than 19% super-tax	30% + no less than 19% super-tax	30% + no less than 19% super-tax	30% + no less than 19% super-tax	
Foreign corporation		63%	50%		

152

Indonesia				
Citizen and resident		20%		same as those provided in income tax law
Domestic corporation		20%		
Nonresident individual		20%		
Foreign corporation		20%		
Japan				
Citizen and resident	10%	10%		provided in the withholding tax table
Domestic corporation	10%	10%		
Nonresident individual	20%	20%		
Foreign corporation	20%	20%		20%
South Korea				
Citizen and resident	12%	12%	1%[5]	
Domestic corporation	12%[6]	12%	1%	
Nonresident individual	15%		1%	
Foreign corporation	15%		1%	
Malaysia				
Citizen and resident				
Domestic corporation				
Nonresident individual	30%			
Foreign corporation	40%			

TABLE 26 (continued)

Countries	Interest	Dividends	Royalties	Rents	Wages and Salaries
Singapore					
Citizen and resident					
Domestic corporation					
Nonresident individual	40%				
Foreign corporation	40%				
Thailand					
Citizen and resident	10%-50%	10%-50%	10%-50%	10%-50%	10%-50%
Domestic corporation	15%-25%	15%-25%	15%-25%	15%-25%	1% of assessable income of government corporation
Nonresident individual	10%-50%	10%-50%	10%-50%	10%-50%	
Foreign corporation	15%-25%	15%-25%	15%-25%	15%-25%	
South Vietnam					
Citizen and resident	18%-30%	18%-30%	24%		only on salaries of members of the armed forces, according to income tax table
Domestic corporation	18%-30%	24%-30%	24%		
Nonresident individual		30%	24%		
Foreign corporation		30%	24%		

Philippines

Citizen and resident

				according to withholding tax table
Domestic corporation				
Nonresident individual	20%	20%	20%	20%
Foreign corporation	30%	30%	30%	30%

---

[1] Domestic corporations include resident corporations engaged in business in that particular country.

[2] Foreign corporations refer to foreign companies not engaged in business in that particular country.

[3] In excess of NT$ 900.

[4] Supertax imposed varies according to whether recipient is subsidiary or not and whether date of registration is before or after April, 1959.

[5] A 15% rate is imposed on interest accrued from nonbusiness loan.

[6] A 15% rate is imposed on occasional assessment.

155

<u>N</u>otes to Chapter 7

1.   Harold M. Groves, <u>Financing Government</u> (New York: Henry Holt & Co., Inc., 1955), p. 163.

2.   Japan Tax Association, <u>Proceedings of the Special Meeting on Tax System and Administration in Asian Countries</u> (Japan: The Association, 1963), pp. 134, 135, 137.

3.   Tax rates start with (1) 3 per cent normal tax of the next Rs 2,000 of total income of Rs 5,000 to a maximum of 25 per cent on excess of Rs 30,000 of total income; (2) 7 per cent supertax on excess over Rs 20,000 of total income to a maximum of 47.5 per cent on excess of Rs 80,000 of total income, and (3) 5 per cent surcharge on excess of Rs 7,500 of total income.

4.   Japan Tax Association, <u>op. cit</u>., pp. 162, 164, 166.

5.   There are three kinds of rates: Rate A, for net income of resident taxpayer, as per outward signs of social prosperity, estimated at not more than Rp 18,000; Rate B, the ordinary rate; and Rate C, rate on the proceeds of a work-relation amounting to a gross income of less than Rp 24,000 annually.

6.   Japan Tax Bureau, <u>An Outline of Japanese Tax</u> (Tax Bureau Ministry of Finance, 1964), pp. 53-58.

7.   Japan Tax Association, <u>op. cit</u>., pp. 192, 193, 195.

8.   Two different tax rates are applicable to wages and salaries.   A progressive graduated tax of 7-35 percent is imposed on ordinary wages and salary received from a definite employer and compensation received from the U.N.: A flat rate of 7 per cent is levied on daily and hourly wages of persons who do not have any definite employer.

9.   Japan Tax Association, _op. cit._, pp. 213–14.

10.   _Ibid._, pp. 238, 240.

11.   _Ibid._, pp. 247, 248.

12.   _Ibid._, pp. 260, 264.

13.   The obligor or payor agrees to pay any portion of the tax due on the interest received by the obligee or payee.

14.   Sections 53 and 54, National Internal Revenue Code Supplement A-Withholding on Wages, Sections 198 to 205, Income Tax Regulations.

15.   The law provides for certain exceptions.

16.   Harvard Law School International Program in Taxation, _Taxation in the Federal Republic of Germany_ (Chicago: Commerce Clearing House, 1963), pp. 461–67.

17.   Harvard Law School International Program in Taxation, _Taxation in the United Kingdom_ (Boston: Little, Brown & Co., 1957), pp. 273–77.

18.   Harvard Law School International Program in Taxation, _Taxation in Australia_ (Boston: Little, Brown & Co., 1958), pp. 173, 229.

19.   Harvard Law School International Program in Taxation, _Taxation in Sweden_ (Boston: Little, Brown & Co., 1959), pp. 594–97.

CHAPTER **8** TAX ADMINISTRATION

Tax administration encompasses: (1) the ascertainment of tax liability, (2) the collection of the tax, and (3) the settlement of tax disputes and the imposition of penalties for violation of tax laws.[1]

The ascertainment of tax liability involves the determination of the tax base and the application of the tax rate. Assessment is made either officially or voluntarily. In the former case, it is done by tax officials, while in the latter, the taxpayer himself assesses his tax liability. As a means of checking the taxpayer's statement, information returns are required by the tax administrator. Since tax rates are usually specified in tax laws, the administrator's job is purely to determine the appropriate tax rate for a particular return. Computation of the tax liability is usually done by the taxpayer, and the tax return is subject to review and verification by tax examiners. In some instances, however, the computation is done by the officers with whom the returns are filed. These officers then send the tax bills to the taxpayers.

Payment of taxes is ordinarily made at the time the return is filed. In some cases, however, one government agency takes charge of assessments while another undertakes the collection of taxes. This is especially true with respect to the collection of real property tax.

Failure to comply with tax laws may occur due to neglect, inadvertence, inability, misunderstanding, or deliberate intent to evade. Administrative and

judicial penalties for such defaults range from the
imposition of interest on the defaulted or delinquent
tax to imprisonment in the more severe cases. When
questions in tax determination arise, it is generally
the courts which act as the final interpreters and
arbiters. However, initial interpretation may be
done by an administrative body.

The framework of the tax administration machinery extends to the country's smallest political sub-
division. The central and local governments, however, have a clearly defined scope with respect to
the administration and enforcement of the different tax
laws. The ultimate responsibility for tax administration is usually vested in the central government,
while different degrees of authority are shared by
the local units, depending on the form of the government and the nature and purpose of the tax law.

A good tax system requires an effective tax administration. A good tax badly administered can become an instrument of injustice; on the other hand,
proper administration can partially offset the de-
merits of a poorly designed tax.

This chapter describes tax administration systems and practices followed in selected Asian countries.[2] Charts illustrating the organization of systems of these countries are integrated with the text.

REPUBLIC OF CHINA

Tax laws in the Republic of China are administered at the central government level by the Tax Department of the Ministry of Finance, and, at the provincial government level, by the Department of
Finance of the provincial government. However, customs duties and salt tax are administered exclusively
by the Customs and Salt Administration.

Presently, about fifteen taxes are levied by
the Republic of China: (1) customs duty, (2) salt
tax, (3) income tax, (4) estate tax, (5) stamp tax,
(6) commodity tax, (7) land tax, including land

valuation tax, (8) business tax, (9) house tax,
(10) title deeds tax, (11) slaughter tax, (12) restau-
rant and amusement tax, (13) vehicle license tax,
(14) household tax, and (15) defense tax. The first
six items are national taxes, while the next eight
items are provincial and local.[3] The defense tax,
which is temporarily levied, is in the nature of a
surtax. As stated earlier, only the salt tax and
customs duties are collected directly by the central
government. Collections from customs duty, salt
tax, and commodity tax go to the National Treasury,
while proceeds from the other taxes are shared in
different ratios by the central and local governments.

In most cases, assessment procedures and methods
of payment are spelled out in the tax laws. Generally, as in the case of the income tax, assessment is
done by the taxpayer himself. The withholding tax
system on income from securities, salaries, interest,
and rents is also one of the features of tax collection.

To encourage honest tax declarations, effective
periods are specified for collection of unpaid taxes,
interest charges, and short payment. Reminders are
sent to the taxpayers fifteen days before taxes are
due. Delinquency charges are imposed for those who
fail to pay within the stipulated deadline.[4]

Taxpayers' complaints and protests against
assessments and other tax decisions pass through review, appeal, and reappeal. If the decision is
still unsatisfactory to the taxpayer, the case is
referred to the administrative court, where final
judgment is rendered.

A provincial tax office under the Department of
Finance supervises and directs the operations of the
local tax bureau, as well as the appointment, dismis-
sal, and transfer of personnel. With respect to tax
personnel matters, such as appointment, training,
transfer, reward, punishment, and retirement, the
Department of Finance follows a set of temporary
regulations prescribed by the Executive Yuan. To
enhance the competence of tax personnel, training

CHART 1 TAX ADMINISTRATION SYSTEM OF THE REPUBLIC OF CHINA

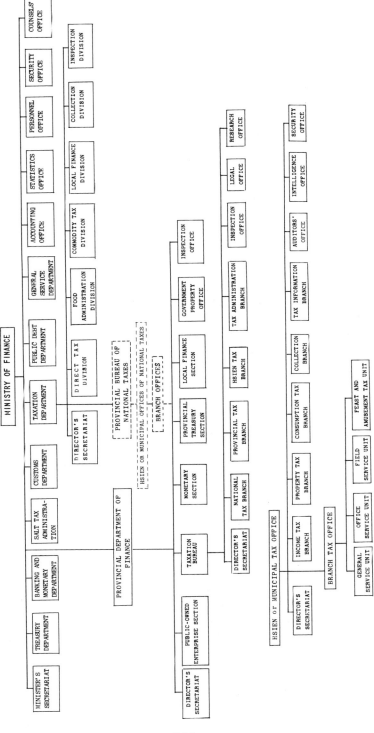

NOTE: As all national taxes have been delegated to the Provincial Department of Finance for unified collection, the stipulated organization of Provincial Bureau of National Taxes and Hsien or Municipal office of National taxes are not in existence now.

programs are provided. Provincial tax agencies usually rotate their personnel so that they can participate alternately in training programs. Examinations
are given by the examination agency, and successful
candidates are trained before they are appointed.
Graduates of special courses in public finance and
taxation given at the National Political University
are appointed after succeeding in the competitive examinations and completing training.

INDIA

Although the primary responsibility for tax
formulation and administration at the central government level pertains to the Department of Revenue in
the Ministry of Finance, these functions are delegated to the Central Board of Revenue.[5] The Board
consists of the Secretary, as Chairman, and four
Joint Secretaries of the Department of Revenue as
members. The various deputy secretaries and undersecretaries of the Department act as Secretaries and
Undersecretaries of the Board. The Board supervises
the administration of central taxes and performs additional functions assigned to it by various tax acts.
Through the Commissioners of Income Tax, the Board
directs and controls the administration of income,
wealth, expenditure, and gift taxes in various parts
of India. It also administers the central excise
tax, the estate duty, and customs duties through the
customs collectors. The state, however, administers
the central sales tax, central stamp duty, and central excise tax on medicinal alcohol and narcotics.

Reports and assessments on income, net wealth,
expenditure, and gifts are done by the same officers,
but by means of separate returns. To ensure proper
assessment, the Board empowers the Inspecting Assistant Commissioners to review and check the work of
the income tax officers. Aside from this function,
Inspecting Assistant Commissioners also approve the
imposition of penalties and supertax on undistributed
profits of privately owned corporations. The work of
the Inspecting Assistant Commissioners is subject to
examination and control by the Director of Inspection.

CHART 2 TAX ADMINISTRATION SYSTEM OF INDIA

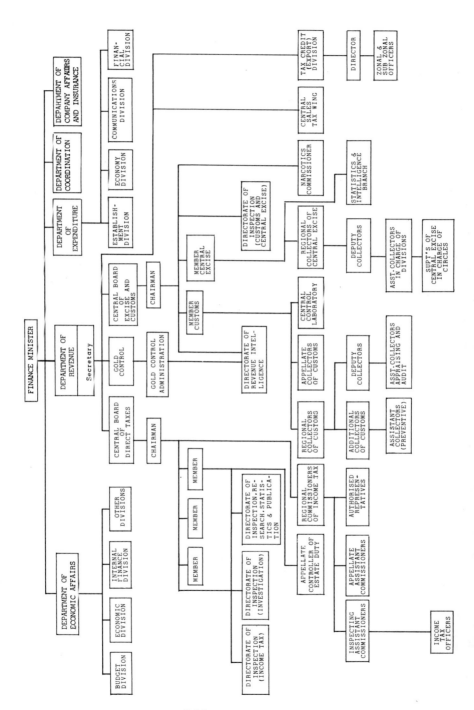

Income tax officers within each jurisdiction
are charged with determining the tax liability of
taxpayers and matters pertaining to assessment.
Their job also includes sending notices of demand
for payment of tax, issuing tax clearance certificates to persons leaving India, and initiating most
of the proceedings for collection of delinquent taxes.

At the local level, income tax officers are
aided by a local staff of Inspectors of income tax,
who investigate and gather evidence from the taxpayers. These officials collect information on income-
producing activities within the jurisdiction of each
income tax officer by compiling lists of houses,
businesses, court cases, government contracts, and
other data available from public sources. An investigation branch staffed by inspectors collects information on important transactions, price changes, construction, purchases of property, contracts, new
businesses, and other pertinent matters which will
aid the income tax officers in their job.

Administrative remedies provided in each tax
law are available to the taxpayer in cases of im-
proper assessment and other tax complaints. The income tax act, for example, allows modification or
revision of income tax assessments. It gives the
taxpayer the right to appeal his case to the Appellate Tribunal, and to refer to a High Court matters
arising out of the orders of the Appellate Tribunal.
The judgment of a High Court may in turn be appealed
to the Supreme Court. Similar remedies are also
available to the taxpayer with respect to assessment
arising from wealth, expenditure, and gift taxes.
For the estate tax, appeals are first filed with Appellate Controllers and then with the Appellate Tribunal. For central excise taxes and custom duties,
the Central Board of Revenue acts as the principal
appellate authority, with the central government as
the highest appellate authority. By authority of
the Constitution, the High Courts can also grant relief from unlawful imposition or collection of taxes.
However, such relief is not generally granted if a
specific and adequate remedy is otherwise available.

To safeguard the interest of taxpayers, special requirements must be met for people to qualify as "income tax practitioners."

Each state has a Board of Revenue headed by the chief revenue authority, except in Punjab, where the chief revenue authority is the Financial Commissioner. Collections are made by the District Collectors, in the case of land revenue, and by the Commissioner or collectors of sales taxes or commercial taxes, in the case of sales taxes. Appellate authority varies from state to state.

JAPAN

The administration of the Japanese tax system falls under the general jurisdiction of the Ministry of Finance.[6] Among the many agencies in this office, direct administration of taxes is delegated to the Tax Administration Agency, the Tax Bureau, and the newly established Customs Bureau. Each of these agencies branches out into several units.

The Tax Bureau is responsible for conducting research and planning and drafting the internal system of taxation. It is also concerned with the estimation and settlement of tax revenue. The Customs Bureau, which was formerly a division of the Tax Bureau, is responsible for conducting research and the imposition and collection of customs duties, tonnage dues, and special tonnage dues. It also controls and regulates imports and exports.

The Tax Administration Agency, headed by a Director and a Deputy Director, has for its main function the assessment and collection of internal taxes. It performs supervisory and controlling functions, such as formulating policies and plans for tax administration practice with respect to the collection of internal taxes. Assessment and collection of national taxes within certain territories and on certain taxpayers are undertaken by the Tax Administration Bureau. It also exercises control and guidance over taxation offices in matters concerning national taxation. As

CHART 3 TAX ADMINISTRATION SYSTEM OF JAPAN

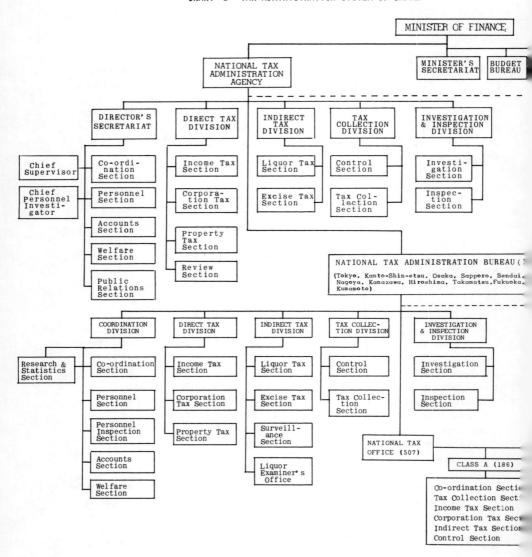

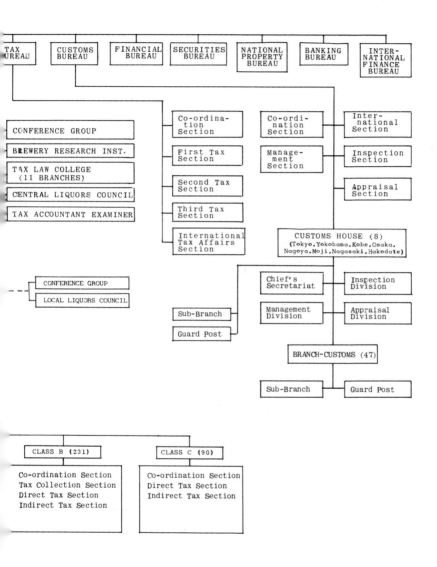

| TAX BUREAU | CUSTOMS BUREAU | FINANCIAL BUREAU | SECURITIES BUREAU | NATIONAL PROPERTY BUREAU | BANKING BUREAU | INTER-NATIONAL FINANCE BUREAU |

CONFERENCE GROUP

BREWERY RESEARCH INST.

TAX LAW COLLEGE (11 BRANCHES)

CENTRAL LIQUORS COUNCIL

TAX ACCOUNTANT EXAMINER

CONFERENCE GROUP

LOCAL LIQUORS COUNCIL

Co-ordina-tion Section

First Tax Section

Second Tax Section

Third Tax Section

International Tax Affairs Section

Co-ordi-nation Section

Manage-ment Section

Inter-national Section

Inspection Section

Appraisal Section

CUSTOMS HOUSE (8)
(Tokyo.Yokohama.Kobe.Osaka.
Nagoya.Moji.Nagasaki.Hakodate)

Chief's Secretariat

Management Division

Inspection Division

Appraisal Division

Sub-Branch

Guard Post

BRANCH-CUSTOMS (47)

Sub-Branch

Guard Post

CLASS B (231)

Co-ordination Section
Tax Collection Section
Direct Tax Section
Indirect Tax Section

CLASS C (90)

Co-ordination Section
Direct Tax Section
Indirect Tax Section

167

a district branch of the Tax Administration Bureau,
the taxation office is responsible for assessment
and collection of internal taxes in the main cities.
Of the several tax administration offices, it is the
one most closely in touch with taxpayers. Taxes
levied by local governments are collected by local
tax-collecting agencies.

Five methods of tax collection are employed in
Japan: self-assessment, official assessment, withholding tax, special collection, and stamp tax.
Under the self-assessment system, the taxpayers themselves determine their tax liabilities, file their
returns, and pay the amount of tax due at the same
time. The self-assessment system is used to collect
direct taxes, such as individual and corporate income taxes, inheritance tax, gift tax, revaluation
tax and part of the securities transaction tax. Under the official assessment system, the government
determines the tax base, computes the tax liability,
and issues a notice requiring the taxpayer to pay
the tax due on a certain date. Tax on income, such
as interest, dividends, or wages, is usually collected through the withholding tax system. Under
this system, those who pay such income are required
to withhold the amount of the tax due from income
recipients. These collections are in turn paid to
the government on behalf of the income recipients.
Under the special collection system, instead of the
payer, it is the recipient who is required to withhold the tax, which he eventually pays to the government at a specific time. This is used to collect
admission taxes and part of the securities tax, to
mention a few examples. The stamp tax, registration
tax, and some securities transaction taxes are collected through the stamp tax system, wherein a taxpayer pays the tax by simply affixing a stamp on the
documents or account books.

In cases of default on the part of the taxpayer,
certain administrative and judicial penalties are
imposed. The administrative penalty consists of an
"interest tax" or "additional tax" which is imposed,
according to the provision of each tax law, on a
taxpayer who has defaulted by failing to file a

return or by filing a false return. Judicial penalties are also spelled out in each of the tax laws.
They usually involve imprisonment and fine. With
respect to the investigation of tax crimes, a "National Tax Evasion Control Law" has been enacted.

A taxpayer can request the taxation office to
reinvestigate a tax case if he is dissatisfied with
an assessment or other tax procedures. If he is dissatisfied with the decision of the taxation office,
he can ask the Director of the Tax Administration
Bureau to reconsider the decision. As a last resort,
he can appeal to the courts, whose decision is final.

PHILIPPINES

The Department of Finance oversees the administration of national taxes in the Philippines. Responsibility for the assessment and collection of
practically all taxes is divided between the Bureau
of Internal Revenue and the Bureau of Customs.

The Bureau of Internal Revenue,[7] headed by a
Commissioner, takes charge of the collection of internal revenue taxes, fees and charges, and dues
arising from forfeitures, penalties, and fines. To
accelerate the assessment and collection of national
taxes, the Bureau maintains fifteen regional offices,
each headed by a regional director. Decentralization has been effected by dividing the Philippines
into seventy-two inspection districts under the
supervision of provincial or city revenue officers.
Collection agents are also stationed in each municipality and city.

The Bureau of Customs, also headed by a Commissioner, is responsible for the collection of customs
duties. In addition, agents of the Bureau act as
collectors of the Bureau of Internal Revenue with
respect to internal revenue taxes on imported articles, such as the advance sales tax, compensating
tax, documentary stamp tax, etc. A customs collector is assigned to every port of entry.

CHART 4   TAX ADMINISTRATION SYSTEM OF THE REPUBLIC OF THE PHILIPPINES

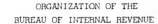

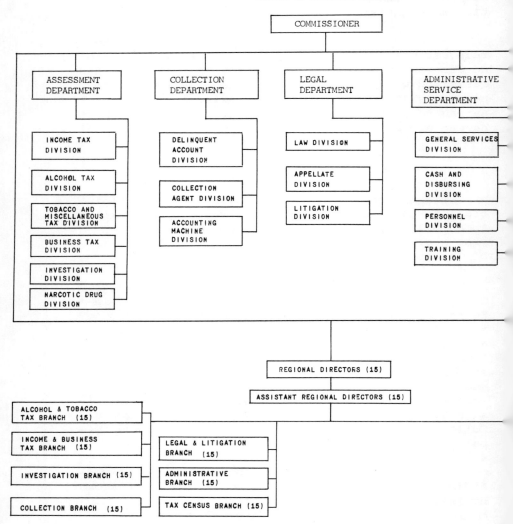

ORGANIZATION OF THE
BUREAU OF INTERNAL REVENUE

COMMISSIONER

ASSESSMENT DEPARTMENT

COLLECTION DEPARTMENT

LEGAL DEPARTMENT

ADMINISTRATIVE SERVICE DEPARTMENT

INCOME TAX DIVISION

ALCOHOL TAX DIVISION

TOBACCO AND MISCELLANEOUS TAX DIVISION

BUSINESS TAX DIVISION

INVESTIGATION DIVISION

NARCOTIC DRUG DIVISION

DELINQUENT ACCOUNT DIVISION

COLLECTION AGENT DIVISION

ACCOUNTING MACHINE DIVISION

LAW DIVISION

APPELLATE DIVISION

LITIGATION DIVISION

GENERAL SERVICES DIVISION

CASH AND DISBURSING DIVISION

PERSONNEL DIVISION

TRAINING DIVISION

REGIONAL DIRECTORS (15)

ASSISTANT REGIONAL DIRECTORS (15)

ALCOHOL & TOBACCO TAX BRANCH (15)

INCOME & BUSINESS TAX BRANCH (15)

INVESTIGATION BRANCH (15)

COLLECTION BRANCH (15)

LEGAL & LITIGATION BRANCH (15)

ADMINISTRATIVE BRANCH (15)

TAX CENSUS BRANCH (15)

170

ORGANIZATION
of the
JOINT LEGISLATIVE-EXECUTIVE TAX COMMISSION

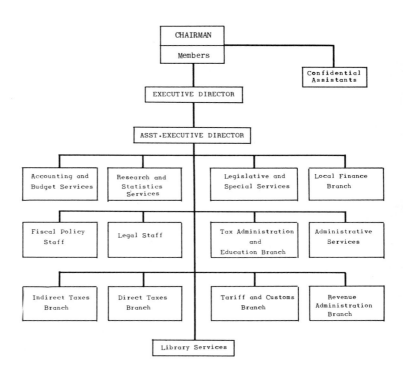

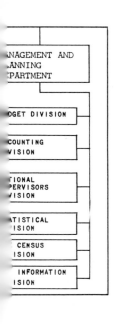

The Joint Legislative-Executive Tax Commission,
a research entity established by law, takes charge
of the formulation of tax policies, conducts research for the purpose of improving the tax system
and tax policy, and recommends reforms or revisions
to improve revenue collection and administration.[8]
It also evaluates all tax measures and revenue proposals.

The powers of the Tax Commission are vested in
a governing body which consists of nine members.
Three members are appointed by the President of the
Philippines, three are senators appointed by the
President of the Senate, and three are congressmen
appointed by the Speaker of the House of Representatives.   The Tax Commission Technical Staff is headed
by an Executive Director who is directly responsible
to the Chairman and the members of the Commission.

There are several methods of tax collection.
The most common, especially in cases where returns
are required to be filed, is the "pay-as-you-file"
method.   At the end of the year, the taxpayer makes
payment at the same time that he files his return.
This is particularly true with respect to individual
and corporate income taxes and other direct taxes.
Other taxes are collected by one of the following
methods: the withholding method, where the payer de-
ducts an amount which represents the tax due from the
taxpayer's income; the official assessment method,
where assessment and collection are done by tax officials, as in the case of most local taxes; or the
special assessment method, where the tax is collected
by the recipient of income, who turns it over to the
government, as is usually done in the case of taxes
on admission to places of entertainment.   A simple
and efficient method of collection is the stamp tax
payment method: Here a taxpayer simply affixes a
stamp on documents and books of account.   Under the
Bureau of Internal Revenue and the Bureau of Customs
are offices which directly take charge of assessment
and collection.

Penalties for tax violation or tax default are
spelled out in the different tax laws.   Administrative

penalties are usually in the form of interest, surcharges, and the so-called compromise payments[9]
which are levied in addition to the original amount
of tax liability. Administrative penalties are generally imposed for failure to file the required tax
return and failure to pay the tax on time, either
willfully or through neglect. Judicial penalties
consist of confinement in jail, payment of fine, or
both. Judicial penalties are usually imposed on taxpayers for rendering false and fraudulent returns
and for tax evasion.

Whenever tax disputes and conflicts arise between the taxpayer and the tax official representing the government, the former can file a petition
with the Appellate Division of the Bureau of Internal
Revenue. This division usually arranges a confronta-
tion between the taxpayer or his counsel and the tax
official, after which it renders a decision. If the
taxpayer is dissatisfied with the decision, he can
file a formal protest with the Commissioner of Internal Revenue contesting the decision of the Appellate Division. If he still has objections to the
opinion of the Commissioner, he can present his case
to the Court of Tax Appeals. If the decision of the
Court of Tax Appeals is still unsatisfactory, it can
be contested by appeal to the Supreme Court, the
highest judicial body, for final judgment.

To encourage efficiency in the administration of
tax laws and enhance competence of tax functionaries,
seminars and intensive training courses are conducted
by the various revenue-collecting agencies of the
government. Before personnel are assigned to the
field, they receive a rigorous three-month in-service
training course covering all aspects of Philippine
taxation. Deserving employees are sent abroad to ob-
serve modern trends and procedures in tax administration. Recently, a Finance Academy has been set up to
provide a more comprehensive training program for
revenue officials. It has for its objectives the development and maintenance of a "desirable high standard of employee performance in the Department of
Finance and its agencies and offices to enable it to
perform more effectively as the principal revenue

raising and collecting arm of the National Government."[10]

It also aims to develop technical skills and improve productive capacity. It seeks to develop personnel for lifetime careers in important branches of the Department of Finance, particularly Career Appraisers in the Bureau of Customs, Career Examiners in the Bureau of Internal Revenue, and Career Treasurers in the treasury services.

Similarly, to encourage honest and up-to-date tax declarations, brochures and pamphlets on taxation are distributed to the public. Extensive tax-consciousness campaigns are also conducted.

THAILAND

The administration of tax laws in Thailand devolves on three departments: the Revenue Department, the Excise Department, and the Customs Department.[11] These offices are under the Ministry of Finance.

The Revenue Department administers and collects general state revenue taxes, including personal income, corporate income, business, and commodity purchase taxes. It supervises the assessment practices of localities in their administration of land and miscellaneous local taxes, and it collects some local taxes on a percentage basis. The Excise Department collects the various excise taxes, including taxes on cement, playing cards, matches, soft drinks, liquor, and tobacco products. The collection of customs duties on imports and exports is performed by the Customs Department. It also conducts searches and inspections to prevent and reduce smuggling. Motor vehicle taxes, alien fees, and duties on land transfer are collected by the Ministry of Interior.

For effective administration of internal taxes, several tax offices are stationed in the nine regions into which the country is divided. The responsibility of levying and collecting local taxes is vested in the Mayor of each municipality. The authority

CHART 5   TAX ADMINISTRATION SYSTEM OF THAILAND

REVENUE DEPARTMENT

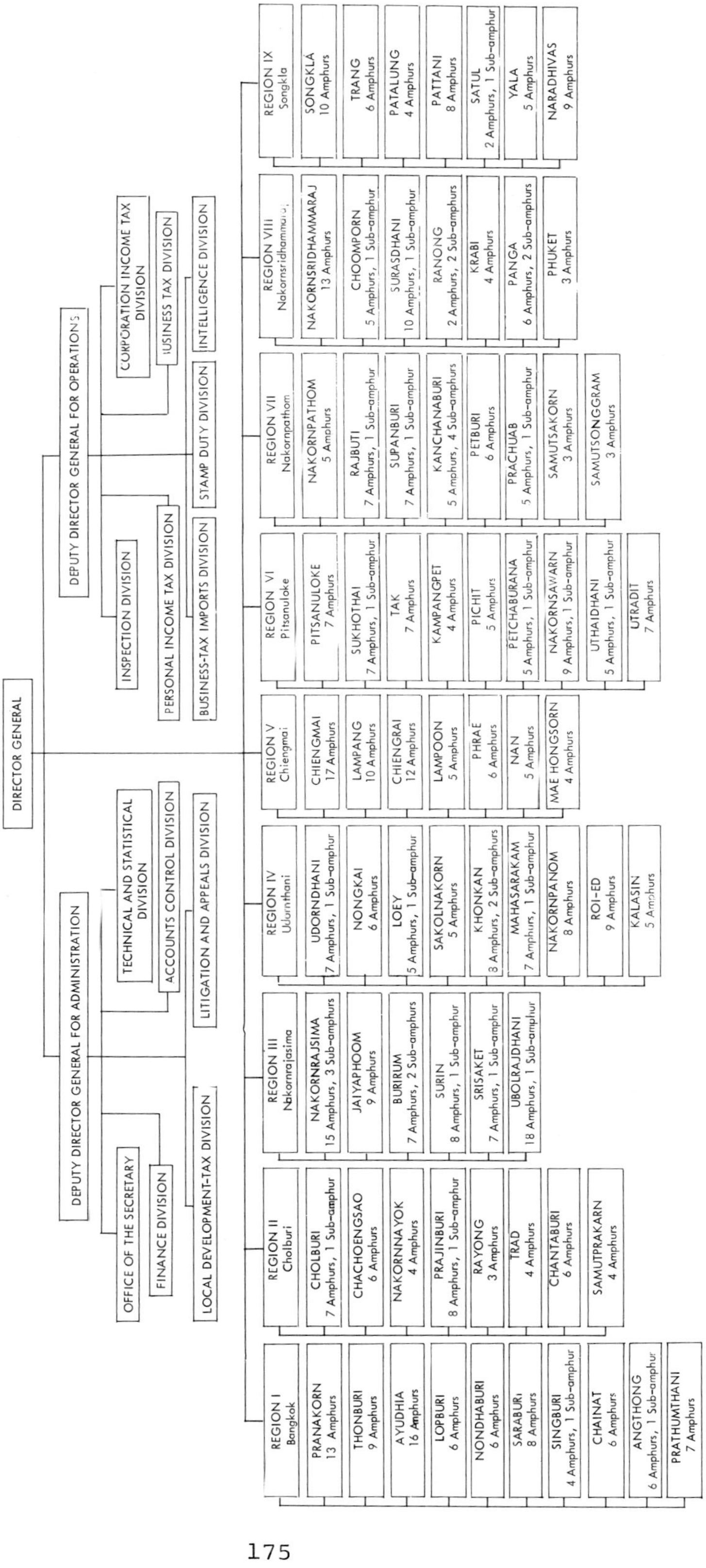

DIRECTOR GENERAL

DEPUTY DIRECTOR GENERAL FOR ADMINISTRATION

DEPUTY DIRECTOR GENERAL FOR OPERATIONS

OFFICE OF THE SECRETARY

FINANCE DIVISION

TECHNICAL AND STATISTICAL DIVISION

ACCOUNTS CONTROL DIVISION

LITIGATION AND APPEALS DIVISION

LOCAL DEVELOPMENT-TAX DIVISION

INSPECTION DIVISION

PERSONAL INCOME TAX DIVISION

BUSINESS-TAX IMPORTS DIVISION

CORPORATION INCOME TAX DIVISION

BUSINESS TAX DIVISION

INTELLIGENCE DIVISION

STAMP DUTY DIVISION

REGION I Bangkok
- PRANAKORN, 13 Amphurs
- THONBURI, 9 Amphurs
- AYUDHIA, 16 Amphurs
- LOPBURI, 6 Amphurs
- NONDHABURI, 6 Amphurs
- SARABURI, 8 Amphurs
- SINGBURI, 4 Amphurs, 1 Sub-amphur
- CHAINAT, 6 Amphurs
- ANGTHONG, 6 Amphurs, 1 Sub-amphur
- PRATHUMTHANI, 7 Amphurs

REGION II Cholburi
- CHOLBURI, 7 Amphurs, 1 Sub-amphur
- CHACHOENGSAO, 6 Amphurs
- NAKORNNAYOK, 4 Amphurs
- PRAJINBURI, 8 Amphurs, 1 Sub-amphur
- RAYONG, 3 Amphurs
- TRAD, 4 Amphurs
- CHANTABURI, 6 Amphurs
- SAMUTPRAKARN, 4 Amphurs

REGION III Nakornrajasima
- NAKORNRAJSIMA, 15 Amphurs, 3 Sub-amphurs
- JAIYAPHOOM, 9 Amphurs
- BURIRUM, 7 Amphurs, 2 Sub-amphurs
- SURIN, 8 Amphurs, 1 Sub-amphur
- SRISAKET, 7 Amphurs, 1 Sub-amphur
- UBOLRAJDHANI, 18 Amphurs, 1 Sub-amphur

REGION IV Udornthani
- UDORNDHANI, 7 Amphurs, 1 Sub-amphur
- NONGKAI, 6 Amphurs
- LOEY, 5 Amphurs, 1 Sub-amphur
- SAKOLNAKORN, 5 Amphurs
- KHONKAN, 8 Amphurs, 2 Sub-amphurs
- MAHASARAKAM, 7 Amphurs, 1 Sub-amphur
- NAKORNPANOM, 8 Amphurs
- ROI-ED, 9 Amphurs
- KALASIN, 5 Amphurs

REGION V Chiengmai
- CHIENGMAI, 17 Amphurs
- LAMPANG, 10 Amphurs
- CHIENGRAI, 12 Amphurs
- LAMPOON, 5 Amphurs
- PHRAE, 6 Amphurs
- NAN, 5 Amphurs
- MAE HONGSORN, 4 Amphurs

REGION VI Pitsanuloke
- PITSANULOKE, 7 Amphurs
- SUKHOTHAI, 7 Amphurs, 1 Sub-amphur
- TAK, 7 Amphurs
- KAMPANGPET, 4 Amphurs
- PICHIT, 5 Amphurs
- FETCHABURANA, 5 Amphurs, 1 Sub-amphur
- NAKORNSAWARN, 9 Amphurs, 1 Sub-amphur
- UTHAIDHANI, 5 Amphurs, 1 Sub-amphur
- UTRADIT, 7 Amphurs

REGION VII Nakornpathom
- NAKORNPATHOM, 5 Amphurs
- RAJBUTI, 7 Amphurs, 1 Sub-amphur
- SUPANBURI, 7 Amphurs, 1 Sub-amphur
- KANCHANABURI, 5 Amphurs, 4 Sub-amphurs
- PETBURI, 6 Amphurs
- PRACHUAB, 5 Amphurs, 1 Sub-amphur
- SAMUTSAKORN, 3 Amphurs
- SAMUTSONGGRAM, 3 Amphurs

REGION VIII Nakornsridhammaraj
- NAKORNSRIDHAMMARAJ, 13 Amphurs
- CHOOMPORN, 5 Amphurs, 1 Sub-amphur
- SURASDHANI, 10 Amphurs, 1 Sub-amphur
- RANONG, 2 Amphurs, 2 Sub-amphurs
- KRABI, 4 Amphurs
- PANGA, 6 Amphurs, 2 Sub-amphurs
- PHUKET, 3 Amphurs

REGION IX Songkla
- SONGKLA, 10 Amphurs
- TRANG, 6 Amphurs
- PATALUNG, 4 Amphurs
- PATTANI, 8 Amphurs
- SATUL, 2 Amphurs, 1 Sub-amphur
- YALA, 5 Amphurs
- NARADHIVAS, 9 Amphurs

175

for collecting local development tax, motor vehicles tax, rice premiums, and surcharges on merchandise or services is vested in the respective departments of the national government. The collections are turned over to the Mayor of each municipality.

As in other Asian countries, several methods of assessment and collection are followed in Thailand. Personal and corporate income taxes and business taxes are paid through the self-assessment procedure, where taxes are paid at the time the returns are filed. Other methods, such as the stamp-tax method and the official-assessment method, are also employed.

Filing of returns is made at the time and in the form prescribed by the Director-General of the Revenue Department.[12] The Director-General also requires in certain cases an annual report and balance sheet. Returns are assessed by either the amphur or the assessment officers. If a tax or a refund is due, a notice is sent to the taxpayer; otherwise, the notice is generally dispensed with. In certain instances, assessment may be made in advance. The Revenue Code empowers the Assessment Officer to review an assessment within five years after the taxpayer has filed the return if indications of false and inadequate information exist.

Appeals are made in the form prescribed by the Director-General. An appeal against the assessment made by the amphur must be filed with the assessment officer within fifteen days from the date the notice is received. If the decision is unsatisfactory to the taxpayer, he may file an appeal with the ChangVad Governor. An appeal against the decision of the ChangVad Governor may be lodged with the court.

Appeals against assessment officers with offices at Dhonburi are filed with the Board of Appeals composed of the Director-General or his representative, a representative of the Department of Public Prosecution, and a representative of the Interim Department. Appeals against decisions of assessment officers from any other area are lodged with the Board of Appeals composed of the ChangVad Governor, the Regional

Revenue Officer, and the ChangVad Public Prosecutor, or their representatives. Generally, a tax or a duty is collected even if a case is under appeal, except in certain cases where payment is deferred by the Director-General.

Failure to file a return is punished with a fine not exceeding two thousand bahts. Making a false and fraudulent return is punishable with an imprisonment of from three months to seven years and a fine of from two to three thousand bahts. A fine not exceeding five thousand bahts or imprisonment not exceeding six months, or both, is imposed on those guilty of willful neglect to file a return, with a view to evading taxes.

SOUTH VIETNAM

Tax administration in South Vietnam is carried out at the central government level and at the local government level.

The responsibility for administering central government taxes is shared by the General Directorate of Taxation, the General Directorate of Customs, and the General Treasury. These offices fall under the jurisdiction of the Secretary of State for Finance. The General Directorate of Taxation assesses and collects most of the internal taxes, which are classified into direct, indirect, excise, and registration taxes. Direct taxes are collected by the General Treasury. All import duties and export taxes are assessed and collected by the General Directorate of Customs.[13] Several branches maintained by these offices are located strategically throughout South Vietnam.

At the local government level, taxes are administered by local tax administration units. A unique feature of the tax administration setup in South Vietnam is the separation of assessment and collection functions with respect to direct taxes.[14] Direct taxes, including income, property, and business license taxes, are assessed by the Directorate General of Taxation, which also prepares the tax rolls.

CHART 6 TAX ADMINISTRATION SYSTEM OF SOUTH VIETNAM

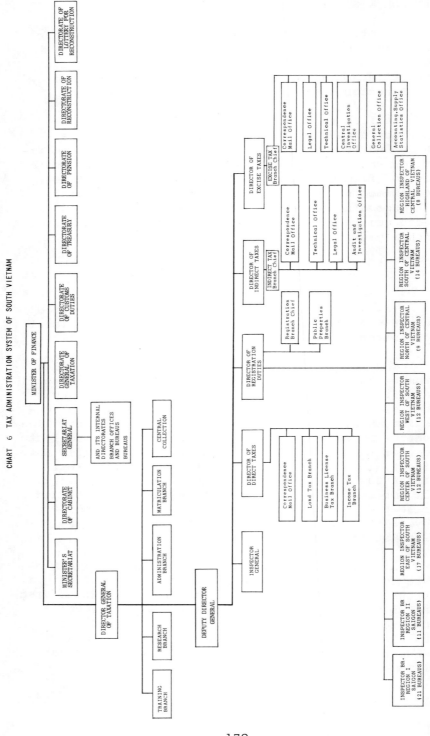

These rolls are then sent to the Treasury, headed by
the National Treasurer, which collects the taxes due.
However, with respect to indirect taxes, registration taxes and excise taxes, assessment and collection are both done by the Directorate General of
Taxation.

The Vietnamese tax system imposes both civil and
criminal tax penalties. Civil tax penalties are imposed in terms of monetary fines and interest, for
ordinary neglect or unintentional failure to file
tax returns on the date due. Penalties are not graduated; that is, a taxpayer may be fined 100 per cent
or 200 per cent, regardless of the length of time
payment is neglected. Criminal tax offenses arise
from fraud or tax evasion.

Several measures are being implemented with a
view to improving the tax administration machinery,
especially by the Directorate General of Taxation.
Decentralization of the twenty-four bureaus of property, business, and excise taxes is already under
way. Machines are being utilized for greater efficiency. A field investigation staff with definite
plans and quarterly programs is being established.

Training programs by the In-service Training
Section for central and local tax officials and an
extensive tax information campaign are conducted to
acquaint both tax officials and taxpayers with
taxation matters.

SINGAPORE

The responsibility for administering taxes in
Singapore pertains to the Customs and Excise Department, headed by a Comptroller, and the Inland Revenue
Department, headed by a Commissioner.[15] In each
case, general supervision and control is exercised
by a Comptroller General in the Federal capital in
Kuala Lumpur. These offices are directly under the
Ministry of Finance. The former takes charge of the
assessment and collection of customs duties and excises on tobacco, petroleum, liquor, admissions to

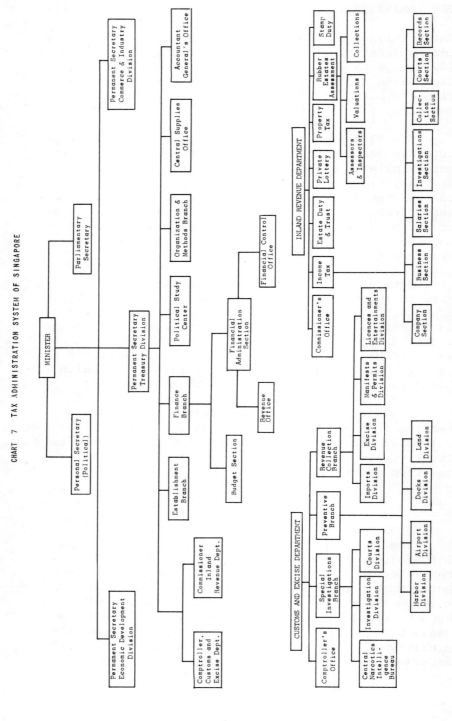

CHART 7 TAX ADMINISTRATION SYSTEM OF SINGAPORE

180

places of entertainment, licenses, and storage of
dutiable goods in government warehouses. The latter
takes charge of the assessment and collection of internal taxes, such as the income tax, the property
tax, and taxes on estates and stamps. The Inland
Revenue Department consists of the Commissioner's
office, income tax, estate duty and trust, private
lottery, property tax, and stamp duty branches. The
Customs and Excise Department is composed of the
Comptroller's office, the special investigations
branch, the preventive branch, and the revenue collection branch. Smaller administrative units are
maintained by the above-mentioned offices.

Definite time periods for payment of self-
assessed or officially assessed taxes are provided
in the tax laws. In certain instances, such as in
the payment of income tax, the Comptroller is empowered to extend the time limit within which payment
is to be made.

Taxpayers are provided with ample safeguards
against undue assessments and collections. In case
of tax dispute, a taxpayer may first appeal his case
to the Board of Review, which is usually composed of
business and professional men appointed by the government. The case then goes to the High Court. If the
decision is still adverse to the taxpayer, the case
can be taken to the Court of Appeals, and finally to
the Privy Council, the highest judicial body in the
British Commonwealth of Nations.[16]

SOUTH KOREA

As in most Asian countries, the over-all administration of taxes in South Korea is the responsibility of the Ministry of Finance. The assessment and
collection of taxes are, however, entrusted to two
offices under it: the Bureau of Customs, which is
responsible for customs duties and excises, and the
Taxation Bureau, which is in charge of all domestic
taxes, both national and local.[17]

CHART 8   TAX ADMINISTRATION SYSTEM OF SOUTH KOREA

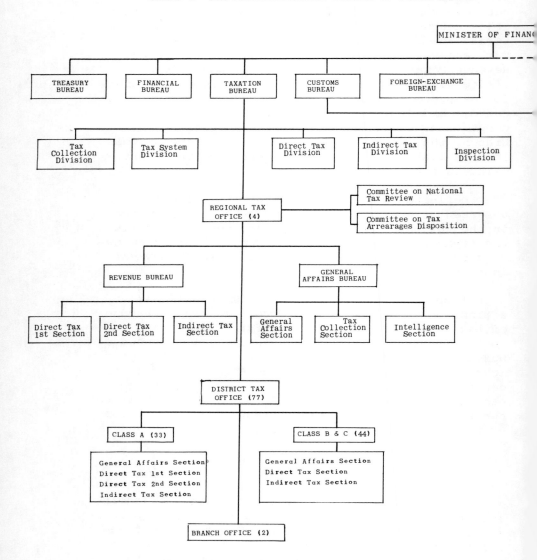

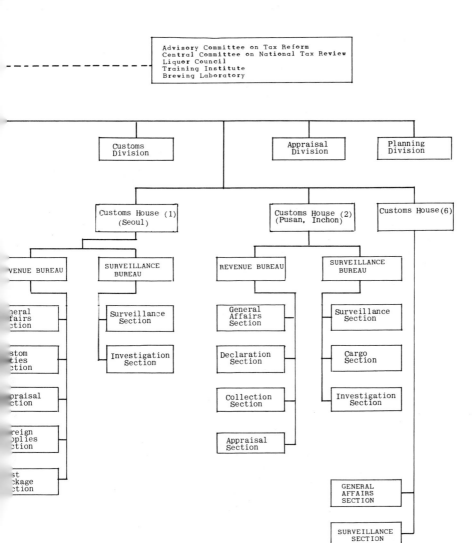

Advisory Committee on Tax Reform
Central Committee on National Tax Review
Liquor Council
Training Institute
Brewing Laboratory

Customs Division

Appraisal Division

Planning Division

Customs House (1)
(Seoul)

Customs House (2)
(Pusan, Inchon)

Customs House (6)

REVENUE BUREAU

SURVEILLANCE BUREAU

REVENUE BUREAU

SURVEILLANCE BUREAU

General Affairs Section

Surveillance Section

General Affairs Section

Surveillance Section

Custom Duties Section

Investigation Section

Declaration Section

Cargo Section

Appraisal Section

Collection Section

Investigation Section

Foreign Supplies Section

Appraisal Section

Post Package Section

GENERAL AFFAIRS SECTION

SURVEILLANCE SECTION

The Customs Bureau maintains nine customs houses which perform, among other things, investigation, surveillance, appraisal, and collection functions. Each customs house has different branch offices, each of which in turn maintains surveillance posts.

The Taxation Bureau has four regional tax offices which are responsible for the regulation, coordination, and supervision of the different district tax offices within their respective jurisdictions. To date, there are seventy-seven district tax offices throughout the country. Within each of the districts, branch offices are strategically located.

Taxes are generally paid voluntarily or on a self-assessment principle. Intensive campaigns are now under way to make taxes understandable to both taxpayers and tax officials. The Tax Delinquent Punishment Law and its Procedural Law impose penalties for violation of any tax law. The National Tax Review Claim Law affords adequate protection to taxpayers against erroneous tax assessments by the government.

INDONESIA

The highest governing body in matters of taxation in Indonesia is the Directorate of Taxes. The Directorate's main function is to coordinate, control, and supervise the work of the various tax administration agencies.[18] Administration of customs duties and excises, however, is entrusted to a separate agency.

Tax administration has a decentralized setup. The territory is divided into four regions for supervisory purposes. Each region is headed by a Regional General Inspector who exercises full autonomous authority for tax management. Four senior officials assist the Chief of the Directorate of Taxes in matters of communication and supervision.

Within each region are district offices called Inspectorates of Finance. The district offices are responsible for sending monthly statistical reports,

progress reports, and reports on conditions and developments with respect to the internal organization,
work output in terms of assessment and collection,
and regularity of operations of the offices.

MALAYSIA

In Malaysia administration of internal taxes is
vested in the Inland Revenue Department which is comprised of three offices: the Income Tax Division,
Estate Duty Division, and Business Registration Division. It is headed by the Comptroller of Inland
Revenue, who acts as the comptroller of income tax,
collector of estate duty, and registrar of businesses.
He is responsible to the Accountant-General for the
administration of the stamp duty offices at Kuala
Lumpur and Penang. The headquarters of the Inland
Revenue Department and the offices that comprise it
are situated in Kuala Lumpur. However, there are
ten branch offices spread throughout the country under the subsidiary control of four regional heads.[19]

Malaysia also maintains jointly with Singapore
and other Commonwealth countries the Overseas Territories Income Tax Office, located at the Grosvenor
Gardens, London, S.W.I., which assesses and collects
taxes on behalf of Malaysia from individuals and companies residing in the United Kingdom.

The tax is due and payable within one month of
the date of service of the notice of assessment.
There is a "pay-as-you-earn" system, under which the
tax payable by employees is automatically deducted
from monthly wages when the tax due exceeds M$240
per year. The same system may be used voluntarily
by people who earn less. A unique feature is the
systematic manual processing of taxpayer's accounts.
In this way, the tax agency concerned keeps in touch
with the taxpayer until the tax is paid. Several
devices are utilized to enhance prompt payment of
taxes. The relatively stringent penalties in terms
of interest and court action in cases of default
serve to forewarn taxpayers about the dangers of not
paying on time. In certain instances, the law even

CHART 9 TAX ADMINISTRATION SYSTEM OF INDONESIA

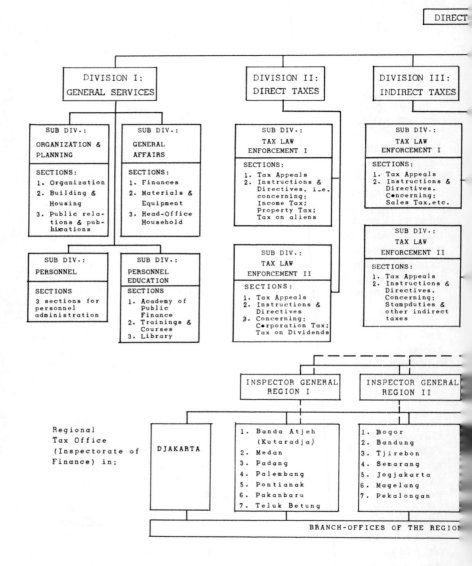

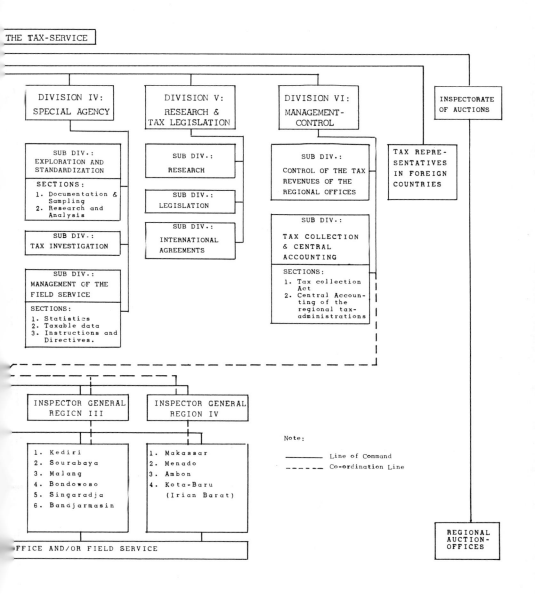

DIVISION IV:
SPECIAL AGENCY

DIVISION V:
RESEARCH &
TAX LEGISLATION

DIVISION VI:
MANAGEMENT-
CONTROL

INSPECTORATE
OF AUCTIONS

SUB DIV.:
EXPLORATION AND
STANDARDIZATION

SECTIONS:
1. Documentation &
   Sampling
2. Research and
   Analysis

SUB DIV.:
RESEARCH

SUB DIV.:
LEGISLATION

SUB DIV.:
INTERNATIONAL
AGREEMENTS

SUB DIV.:
CONTROL OF THE TAX
REVENUES OF THE
REGIONAL OFFICES

SUB DIV.:
TAX COLLECTION
& CENTRAL
ACCOUNTING

SECTIONS:
1. Tax collection
   Act
2. Central Accoun-
   ting of the
   regional tax-
   administrations

TAX REPRE-
SENTATIVES
IN FOREIGN
COUNTRIES

SUB DIV.:
TAX INVESTIGATION

SUB DIV.:
MANAGEMENT OF THE
FIELD SERVICE

SECTIONS:
1. Statistics
2. Taxable data
3. Instructions and
   Directives.

INSPECTOR GENERAL
REGION III

INSPECTOR GENERAL
REGION IV

Note:

———————— Line of Command
— — — — — Co-ordination Line

1. Kediri
2. Sourabaya
3. Malang
4. Bondowoso
5. Singaradja
6. Bandjarmasin

1. Makassar
2. Menado
3. Ambon
4. Kota-Baru
   (Irian Barat)

REGIONAL
AUCTION-
OFFICES

OFFICE AND/OR FIELD SERVICE

187

CHART 10 TAX ADMINISTRATION SYSTEM OF MALAYSIA

DEPARTMENT OF INLAND REVENUE

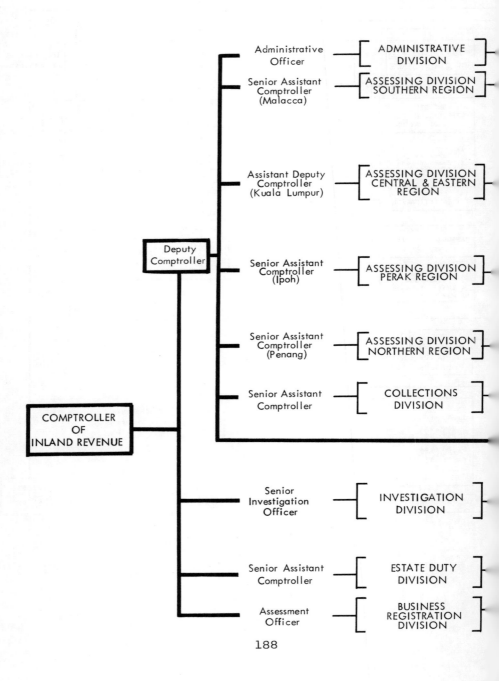

188

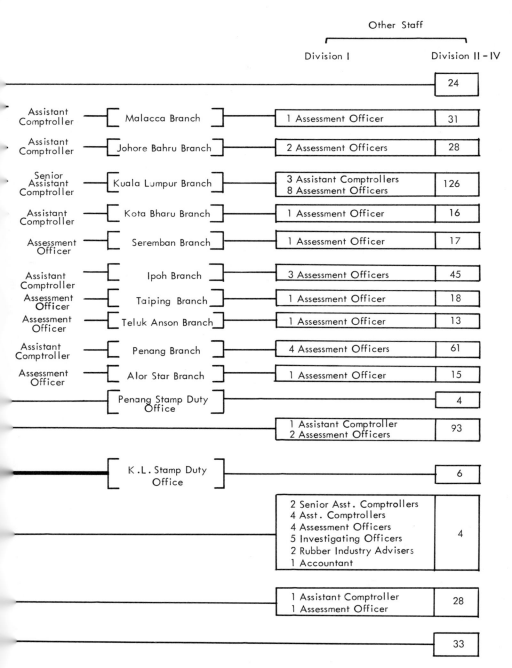

			Other Staff	
			Division I	Division II – IV
				24
Assistant Comptroller	Malacca Branch		1 Assessment Officer	31
Assistant Comptroller	Johore Bahru Branch		2 Assessment Officers	28
Senior Assistant Comptroller	Kuala Lumpur Branch		3 Assistant Comptrollers 8 Assessment Officers	126
Assistant Comptroller	Kota Bharu Branch		1 Assessment Officer	16
Assessment Officer	Seremban Branch		1 Assessment Officer	17
Assistant Comptroller	Ipoh Branch		3 Assessment Officers	45
Assessment Officer	Taiping Branch		1 Assessment Officer	18
Assessment Officer	Teluk Anson Branch		1 Assessment Officer	13
Assistant Comptroller	Penang Branch		4 Assessment Officers	61
Assessment Officer	Alor Star Branch		1 Assessment Officer	15
	Penang Stamp Duty Office			4
			1 Assistant Comptroller 2 Assessment Officers	93
	K.L. Stamp Duty Office			6
			2 Senior Asst. Comptrollers 4 Asst. Comptrollers 4 Assessment Officers 5 Investigating Officers 2 Rubber Industry Advisers 1 Accountant	4
			1 Assistant Comptroller 1 Assessment Officer	28
				33

189

permits the Department to collect the tax if an assessment is under appeal.

The method of assessment is also geared to facilitate prompt collection. Although the tax is payable in terms of current income, the liability is usually measured by reference to the previous year's income. "Transitional complications" are usually encountered, however, with respect to the determination of new forms of income and "closing" sources of income. After the source of income has been established for two or three years, succeeding tax liability can easily be computed. The early computation of the tax is also made possible by accepting as the basis an accounting year which does not coincide with the calendar year.

Any objection to an income tax assessment must be made in writing to the Comptroller within one month. If a taxpayer is dissatisfied with the decision of the Comptroller, he may appeal to the Federation Income Tax Board of Review, which hears the case "in camera." If the Comptroller or the taxpayer is dissatisfied with the decision of the Board of Review, either party may appeal to the Courts.

Several measures are being adopted by Malaysia to minimize tax evasion, such as the imposition of heavy penalties on violators and wide publicity of antitax-evasion campaigns. In some instances concessions are granted by the Department. Employees who fail to pay on time are not normally prosecuted; instead, the tax due is deducted from their salaries. Where the evader is prepared to cooperate in assessing his true liability, the Department accedes to an out-of-court settlement.

CONCLUSIONS AND OBSERVATIONS

In view of the growing awareness of the vital role which taxation plays in a developing economy, substantive and major reforms in tax administration are being undertaken. These reforms are fashioned along the classic requirements of a good tax system: certainty, convenience, and economy.

To a great extent, difficulties in tax administration are traceable to ambiguities in the tax laws,
particularly with respect to the definition of the
tax base and the manner and time of payment. Confus-
ing provisions of tax laws not only invite indiffer-
ence on the part of taxpayers, but also encourage
tax avoidance or evasion. Faulty legislation and
conflicting interpretations by tax officials and
judicial agencies compound the problem further. Opposition is generally strong on the initial levying
of the tax, but it gradually wanes as taxpayers become familiar with the tax law and administrative enforcement settles down to an efficient routine.[20]

In all of the countries considered, great efforts are being made by tax authorities to familiar-
ize taxpayers with the various tax laws. In South
Korea and Malaysia, intensive campaigns are under
way to acquaint both taxpayers and tax administrators with the tax laws. In the Philippines and in
Japan brochures and pamphlets on existing tax laws
are being distributed to the public, while new taxes
are given publicity through the radio, newspapers,
and other means of mass communication. Regulations
and decisions on tax disputes are also made available to the public.

Several schemes, designed for the convenience
of both taxpayers and tax administrators, are also
being incorporated in the tax administration systems
of these countries. The advantages offered by the
withholding tax system have led to its wide acceptance in many Asian countries. For instance, among
the major tax reforms initiated in the Republic of
China is the withholding tax system. In Japan,
India, and the Philippines such a scheme has already
long been incorporated in their respective tax administration systems. In Malaysia payment through the
withholding tax system is applied to wages, dividends,
and in certain circumstances to interest. Installment or quarterly payments are convenient schemes
resorted to in order to help hard-pressed taxpayers
who would otherwise have to make a single lump payment at the end of the year. In the Philippines, income tax and transfer taxes may be made in two

installments, if the amount exceeds a certain stipulated figure during any taxable year. The tax administration system of Japan allows a similar concession
to taxpayers.

Rigid time limitations for the payment of taxes
are not uncommon sources of taxpayer inconvenience.
In Malaysia and Singapore the Comptroller is empowered to extent the time limit within which tax payment may be made. In the Philippines indisposition
of a taxpayer due to sickness or accident may be
grounds for the Commissioner to extend the deadline
for tax payment, while in Thailand the Director-
General is empowered to defer tax payment in certain
cases. To encourage prompt collection and for the
convenience of taxpayers, a unique scheme is being
utilized in the Republic of China. Fifteen days before the deadline for tax payments, reminders are
sent out to taxpayers.

Overcentralization of tax administration may
compel taxpayers to travel far and wait for a long
time to file returns and make tax payments. This
has given rise to the necessity of decentralizing
the tax administration machinery. All of the countries in this study have a decentralized setup to
take care of the administration of taxes at the local
government level. For instance, in South Vietnam decentralization of the twenty-four bureaus charged
with the collection of property, business, and excise taxes is already being undertaken. Malaysia
has established an overseas office in London to
serve Malaysian residents who want to have their liabilities assessed there. The Office of International
Operations, which was recently set up by the Bureau
of Internal Revenue in the Philippines, has for its
main task the servicing of Filipino taxpayers deriving income from sources outside the Philippines.

A major source of taxpayers' and tax administrators' inconvenience is the shortage of competent
staff and lack of equipment. These problems are
gradually being met through training courses for tax
personnel and the mechanization of certain phases of
tax administration. In the Republic of China tax

personnel are recruited through examinations. Before successful examinees are assigned to the field,
they are required to undergo training. In Japan the
Tax Law College and its branches in several cities
conduct training courses in tax administration. It
offers a special one-year course, a one-year superior
course, and a short-term course of training. The
newly established Finance Academy in the Philippines,
which conducts similar training courses for tax officials and other finance personnel, seeks to enhance
competence in tax administration. Some of the countries send their tax officials abroad for further
studies and observations.

Mechanization of certain phases of tax work, especially verification and audit of tax returns, is
gaining ground. It may be mentioned that convenience
can be greatly facilitated by such schemes as service
by mail to save waiting in line, evening tax office
hours, prompt answers to tax queries, and frequent
audits.[21]

Tax administration entails both administrative
and compliance costs. Administrative costs are those
incurred by the government in enforcing tax laws.
Compliance costs are those incurred by taxpayers in
complying with their tax liabilities. For purposes
of convenience and efficiency, these should be reduced to the lowest practicable limit. With respect
to administrative cost, however, this does not mean
that the lower the cost, the more efficient the tax
machinery. It is generally the case that the lower
the administrative cost, the less satisfactory is
the administrative result.[22]

Because of the growing complexity and the expanding scope of tax administration in Asian countries, the cost aspect is particularly significant.
The self-assessment system and the pay-as-you-file
system have substantially reduced administrative
cost. Part of the tax reform presently being contemplated by the Republic of China is to utilize voluntary tax compliance to a greater degree, by the
adoption of the self-assessment and pay-as-you-file
systems. In South Vietnam this is also one of the

major features of its tax reform.   Increased utilization of machines is also being undertaken in order
to improve the work-flow.   In the Philippines, plans
are afoot to install electronic machines to handle
the processing of tax returns.   This is intended not
only to facilitate and increase work output, but
also to reduce the cost of personnel needed for
audit and review.   Much can be also achieved at lower cost from a well-planned monthly or quarterly
work program, such as the one introduced in South
Vietnam.

If tax administration is to be effective, it
should enhance or promote the just and equitable enforcement of tax laws.   A tax administration system
which allows considerable tax evasion loses much of
its usefulness.   Injustice arises from the fact that
some taxpayers can go scot-free while others are
made to bear the tax burden.

Large-scale tax evasion and avoidance in many
of the countries have prompted tax authorities to
wage an all-out drive against tax law violators.   In
Japan special procedures for investigation and handling of direct and indirect tax evaders are stipulated in the National Tax Evasion Control Law.   Under this law, tax officials are authorized to search
for indirect tax evaders by means of warrants secured
from the court.   If a direct evader is involved, the
tax official can hand over the case to the prosecutor
immediately after investigation.   In South Korea penalties for offenses committed in violation of any
tax law are spelled out in the Tax Delinquent Punishment Law and the Procedural Law.   Adequate protection for taxpayers against erroneous tax assessment
by the Government is provided under the National Tax
Review Claims Law.   In Thailand, Singapore, Indonesia,
India, and the Philippines heavy penalties are imposed on tax violators.   However, in all these countries, administrative and judicial remedies are available to taxpayers who might have been assessed im-
properly or unjustly.

Notes to Chapter 8

1. Harley L. Lutz, "Tax Administration," Encyclopaedia of the Social Sciences, XIV (New York: The
Macmillan Company, 1935), 526-28.

2. For an interesting work on this topic, with
particular emphasis on underdeveloped countries, see
Stanley S. Surrey, "Tax Administration in Underde-
veloped Countries," University of Miami Law Review,
XII (Winter, 1958), 158-88. Also appearing in Read-
ings on Taxation in Developing Countries, ed. by
Richard Bird and Oliver Oldman (Baltimore: The
Johns Hopkins Press, 1964), pp. 503-44.

3. Han Lih-Wu, Taiwan Today (Taipei: Hura Kuo
Publishing Co., 1964).

4. China Yearbook, 1963-1964 (Taipei: China
Publishing Co.), pp. 322-25.

5. Harvard Law School International Program
in Taxation, Taxation in India (Boston: Little,
Brown & Co., 1960), pp. 64-72.

6. Japan Tax Bureau, op. cit., pp. 187-93.

7. The creation of the Bureau of Internal Revenue was provided by Commonwealth Act No. 466 (approved June 15, 1939). However, a major revamp of
the Bureau was effected in January, 1967. The number
of Regional Offices (now Revenue Regions) was increased from fifteen to twenty. The number of Inspection Districts (now Revenue Districts) was increased from seventy-two to ninety. A new Special
Operations Department was created containing three
divisions: the International Operations Division
(formerly Office of International Operations), the
Anti-Smuggling Unit (formerly under the North Manila
Regional Office), and the Special Investigation Division (formerly under the Assessment Department).
The addition of another Deputy Commissioner for Administration is being considered. Should this be
approved, the present Deputy Commissioner would take
charge of operations.

8. Republic Act No. 2211, May 15, 1959.

9. General Circular No. 239, March 12, 1957.

10. A Study in Establishing a Finance Academy
(Manila: Department of Finance, 1964), pp. 5-6.

11. Japan Tax Association, op. cit., pp. 61-68.

12. Sanan Kettudat and Vid Tantayakul, The
Revenue Code, October, 1961 (Bangkok, Thailand), pp.
12-19.

13. Taylor, op. cit., p. 2.

14. Ray E. Davis, Progress Report on Accomp-
lishments in 1962 including Work Program for 1963 and
Recommendations of Vietnam Directorate General of
Taxation (Saigon: United States Operations Mission-
AID).

15. Japan Tax Association, op. cit., p. 57.

16. Ibid., pp. 33-37.

17. Loc. cit.

18. Ibid., pp. 22-23.

19. Malaysia Department of Inland Revenue,
Annual Report 1961, p. 1. The establishment of a
section for legal matters (to be headed by a Deputy
Commissioner) is proposed for 1967. Under this proposed reorganization, the Commissioner General would
be assisted by two Deputy Commissioners General and
the two Commissioners for Sabah and Sarawak--the latter two positions having been created since independence.

20. William J. Shultz and C. Lowell Harriss,
American Public Finance (7th ed.; Englewood Cliffs,
New Jersey: Prentice-Hall, 1959), pp. 212-15.

21. Ibid., pp. 215-16.

22. Ibid., pp. 216-18.

CHAPTER **9** TAX INCENTIVES*

The quest of many Asian countries for faster economic development has led to the utilization of tax
concessions to divert the flow of resources from activities with little or no developmental merit to those
which are more productive and desirable. In like manner, tax concessions have also been utilized in many
foreign-exchange-deficient countries as a means of
channeling capital away from luxury imports and/or consumption to economically desirable investments or consumption. Tax laws have also been enacted to promote
a variety of nonindustrial activities, such as private
saving, housing construction, and tourism.

Thus, the major significance of tax incentives
lies in their utilization as a means of promoting selected activities, the encouragement of which is considered of high priority. Such tax statutes or provisions can be found in many Asian countries, either as
an integral aspect of a development program or as special measures operating independently. These tax
holidays are cast in a variety of forms, the most
common of which are partial or complete exemptions,
usually for a specified period of time, covering one
or several types of taxes. They may include special
allowances in the form of accelerated depreciation
under individual and corporate income taxes.

In the Republic of China major tax benefits,
such as exemption from or reduction of income tax,
business tax, and customs duties, and special depreciation allowances, are given to new or expanding
enterprises conforming to certain criteria regarding

*In 1967, the Philippines passed the Investment
Incentives Act designed to direct investments to preferred areas and encourage the inflow of external
capital. See Appendix XII, p. 410, for features of
the act.

their expected contribution to the economic development of the country.

Tax relief in Ceylon is also largely selective.
The Minister of Finance determines which projects are
eligible for tax concessions. Projects are also appraised in terms of their expected contribution to
the economic development of the country. Among the
tax reliefs granted, the major ones relate to exemption from income tax, concessionary rates of duty on
imports of raw materials for certain industrial activities, and liberal depreciation allowances. In
the field of agriculture, the major tax benefit is
the deduction of the total replanting expenses in
growing rubber, tea, and cocoa from taxable income.

Incentive taxation in India is granted to new
industrial enterprises, as well as existing enterprises undertaking expansion, provided that the new
unit is not a renovation or replacement of existing
capital. Enterprises run by cooperatives are accorded the largest tax reliefs. Next are certain
basic industries specified in the fifth schedule of
the Income Tax Act of 1961. The major tax incentives take the form of exemption from income tax,
special depreciation allowances, deduction and
carry-forward of losses, and some special concessionary rates on intercorporate dividends.

In Indonesia industrial and agricultural enterprises run by cooperatives and government entities
receive the major tax reliefs. These include exemptions from income tax, special depreciation allowances, and concessionary tariff rates which are much
lower than those generally applied to other entities.

In Japan "new important products," especially
those destined for export, as well as "important
patents or know-how," are given top priority in the
incentive scheme. The special tax reliefs take the
form of exemption from income tax, special depreciation allowances, and special tax reduction for the
use of important foreign patents or know-how.

In Malaysia new or expanding vital industries

are exempt from the payment of income tax. The exemption extends to dividends from profits earned
during the tax-relief period, whether paid during or
after the tax-relief period. Liberal depreciation
allowances on plants and factories are also granted
to such industries.

In the Philippines tax legislation primarily encourages the establishment and growth of basic industries, overseas shipping, and the development of the
mining industry. The statutory tax reliefs provide
for full exemption in the initial stage, subsequently followed by diminishing exemptions. The exemption relates to the income tax and all taxes inci-
dent to the importation of such things as machinery,
spare parts and accessories, and raw materials.
Basic industries are accorded exemption from only
four kinds of tax: import duties, compensating tax,
special import tax, and foreign-exchange tax. Prior
to the enactment of the Basic Industries Law, new
and necessary industries established under Republic
Act No. 35 (approved September 30, 1946) as amended
by Republic Act No. 901 (approved June 20, 1953)
were exempt from the payment of all internal taxes
(income tax, compensating tax, special import tax,
and customs duties). With the amendment of Republic
Act No. 901[1] and its expiration on December 31, 1962,
only overseas shipping enjoys exemption from income
tax. A number of entities, such as developmental
authorities, corporate enterprises, and specific business firms, have also been extended tax concessions
through express provisions of the National Internal
Revenue Code and certain special tax legislations.[2]

In Singapore only "pioneer industries"[3] qualify
for tax exemption. The major tax benefit is exemption from the payment of income tax. As in Malaysia,
the exemption extends to dividends paid out of exempt profit. Losses incurred during the tax-relief
period are deductible against any profit earned in
the following taxable year. Recently, a system of
liberal depreciation deduction has also been con-
ceded to such industries.

The income tax law of South Korea provides

exemption for such important enterprises as oil refining, manufacturing of steel ships or artificial
fertilizer, and electric power generation. Tax re-
ductions are also provided for retained earnings of
corporations to be used for expansion purposes.
Profit-seeking enterprises aimed at earning foreign
exchange are also given tax deductions.

In South Vietnam exemptions were originally limited to industrial and agricultural enterprises,
priority being given to those areas of investment
recommended in the economic development plan. In
practice, however, tax exemptions have been extended
to such industries as fishing and transportation.
The major taxes from which a qualified enterprise
may be exempted are tax on profits, production tax
and customs duties on imported capital goods, registration tax for new companies, and land tax on property for industrial plants and for cultivation of
crops other than rice. A system of liberal depreciation allowances has also been recently adopted.

In Thailand the major tax benefits take the
form of exemption from or reduction of income tax
and tariff duties on imports of machinery, component
parts and accessories, and raw materials for use in
certain industrial activities. The industries are
classified into Groups A, B, and C in the order of
priority.[4] Priority Group A receives the biggest
tax reliefs.

MAJOR TAX INCENTIVES

The major tax incentives common to the countries studied are: (1) exemption from income tax,
(2) exemption from customs duties, and (3) special
depreciation allowances (reinvestment allowances and
accelerated depreciation allowances). The special
features of these tax incentives are discussed below.

Exemption from Income Tax

The exemption from income tax payment is generally subject to a time limit, since said exemption

primarily aims to provide temporary encouragement to
new investments and not to subsidize long-run operations of enterprises.

The Philippines gives the longest tax-relief
period. For instance, enterprises engaged in overseas shipping and in the construction of modern
boats are exempt for a period of ten years.[5] The exemption period has recently been extended for another five years, making a total of fifteen years.[6]
A ten-year period of exemption was also given to new
and necessary industries organized under Republic
Act No. 901 (as amended), which expired on December
31, 1962.

One striking feature about Philippine tax-exemption laws, especially as regards income tax, is the
provision that where the enterprise, agricultural or
nonagricultural, is operated by cooperatives, the income tax exemption (including all other taxes and
fees of whatever nature) has no time limit. To be
entitled to an exemption, the law requires that nonagricultural cooperatives own net assets not exceeding ₱500,000. No limitation on net asset ownership
is provided in the case of agricultural cooperatives.[7]

In India income of new enterprises is generally
exempt for a period of five years. However, if the
new industrial undertaking is operated by a cooperative, the tax-relief period is seven years.[8] Ceylon
provides a maximum tax-relief period of six years.
The exemption was originally granted only to selected
enterprises, such as deep-sea fishing and private
corporations financed and owned jointly with the government. Later, it was extended to twenty-five other
new industries, such as those engaged in the production of beer and other malt liquors, cement, asbestos,
rayon, nylon, etc.[9] In South Korea the maximum exemption period is also six years. The exemption applies to oil refining, manufacture of steel ships or
artificial fertilizer, and power generation.[10] In
South Vietnam the general tax-relief period for new
and expanding enterprises is five years. However,
priority and basic investments are generally exempt
for periods longer than five years.[11]

Other countries adopt a maximum tax-relief
period of either five years (Singapore, Thailand, the
Republic of China, and Malaysia) or three years (Indonesia and Japan).[12] Only "pioneer industries" in
the case of Singapore and "promoted industries" in
the case of Thailand are granted the maximum five-
year tax-relief period. In the Republic of China,
the five-year maximum exemption period is generally
applicable to income of selected industries, such as
export, oil refining, mining, woods and fishery, rubber, copra, tin, and bauxite. The three-year maximum
period in Japan is applicable to income from "new important products."

In Malaysia pioneer industries with fixed capital expenditure on factory and machinery of $250,000
in Malaysian money (about $83,000) or more are granted
tax relief.[13] The length of period within which tax
relief may be enjoyed depends on the amount of fixed
capital expenditure incurred on factory and machinery.
A two-year relief period is granted to pioneer industries with fixed capital expenditure of over $250,000;
on those with over $500,000, three years; and on
those with $1 million, five years. Alternative or
additional tax-exemption privileges in terms of enhanced capital allowances are also provided. Under
this scheme, maximum relief is given to an industry
by permitting it to write off its qualifying capital
expenditure at the rate of 20 per cent annually for
five years.

It is apparent that with the exception of the
Philippines and, to a certain degree, India, Ceylon,
and South Korea, the common practice among the countries under study is to set five years as the maximum tax-exemption period, particularly on income or
profits of new and expanding priority industrial undertakings. Reasons for limiting the tax-exemption
period vary among countries, ranging from the difficulty of administration to the idea that longer
periods are rather costly on the part of the government.

Experience shows that only a few industrial undertakings are able to make substantial profits in

the early years of operation. Therefore, it is believed that the five-year exemption period is too
short a time to present an appealing investment climate. A relatively short exemption period may not
appear sufficiently attractive to the serious investor who will eventually face what will seem to him a
high tax rate. Besides, it is obvious that the
shorter the period of exemption, the lesser are the
prospective benefits.

Thailand and South Vietnam directly relate the
tax exemption to the profitability of investment;
that is, the tax-relief period starts in the year
the tax-exempt enterprises earn a net profit. All
other countries considered differ in that they adopt
the "beginning period of operation." It may be sur-
mised that since the tax-exemption period is limited,
the choice of the time when the tax-exempt status
will take effect can significantly affect the tax relief the enterprise will actually enjoy. Manufacturing enterprises, especially those which involve
large pre-operating expenses, usually incur losses
in the early years of operation. These enterprises,
therefore, will not actually enjoy any tax relief
during the years losses are incurred if the limited
tax-exempt status is made effective in the early
years of operation. Under such a condition, it
seems advisable to initiate a tax-relief status similar to that in South Vietnam and Thailand, where the
tax exemption begins in the year the tax-exempt enterprise earns a net profit. Two approaches may be
adopted: Profits may be totally or partially exempted
for a certain period of time, or the exemption may be
limited only to the extent of losses or a certain percentage of losses incurred during the initial years
of operation.

In addition to temporary tax exemption, particularly on profits, India and Singapore have provided
for the carrying forward of net operating losses
against future taxable income. In India the business loss of one year is allowed to be carried forward and set off for eight successive years, after
which the unabsorbed loss will lapse.[14] In Singapore carry-forward of business loss is limited to

the period (five years) during which the tax-relief status is effective.[15] From the point of view of the investors, this concession is directly related to the profits they expect to make in the future. As such, their inclusion in the tax-incentive scheme is worth considering.

Potential investors are often afraid to put their money in high-risk ventures because they know that by the time they become well established, they will have to pay high taxes, with inadequate returns to compensate for risk and losses shouldered during the initial years of operation. On the other hand, if investors know that losses incurred during the initial years will be deducted from taxable profits in the later periods, presumably even without temporary tax exemptions, more investments in desirable industries might be made. On the other hand, a temporary tax exemption from payment of income tax will not result in increased profits if the enterprise suffers losses during the tax-relief period. Net operating loss carry-over will be reduced to a passive incentive scheme in cases where firms expect and do realize profits during the tax-relief period.

Where the start of the tax-relief period is the "beginning period operation," an efficient tax-incentive scheme will require a combination of both temporary income tax exemption and a system of net operating loss deduction; for in this instance, whether the enterprise suffers losses or realizes profits, it is assured of a temporary tax-relief in its initial operation. This scheme, however, is costly on the part of the government because of the attendant large losses in revenue, especially when it applies to a number of industries.

In a country which grants exemption to new manufacturing, while allowing the gains from more speculative ventures to go untaxed (or taxed at comparatively lower rates), income tax exemption will become merely an attempt to equalize the prospective returns from alternative investments, rather than a positive move favoring investments in manufacturing. would be better to have a selective tax-incentive scheme for limited areas of high-priority economic activity. The speculative investor is not likely to be impressed with new opportunities in manufacturing so long as his gains in the customary lines of endeavor continue to enjoy exemption or relatively low tax rates.

Exemption from Customs Duties

Customs duties in the Asian countries are generally heavy on luxury goods and light on essential consumer and producer goods (such as food and clothing, machinery, and industrial equipment). However, specific tax legislations exempting imports of important industries can be found in many of these countries. The relief from customs duties takes the form of total or partial rate reduction. It is usually selective and given with greater frequency than income tax exemption, primarily because customs duties function not only for raising of revenue, but for the protection of domestic manufactures from competitive imports and the conservation of foreign exchange.

In Indonesia, for example, imports of national enterprises engaged in important industries, such as oil, mining, wood, fishery, rubber, copra, tin, and bauxite are subject to special or low rates of duties for a period of five years. Commodities are also classified into groups to implement easily the tax exemption and control program. Essential commodities falling under Group A are food, clothing, fertilizer, raw cotton, etc. These commodities are completely exempt from the payment of import duties. They are subsidized at the preferred rate of U.S. $1 = Rp 45, which is very much lower than the market rate of U.S. $1 = Rp 200. With respect to other commodities (not falling under Group A) for which the government is still granting import licenses, the exchange rate is also U.S. $1 = Rp 45, but the import duty ranges from 20-30 per cent. All other commodities subject to import restrictions are taxed at 100 per cent of the import duty, at the market rate of exchange of U.S. $1 = Rp 200.[16]

In Thailand a "promoted person"[17] is exempt
from the payment of import duties and business taxes
on machinery, component parts, and accessories which
are required for an approved industrial project.
The exemption is extended to prefabricated factory
structures to be installed for the carrying on of an
industrial activity. It does not cover items produced in the country in sufficient quantity and of
comparable quality and price.[18] Supplementary to
tax incentives is the prohibition or imposition of
increased import duties on products of the same kind
as those produced locally by the promoted person.[19]

In South Korea importation of production goods
and industrial equipment that are available in the
country and are of comparable quality are heavily
taxed.[20] However, imports of certain machineries
and construction materials which are not available
in the country are tax exempt. Machineries imported
for new installations are totally exempt until the
completion of such installations. Those imported
for replacement or maintenance are generally exempt
for a period of five years, extendible to eight
years.[21]

In 1963, Ceylon recognized twenty-five new industries in the private sector as "approved projects,"
granting them income tax exemption and concessionary
rates of duty on imports of raw materials. The approved industries include razor blade, beer and other
malt liquors, asbestos, cement products, finishing of
rayon, nylon, and other synthetic fibers, refrigerators, and clocks.[22] The government also grants duty
relief to encourage the development of the export
trade in manufactured goods. Tax relief is divided
into three stages. In the first stage, goods produced locally and raw materials imported for their
manufacture are given a 100 per cent rebate of duty,
instead of the 87 per cent rebate to which they are
presently entitled. In the second stage, additional
tax relief is given to manufacturers using 100 per
cent local materials. In the third stage, a "comprehensive scheme" is introduced.[23]

In South Vietnam imports of capital equipment

for establishing a new enterprise or expanding an existing one are exempt from customs duties which, according to the circular of the Directorate General
of Planning, range from 15 to 25 per cent of the C.I.F.
price,[24] and from production tax which ranges from
15 to 35 per cent.[25] The exemption applies to both
domestic and foreign capital.[26]

In the Republic of China new investments are
not exempt from the payment of import duties. However, the law provides for the installment payment
of customs duties after the imported machinery and
equipment are put into operation.[27]

In the Philippines basic industries enumerated
in the Basic Industries Law[28] are totally exempt
from payment of the special import tax, compensating
tax, and customs duties with respect to imports of
machinery, spare parts, and equipment from June 22,
1961, to December 31, 1965, after which a gradual decrease of exemption will commence, beginning January
1, 1966, up to December 31, 1970. Thereafter, all
basic industries will be taxed in full.[29] The Philippine overseas shipping business is also exempt
from the payment of said taxes (including income
tax) with respect to imports of engines, spare parts,
accessories, supplies, and raw materials for the re-
pair and construction of vessels. Originally, the
full exemption was for a period of ten years commen-
cing September 8, 1955. But it was extended for another five years upon the expiration of the period
of ten years as originally provided.[30] During the
third session of the Fifth Philippine Congress, a
law exempting the textile industry from payment of
the same taxes was approved.[31] The exemption is applied to imports of natural and synthetic raw fibers
and chemicals, dyestuffs, and spare parts, as well
as the manufacture and sale of finished products.

Special Depreciation Allowances[32]

In the selected countries, depreciation allowances usually take two general forms: (1) those related to capital expenditure without prejudice to
normal depreciation, and (2) those designated as

accelerated depreciation, which essentially change
the normal time pattern of depreciation deductions.
The former frequently takes the guise of "investment
(or reinvestment) allowances," which are deductions
from taxable income in the first or early years of
service of a stipulated percentage of the cost of
assets, such as buildings, plant, and machinery.[33]
These allowances do not reduce the basis for subsequent depreciation deductions allowed under ordinary
tax law. The latter does not represent any addition
to the normal depreciation allowances. It simply
permits the taxpayer to exhaust his total normal depreciation deductions over a specified number of
years, which usually constitute a period shorter
than the anticipated life of the asset. It can permit a taxpayer complete freedom in choosing the percentage of the cost of assets he elects to deduct
from income in any year (unless the annual percentage
deduction is specified by the law).

Investment Allowance

Investment allowance is popular among the countries in Asia. Typically, allowances are tied to
the acquisition of selected assets and are given
only in the year of acquisition.

The manner in which allowances are limited
varies. In Malaysia, India, South Vietnam, Ceylon,
Singapore, Japan, and South Korea the maximum allowance in any year is either the whole amount or a
specified percentage of the cost of approved assets
in the year acquired.

Among the countries using the cost of acquired
assets as the basis for allowances, only Malaysia
and Singapore allow the full value of the approved
assets. In Malaysia the whole of the qualifying expenditure on plant and machinery bought during the
income tax-relief period and in use after such period
is deemed to have been incurred on the first day of
the taxable period. If the total allowable capital
expenditure is not exhausted during the first taxable
period, the remainder can be carried forward against
the succeeding taxable period. Hence, if the capital

expenditure has been heavy, this privilege may mean
that, in addition to the exemption period of five
years, no tax will be payable in the sixth year, and
possibly beyond that. Essentially, the same scheme
operates in Singapore.

The rest of the countries adopting the cost of
acquired assets as the basis for the deductions allow only a portion of the value of the approved
assets. In Japan 33 1/3 per cent of the acquisition
cost is allowed on plants and equipment. In South
Vietnam 20 per cent of the acquisition cost is allowed on fixed assets used as industrial equipment.
India allows 20 per cent on new machinery and plant,
and 40 per cent on new ships. The unused portion of
the allowance may be carried forward and set off
against the taxpayer's total income in succeeding
years for a maximum of eight years.[34] In South Korea
the allowance is 50 per cent of the reserve funds set
aside for the purpose of production capacity expansion.[35] Ceylon allows 20 per cent for assets (usually building and plant) used in new business or for
expansion of an existing business. If the business
undertaking is an "approved project," the allowance
is 40 per cent of the cost of the assets.[36]

In certain other countries, including Indonesia
and the Republic of China, the amount of the allowance is based on taxable income. These countries do
not allow total deduction. The amount of the allowance in any year is limited to a specified percentage
of the taxable income. In the Republic of China when
a productive enterprise invests its undistributed
profits for the taxable year in machinery and equipment for production or rendition of services, the
value of the assets deductible from taxable income
is limited to 25 per cent of the taxpayer's total income for the taxable year.[37] In Indonesia the limit
is also 25 per cent of the taxpayer's taxable income
for the year. The allowed capital expenditures are
classified into eight groups. A 100 per cent deduction, however, is allowed if the investments are
used to increase production in the fields of industry, agriculture, mining, and transportation. This
will be permitted at a rate of 25 per cent annually
for a period of four years.

The grant of investment allowance as practiced
in most Asian countries is based either on the taxable income or on the cost of approved assets. When
the allowance is based on the cost of approved assets,
the government can better select specific types of
assets for preferential treatment than when it is
based on taxable income.[38] This may help encourage
investment expenditures in high-priority areas.

Unless there is a carry-forward provision like
that in India, Malaysia, and Singapore, either method
is of value only to those taxpayers with sufficient
taxable income from which to take the permissible deduction. In many Asian countries, investment allowance is usually granted to new industries which require large sums of capital outlay and pre-operating
expenses. These industries often earn only small
profits or even sustain losses for a number of years,
due to lack of demand for their product. Without
the appropriate carry-forward provision, such a system of investment allowance will become merely a
passive incentive scheme. Presumably, it might even
cause such industries to postpone the acquisition of
new assets until income is sufficient to permit the
maximum tax benefit. For example, instead of buying
lands and constructing industrial buildings for its
administrative and executive offices, an enterprise
may find it more advantageous to simply rent.

Accelerated Depreciation Allowance

Like investment allowance, there are several
forms of accelerated depreciation. For example, accelerated depreciation provisions can permit a taxpayer complete freedom in choosing the percentage
value of the depreciable assets he elects to deduct
from income during any taxable year. Usually, the
number of years under which the total depreciable
value may be accelerated is specified in the law.
This form of accelerated depreciation obtains in
Indonesia and India.

In Indonesia capital expenditures incurred before March 31, 1959, may be depreciated over a period
of three years,[39] while in India, the period is five
years for new expenditures.[40]

Another form of accelerated depreciation speci-
fies the initial percentage allowance (rates), after
which the balance may be written off normally over
the years. This form is typical in a number of countries in Asia. Most of these countries allow a lower
initial percentage, ranging from 10 to 25 per cent
of the value of the depreciable assets. For instance,
in Singapore and Malaysia, 10 per cent is allowed for
industrial buildings and 20 per cent for machinery
and plants.

The most liberal initial depreciation allowance
is found in Ceylon, under the so-called lump-sum depreciation allowances. All plants, machineries, and
buildings purchased after March 31, 1957, can be depreciated in lump-sum in the year of acquisition.
The lump-sum is calculated as the discounted value
of the total depreciation allowable under the declining balance method over the life of the asset. In
order to simplify computations, all assets are
grouped into four classes, with the following lump-
sum depreciation allowances:

Industrial building	33-1/3%
Durable plant and machinery	50%
Normal machinery	66-2/3%
Short-lived equipment	80%

When the initial depreciation allowance exceeds current income, the excess can be carried forward
against taxable income of future years, in addition
to the normal depreciation due for the year. There
is no limitation on the number of years of carry-
forward.[41]

Specification of the time period or the rate of
the accelerated depreciation directly affects the
tax concessions which enterprises expect. Where the
time period is specified, the taxpayers can better
avoid high taxes in the future due to price changes
than where the rate of initial allowance is specified. For example, if prices increase during the
period when a taxpayer is allowed to claim depreciation ratably, he can select which rate to apply in

any year. This permits him to reserve a higher rate
of deduction from taxable income when prices are relatively high, and so avoid paying a higher tax on
profits which must have gone up too because of the
price increases. It is obvious that such tax avoidance will not occur where the rates are specified.

Adequate information on the system of accelerated depreciation allowance in the other countries
under study is unavailable. It is therefore impos-
sible to state whether most of them provide for the
carrying forward of the excess of the accelerated deduction in the years when normal depreciation will
have been effective. Nevertheless, it is clear that
an inadequate carry-forward provision may significantly reduce the benefits investors may gain from a
given system of accelerated depreciation. This is
particularly true where the taxpayer does not have
sufficient income against which to offset the deduction.

The rationale behind any system of accelerated
depreciation as an incentive scheme for investments
is that it makes investment in depreciable assets
more liquid and generally diminishes the risk attendant to the business venture. It enables the investors to recover the invested capital at an earlier date, enhancing their ability to undertake expansion and replacement expenditures, because part of
the earnings which otherwise would have to be paid
to the government remains in their hands.

A common argument, however, is that accelerated
depreciation generally raises the prospective rate
of return of any given investment. The funds that
would otherwise be turned over to the revenue authorities may be invested at a profit.[42] An analysis of
the effects of accelerated depreciation on the rate
of return do not lead to any definite conclusion.
It would be necessary to appraise the elasticity of
investment demand with respect to an increase in the
rate of return, while taking into account the risk
factors and the over-all financial capacity of the
business, which more or less indicate the anticipated rate of return.

OTHER TAX RELIEFS

Tax Exemption of Dividends

Many countries have extended the income tax exemption to dividends paid to shareholders. This practice is found in Ceylon, India, Singapore, and Malaysia.[43] The amounts qualified for exemption are limited to dividends paid out of profits realized during the income tax-relief period. They are, however, included in the individual shareholder's "total income" for the purpose of determining the rate applicable to his "other" income.

The Republic of China does not exempt dividends paid out of tax-exempt profit in the computation of income tax. However, dividend incomes of a tax-exempt enterprise from investments made in nonexempt enterprises are not treated as taxable income.[44] In the Philippines, only 25 per cent of the dividends received by a domestic company or resident foreign corporation from a domestic corporation is subject to tax.

A system of tax reduction or exemption for intercorporate dividends obtains in India. Dividends received by a parent company from its subsidiaries are taxed at rates lower than those applicable to other income of the company.[45] Also, dividends received by any company from an Indian company engaged in certain basic industries specified in the fifth schedule of the Income Tax Act of 1961 are exempt from the payment of the supertax.[46] Dividends from newly established industries and hotels are partially exempt; those paid by cooperative societies are completely exempt.

Tax Exemption of Foreign Technicians

In Ceylon foreign scientists and technicians are exempt from income tax if employed in a corporation wholly financed by the government. They are exempt for the first three years of their employment if employed in an "approved" corporation or industrial undertaking.[47] Under the Finance Act of 1961 of

India, complete exemption from income tax is also
provided for the salaries of foreign technicians.
Technicians having specialized knowledge in industrial and business management techniques are exempt
for a period of six months from the date of arrival
in India, provided their service contracts have been
approved by the Central Government.[48] Other technicians who do not meet the above qualifications are
exempt for a period of 365 days.[49] In the Republic
of China aliens are generally required to pay only
10 per cent of the usual income tax.[50] In the Philippines special laws grant income tax exemption to
foreign technicians and personnel of the International Rice Research Institute and the Ford Foundation on their salaries and stipends in dollars.[51]

     The exemption of foreign technicians and person-
nel from payment of the tax on salaries and stipends
is primarily aimed at inducing them to come and render service for the social and economic development
of the country.

Special Tax Privileges for Exports

     The tax exemption from or reduction of income
tax on export income has been generally adopted in
Asia to develop and promote export industries for
the earning of foreign exchange. Among the countries adopting such exemption are Thailand, Ceylon,
India, and South Korea.

     Some countries have also adopted exemptions
from or reduction of taxes affecting export commodities. In South Korea, for example, customs duties
are not generally levied on export commodities.[52]
Commodity tax is also waived on taxable commodities
destined for export.[53] Recently, Indonesia abolished
her 10 per cent export duty.[54] In Thailand, exports
of "promoted" industries are either exempt from or
enjoy a preferred rate of export duty. The period
of exemption is at the discretion of the Board of Investment.[55] In the Philippines, tariff duties are
not levied on export commodities. Also, articles
subject to the percentage tax are exempt if destined
for export.[56]

The Republic of China has a different scheme for her export industry. To encourage exports, a deduction from taxable income of 2 per cent of the total amount of export proceeds is permitted.[57] The concession seems to have been given only to those industries whose production scale, capital equipment, and technical and managerial competence approximate world standards, and whose products compete in the export market in terms of cost and quality. Examples of these industries are textiles, plastics, glass, cement, paper, plywood, aluminum, and the contemplated petrochemical industry.[58]

CONCLUSION

Tax concessions have become an integral feature of the taxing patterns of many Asian nations. They lead to growth and stability by encouraging new investments and reinvestment in a favorable investment climate. Thus, the major tax incentives in the countries under study apply to many fields of investment. For example, incentives are accorded "pioneer industries" in Malaysia and Singapore, "promoted industries" in Thailand, and "new, necessary, and basic" industries in the Philippines. Obviously, however, tax incentives are only one of many factors which promote investment. As such, they may assume only a marginal role in attracting capital to productive investment.

The attraction of domestic and foreign investments depends on such factors as the potential market for the products, either at home or abroad; availability of credit facilities, skilled labor, technicians, and managers; adequate supply of cheap raw materials, transportation, and communication; and the availability of power, health, and educational facilities. In Mexico a combination of these factors induced foreign as well as domestic investors to make the basic decision to invest even before learning of the tax incentives to which they would be entitled.[59] Government officials in Puerto Rico were also of the opinion that even without the 1954 Tax Exemption Act, quite a large number of firms

would have invested.[60]   Apparently, in many Asian
countries the investment climate is susceptible of
improvement.   This could be the primary reason why
many of these countries use incentive schemes.   However, the absence of the factors mentioned previously
is the major obstacle to potential investments.
Therefore, tax incentives may have only a tangential
bearing on the level of new investments.

Viewed from this perspective, tax incentives
have their limitations.   The desirable effects of incentive taxation, for example, may not compensate
for the intricate administrative problems connected
with the tax exemption laws.   Experience also shows
that they may lead to ineptitude, arbitrariness, and
even corruption.   The laborious administrative problems, inefficient administration, arbitrary benefits,
and harassing practices which may occur tend to make
the existing investment climate even more unfavorable.   Obviously, they certainly do not improve an
investment climate that has become unattractive because of unpredictable government economic policies
and the apparent inability of the government to maintain political, social, and economic stability.   A
less-developed economy with clear-cut economic policies administered efficiently might keep its investors less frustrated, and thus promote investments
and obtain greater revenues.

Also, incentives will not induce investment to
an appreciable extent when potential investors cannot readily locate the business data pertinent to
their projected ventures, or when they cannot ascertain the latest tax laws.   Few governments maintain
facilities either domestically or abroad for systematically identifying investment opportunities and
bringing them to the attention of potential investors.
Many less-developed countries also do not appreciate
the incentive aspects of a comprehensive compilation
of basic laws to the potential investor.   This can
be done through an investment-incentive law which de-
lineates the rights and guarantees accorded domestic
and foreign investors.

A careful re-examination of the various tax-
incentive schemes is needed. It should be done in con-
junction with an assessment of the various countries,
to disclose restraints to development and ascertain
suitable incentive devices. While many Asian countries have passed concessionary tax laws, these have
produced meager results as a rule, and at the expense
of the government coffers, at that. The loss of
revenue becomes a real problem in less-developed countries with ambitious development programs to finance.

Accordingly, tax incentives should not be designed as a permanent fixture in the economy. They
should be temporary, and should trigger the establishment of selected new and necessary industries
which can broaden the economic base.

Tax concessions such as exemption from income
tax, sales, and import duties should be discouraged.
Instead, schemes such as a system of net operating
loss carry-over and accelerated depreciation may be
adopted. These incentive devices have a direct bearing on new industries, since a large number of desirable industries suffer losses in the early years
of operation. These tax incentives may also result
in revenue loss for the government. Nevertheless,
the losses in revenue involved in this case are to
be preferred to losses due to exemption from income
tax and customs duties. Income tax exemption may be
used by profit-earning enterprises which do not need
it in the first place. Similarly, exemption from
customs duties lacks selectivity, in that both
profit-making and money-losing firms are eligible
for exemption.

Notes to Chapter 9

1. Republic Act No. 2351, amending Republic Act No. 901 so as to subject the income of new and necessary industries to the full payment of the income tax, was approved June 20, 1959.

2. An extensive account of Philippine tax incentives is presented in a study of the Joint Legislative-Executive Tax Commission, conducted in 1965, entitled "An Examination of the Tax Exemption Laws in the Philippines." See also Tax Exemption Laws in the Philippines (1966), a brochure prepared by the Joint Legislative-Executive Tax Commission.

3. "Pioneer industries" include the approved investments which are eligible for tax relief because of their expected or actual contribution to the country's needs and its development program.

4. Industrial activities under Group A are those which are vital or necessary to the economy of the country, as designated by ministerial regulation defining the categories, sizes, or other conditions applicable to this classification; under Group B are those which are less vital and necessary to the economy of the country, as designated also by ministerial regulation, etc.; under Group C are those other than the industries classified under Groups A and B, the categories and sizes to be defined by announcement of the Board of Investment.

5. Republic Act No. 1407, approved September 9, 1955, otherwise known as "The Philippine Overseas Shipping Act of 1955."

6. Republic Act No. 4146, approved June 20, 1964. It extends the period within which a qualified person, association, or corporation is exempt from the payment of income tax on income derived from his or its shipping operations for another five years after the expiration of the period of ten years, as originally provided.

7. Republic Act No. 2023, approved June 22,
1957, and Public Act No. 3425, approved December 9,
1927. The activities these Acts encourage cover the
promotion of industrial and agricultural production,
their marketing and distribution, the purchase, hiring, and use of machinery and equipment, and the
financing of such activities on an organized or cooperative basis.

8. The Investment Center, Investing in India
(India: New Delhi National Insurance Bldg., 1962),
p. 49. See also, India (Republic), Report of the
Ministry of Finance, 1961-1962, p. 2.

9. H. E. R. Abayasekara, "Plans to Boost Exports," Far Eastern Economic Review, XL (April 11,
1963), 61.

10. A Guide to Investment in Korea, op. cit.,
p. 122.

11. David Cole, "Tax Exemption for New Investments in Vietnam," Michigan State University Vietnam
Advisory Group, 1960. (Mimeographed.)

12. See, for example, Investment Laws of the Republic of China, September, 1960, pp. 7-40; Promotion of Industrial Investment Act, B.E. 2505 (1962),
Bangkok, Thailand, pp. 12-24.

13. "Tax Changes Within Malaysia." Paper presented to Parliament on November 25, 1964, with the
Budget Speech of the Minister of Finance, Malaysia.

14. Investing in India, op. cit., pp. 64-65.

15. Pioneer Industries (Relief from Income Tax)
Ordinance, 1959, Secs. 9 & 19.

16. "New Trade Measures in Indonesia," The Far
Eastern Economic Review, XXXV (November, 1960), 256,
258.

17. A "promoted person" is an applicant for expansion of an industrial activity who has been granted a promotion certificate by the Board of Investment [B.E. 2505, Secs. 15, 16].

18. Ibid., Secs. 19(2), 19(3).

19. Ibid., Secs. 23(1), 23(2).

20. Korean Ministry of Foreign Affairs, Trade and Investment Guide to Korea, 1963, p. 82.

21. "Korea Invites Foreign Capital," Korean Report, II (March, 1962), pp. 6, 7.

22. Abayasekara, op. cit., p. 61.

23. Ibid.

24. Cole, op. cit., pp. 2-5.

25. "Production tax" is levied on both imported and internally produced products. Taylor, op. cit., pp. 10-16.

26. Colombo Plan for Cooperative Economic Development in South and Southeast Asia, Sixth Annual Report (Colombo, 1957), p. 172.

27. Investment Laws of the Republic of China (September, 1960), p. 25. See also Statute for Encouragement of Investment, Art. 18.

28. Republic Act No. 3127 authorizing the exemption of basic industries from the payment of certain taxes, etc., was approved on June 17, 1961. It was later amended by Republic Act No. 4095, approved June 17, 1964, in order to exclude certain industries considered basic under the original law and to extend the period of exemption up to December 31, 1970.

29. Some of the basic industries included in the Act as amended are: iron and steel, nickel and

aluminum industries; chemical industries, such as
antibiotics and fungicides, including cement manufacture and fertilizers; deep-sea fishing, shipbuilding
and dry-docking; cattle and dairy industries; canning
of food products out of local raw materials; manufacturing or processing of cereals.

30. See Republic Act No. 1407, approved September 4, 1955, otherwise known as "The Philippine Overseas Shipping Act of 1955," as amended by Republic
Act No. 4146, approved June 20, 1964.

31. See Republic Act No. 4086, approved June
18, 1964. Said Act supersedes Republic Act No. 1392
as amended by Republic Act Nos. 1768 and 2353, otherwise known as "An Act Exempting Textiles of 100 percent Philippine Ramie Fiber from the payment of Duty
and Special Import Tax, etc.," which expired on December 31, 1960.

32. See also Chapter 4.

33. Jack Heller and K. M. Kauffman, Tax
Incentives for Industry in Less Developed Countries
(Cambridge: The Law School of Harvard University,
1963), p. 152.

34. Income Tax Act of India (1961), Sec. 33.

35. A Guide to Investment in Korea, op. cit.,
pp. 123, 124.

36. Goode, op. cit., p. 332.

37. Heller and Kauffman, op. cit., p. 29. See
also Statute for the Encouragement of Investment,
Art. 7, par. 1.; Investment Laws of the Republic of
China (September, 1960), p. 13.

38. Ibid., pp. 30, 31.

39. International Chamber of Commerce, Taxation and Developing Nations (Paris: The Chamber,
1959), p. 18.

40. Ibid., pp. 10, 22.

41. Goode, op. cit., p. 332.

42. Heller and Kauffman, op. cit., p. 156.

43. Investing in India, op. cit., pp. 49-51; International Chamber of Commerce, op. cit., pp. 10-20.

44. Statute for Encouragement of Investment, Art. 8.

45. Under the Income Tax Act (1961) of India, the parent (or a holding) company and its subsidiary companies are considered separate entities and are taxed separately.

46. See India (Republic), Report of the Ministry of Finance, 1961-1962, p. 2.

47. Goode, op. cit., p. 333.

48. Report of the Ministry of Finance, 1961-1962, loc. cit.

49. Investing in India, op. cit., p. 70.

50. Statute for the Encouragement of Investment Act, Art. II.

51. See Republic Act Nos. 2707 and 3538. It may also be cited that according to staff members of the Ford Foundation in Manila, all their foreign technicians and personnel are generally exempt from income tax in the countries of Southeast Asia, Africa and Europe where the Foundation holds offices.

52. Trade and Investment Guide to Korea, 1963, loc. cit.

53. "Commodity tax" is an excise levied on an ad valorem basis on specified goods both domestic and imported. See A Guide to Investment in Korea, pp. 123-24.

54. "Indonesia's May 27 Reform," Far Eastern
Economic Review, XL (June 13, 1963), 600-603.

55. Promotion of Industrial Investment Act,
B.E. 2505 (1962), Sec. 23(3), (4).

56. National Internal Revenue Code, Sec. 188(e).
"Percentage Tax" is imposed on the manufacturer's
level. The tax rate is applied on the Gross Selling
Price and is payable within twenty days after the
end of each month (Sec. 183).

57. "Foreign Trade Aspects of the Economic Development Plans of ECAFE Countries," Economic Bulletin for Asia and the Far East, XIV (June, 1963), 12.

58. China (Republic) Ministry of Economic Affairs, The Industrial and Mining Program under
Taiwan's Third Four-Year Plan (December, 1961), p. 6.

59. Heller and Kauffman, op. cit., p. 65.

60. Kenneth M. Kauffman, "Income Tax Exemption
and Economic Development," National Tax Journal, III
(September, 1960), 263.

10

Regulation and development of exports in the context of the economic growth of the developing ECAFE countries is important because exports constitute the major source of foreign-exchange earnings, and there is a widening gap between exchange earnings and import needs.

External loans and grants are essential in financing the import requirements for desirable rates of capital formation, but these can be no substitute for trade. Exports still provide the major portion of the total foreign-exchange receipts.

Again, while foreign aid and loans help to bridge the foreign-exchange gap, the burden of debt service payments of interest and principal will have to be met primarily out of export earnings.

In view of the need for an increasing and stable flow of foreign-exchange resources, many ECAFE countries have adopted various measures to promote their export trade. The most important measures are special credit accommodation for exports, export insurance schemes, differential exchange rates, multiple currency practices, industry grants, government subsidies, state trading, and trade agreements.

SPECIAL CREDIT ACCOMMODATION FOR EXPORTS

The development of a large export volume to relieve pressure on foreign-exchange reserves is an arduous process requiring adequate financing. Finding new markets and expanding the existing ones require

costly market surveys, intensive advertising, participation in international trade fairs, and other related sales promotion activities. A larger working
capital to finance production and an expanded scale
of operations is also needed.

Exports on a deferred payment basis are being
increasingly resorted to in foreign trade. This has
arisen because of the foreign-exchange shortage;
hence, the supplier's credit assumes great importance. Exporters need credit while awaiting payment
from foreign buyers. Without the necessary insurance guaranty, commercial banks are not prone to finance this type of exportation. The government,
therefore, should either establish a specialized institution for this purpose or endeavor to underwrite
a larger credit volume by the banking system against
export sales.

Among the ECAFE countries, Japan seems to be
the only country that has an export and import bank
similar to that of the United States. It was established primarily to finance the long-term credit requirements of export industries, particularly those
engaged in the manufacture of machinery and equipment. The bank is noted for the financing of exports on a deferred payment basis. The inclusion of
this type of exportation in the financing operation
of the bank has significantly contributed to the expansion of Japanese exports.[1]

To a degree, Indonesia accommodates her exporters through an institution similar to the Export and
Import Bank of Japan. The Bank Negara Indonesia was
established primarily to extend credit to exporters
and importers. Recently, four additional private Indonesian banks were designated by the government as
foreign-exchange banks to extend accommodation to
those engaged in foreign trade.[2]

In the Philippines a gradual decontrol of foreign exchange was instituted in April, 1960. This
has resulted in a de facto devaluation of the Philippine currency, to the benefit of the export sector.
The freeing of the rate of exchange has been viewed

as sufficient incentive for the expansion of the export industry.[3] In fact, fears of the inflationary "push" coming from the export sector due to the windfall incomes brought about by higher export proceeds have been expressed, leading to a clamor for a system of selective export taxation.

Most ECAFE countries rely on both the existing commercial banks and a system of exchange controls, differing from one country to another, for a selective allocation of credit and foreign-exchange resources among priority sectors. The government also plays an even more important role in providing assistance to major export industries. This largely takes the form of direct subsidies to industries.[4]

In India the Reserve Bank has established the Industrial Finance Corporation of India, which provides medium- and long-term loans to industries, and the Refinance Corporation, which gives relending facilities to banks against medium-term credit granted by them to medium-sized industrial units in the private sector. It also grants advances to sixteen trade-oriented foreign banks, members of the so-called scheduled banks, for purposes of issuing loans to exporters against export bills. These bills are merely collected instead of discounted.[5] Ordinarily, accommodations in the money market are granted only against the security of discounted commercial or trade bills.

In South Vietnam and Ceylon the paucity of financial institutions is striking. There are very few commercial banks, the majority of which are foreign owned with head offices abroad. In South Vietnam, for example, there were only ten private commercial banks in 1960. Of these, eight were foreign banks. The prevalence of colonial banking in these countries leads to the concentration of credit on expatriate primary-producing enterprises such as foreign-owned plantations.[6] Their conventional requirement that loans be backed up by adequate collateral leaves large sectors and enterprises completely outside of the money sphere.

Because these institutions failed to provide
capital for development on a significant scale, the
National Bank of Vietnam found it necessary to enter
the field of commercial banking, by associating itself with the Commercial Credit Bank of Vietnam.
Since July 30, 1958, the latter has been empowered
to deal in long-term and medium-term finance.[7]

Statutory law in Ceylon prohibits its Central
Bank from engaging in commercial banking. This problem was met through the establishment of the Development Finance Corporation, in 1956, which has been
empowered to finance new industrial projects.[8] Selective credit expansion is used sparingly. It usually
takes the form of directives or moral suasion, dis-
couraging certain types of credit operations, or
seeking the cooperation of commercial banks for
nationally desirable purposes.

In the Republic of China and South Korea statutory laws required banks to classify their loans according to a schedule separating credit for agriculture, raw material import, inventories, export, marketing, stock-exchange financing, real estate mort-
gage, etc.[9] This setup puts the Central Banks of
these countries in a better position to initiate
selective credit control and expansion, particularly
in favor of the export sector. The Bank of Taiwan
also provides extended rediscounting facilities or
advances to commercial banks which extend loans for
stimulating exports.[10] Beginning in March, 1962,
loans for exports were required to be classified
into line of credit on a project basis, and working
capital on a transaction basis. While the Bank of
Taiwan has increasingly extended loans to the export
sector since 1957, and will continue doing so in the
near future, it was expected that the new form of
lending will be a successful complementary measure.[11]
In most countries of the region, the growth of agricultural cooperatives owes much to government support, by encouragement and financing. Cooperatives
have been largely instrumental in meeting the recurring credit requirements of small cultivators on
reasonable terms and in accordance with commercial
principles, as well as the speedy introduction of
better farming and marketing methods, mechanization

of agriculture, and efficient supply of raw materials,
on a wider scale.

In the Republic of China governmental services
such as the distribution of chemical fertilizers and
improved seeds selected by experimental stations are
effected promptly through cooperatives. In Vietnam
cooperatives have greatly facilitated the mechanization of agriculture. To increase membership in the
cooperative societies, cooperatives receive first
priority in loans.[12]

In Japan cooperatives are the most important institutional financiers of agricultural credit. About
90 per cent of the deposits of, and loans to, Japanese farmers are handled by cooperatives.[13]

In most countries of the ECAFE region, however,
cooperatives have a long way to go before reaching
the Japanese level of performance in this field. In
India, for example, local money-lenders still account
for an overwhelming proportion of the loans raised by
the average farmer.[14] Nevertheless, it is the consensus that the cooperative organization is the only
effective way of providing an integrated rural credit
in Asia.

Institutions other than cooperatives have also
been developed in recent years to provide agricultural credit. In an attempt to integrate rural
credit in South Korea, the new National Agricultural
Cooperative Federation created by the Farmers Cooperative Law was merged with the Korean Agriculture
Bank.[15]

EXPORT INSURANCE SCHEMES

A recent institutional development in the domain
of international trade is the insurance of export
risks arising from a sudden decrease in export prices,
insolvency or protracted default of the buyer or importer, nationalization, currency depreciation, exchange controls, war, etc. Because of their very
nature, export risk insurance is not commonly

accepted by private insurance firms. For this reason, the export-risk insurance business has become a
governmental concern. Countries pioneering in this
kind of insurance system are Great Britain, Germany,
France, the United States, and Japan.[16]

Today the consensus is that an export-risk insurance system is of major importance in international
trade. It can prevent the disruption of trade in
cases where exporters would have been unable to maintain their business due to increasing uncertainty.
Thereby enabled to assume great risks, exporters can
expand their business turnover without jeopardizing
their financial position. Insured risks also improve the financial position of the exporters, as
private commercial banks are more prepared to finance
the underlying transactions.[17] Accordingly, insurance policies can be used by the exporters as collateral for additional credit accommodations, thereby expanding their financial horizons.

In the late 1950's, some of the ECAFE countries
adopted an export insurance guaranty scheme substantially similar to that of the industrialized countries. In India, for example, through the Export
Risks Insurance Corporation, Ltd. (established in
July, 1957), the government issued four types of insurance policies to exporters: shipments comprehensive risk, shipments political risk, contracts comprehensive risk, and contracts political risk. The
Corporation covers 85 per cent of the producer's export proceeds for political risks, and 20 per cent
for commercial risks.[18]

The Republic of China has a system of risk insurance. The Central Trust of China, backed by the
Foreign Exchange and Trade Control Commission, under-
writes two types of export-risk insurance:[19]

(1) General export insurance, which insures
against losses incurred by the exporter due to inability to deliver the goods, or to collect the proceeds therefrom owing to hazards, such as sudden
trade restrictions and war, which are beyond the control of either party to the contract;

(2) Consignment export insurance, which insures against losses incurred due to the inability of the exporters to sell beyond, or equal to, the export quotations.

In Japan in addition to these two types of risk, the Export Insurance Law requires the government to insure against another risk: the losses suffered by a producer-exporter who, after exporting samples for the purpose of exporting goods, and disbursing neces- sary expenses for advertisement, is unable to export the goods and recover these expenses. This type of insurance is commonly called "overseas advertisement insurance." The maximum amount collectible under this insurance is 50 per cent of the amount disburs- able for advertisement as stipulated in the contract.

Another form of export-insurance system that has recently developed in foreign trade is the so- called export credit insurance. The pioneers of this insurance scheme are the countries of Western Europe, such as West Germany, Austria, France, Italy, and the United Kingdom. This form of insurance was orig- inally aimed at securing the sales of equipment on a deferred payment basis to underdeveloped countries.[20] Owing to their foreign-exchange shortage, underde- veloped countries would otherwise be able to buy only "essential" goods on credit. This insurance, which usually covers 70 to 90 per cent of the amount of sale, has greatly stimulated the flow of equip- ment to underdeveloped countries.

The export-credit insurance system brings the banker and the credit insurance company together to enable the exporters to grant credit to their buyers, thereby facilitating trade which otherwise would not have taken place.[21] Occasionally, a banker may be unwilling to finance an export on transaction. If the risk is covered by a deferred payment basis be- cause of the risk connected with such export credit guarantees, the banker will be prepared to finance the underlying transaction. Like insurance of ex- port risk, therefore, the export-credit insurance scheme will generally expand export turnover and widen the financial horizons of exporters.

Notably, with the exceptions of Japan and the Republic of China, export-credit insurance schemes are nonexistent in the countries of the ECAFE region.[22] Even the system adopted in Taiwan is limited to the insurance of advances made by banks to exporters, such as production and raw material loans.[23] Only Japan has included in her export-credit insurance scheme the sale of goods on a deferred payment basis. This is practiced under the so-called export bill insurance.[24]

Under this type of insurance, an authorized foreign-exchange bank (which made advance payment to the exporter) is entitled to compensation by the Japanese Government for such amount remaining unpaid to the bank at the maturity of the documentary bill purchased from a drawer (the importer). The insurable value in this case is the sum stated in the bill, and the amount collectible under the insurance is 80 per cent of this amount.

The export-credit insurance system in Japan also includes the so-called export finance insurance. Under this type of insurance, a bank which has made a loan or a bill of discount to finance an exporter or producer is entitled to compensation by the government for such uncollectible amount brought about by the inability of the exporter to deliver the goods, or by his inability to collect the export proceeds. The amount collectible under this insurance is 80 per cent of the insurance value.

The Supreme Council of Japan has recently considered extending the periods of deferred export payment and granting special considerations by way of payment terms for exports to Southeast Asia, Latin America, and the Soviet Bloc.[25]

DIFFERENTIATED EXCHANGE RATES AND MULTIPLE CURRENCY PRACTICES

Thailand (until 1955), Cambodia, the Republic of China, Indonesia, South Korea, and South Vietnam offer important illustrations of countries with

multiple currency practices which involve indirect
export subsidies. These take the form of either partial or complete retention of export proceeds by exporters for sale in the open market, or differential
favorable official-exchange rates for exports which
are administered by exchange control authorities.
In Indonesia, for example, the old export duty of 10
per cent has been abolished, and exporters now get
Rp 315 per U.S. $1 worth of export (f.o.b. value),
which is seven times greater than the old rate of Rp
45 per U.S. $1 for export proceeds; 5 per cent can
be retained by the exporter to use at will.[26] In Nationalist China besides a preferential rate of exchang
for export proceeds, private exporters receive a certificate of exchange which represents a claim for a
certain amount of premium for each unit of foreign
currency brought into the country.[27] Industrial
firms which manufacture articles for export are permitted to retain 80 per cent of their foreign-exchange earnings with which to pay for their imports
of raw materials. They may also ask government trading agencies to export the products for them, in
which case they can obtain raw materials for their
exports on a loan basis.[28] In South Korea exporters
of manufactured goods are not only allowed to buy
foreign exchange needed for the importation of necessary raw materials at the preferential official rate
of 130 hwan to U.S. $1, but are also entitled to im-
port other goods in amounts corresponding to the
gross exchange accruing from the export.[29] In addition, they receive export subsidies from the government ranging from 5 to 60 hwan for each U.S. dollar
of net earning.[30] In South Vietnam exporters are
permitted to keep foreign exchange up to 15 per cent
of their sales proceeds with which to pay for specified imports (about fifty items) without applying
for foreign exchange at the National Exchange Office.[31]

     In undertaking a multiple currency scheme, a
distinction is often made between different commodities in terms of rates or percentages of exchange
which can be retained. In Cambodia the percentages
of export earnings retained by exporters vary not
only between commodities, but also between countries

to which exports are destined, depending upon the
currency areas they belong to. Under South Korea's
export subsidization scheme, exporters automatically
receive bonuses ranging from 100 to 250 hwan for
each dollar earned through exports. Commodities exported for the first time get the largest bonus; existing exports sold to new markets and handicraft
items are given the second prize of 200 hwan to one
dollar.[32] The South Korean Government also put into
effect on January 16, 1963, a special link system
under which a trader who exports certain types of
goods is also authorized to import certain high-
profit commodities, such as nylon yarn, watches, and
ball point pens, a privilege not granted to general
export-import traders. In addition, if a trader
bartered for certain products with Japanese ammonium
sulphate fertilizer, he is eligible to import other
commodities corresponding up to 50 per cent of the
value of the exports involved.[33] In Indonesia in addition to the 5 per cent retention scheme allowed to
all exporters, 15 per cent of export earnings can be
retained by exporters engaged in rubber production.
Nonproducer exporters of rubber are provided with a
secured import license of 10 per cent of their export earnings, which they can use for the importation
of essential and semiessential goods.[34]

INDUSTRY EXTENSION GRANTS
AND GOVERNMENT SUBSIDIES

Subsidies have not been used to a great extent
in Asian countries. They have not been considered,
particularly in agriculture, because the domestic
manufacture of import substitutes has claimed greater
attention.[35] Instances of their use are to be found,
however, in the major export industries. The reason
is obvious: Capacity to import "essentials" largely
depends on capacity to export. Heavy imports of essential producer and consumer goods for their development programs have left most of the Asian countries
in a state of chronic international reserve drainage.
Meanwhile, domestic capital available for internal
finance is rather limited. Scarcity of long-term
financing underlines the need to finance some priority

industries with careful concentration for a certain
number of years. Necessarily, the major export industries must receive special attention.

In India besides long-term loans for replanting
and extension of old tea-growing areas, the government grants subsidies for transport and fertilizer
to the tea producers of Cachar and Tripura. Through
the Industrial Development Corporation and the Coffee
Board, coffee and jute producers in Mysore, Madras,
and Kerala are also provided with adequate funds for
the modernization of their equipment and to assist
them in carrying on intensive promotional publicity
for jute and coffee in foreign countries.

In Malaysia replanting of rubber started early in
the 1950's. Small holders were provided with high-
yielding planting materials, and an outright grant
of Malaysian $500 per acre of replanted rubber was
granted for a period of seven years. The associated
government subsidies to the rubber industry came to
67 per cent of the total public investment in agriculture.[36]

While Malaysia depends on rubber, she is making
substantial advances as a tea producer.[37]

In Ceylon the government has taken various measures to promote tea production. The rehabilitation
scheme introduced in 1959 is being continued. Under
this scheme, a subsidy of Rs 2,500 to 3,500 per acre
is given to estates under one hundred acres to promote more intensive cultivation of tea. A subsidy
of Rs 3,500 is offered to plantations over one hundred acres for each new acre brought under cultivation. Another subsidy scheme is being formulated
for small holdings of about two acres each.[38]

In the Republic of China substantial assistance
has been recently provided for the Taiwan Sugar Corporation to raise yields through mechanization and
new fertilizing methods, and to improve efficiency
in the refineries with new extracting and processing
equipment. Direct U.S. aid to the sugar industry
was also given. For example, aid in the year 1957

totaled U.S.$ 3,049,000 and NT$ 4,705,400. These
amounts were generally used to procure automatic
sugar scales, boilers, generators, high-speed cen-
trifugals, alcohol locomotions, and equipment to
transport sugar cane from plantations to the mills.
Equipment valued at U.S.$ 246,000 procured through
the Agency for International Development greatly improved the productivity of the pineapple-canning industry. The new equipment includes stainless steel
slicing tables, modern canning and juice-making
equipment, aluminum screens, and window glass.

To support the program for increased production
of bananas, the Foreign Exchange and Trade Control
Commission extends to growers production loans ranging from NT$ 6,000 to 15,000 per hectare.[39]

In 1961 Thailand undertook an extensive program
of rubber plantation subsidy. As an initial step, a
Rubber Plantation Aid Fund was set up on December 5,
1960. During the first year in operation, the Fund
gave out 55,325,000 baht as subsidies to 1,867 owners of rubber plantations covering an area of 37,150
rai. In 1962, of the 3,013 applications received,
covering an area of 55,533 rai, 1,450 applicants
with an area of 17,618 rai were given subsidies
amounting to 28,427,000 baht.[40]

Regarding her sugar industry, in a January, 1963
meeting of the Research Sub-Committee of the Office
of the Sugar Industry Aid Fund, Thailand planned to
spend the following sums in aid to sugar growers:
952,000 baht for disease and pest destruction; 9 million baht for the purchase of fertilizer at subsidized prices; 5,383,400 baht for the procurement of
agricultural tools and implements; and 2,144,555
baht for the establishment of an experimental sta-
tion for sugar cane growing. These programs will be
implemented by stages.[41]

Price subsidy has claimed greater attention in
some Asian countries. The primary intent of this
scheme is to minimize the disadvantageous impact of
export price fluctuations in the world market on the
primary producer-exporting sector. During periods

of unfavorable export prices, the general reaction
of growers and producer-exporters is to limit their
scale of operation, so that only a few of them can
adjust operation and output in the ensuing period of
favorable prices. The inflexibility of major export
commodities (which are mainly agricultural products)
makes them unable to follow the movement of export
prices efficiently. Agricultural products are heavily dependent upon climatic conditions. If producer-
exporters are assured of prices above the dwindling
export prices during periods of slackening market demand, the tendency to limit the scale of their operation and production will be minimized, thereby leading to a better adjustment in output in the ensuing
"busy" market period.

The price-subsidy scheme adopted in Thailand is
undertaken by the so-called Government Warehouse Organization, which makes purchases at subsidized rates
to stabilize prices during periods of dwindling market demand. Subsequently, the Organization may export its stock of export commodities. During periods
of favorable export prices, the Organization usually
abstains from trading, and trade is completely left
to private exporters. In fixing the support price
for each commodity, the Organization takes into consideration the general level of prices in the world
market and the cost of transportation from the area
of production to the market.[42]

South Vietnam has a different approach to the
rice price-support scheme. During unfavorable market conditions, the government gives exporters the
difference between the export price which would pre-
vail in normal conditions and the actual selling
price in the international market. In return, exporters are required to turn in the entire foreign-
exchange proceeds to the government. Of these proceeds 34 per cent are used by the government to import goods essential to her development program
other than those financed by U.S. funds.[43]

In South Korea the Farm Product Maintenance
Law[44] provides for the purchase by the government of
such products as rice, barley, cotton, and others as

determined by the Ministry of Agriculture and Forestry, when such purchase is necessary to enable the farmers to sell their products at a price above the production cost. This law not only aids the farmers, but also encourages greater agricultural production.

STATE TRADING

State trading has grown in importance in the ECAFE region in recent years. In some countries where the export and import trade was formerly in the hands of foreign firms and where the gradual disappearance of such alien firms has not been replaced by domestic enterprises, state trading has been an important supplement to private trade. It has also provided an alternative outlet for trade which passed through "entrepôt countries."[45]

In numerous instances, state trading has played an important role in the promotion of exports. State trading enterprises which command large resources, financial and technical, can reduce the cost of marketing. This, for example, is the case with the Indian State Trading Corporation, which handles the bulk of trade in manganese and iron ore. They can also stimulate production for export by providing a regular marketing outlet, as well as financing and specifications, for small producers of export commodities. In some cases, state trading enterprises can even undertake production to ensure regular supply, as in the case of the Taiwan Sugar Corporation.[46]

State trading enterprises are particularly helpful in providing export producers with funds and materials. This is true, for example, in Indonesia and India. In its early years, the Indonesian Copra Fund supplied funds to small exporter-producers. The State Trading Corporation in India has also been extending credit to exporters and allocating among them the short supply of shipping space, as well as internal railway transportation.[47]

State trading organizations can also exercise strong bargaining power, especially when private

exporters are small and unorganized. With greater
access to technical expertise regarding market conditions, as well as their larger resources, they can
afford to assume calculated risks in introducing new
products into the world market and promoting traditional exports to new destinations, thus paving the
way for private traders. For example, the State
Trading Corporation in India is credited with finding new markets for iron and manganese ore in Italy,
Yugoslavia, and Hungary, as well as promoting exports
of shoes, tobacco products, and woolen textiles to
the Soviet Bloc.[48]

State trading organizations also serve as a
medium for subsidizing exports in their bid to enter
the world market. They can buy at the internal market price from private traders or export industries
and sell at a lower price abroad, so as to successfully compete with other suppliers. In Indonesia
direct purchases of state-authorized trading companies from exporter-producers have been emphasized not
only for such purposes, but also to keep intermediate traders from dealing in export products.[49]

In some instances, state trading has been undertaken to fulfill contracts under trade agreements.
In Ceylon state trading is confined to the export of
rubber to Mainland China under a trade agreement.
In India since July, 1957, all iron ore exports have
become a monopoly of the state trading corporation,
which has long-term contracts with Japan and Czechoslovakia. In Indonesia state trading corporations
expanded with the growth of bilateral trade agreements. In these countries, state trading and bilateral trade agreements deal almost entirely with traditional exports, but India has also attempted to increase its exports of manufactured goods.[50]

TRADE AGREEMENTS

Bilateral trade agreements are popular among
the countries studied. They cover single or multiple commodities and invariably include bulk-purchase
contracts.

As of 1961, there were about thirty-seven bilateral trade agreements between countries within
the ECAFE region (which includes the selected countries), of which twenty-three were between private
enterprise economies and fourteen between them and
the centrally planned economies within the region.[51]

As for extraregional trade agreements, private
enterprise economies of the ECAFE region in 1959 had
twenty-five trade agreements with the U.S.S.R. and
the Eastern European countries, thirteen with Western European countries, and thirteen with the rest
of the world.

Trade agreements with advanced countries mainly
have taken the form of exchanging primary exports
for manufactured goods, with the proportion of capital goods increasing in importance. Generally speak-
ing, the selected countries have exchanged rice (Thailand), iron ore (India), rubber and tea (Ceylon), etc.,
for imports of foodstuffs and manufactured goods of
all kinds.

Multilateral trade agreements are also common.
Examples of these agreements are the International
Agreement on Tea, which lapsed in 1955, and the International Tin Agreement. The International Tin
Agreement operates by country export quotas and an
international buffer stock designed to undertake
open market sales and purchases to stabilize prices.[52]

Trade agreements occupy an important place in
the domain of international trade. They promote
short-term stability in export prices by fixing
volumes and prices of particular export commodities
while the agreements are in effect. Unfortunately,
these agreements have mainly covered single commodities and are valid for only a short period. Even
within the period, the usual practice has been to
negotiate for the price level every year.[53] To become effective price stabilizers, such agreements
must cover a significant number of important export
commodities and remain valid for long periods.

The primary role of trade agreements, however,

seems to lie in finding new markets or promoting new exports. Trade agreements enable contact between the governments of various countries at the highest level, and foster a better appreciation of each other's problems and economic interests. They also encourage private traders to seek additional trade contacts in the partner countries. This seems to be the Indian experience, as reported by the Export Promotion Committee.[54]

Minor or supplementary exports of the region are also directly promoted under trade agreements, such as tapioca from Indonesia to Czechoslovakia and East Germany, and cashew nuts from India to the U.S.S.R.[55]

Trade agreements have also been used to facilitate a settlement of trade in local currencies when exporters are not conversant with the currency and banking systems of the trading partners. Foreign banks have opened accounts in local currency to receive and make payments, the balance being met in foreign currency at the level of the Central Bank. This has been done in India in regard to trade agreements with the centrally planned economies. Often, trade agreements are linked up with long-term capital financing in order to facilitate the import of capital goods.[56]

OBSERVATIONS AND CONCLUSION

The countries studied have made use of several schemes to promote export trade. However, most of the governments of these countries have not even attempted to imitate, much less adopt, certain incentive measures that have proved to be effective in increasing foreign-exchange earnings through greater export volume. A good example of this would be the establishment or nonestablishment of an export-import bank to finance medium- and long-term credit requirements of export industries. The Philippines has no institution that could be aptly called an export-import bank.

Of the various institutional financiers of agricultural credit, cooperatives are the ones most relied upon. Cooperatives figure prominently in the export incentive schemes of almost all of the selected countries. Japan, the Republic of China, the Philippines, and South Korea have placed great reliance on cooperatives to provide financial and other forms of assistance to their agricultural producer-exporters. This is particularly significant in view of the fact that the majority of the countries under study chiefly export agricultural products.

Few of the selected countries have kept up with a recent development in the field of export trade--the insurance of export risks. A common excuse for not adopting export insurance schemes on the part of the countries concerned is the gravity of the risks involved. The virtual nonexistence of an export-risk insurance system in these countries can be cited as an important factor in the slow growth of their export business. The reason for this is obvious: The inability to assume excessive risk on the part of the exporters creates a veritable obstacle in expanding their turnover, since, in the process, financial difficulties are likely to be encountered. The exceptions to this are Japan and the Republic of China.

Some countries have undertaken multiple currency practices to provide indirect export subsidies. Unlike the Philippines, where the export sector has benefited from the lifting of exchange controls while causing maladjustments in the financial position of other sectors, the multiple currency scheme employed in other countries has been on a selective basis. Hence, exporters are benefited without simultaneously impairing the interests of other sectors of the economy.

Direct grants and government subsidies have gained the attention of a minority of the countries. Nevertheless, these grants and subsidies have been concentrated in the major export industries. However, these countries are becoming more conscious of the need for assisting the export sector as a part of the over-all drive for economic development. Judging

from what has been done so far, it appears that the
efforts of the selected countries in aiding their
export industries will result in a handsome pay-off
in the future. The Philippine Government can, with
reason, lay claim to having exerted substantial efforts in helping the country's major export industries through grants and subsidies.

The Philippines must exert still greater efforts to promote the growth of its exports. Too
much emphasis on such measures as outright tax exemptions should be reduced to a minimum in favor of
other incentive schemes. Tax exemption privileges
at times do not increase export production, since
they can be utilized instead as an effective device
for dodging taxes which otherwise would be required
of the export producers. Moreover, the nonpayment
of taxes due to tax privileges reduces the capacity
of the government to finance projects consonant with
the general development program. The Philippine Government has yet to learn the favorable effects on export production of provisions for accelerated depreciation and the carry-over of losses. The former
allows producers to recover their capital investment
more quickly, especially during times of uncertainty.
The latter makes it possible for businessmen to recover losses incurred during certain periods. This
is done by deducting all or a part of the losses incurred in previous years' operations from profits
realized during subsequent periods, and using the
difference as the tax base. Provisions for the carry-
over of losses would help businessmen plan expansions
in their scale of operations in advance, without fear
of suffering tremendous losses, which otherwise could
never be recovered during profitable periods.

The Philippine Government must realize the need
for a systematic adoption of export incentive schemes.
The growth of exports forms an inextricable and very
significant part of efforts to achieve greater national economic development. More particularly, the
need to tap all sources of foreign exchange cannot be
overstated, for the export sector requires adequate
assistance from the government.

Notes to Chapter 10

1. "Problems of Industrialization in Relation to Economic Development in the Countries of Asia and the Far East," Economic Bulletin for Asia and the Far East, IX (December, 1958), 23, 24.

2. Benjamin H. Higgins and William C. Hollinger, "Central Banking in Indonesia" in S. Gethyn Davies (ed.), Central Banking in South and East Asia (Hongkong: Hongkong University Press, 1960), pp. 53-77.

3. Full decontrol took effect in 1964 and by this time the rate of exchange had almost doubled, i.e., from ₱2.00 = $1.00 to ₱3.90 = $1.00.

4. A discussion is devoted to this topic in succeeding pages.

5. S.L.N. Simha, "Central Banking in India," in Central Banking in South and East Asia, op. cit., pp. 31-52, 45, 46.

6. Edward Nevin, Capital Funds in Underdeveloped Countries (London: Macmillan & Co. Ltd., 1961), pp. 49-50.

7. Bui Van Thinh, "Central Banking in Vietnam," in Central Banking in South and East Asia, op. cit., pp. 183-89.

8. Michael Greenberg, "Central Banking in Ceylon," ibid., pp. 9-26.

9. See T. K. Chang, "Central Banking in China" and Byong Kuk Kim, "Central Banking in Korea," ibid., pp. 27-30, 87-110.

10. "Economic Development and Planning," Economic Bulletin for Asia and the Far East, XIV, No. 3 (December, 1963), 74.

11. Bank of Taiwan Annual Report, 1962, p. 19.

12. Tan That Thiem, "Economic Development in South Vietnam," The Malayan Economic Review, VI, No. 1 (April, 1961), 55-70; Tran-Ngoc-Liem, The Growth of Agricultural Credit and Cooperatives in Vietnam, a speech delivered before the American Friends of Vietnam Conference, Vietnam, Oct. 24, 1959, reprinted in Commissariate General for Cooperatives and Agricultural Credit, 1960, pp. 6, 7.

13. U.N., Economic Survey of Asia and the Far East, 1961, Ch. II, pp. 61, 62.

14. Ibid.

15. A Guide to Investment in Korea, op. cit., pp. 43-46.

16. Paul Alpert, Economic Development: Objectives and Methods (New York: Free Press of Glencoe, 1963), pp. 240-41.

17. "Problems of Industrialization in Relation to Economic Development," op. cit., p. 24.

18. "Commercial risks" refer to the insolvency or protracted default of the buyer or the importer. "Political risks," on the other hand, include the delay or stoppage in the transfer of foreign-exchange transactions due to war or revolution in the importer's country, sudden imposition of government regulations preventing the import of goods, war, and other similar restrictions and developments occurring outside the exporting country.

19. China (Republic) Foreign Exchange and Trade Control Commission, Foreign Exchange and Trade Handbook 1961 (Taipei: The Commission, 1961), pp. 68-71.

20. Alpert, op. cit., p. 240.

21. "The Economic Function of Credit Insurance," U.N. Trade Promotion News (March, 1956), pp. 5-7.

22. U.N. Trade Promotion News (February, 1956), p. 5. See also "Economic Development and Planning,"

Economic Bulletin for Asia and the Far East, XLV (December, 1963), 74.

23. Foreign Exchange and Trade Handbook 1961, op. cit., pp. 5-7.

24. This insurance covers only those transactions financed by authorized foreign-exchange banks other than the Export-Import Bank of Japan. The Export-Import Bank of Japan finances exports on a deferred-payment basis regardless of the backing of any form of insurance.

25. Kazuo Takita, "New Steps to Boost Exports," Far Eastern Economic Review, XL (June 6, 1963).

26. "Indonesia's May 27 Reform," op. cit., pp. 600-603. See also "Another Batch of Reforms," Far Eastern Economic Review, XL (June 6, 1963), 526.

27. "Relationship Between Agricultural and Industrial Development: A Case Study on Taiwan, China, 1953-1960," Economic Bulletin for Asia and the Far East, XIV (June, 1963), 53.

28. U.N. Trade Promotion News (September, 1956), p. 11.

29. A manufacturer who has gained gross proceeds of $120,000 from exportation of goods for which he has already used $100,000 for the import of necessary raw materials is given the right to import still another $120,000 worth of any other goods.

30. Han Nae Bok, "Can Korea Hold the Line?" Far Eastern Economic Review, XLI (September 19, 1963), 739.

31. U.N. Trade Promotion News (August, 1956), p. 12.

32. Ibid., p. 186.

33. Han Nae Bok, op. cit., p. 740.

34.   "Indonesia's May 27 Reform," loc. cit.

35.   U.N. Economic Survey for Asia and the Far East 1961, Ch. I, pp. 30, 31.   However, emphasis on manufactures to serve domestic markets has sometimes led to new exports.

36.   Ibid., Ch. I, p. 26.

37.   Far Eastern Economic Review, XLI, No. 6 (August 8, 1963), 349.

38.   Ibid., p. 347.

39.   Ibid., p. 354.

40.   Bank of Thailand Monthly Report (April, 1963), p. 17; ibid. (March, 1963), p. 17.

41.   Ibid. (February, 1963), p. 19; ibid. (June, 1963), p. 26.

42.   "Six-Year Economic Development Plan," Thai Chamber of Commerce Journal, XIV (November, 1960), 79, 80.

43.   U.N. Trade Promotion News (January, 1957), p. 16.

44.   A Guide to Investment in Korea, op. cit.

45.   "Economic Planning and Development," op. cit., p. 74.

46.   Ibid.

47.   Ibid.

48.   "State Trading by Underdeveloped Countries," Law and Contemporary Problems, XXIV (Summer, 1959), 476.   See "Economic Planning and Development," op. cit., pp. 74, 75.

49. In addition, it was proposed in late 1961
that a regulation be passed which will prohibit non-
exporters from keeping stocks of export products for
a period of two months so as to prevent hoarding, especially by speculators. It was believed this measure will compel producers to sell directly to authorized state trading companies. See Soekanto Sajidiman,
"Indonesia's New Trading System," Far Eastern Economic
Review (December 7, 1961), 461.

50. Ibid.

51. "Economic Development and Planning," op.
cit., p. 75, n. 39.

52. Ibid., p. 62; see also Elmer M. Harmon,
Commodity Reserve Currency (New York: Columbia University Press, 1959), pp. 32-35.

53. Alpert, op. cit., pp. 214-19, 221-23.

54. See Report of the Export Promotion Committee, 1957, pp. 55-59.

55. "Economic Development and Planning," loc.
cit.

56. Ibid., p. 75.

11 REVENUE, EXPENDITURE, AND PUBLIC DEBT PATTERNS

INTRODUCTION

The government, through the nature and level of public expenditure, taxation, and public debt, directly and indirectly influences the allocation of resources. Fiscal policy provides a system by which such influence on the economy can be directed to attain a predetermined objective. A comparison of the experiences of different countries in the fiscal policy field might well suggest the pattern of government fiscal action most suited for a given national objective.

The revenue, expenditure, and borrowing patterns of a country are heavily influenced by its institutional milieu. Correspondingly, what constitutes an appropriate action for one country may not be suitable to another. However, as the national efforts of the selected Asian countries are geared toward the acceleration of economic development, the problem of data comparability is reduced to manageable proportions.[1] Another problem that renders international comparison difficult pertains to the paucity of reliable and comparable data. Most of the statistics on government revenue and expenditure for this study have been abstracted from United Nations publications, particularly those of the ECAFE.

In deriving conclusions from the data, three salient considerations must be kept in mind: (1) not all accounts are final; some are estimates; (2) the composition or coverage of an account sometimes varies from country to country; and (3) within a given fiscal year, some accounts are not available.

248

Although the revenue, expenditure, and public debt
patterns of the central government of selected Asian
countries are dealt with separately, the subject
division is merely an expository device. In actual-
ity, these phases of government participation in economic activity are intertwined.

Centralized developmental planning represents a
major force that heavily influences the revenue, expenditure, and public debt patterns of the selected
Asian countries. The actual extent of planning
varies from country to country. In general, however,
planning consists mainly of formulating programs to
be implemented in the public sector and setting production and investment targets for the private sector. Infrastructure outlays are shouldered by the
government, while the private sector is called upon
to engage directly in productive activities. In addition to providing capital outlays, some governments
actually participate in production, or directly influence patterns of production and investment by establishing priority areas supported by tax holidays,
credit assistance, and other incentives.

Development programs, of necessity, require
huge financial resources, both in domestic and foreign currencies. Table 27 indicates the financial
resources expressed in dollars that must be marshaled
for the effective implementation of the various programs of the selected Asian countries.

It can be seen that the development plans of the
countries concerned call for a substantial portion of
their national income, except in the case of Thailand.
Nationalist China's Third Four-year Plan, 1961-65,
needs to marshal 21 per cent of her national income.
Compared to the average ratio of government revenue
to national income for the period 1958-62, which was
14 per cent (see Table 29), a concerted effort is
clearly necessary to bring the program to fruition.
India faces a similar situation. Its Five-year Plan
for 1961-66 requires 17 per cent of national income,
while the ratio of government revenue to national income for 1958-62 amounted to only 8 per cent. In
the case of Thailand, the annual average cost of its

TABLE 27

Development Plans of Selected Asian Countries

Country	Plan Period	Annual Average Cost in Million U.S. $	Exchange Rate[a]	As a Per Cent of National Income[b]
Republic of China	Third 4-year plan 1961-65	313	NT$ 40	21.3
India	Third 5-year plan 1961-66	5,080	Rs 4.8	16.7
Indonesia	First 8-year plan 1961-69	662	Rp 45	11.1
Malaysia	Second 5-year plan 1961-66	326	M$ 3	19.5
Philippines	5-year program 1963-67	617	₱ 3.90	18.7
Singapore	First 4-year plan 1961-65	70	M$ 3	...
South Korea	First 5-year economic plan 1962-66	208	Won 130	11.1
Thailand	First 6-year plan 1961-67	100	Baht 20.5	3.8

[a]Equivalent of a U.S. dollar as of April, 1963.

[b]Annual average cost as a per cent of 1962 national income.

Source: Dick Wilson (ed.), Far Eastern Economic Review 1964 Yearbook (Marina House, Hongkong: Far Eastern Economic Review Ltd., 1964), p. 31.

Six-year Plan (1961-67) as a percentage of national income amounts to a low 3.8 per cent. For 1958-62, the ratio of its government revenue to national income registered a comparatively high 15 per cent.

The table also points out that while Indonesia, Singapore, South Korea, and Thailand have just begun centralized development planning, the Republic of China and India are now working on their third long-range plan, and Malaysia on its second. Ceylon presently has a Ten-year Plan (1959-68), and Japan has embarked on a Ten-year Income Doubling Plan for 1961-70. The Philippines has had long experience in drawing up economic plans, dating back to 1934.[2]

PATTERNS OF GOVERNMENT REVENUE

The ratio of government revenue to national income and its composition for the five-fiscal-year period 1958-62 are given in Table 28. The share of the public sector in national income is, among other indicators, a measure of its participation in economic activity.[3] Aside from meeting expenditure requirements, the revenue system of a country represents a veritable anti-inflationary instrument. As the greater portion of government expenditure is generally a continuing commitment, anti-inflationary measures can better be implemented with an effective revenue system. The revenue system, especially in the case of taxation, can also be utilized as an incentive or disincentive scheme. The latter is clearly exemplified by sumptuary taxation, while tax holidays illustrate the former.

On the average, Cambodia, Ceylon, and Malaysia have registered the highest percentages of government revenue to national income. These countries have appropriated a little more than one-fifth of their national product to finance government services. In India, revenue accounts for a conspicuously low 8 per cent. In the case of Indonesia, the Philippines, South Korea, and Thailand, the percentage ranges from 12-17 per cent. In Japan, where the level of economic development compares favorably with the

TABLE 28

Average Percentages of Government Revenue, Expenditure, and Saving
of Selected Asian Countries, FY 1958-62

	Cambodia	Ceylon	India	Indonesia	Japan	Malaysia	Philippines	Singapore	South Korea	South Vietnam	Thailand
Total Revenue	20.6	22.9	8.1	17.2	15.9	22.5	11.5	...	15.4	...	14.9
Nontax revenue	25.1	11.2	41.5	28.3	6.0	17.0	19.2	29.3	13.9	19.2	10.4
Tax revenue											
Tax on income and wealth	13.0	24.0	27.7	26.1	55.6	21.3	23.1	40.0	18.9	7.9	9.4
Land tax	0.6	0.8	–	–	–	–	–	–	6.8	2.1	–
Customs duties	36.9	59.8	25.3	13.6	5.0	66.3	29.4	41.2	15.9	32.8	41.4
on import	32.6	33.0	22.0	10.0	...	40.9	29.4	41.2	...	30.9	33.4
on export	4.3	26.8	3.3	3.6	...	25.4	–	–	...	1.9	8.0
Transaction and cons. taxes	37.3	11.0	...	⎫	32.6	3.4	18.4	10.5	28.5	46.5	30.2
Licenses, stamps, etc.	8.2	2.1	...	60.3	2.7	7.9	22.3	6.6	2.9	7.1	3.0
Other tax revenues	4.1	2.3	47.0	⎭	4.2	1.3	6.8	1.8	27.0	3.6	16.0

Total expenditure	20.8	30.8	13.2	25.7	15.1	27.0	11.8	...	28.0	...	16.1
Defense	30.8	4.1	15.8	35.4	9.3	12.0	14.4	2.6	29.0	39.3	19.9
Subsidies	-	9.8	1.4	...	1.4	4.4	2.6	-	2.3	-	0.2
Economic services	4.7	10.3	...	5.3	2.3	...	14.6	6.6	2.6	...	8.5
Social services	24.8	25.0	...	8.2	21.3	21.3	29.7	36.6	15.5	...	24.3
Contributions to provincial and local government	...	2.0	8.3	...	24.0	-	7.0	-	3.8	...	1.5
Other current expenditures	30.3	19.1	21.6	45.3	19.2	34.1	11.8	26.3	13.2	40.3	26.3
Investment	9.3	27.0	28.0	5.9	22.2	28.2)	17.4	28.0	11.4	20.4	18.5
Loans and advances (net)	...	2.8	25.0	...	0.3	)	2.6	...	22.1	...	0.8
Saving	(16.6)	5.5	22.8	(21.8)	25.8	13.1	16.8	...	(24.0)	(41.9)	12.0

Note:
1. Total revenue and total expenditure are shown as a per cent of national income.
2. Nontax revenue is shown as a per cent of total revenue.
3. The components of tax revenue and total expenditure are shown as a per cent of their respective total.
4. Saving is shown as a per cent of total revenue.

Sources: See Appendixes XII and XIII.

Western hemisphere, government revenue amounts to 16 per cent of national income.

The phenomenon of a low ratio of government revenue to national income gives cause for concern because the legitimate expenditure needs of these developing economies are expanding rapidly. This is not to maintain that revenue ought to balance expenditure. If government expenditure increases faster than government revenue, the difference must be made up by a correspondingly faster increase in private saving than in private investment.[4]

On a fiscal year basis, government revenue as a per cent of national income has generally been increasing, although at a very slow pace (Table 29).[5] This indicates that the increase in national income, a relatively good measure of taxable capacity, has not been effectively tapped by the public sector to finance expanding expenditure needs. In Cambodia, South Korea, Malaysia, and South Vietnam, government revenue has decreased on a percentage basis, and on an absolute basis as well. Indonesia presents a marked exception to this picture. From a low 15 per cent in 1959, the percentage of government revenue jumped to 24 per cent in 1960, or an increase of about 55 per cent. For fiscal year 1961, the percentage rose to 26 per cent. This is mainly attributable to the principle of "guided economy," a concomitant of the "guided democracy" instituted in 1959, whereby resources are brought into the public sector and considerable restrictions are placed on private enterprise.[6]

Government revenue necessarily represents a reduction from the resources of the private sector. It is raised either through taxation or nontax sources, such as administrative income, and grants and aids. There is no precise ratio between these two sources that will best attain national goals. Much doubt arises, however, as to a country's claim to a private enterprise economy when a substantial portion of its revenue is derived from, for example, rental and monopoly sources. In developing economies, reliance on nontax sources is occasioned by economic

and noneconomic factors, such as heavy dependence on
a few agricultural exports which the state seeks to
protect, weak taxing power of the state, and, in
some instances, outright veering toward socialism.

TABLE 29

Government Revenue and Expenditure as a
Per Cent of National Income; Saving
as a Per Cent of Government Revenue

	1958	1959	1960	1961	1962	Average
Cambodia						
Revenue	18.5	21.2	21.1	21.9	20.5	20.6
Expenditure	18.5	26.6	28.2	29.3	30.2	26.6
Saving	15.6	(8.1)	(27.0)	(25.8)	(37.9)	(16.6)
Ceylon						
Revenue	22.1	21.7	22.3	23.8	24.5	22.9
Expenditure	27.2	29.6	30.3	32.2	34.6	30.8
Saving	17.5	1.6	0.8	0.6	6.9	5.5
China, Re-						
** public of**						
Revenue	16.6	16.3	...	12.6	11.8	14.3
Expenditure	16.5	18.2	...	14.7	14.8	16.0
Saving	...	...	...	...	...	...
India						
Revenue	7.3	7.5	7.6	8.4	9.6	8.1
Expenditure	12.7	13.2	12.2	12.9	15.1	13.2
Saving	22.5	20.0	21.8	23.6	26.2	22.8
Indonesia						
Revenue	13.4	15.1	23.6	26.2	...	19.6
Expenditure	20.3	21.9	27.3	33.3	...	25.7
Saving	(46.2)	(38.7)	(8.3)	(15.6)	...	(21.8)
Japan						
Revenue	15.9	15.5	15.2	16.3	16.4	15.9
Expenditure	14.6	15.4	14.8	14.7	16.0	15.1
Saving	21.4	23.0	25.4	32.9	26.2	25.8

TABLE 29 (continued)

	1958	1959	1960	1961	1962	Average
Malaysia						
Revenue	20.9	22.5	24.5	22.1	...	22.5
Expenditure	26.7	25.1	25.1	31.0	...	27.0
Saving	3.3	16.0	21.9	11.3	...	13.1
Philippines						
Revenue	10.8	10.5	11.9	12.0	12.3	11.5
Expenditure	11.5	10.4	11.4	13.0	12.6	11.8
Saving	16.2	17.4	19.4	15.3	15.7	16.8
South Korea						
Revenue	13.2	16.7	17.6	14.1	15.3	15.4
Expenditure	27.0	15.8	24.0	29.3	33.7	28.0
Saving	(34.8)	(16.0)	(4.5)	(40.8)	(23.7)	(24.0)
Thailand						
Revenue	15.1	14.8	14.6	14.7	15.5	14.9
Expenditure	16.2	15.7	14.5	16.7	17.9	16.1
Saving	9.8	12.8	18.6	8.6	10.0	12.0

Source: See Appendixes XII and XIII.

The average ratio of nontax revenue to total revenue of selected Asian countries varies markedly, from a high two-fifths in the case of India to a low one-sixteenth in the case of Japan (Table 28).   Cambodia, Indonesia, and Singapore derive a little more than one-fourth.   Thailand and Ceylon depend on nontax sources to the extent of one-tenth of their total revenue.

The data on hand enable us to discuss five kinds of revenue: tax on income and wealth, land tax, tax on foreign trade (import and export duties), transaction and consumption taxes, and miscellaneous taxes (licenses, stamps, registration fees, and others). In the following discussion, these broad categories of taxes are related to tax revenue. Necessarily, these percentages will be lower if such taxes are related to total revenue.

The percentage of tax on income and wealth, consisting of income and gift taxes, to total tax revenue of selected Asian countries indicates, except in the case of Japan, the minor role played by this source in bringing in revenue to the national coffers. This situation is the converse of that obtaining in developed economies, where tax on income and wealth contributes two-thirds or more of the total tax revenue. Five factors in developing economies have brought about this situation: (1) low level of income, (2) low marginal income tax rates, (3) high level of personal exemptions, (4) low level of efficiency in the collection machinery, and (5) political preference for "hidden taxes."

The almost universal preference for "direct taxes" (tax on income, wealth, and land) needs examination. The special features of direct taxes, such as discrimination of taxpayers with respect to their ability to pay, built-in flexibility, and relative nonshiftability, are indeed desirable. These features are not peculiar to direct taxes alone. Furthermore, since the coverage of direct taxation is particularly limited in developing economies, while government expenditure is progressively on the rise, it is exigent to tap other sources of revenue through indirect taxation. The limited coverage of tax on income and wealth presents a formidable problem. While welfare considerations demand that those with the ability to pay bear a greater burden of the cost of government, revenue needs call for taxes which do not vary directly with income. This situation arises because such taxes are usually highly productive. This state of affairs need not be alarming. In developing countries, the major problems are uneven distribution of income and the need for enlarging income.

When the proportion of tax on income and wealth to tax revenue is considered, Japan, with an average of 56 per cent, ranks first. Singapore and India

come next with 40 and 28 per cent, respectively.
Indonesia, the Philippines, and Ceylon obtain a
little less than one-fourth of their tax revenue
from taxes on income and wealth. Of the countries
under study, South Vietnam depends least on tax on
income and wealth, for it derives only an average of
8 per cent of its tax revenue from this source.

Land taxes contribute an insignificant portion
to tax revenue of the selected Asian countries. Except for South Korea and South Vietnam, which derive 7 and 2 per cent, respectively, revenue contribution of land taxes to the national treasury is
either nil or negligible. In certain cases (the
Philippines, for example),[7] the land tax accrues entirely to the local governments. The coverage of
land taxes varies from country to country. Land
taxes are based on farm output, as in the case of
the Republic of China and South Korea, or on capital
value of the land and equipment, as in the case of
Thailand and the Philippines, or on a combination of
the two, as in the case of India.

Revenue from foreign trade (taxation of imports,
exports, or profits from state trading of imported
items) constitutes a substantial portion of total
tax revenue, except in the case of Japan, Indonesia,
and South Korea. During the period under study,
these countries derived only 5, 14, and 16 per cent,
respectively, from this source, whereas the others
obtained from 20 to 66 per cent. Taxes on foreign
trade are levied to achieve one or a combination of
the following objectives: (1) provide revenue,
(2) improve balance-of-payments accounts, (3) ration
scarce foreign exchange, (4) curtail inflationary
tendencies, (5) encourage and protect certain domestic industries, and (6) facilitate the flow of capital equipment. For those countries which strive to
attain these objectives simultaneously, a dilemma
inevitably arises because they are not complementary.
Revenue needs may demand low import duties, but such
a move conflicts with the policy of protection of
domestic industries.[8]

The export tax presents a special feature of

the tax system of some Asian countries. Revenue arising from this source is quite substantial, especially
in Indonesia, Ceylon, Malaysia, and Thailand.[9] Besides bringing in revenue, the export tax presents
an effective tool in minimizing sharp fluctuations,
caused by both supply and demand factors, in the
volume and price movements of primary export commodities.[10] Asian countries, except Japan, face a common
problem of dependence on a few primary exports. If,
for example, revenue from the export tax is directed
to the development of industrial products, export
diversification can well be facilitated.

The determination of the rate and base for the
export tax presents a serious problem. Primary exports are quite competitive, so that an increase in
price resulting from an attempt to shift the tax may
mean the loss of the market. On the other hand, an
abnormally low tax will be ineffectual as a revenue
producer and as a countercyclical instrument.[11]

Another substantial source of income for the
majority of the selected countries pertains to transaction and consumption taxes. These taxes include
excise duties, turnover taxes (sales taxes), and entertainment imposts. The high revenue productivity
of these taxes arises not so much from high rates
but from their general scope. Except for food and
basic necessities, the sale or manufacture of all
commodities is subject to tax. To incorporate the
ability-to-pay principle, differential rates are imposed, depending on the essentiality of the commodity. While taxes on foreign trade are designed to
attain several objectives, transaction and consumption taxes are generally imposed for revenue purposes. These taxes should therefore be levied on
those services and commodities with a low price elasticity (a decrease in price is accompanied by a less-
than-proportionate decrease in quantity demanded)
and a high-income elasticity of demand (an increase
in income is accompanied by a more-than-proportionate
increase in quantity demanded).

In developing economies, transaction and consumption taxes have a decided advantage over the

income tax in curtailing purchasing power, which is
desirable during inflationary periods. This is due
to the limited coverage of the latter, owing to several factors mentioned earlier, while the former
reaches almost everyone, regardless of income status.
If, in developed countries, a sales tax is justified
to keep from raising the already high income tax
rates, the sales tax in developing economies precise-
ly compensates for the inadequacy of the income tax.

Indonesia and South Vietnam derive a little more
than one-half of total tax revenue from transaction
and consumption taxes. By contrast, this source contributes a mere 4 per cent in the case of Malaysia.
Other countries lie between these extremes, with the
concentration at the upper range.

Licenses, stamps, and other sources as a per
cent of total tax revenue differ markedly, because
the composition and coverage of these taxes differ
markedly. In the case of the Philippines, licenses,
stamps, and other sources contribute 21 per cent to
tax revenue, but this includes business taxes. In
the case of South Vietnam, business taxes are accounted for in transaction and consumption taxes.
The tax on foreign exchange is included in other tax
revenue in South Korea, but it is accounted for in
transaction and consumption taxes in Indonesia.

PATTERNS OF GOVERNMENT EXPENDITURE

Although government revenue has been generally
on the rise, government expenditure, except in Japan,
still outstrips revenue, so the governments concerned are operating with a deficit (shown as negative balances in Appendix XIV). There is, however,
nothing undesirable in this situation. Budgetary
deficit per se is not a dead weight to economic development. The purpose for which the deficit was incurred, the method of financing, and its over-all
effect on economic activity are relevant factors. A
deficit resulting from the construction of a hydro-
electric plant, for example, need not alarm the most
ardent advocates of government parsimony. On the

other hand, there ought to be much apprehension
about deficits arising from misuse of funds.

The percentage of government expenditure to
national income is on the increase (Table 29). For
some countries, such as the Republic of China, South
Korea, and Thailand, it has declined. These countries experienced increases in absolute amounts, in-
dicating that the increase in government expenditure
lagged behind the increase in national income. Ceylon, with an average of 31 per cent, has the highest
percentage of government expenditure to national income, followed by South Korea, Malaysia, and Cambodia,
which have all contributed a little more than 25 per
cent. The Philippines has contributed least to
national income, with 12 per cent.

The gross national product equation, $Y = C + I + G$
(exports assumed equal to imports), states that income
varies directly with government expenditure. Why,
then, does not the government spend itself to prosperity? It is not a truism that any increase in government expenditure would increase the national income.
For instance, an increase in government expenditure
occasioned by an equal decrease in private consumption and investment will not provide an increase in
income, but only indicates a change in the sector
utilizing the income. Assuming that private consumption and investment remain constant, an increase in
government expenditure will result in an increase
only in monetary income, if production stays at the
same level. It follows that only government expenditure aimed at increasing output results in an increase in real income.

As has been stated, the level and pattern of
government expenditure are heavily influenced by noneconomic factors. In the case of Ceylon, Cambodia,
and Indonesia, the high percentage of expenditure to
national income manifests the desire of the government to expand its influence on economic activities.
On the other hand, the containment of the public sector partially explains the low percentage in the
case of Japan and the Philippines. Over-all, however, the increasing percentage of government expendi-

ture to national income lends support to Adolph
Wagner's assertion that government participation in
economic activity regularly increases, both extensively and intensively. [12]

Table 28 presents the components of government
expenditure of selected Asian countries. The presentation uses an admixture of economic and functional
classification. The former subdivides government expenditure into current and capital outlays, while
the latter indicates expenditures on a definite area,
such as economic services, defense, and others. It
is possible to have a combined functional-economic
classification, but the data on hand lump all capital outlays into two accounts--investment, and loans
and advances (net)--regardless of functional destina-
tion. Current outlays are classified functionally.

Defense expenditures of the selected Asian countries as a per cent of total government expenditures
vary considerably, depending upon conditions of
peace and order. As expected, countries such as Cambodia, Indonesia, South Korea, and South Vietnam,
which are either experiencing internal strife or are
engaged in military build-up, devote a greater part
of their resources to defense. Such expenditure is
financed mainly out of grants and aids, so that it
does not exert a heavy pressure on domestic sources.
These grants and aids could have been utilized to
meet developmental outlays. Whereas Cambodia, Indonesia, South Korea, and South Vietnam direct from 31
to 39 per cent of total expenditure to defense outlays, Ceylon and Singapore expend only 4 and 3 per
cent, respectively.

Subsidies as a per cent of total expenditure
are substantial only in Ceylon, which devotes one-
tenth of total expenditure for this purpose (food
subsidy). In India, subsidies are given to imported
steel. The Philippines grants subsidies on food
items and tobacco, although expenditure for this account is not as substantial as in Ceylon.

Current expenditure on economic services, which
includes agriculture, industrial development, public

works, and commerce, constitutes a surprisingly small
percentage of total expenditure. This is probably
due to the fact that the bulk of total expenditure on
economic services is in the form of capital outlay.
There is no breakdown of the capital accounts (investment, and loans and advances) to ascertain what portion of total capital outlay pertains to economic
services. Also, in the case of a public works project
such as a dam or a highway, total expenditure, whether
in the form of salaries, administrative expenses, or
machineries, is treated wholly as capital expenditure.
Thus the classification of current expenditure on
economic services represents expenses incurred independent of a development project. Except for the
Philippines, which allocates 15 per cent of total expenditure to economic services, this account claims
a meager 2 to 10 per cent of total expenditure for
the other countries.

The case for social services contrasts considerably with economic services. While the latter, on
the average, constitutes less than one-tenth of total
expenditure, the former, except in the case of Indonesia and South Korea, claims from two-tenths to a
little less than four-tenths of total expenditure.
This situation may be explained by the fact that expenditure on social services, which includes education, health, labor, and social welfare, is mainly
current. Once the construction of school buildings,
hospitals, and other equipment necessary to carry
out the social program has been undertaken, the maintenance of these services requires current expenditure.

Given a situation of peace and order, internally
and externally, expenditures on economic and social
services vie with each other for the greater share
of total expenditure. In the advanced economies, improvements in social welfare were preceded by advances in economic conditions. In developing countries,
however, the knowledge of present western social welfare standards has produced a "demonstration effect,"
resulting in a high demand for social welfare services.
Of necessity, expenditure on social services means
fewer resources for economic development purposes.

On the other hand, the urgency of social development expenditure precludes its postponement until after economic development has been attained. By its nature, this situation calls for a political decision. This problem represents a conflict between a short-run and long-run national preference. If a nation wants more social services, it may have to be content with a slower rate of economic development.

Contributions to provincial and local governments constitute a small portion of total expenditure. Japan, however, presents a notable exception, for it allocates one-fourth of total expenditure for this purpose. This situation has probably arisen because the national government possesses more than enough resources to defray national commitments. In the case of other governments, these grants and aids to local authorities are almost precluded, since their income has lagged behind their expenditure. India, with 8 per cent, and the Philippines, with 7 per cent, contribute quite substantially to local government resources. In the Philippines, the apportionment of some internal revenue taxes to local authorities is embodied in the tax code.

Other current expenditure, consisting mainly of general administration, has consistently risen with the growth in total expenditure. Offhand, three major factors explain this phenomenon: (1) population increase, (2) intensive and extensive participation of government in economic activity, and (3) general price increases (the same amount of resources must be secured at higher prices). Parkinson's law (administration continues to grow on its own, regardless of the function to be performed) is another factor in this increase in general administration. Work, it seems, is created to provide employment to new entrants and promotions to those already employed. Compounding this situation is the persistent demand of public employees for salary increases (which also holds true in the private sector, but to a lesser degree), resulting in an ever-increasing wage bill.

The Philippines and South Korea have the lowest percentages of other current expenditure to total

expenditure. While other countries allocate an average of from two-tenths to four-tenths, the Philippines and South Korea expend only a little more than
one-tenth.

Capital outlays of selected Asian countries are
lumped together in investment, and loans and advances
(net) accounts. The importance of capital formation
for economic development is certainly realized by
these growth-conscious countries. Their success in
channeling a greater portion of their resources to
this area, however, has not been impressive. As a
matter of fact, a majority of these countries experienced a decrease in the percentage of their capital
outlays. In Ceylon, India, South Korea, and South
Vietnam, there was also a decrease in absolute amount.

There are no data available on the composition
of total capital outlays, but it is highly probable
that the major portion of such outlays is of the infrastructure type (transportation, communication,
and power facilities). The facts that these outlays
are crucial to general economic development and that
the private sector can be least expected to engage
in these areas make it imperative for the government
to undertake such expenditure.

India, with an average of 53 per cent, has the
highest percentage of capital outlay to total expenditure. Loans and advances (net), which are mainly
granted to provinces, local authorities, and public
and private undertakings for capital outlay constitute about one-half of this. South Korea places
second with 34 per cent. Indonesia has the smallest
capital expenditure, because about 80 per cent of
its total expenditure is channeled into only two ac-
counts--defense and other current expenditure.

At this point, an analysis of the importance of
current expenditures vis-à-vis capital expenditures
is relevant. By definition, the former yields a
once-and-for-all service, while the latter creates
new assets which yield continuous or recurring services. The distinction between the two seems to
have been overemphasized. The ability to provide

for the growth of income is not confined exclusively
to capital expenditures. What is of interest pertains not to the expenditure per se, but to its effects on employment and production. Current expenditures on disease control or education may possess
equal or higher growth potential than capital outlays on roads and highways. Capital formation heavily influences the functioning and growth of the
economy. Moreover, an increase in capital outlays
of the public sector is not significant in itself.
It must be assessed in relation to existing economic
and noneconomic factors.

Savings in the public sector, defined as the excess of total government revenue over total current
expenditure, can also be gleaned from Table 28. If
total current expenditure exceeds total revenue,
there is dis-saving. Of the ten countries where
data are available, Indonesia, South Korea, and
South Vietnam consistently experienced dis-saving
for the five-fiscal-year period, 1958-62. Cambodia
dis-saved for the fiscal years 1959-62. Dis-saving
indicates that the governments concerned have expended their total income (revenue), plus a part of
past saving. If there was no saving to draw upon,
these governments must have financed such excess of
expenditure over revenue by borrowing or by printing
new money. [13] Of necessity, government dis-saving is
a reduction of the total saving of the economy.

India, Japan, Malaysia, the Philippines, Thailand, and Ceylon operated with saving, and thus
added to the capital stock of the economy. Except
for Ceylon, which saves 6 per cent of total income,
the others allocate a sizable portion of their income to saving. Japan saves a little more than one-
fourth of its income, while Thailand saves one-eighth.
In the case of India, the Philippines, and Malaysia,
saving accounted for 13-23 per cent of government
revenue.

The capital needs of an economy, as they relate
to the goal of economic development, cannot be overemphasized. Unless concrete steps toward this objective are undertaken, capital formation will not occur.

Saving does not necessarily present the only key to economic development. The volume of saving in the whole economy must be attended by several other economic and noneconomic factors, such as mobilization of saving, sufficient supply of entrepreneurs, and national adaptability to innovations, for it to be an effective agent of economic development.

PUBLIC DEBT

The negative balances shown in Appendix XIV indicate that government revenue has not been able to keep pace with government expenditure. This deficit could have been financed through past saving, but there is reason to believe that public debt has been heavily relied upon. Data on public debt (internal and external), available for five of the twelve countries, are given below.

TABLE 30

Gross Public Debt of Selected Asian Countries

	Public Debt	Period	As a Per Cent of National Income
Ceylon (million rupees)	2,267.1[a]	September 30, 1961	39
India (million rupees)	61,713	March 30, 1961	40
Japan (thousand million yen)	521	March 31, 1961	4
Philippines (million pesos)	2,227.6	July 31, 1961	19
Thailand (million baht)	6,380.3[b]	December 31, 1960	13

[a]Net of sinking fund.

[b]Internal debt only. External debt amounted to £0.5 (M) and U.S.$ 36.1 (M).

Source: United Nations, Statistical Yearbook 1961.

Besides the coverage of the seven other countries, there is a need to obtain a cross-classification of the composition of public debt[14] (i.e., developmental and budgetary, short-term and long-term, internal and external, bonded and nonbonded debt), annual interest payments, holders of public debt, and others. The absence of data on these aspects necessarily restricts the discussion.

Table 30 shows that in Japan, public debt as a per cent of national income stands at a mere 4 per cent. This is not surprising considering that Japan, for the fiscal years 1959-61, consistently achieved a budget surplus; i.e., government revenue more than covered total government financial commitments. For Ceylon and India public debt constitutes two-fifths of national income.

Much apprehension clouds the issue of public debt. More often than not, it is associated with the burden of interest payment and capital amortization, while the benefits arising from its effective utilization are overlooked. Public debt per se does not constitute a burden on the economy. To the extent that the advantages derived outweigh the disadvantages, public debt need not worry any sector of the economy.

The percentage of public debt to national income is not in itself economically significant. The debt capacity of the economy is subject more to qualitative than quantitative restrictions. It is surprising to note, for example, that the United Kingdom in 1960 had an outstanding debt of a little more than one-and-a-half times its national income. As of 1960, the percentage of public debt to national income of some economies were: Australia, 72 per cent; Canada, 77 per cent; and the United States, 69 per cent. The general statement, therefore, that economic development would entail a large public debt (as in the case of the United Kingdom) or that economic development need not call for public debt (as in the case of Japan) would be misleading. The capacity to bear an increasing public debt rests on a number of economic and noneconomic factors, such

as: growth of the economy, debt management, distribution of debt, cooperation of financial institutions with the government, level of taxation, and
the increasing acceptance of compensatory finance.

SUMMARY

1. The revenue, expenditure, and borrowing patterns of the countries under study are heavily influenced by centralized development planning. To the
extent that deliberate government participation in
economic activity has been looked upon as a complement to free enterprise, the level and pattern of
government revenue, expenditure, and debt have been
correspondingly altered. The present development
plans of the countries concerned portray the current
school of thought that for national economic development to proceed at the desired rate, conscious and
active participation by the public sector is necessary.

2. Government revenue of the selected Asian
countries under study is a low percentage of national
income. For the five-year fiscal period 1958-62, it
has generally been on the increase, although at a
very slow pace. Cambodia, Ceylon, and Malaysia,
registering the highest percentages of government
revenue to national income, have appropriated a little more than one-fifth of their national product to
finance government services. Other countries registered 8-17 per cent.

3. Total government revenue consists mainly of
tax revenue. Nontax revenue contributed heavily in
the case of India (42 per cent). Singapore, Indonesia, and Cambodia derived 29, 28, and 25 per cent,
respectively, from this source. Japan, with 6 per
cent, depends least on nontax sources.

4. The tax on income and wealth, except in the
case of Japan, makes a relatively low contribution
to tax revenue. This situation arises chiefly because of: (1) low level of income, (2) low marginal
income tax rates, (3) high level of personal exemp-

tions, (4) low level of efficiency in the collection machinery, and (5) political preference for "hidden taxes." Japan derives 56 per cent from the tax on income and wealth. Indonesia, the Philippines, and Ceylon obtain a little less than one-fourth. South Vietnam, with 8 per cent, depends least on this source for revenue purposes.

5. Revenue from foreign trade is significant, except in the case of Japan, Indonesia, and South Korea. While others obtain from one-fifth to two-thirds of tax revenue from this source, these countries derived only 5 per cent, 14 per cent, and 16 per cent, respectively. Transaction and consumption taxes similarly contribute significantly to total revenue. Cambodia, Japan, South Korea, South Vietnam, and Thailand derive 30 per cent or more of total revenue from this source.

6. In developing economies, indirect taxation must be relied upon as the main source of revenue. This phenomenon exists because of the limited coverage of tax on income and wealth. Indirect taxation finds justification in developed economies in the already high income tax rates; and in developing economies, it compensates for the inadequacy of income and land taxes.

7. Government expenditure, except in Japan, still outstrips government revenue so that the governments concerned are operating with deficits. Budgetary deficit, however, does not by itself indicate something economically significant. The purpose for which the deficit was incurred, the method of financing, and its over-all effects on economic activity are the more relevant factors to consider.

8. On the whole, government expenditure as a per cent of national income has been increasing. This trend lends support to the assertion that government participation in economic activity regularly increases, extensively and intensively. Ceylon contributes most to national income, with 31 per cent, while Japan contributes only half this percentage. The share of South Korea, Malaysia, and Cambodia in

their national income amounted to a little more than one-fourth. The Philippines, with 12 per cent, contributes least to national income.

9. The data on hand present an admixture of economic and functional classification of government expenditure. The pattern obtaining in the case of current expenditure on social services contrasts markedly with that of economic services. While the latter constitutes less than 10 per cent of total expenditure, the former, except in the case of Indonesia and South Korea, claims from 10 to a little less than 40 per cent. This pattern may be explained by the fact that expenditure on social services is mainly current.

10. Other current expenditure, such as general administration, grew with the rise in total expenditure. This situation may be explained by: (1) population increase, (2) intensive and extensive government participation in economic activity, and (3) the general increase in the level of prices.

11. Capital outlays of the countries under study are lumped under either investments, or loans and advances (net). The governments concerned have not been allocating a greater portion of their resources to capital formation. Not only has there been a decrease in the percentage of capital outlay, but also a decrease in absolute amount, in the case of Ceylon, India, South Korea, and South Vietnam. Capital formation heavily influences the functioning and growth of the economy. The increase in capital outlays of the public sector does not by itself present anything quite significant. It must be assessed in relation to relevant economic and noneconomic factors.

12. Saving of the public sector, defined as the excess of total government revenue over total current expenditure, appears to be substantial in the case of Japan and India. These countries allocated 26 and 23 per cent, respectively, of their resources for this purpose. Indonesia, South Korea, and South Vietnam consistently encountered dis-saving.

They not only expended their total income, but also
utilized part of past savings. Other sources of
financing are foreign grants and aids, printing new
money, and public debt.

13.   Data on public debt are available for only
five of the countries under study. Debt for Ceylon
and India constitutes two-fifths of national income;
in the case of Japan, a low 4 per cent. For the
Philippines and Thailand, public debt stands at 19
and 13 per cent, respectively. Public debt per se
does not, however, constitute a burden on the economy.
It has to be related to the growth of the economy,
debt management, and the increasing acceptance of
compensatory finance.

Notes to Chapter 11

1.   In the following discussion, no attempt has
been made to convert the data on hand to a single
unit of currency which will facilitate comparison.
Although the free-market current exchange rate
measures quite accurately the parity between goods
exchanged in foreign trade, it is an inadequate in-
dicator of the internal purchasing power of the different currencies. Except for Table 27, comparison
is therefore undertaken through the use of percentages.

2.   The Philippines in 1962 introduced the Five-
year Integrated Socio-Economic Development Program
for 1963-67. Although there have been several plans
of the same nature in the past, such plans have as a
rule not transcended the blueprint stage.
    The Five-year Program outlines the invest-
ment target for both the private and the government
sectors for the attainment of an average annual
growth rate of more than 6 per cent for the five-
year period. It should be mentioned that the basic
features of this program have been incorporated with
certain modifications in the draft of the four-year
economic program for the Philippines (FY 1967-70) of
the Marcos Administration.

3. The size and growth of the public sector is ordinarily reckoned in terms of government expenditure rather than of revenue. These two magnitudes suffer from a common shortcoming: Government participation in economic activity includes various actions, such as monetary decisions, that may not be reflected in government revenue or expenditure accounts.

4. This observation can be symbolized as:
   (1) $C + I + G = C + I + G$.
   (2) $C + I_g + I_p + G = C + S_g + S_p + R$, where the sub-letters g and p correspond to the government and private accounts, respectively, and R denotes government revenue. Eliminating consumption (C) from both sides of the equation,
   (3) $I_g + I_p + G = S_g + S_p + R$.
It can be seen, therefore, that if government current expenditure is greater than government revenue, i.e., $G > R$, then private saving should correspondingly be greater than private investment.

5. For the average annual growth rate of national income, see Appendix XIII.

6. In March, 1963, a new program embodied in the Economic Declaration ("Dekon") was introduced wherein participation of private enterprise was given due consideration.

7. Local governments, including chartered cities, are empowered to impose a tax of 1-2 per cent upon the assessed value of the real property situated under their jurisdiction. Local governments derive less revenue from the real property tax than from apportionments and grants from the national government.

8. The emergence of a very complicated tax system common to developing economies can be seen from a better perspective by considering the fact that multifarious taxes have been imposed to attain several objectives which are sometimes at variance with one another.

9.   There has been a proposal to impose a tax
on Philippine exports on a selective basis. The objectives are two-pronged: for revenue and for the
promotion and diversification of export products.
It is envisioned that a good bulk of the proceeds
from the export tax shall be utilized for research
designed to benefit the export industries. Similarly, it is intended that a higher tax be imposed on
raw materials than on semiprocessed and completely
manufactured exports, to encourage local processing.
Furthermore, the proposed export tax would serve as
a countercyclical tool to offset the increased purchasing power of the export sector arising from the
de facto devaluation of the currency.

10.   Fluctuations on the supply side are caused
by several domestic factors, such as climatic conditions, and on the demand side, by booms or recessions
in the importing country.

11.   See Kenneth J. Rothwell, "Taxes on Exports
in Underdeveloped Countries," Public Finance, XVIII
(Sept.-Dec., 1963), 310-25.

12.   Philip E. Taylor, The Economics of Public
Finance (3rd ed.; New York: The Macmillan Company,
1961), p. 48.

13.   Another source of financing pertains to
foreign aid. Appendix XIV indicates that the countries under study have had substantial assistance
from the United States. Other countries, such as
Ceylon, India, and Indonesia, receive economic and
defense aid from other foreign powers.

14.   Of the total public debt of the Philippines
in 1962, 92 per cent was held internally, and 8 per
cent came from external sources. Of the outstanding
internal public debt, 25 per cent was devoted to budgetary purposes and 75 per cent to developmental.
Long-term public debt accounted for 63 per cent,
middle-term public debt, 14 per cent, and short-term
public debt, 23 per cent. Bonded debt constituted 41
per cent, and nonbonded debt, 59 per cent of the total
debt held by the national government, the local governments, and government-owned or -controlled corporations.

CHAPTER **12** PHILIPPINE GOVERNMENT
EXPENDITURE AND
TAX REVENUE PATTERNS *

GOVERNMENT EXPENDITURES--
PATTERNS AND TRENDS

The functional classification adopted here is
based on the accounts appearing in the Reports of
the Auditor General to the President of the Philippines. Some modifications to conform to more ac-
ceptable conceptual criteria have been made. For
some time now, the functional classification of expenditures in the budget and the reports has followed a five-fold system consisting of economic development, social development, national defense,
general government, and debt service. Expenditures
for peace and order are included under defense and
pensions and gratuities, under general government.

There seems to be no conceptual justification
(except statistical convenience) for segregating national defense from general administration, and for
lumping the maintenance of peace and order under defense expenditures. Expenditures for pensions and
gratuities do not seem to fit in conceptually under
general government expenditures, since such payments
are for past services. The writers believe that the
separate categorization of debt service has no mean-
ing in a functional sense, unless the specific

---

*This chapter was coauthored by Angel Q. Yoingco
and Antonio O. Casem, Jr., Chief Economist of the
Joint Legislative-Executive Tax Commission, Manila.

TABLE 31

Expenditures of the Republic of the Philippines,
by Function, FY 1955-62 (Thousand Pesos)

	1955	%	1956	%
TOTAL	988,540		1,165,023	
Economic Development	243,639	24.65	404,157	34.70
a) Transport and communication	95,458	9.66	161,749	13.90
b) Agriculture and natural resources	73,467	7.43	129,876	11.15
c) Commerce and industry	46,844	4.74	72,975	6.26
d) Other economic development	27,871	2.82	39,557	3.40
Social Development	298,728	30.22	343,036	29.44
a) Education	228,263	23.09	244,794	24.70
b) Public health and medical care	53,714	5.43	72,502	7.96
c) Labor and welfare	16,751	1.70	25,740	2.21
General Administration	360,375	36.50	329,705	28.30
a) General government	153,345	15.51	115,170	9.89
b) National defense	133,868	13.54	126,998	10.90
c) Administration of justice	12,821	1.30	13,495	1.16
d) Maintenance of peace and order	52,153	5.28	65,489	5.02
e) Legislative services	8,188	0.83	8,553	0.73
Miscellaneous	85,798	8.68	88,125	7.56
a) Debt service	63,634	6.44	66,749	5.73
b) Pensions and gratuities	22,164	2.24	21,376	1.83

1957	%	1958	%
1,252,020		1,292,299	
419,102	33.47	397,407	30.75
207,413	16.57	188,339	1.46
118,813	9.50	135,039	10.50
41,782	3.31	49,270	3.81
51,094	4.08	24,759	1.92
409,345	32.69	430,052	33.28
287,754	22.98	293,511	22.72
93,153	7.44	96,315	7.45
28,438	2.27	40,166	3.11
325,615	26.01	391,488	34.29
111,995	8.95	147,969	11.45
137,530	10.98	153,724	11.89
17,565	1.40	18,959	1.46
49,612	3.96	60,173	4.66
8,913	0.71	10,663	0.83
97,958	7.82	73,352	5.67
93,753	7.49	70,177	5.43
4,205	0.34	3,175	0.24

TABLE 31 (continued)

	1959	%	1960	%
TOTAL	1,224,925		1,440,667	
Economic Development	334,349	27.29	412,548	28.69
a) Transport and communication	178,716	14.58	212,281	14.73
b) Agriculture and natural resources	94,070	7.67	115,860	8.04
c) Commerce and industry	31,376	2.56	29,725	2.06
d) Other economic development	30,187	2.46	54,676	3.76
Social Development	442,071	36.08	512,057	35.54
a) Education	305,350	24.92	357,157	24.79
b) Public health and medical care	99,239	8.10	110,121	7.64
c) Labor and welfare	37,482	3.05	44,779	3.10
General Administration	390,330	31.36	418,659	39.06
a) General government	138,531	11.30	156,265	10.84
b) National defense	151,052	12.33	153,396	10.64
c) Administration of justice	20,273	1.65	21,680	1.50
d) Maintenance of peace and order	66,797	5.45	72,921	5.06
e) Legislative services	13,677	1.11	14,397	1.00
Miscellaneous	58,174	4.74	97,402	6.76
a) Debt service	54,855	4.47	79,682	5.53
b) Pensions and gratuities	3,319	0.27	17,720	1.22

Sources: Reports of the Auditor General to the President of the Philippines.

1961	%	1962	%	Average % Total
1,674,985		1,767,700		
529,737	31.62	463,410	26.21	29.66
269,777	16.10	236,244	13.36	29.67
129,003	7.70	108,017	6.11	8.51
69,548	4.15	77,964	4.41	39.16
61,409	3.66	41,185	2.32	
616,143	36.78	667,189	37.74	33.97
411,993	24.59	467,070	26.41	24.28
133,432	7.96	145,007	8.20	7.52
70,726	4.22	55,162	3.12	2.85
451,457	22.95	519,106	29.36	29.73
172,764	10.31	210,612	11.91	11.27
156,158	9.32	160,387	9.08	11.10
26,035	1.55	28,053	1.63	
79,827	4.76	90,494	5.11	
16,673	1.00	28,660	1.62	
77,649	4.63	117,995	6.67	6.55
68,400	4.08	115,759	6.51	
9,249	0.55	2,236	0.12	

Note: Figures may not add up to totals due to
       rounding.

279

purposes for which borrowed funds are spent can be
determined. Hence, gratuities and debt service are
lumped together under a separate category.

The functional classification is rather loose,
since the aforementioned sources do not contain a
sufficiently detailed breakdown of expenditures
which would permit more conceptually valid group-
ings. However, it is hoped that the rather crude
classification will be of some value in the determination of social and economic policy.

The results of these rearrangements appear in
Table 31. Three things are discernible from the
evidence: First, except for 1959, the total level
manifests a consistent rise from about ₱1 billion
in 1955 to about ₱1.8 billion in 1962, or an increase of about 80 per cent. Population increase,
which has averaged 3.2 per cent in the last few
years, has no doubt contributed to this absolute
rise. This is especially true of expenditures which
are a function of population growth. For example,
the outlay for education almost doubled during the
period covered; the same holds true for public
health and medical care. General government expenditures increased from ₱153.3 million in 1955 to
₱210.6 million in 1962.

A relatively large share is accounted for by
social and economic services. On the average, social expenditures constitute 33.9 per cent of the
total, while economic services make up about 29.7
per cent. The sizable portion given to social expenditures does not indicate any ideological predi-
lection toward welfare expenditures of the unproductive and redistributive type as practiced in many
advanced countries (and some less-developed countries, such as Ceylon), because the bulk of social
services expenditure (about 72.2 per cent on the
average) actually goes to education. Furthermore,
of the amount going to welfare and labor, part can
be said to contribute to the improvement of labor
productivity.

This pattern of social expenditures conforms
with the fact that education is of vital significance to development. The only disagreement in this
regard relates to which type of education should be
given greater emphasis; e.g., the general-literacy
type, or the more technically oriented type designed
to create or improve specific skills in the labor
force. In the Philippines the bulk of education expenditure goes toward the fulfillment of a constitutional mandate providing for free public primary in-
struction. This is indicated in Table 32, which
shows the distribution of national government expenditures by organization for the fiscal years 1963-65.
(Education expenditures largely emanate from the national government; hence, the issue of the representative quality of central expenditures is beside the
point.) This table shows that about 88 per cent of
the budget goes to six departments: education, public works, national defense, Office of the President,
finance, health, and agriculture, with education assuming the leading position. For 1963, the Department of Education received the biggest portion of
total expenditures, 24 per cent. If the expenditures for the state universities and colleges are
included, the percentage rises to 26 per cent.

Despite the relatively high ratio of education
expenditures in absolute terms it is still inadequate to meet requirements, as shown by even a cursory look at public elementary education statistics. Studies conducted by the Tax Commission[1]
reveal, among other things, that: (1) out-of-
school children from 1955 to 1963 totaled an average
of over 300,000; (2) an estimated additional expenditure of ₱20 million would be necessary to provide
new classes and defray overhead expenditures; (3)
"about one-quarter of the public school population
is housed in temporary, rented or borrowed buildings," and "about one-third of the school population
is not provided with adequate teaching materials";
and (4) that classes are oversized and children at-
tend only half-day classes.

TABLE 32

Expenditures of the National Government
Classified by Organizations, FY 1963-65
(All Funds Combined in Million Pesos)

Departments	FY 1963 Actual	FY 1964 Estimate	FY 1965 Estimate
1. Congress of the Philippines	34.9	42.4	42.4
2. Office of the President	243.3	269.7	237.6
3. Office of the Vice-President	0.1	0.1	0.1
4. Department of Foreign Affairs	12.7	16.3	17.5
5. Department of Finance	180.8	245.1	398.5
6. Department of Justice	39.4	48.8	50.1
7. Department of Agriculture and Natural Resources	77.0	83.3	102.9
8. Department of Public Works and Communications	346.3	372.9	480.2
9. Department of Education	445.4	512.2	530.8
10. Department of Labor	4.9	6.1	6.1
11. Department of National Defense	248.3	262.5	269.9
12. Department of Health	90.2	90.0	91.8
13. Department of Commerce and Industry	18.1	24.0	26.0
14. Department of General Services	10.1	10.8	12.1

(continued)

TABLE 32 (Continued)

Departments	FY 1963 Actual	FY 1964 Estimate	FY 1965 Estimate
15. Office of Economic Coordination	0.6	0.7	0.7
16. University of the Philippines	24.4	29.1	28.9
17. Mindanao State University	0.7	2.0	2.5
18. National Science Development Board	7.5	8.2	9.8
19. Philippine Normal College	2.0	2.4	2.5
20. Philippine College of Commerce	1.3	1.7	1.6
21. Central Luzon Agricultural College	1.0	1.4	1.4
22. Mindanao Agricultural College	0.9	1.0	1.0
23. Mindanao Institute of Technology	0.9	1.1	1.1
24. Samar Institute of Technology	0.8	0.9	0.9
25. Philippine College of Arts and Trades	1.2	1.4	1.3
26. Itawes Agricultural College	0.1	0.2	0.2
27. Cagayan Valley Institute of Technology	-	0.5	0.5
28. Zamboanga Normal College	-	0.6	0.7
29. Philippine Merchant Marine Academy	-	0.3	0.6

(continued)

283

TABLE 32 (Continued)

Departments	FY 1963 Actual	FY 1964 Estimate	FY 1965 Estimate
30. Philippine Science High School	–	–	0.3
31. Palawan National Agricultural College	–	0.2	0.3
32. General Auditing Office	5.6	7.4	7.7
33. Commission on Elections	4.4	14.9	25.8
34. Supreme Court of the Philippines	1.8	2.3	2.3
35. Court of Appeals	2.3	2.7	2.7
36. Presidential Electoral Tribunal	0.2	0.2	0.2
37. Contingent Fund	11.5	11.0	10.0
38. Salary-Adjustment Fund	3.4	38.0	44.4
39. Foreign-Exchange Fund	10.0	15.2	20.0
40. Calamity Fund	20.0	18.0	10.0
41. Foreign-Assisted Project Peso Support Fund	–	4.5	5.0
42. Consultant's Fund	–	4.0	5.0
Total Expenditures	1,852.1	2,154.1	2,453.4

Source: Budget Document, FY 1965, p. 22A.

The fact that education expenditures are mainly intended to promote general literacy rather than
to meet more immediate technological needs is no indictment against the public education expenditure
policy. At the initial stages of development, any
such indictment does not seem to be warranted.   Education, by its very nature, is an investment in
human capital and has a leavening effect upon future
growth and development. This may well invalidate
current warnings to the effect that social expenditures should give way to expenditures on areas which
are immediately growth-promoting. The latter argument fails to realize that education is essential in
the shaping of basic attitudes conducive to increasing future productivity. There is no denying, however, that as development gathers momentum, there is
the need to provide for the acquisition of more specialized skills via the educational system.

A third point to be noted is that development
expenditures occupy a relatively large share, averaging about 30 per cent. The trend of this item is
more or less erratic. However, within the period
covered, the absolute amount has increased tremen-
dously, from ₱243.6 million to ₱463.4 million, or
90 per cent, a fact indicative of the attempts being
made to meet the pressing demands of a developing
economy. A large portion of total development expenditures (47.9 per cent) goes to the development
of transportation and communication.   In Table 32,
the importance given to this category is indicated
by the key position of the department of public
works and communications, which accounts for 18 per
cent of total national government expenditures. No
detailed analysis of this particular item is available, but the expenditures are probably of the basic
infrastructure type crucial to development. The
second position goes to expenditures for agriculture
and natural resources. Whether this relative distribution is desirable or not is debatable. But
there appears to be some basis to the contention
that the proportion should be the other way around,
in view of the fact that agricultural production
lags behind requirements. The argument is that a

more aggressive role on the part of the government
is necessary to increase agricultural productivity,
if only to minimize the importation of food and
other agricultural products. The importation of
rice, for instance, by a rice-producing country like
the Philippines lends further validity to this contention.

The huge relative share of general administration is due to the sizable portion which goes to defense expenditure and general government, roughly
averaging 37 per cent each of general administrative
expenditures. These two, taken together constitute
22.4 per cent of total government expenditures,
which is an appreciable dent by conservative standards. The optimum amount necessary for orderly
housekeeping is difficult to determine. But current
observation points to the fact that the wage bill is
inflated owing to the intrusion of politics in the
civil service. It is believed that there is a wide
latitude for improving the efficiency of the civil
service. However, the inflation of the wage bill
may be attributed to the operation of Parkinson's
Law, which states that administration grows on its
own regardless of the extent of functions performed.

Defense expenditures are more or less stable at
this period because of relatively stable peace-and-
order conditions. However, it is believed that the
share of defense is high, consisting of 37.4 per
cent of general administration and 11.1 per cent of
total expenditures. This is not to say that defense
expenditures are unproductive per se, but excessive
defense expenditures in less-developed countries
like the Philippines do not usually provide economic
gains. They do not stimulate private investment as
is the case, for instance, in the United States,
where defense contracts sustain many private industries.

The large amount going to defense appears to be
a carry-over of huge outlays which were necessary to
quell the Communist rebellion some years back. The
retention of this relatively large amount under

present conditions seems to suggest that it is easier
to find expenditure outlets than to curtail them
once they are started. There is weight to the contention that defense expenditures should be pared
down to a minimum to release resources for other
areas of economic activity, and that the basic defense needs be left to foreign aid and existing mu-
tual defense arrangements.

GOVERNMENT EXPENDITURE AND
NATIONAL INCOME

Studying government expenditures in absolute
terms can provide some insights into the nature of
the government's participation in the economy. But
a more meaningful approach would be to determine the
government's share in aggregate output--the share of
the government in the total pie, so to speak. Table
33 shows the proportion of government expenditures
to the national income of the Philippines and eight
other countries.

Extreme caution has been taken in interpreting
the figures to avoid statistical pitfalls. National
income statistics of many of the less-developed countries are unreliable; conceptual and statistical
treatments vary from country to country, thus limiting international comparability; and, furthermore, no
functional classification of expenditures on a consolidated basis is readily available. In this regard, a cross-check of the Philippine case reveals
no substantial discrepancy between the consolidated
total and the national government total, owing to
extreme centralization in government finance activities. If the same assumption for the other countries which are more or less of a similar degree of
centralization is adopted, comparability becomes
less tenuous. However, in view of these difficulties, the conclusions or inferences drawn from the
available data should be taken as general approximations.

TABLE 33

Comparative Ratios of Government Expenditures and Tax Revenues to National Income of Selected Asian Countries, 1955-62

	1955	1956	1957	1958	1959	1960	1961	1962	Average	Growth Rate
Burma										
Tax Revenue/National Income	28	23	25	28	28	26	24	29	26	0.7
Government Expenditure/National Income	15	15	20	18	15	22	17	18	18	3.1
Ceylon										
Tax Revenue/National Income	–	21	21	20	19	20	21	22	27	0.5
Government Expenditure/National Income	–	25	29	28	30	30	32	35	28	4.8
India										
Tax Revenue/National Income	–	–	4	6	4	–	5	6	5	6.5
Government Expenditure/National Income	–	17	19	13	13	–	13	15	15	(5.2)
Indonesia										
Tax Revenue/National Income	8	9	8	8	12	18	16	–	11	14.9
Government Expenditure/National Income	13	14	15	20	22	27	33	–	22	17.4
Japan										
Tax Revenue/National Income	–	13	13	15	15	14	15	15	14	2.4
Government Expenditure/National Income	–	14	13	15	15	15	15	16	15	2.5

Malaysia										
Tax Revenue/National Income	18	19	17	16	18	20	17	–	18	(0.1)
Government Expenditure/National Income	23	26	25	27	25	25	31	–	26	3.0
South Korea										
Tax Revenue/National Income	7	11	9	11	16	15	11	12	11	7.0
Government Expenditure/National Income	16	22	25	27	26	24	30	35	25	8.5
Thailand										
Tax Revenue/National Income	11	12	13	19	13	13	14	14	13	2.5
Government Expenditure/National Income	14	15	16	16	16	14	17	18	16	2.4
Philippines										
Tax Revenue/National Income	8	8	9	8	9	9	8	9	9	0.7
Government Expenditure/National Income	13	14	14	14	12	13	14	14	14	0.2

Sources: Economic Bulletin for Asia and the Far East, 1960-1963; U.N. Statistical Yearbook, 1956-1961.

The ratio of expenditure to national income in less-developed economies generally does not exceed 15 per cent. Table 33 indicates this. But, as in many empirical investigations, one is liable to come across unexpected findings. This is true in Ceylon, the Federation of Malaysia, Indonesia, and South Korea, which register ratios comparable to the observed ratio of over 20 per cent in the more-developed countries. In Ceylon and Malaysia this can be partly explained by their ability to tax exports, the mainstay of their economies. In Indonesia this is probably a result of not only the prosecution of "guided democracy," which has placed restrictions on private enterprise, but also of a large standing army. The case of South Korea can be ascribed to defense expenditures designed to keep the country on a constant war footing. Burma's ratio is also believed to be on the high side, and may well be due to socialistic proclivities of the government.

Of these, only Indonesia and South Korea manifest comparatively high rates of growth, in the ratio of expenditures to national income--17.4 and 8.5 per cent, respectively. The corresponding rates of growth for the other countries do not exceed 5 per cent. As an approximate tendency, this lends credence to the hypothesis that, under normal conditions, the extent to which the government can appropriate resources is limited by a country's productivity. The prevalence of abnormal conditions in Indonesia and South Korea, in the form of deliberately imposed restrictions and the threat of war, probably accounts for their growth rates, which are higher than they might be expected to be under normal conditions. Outside of these extraordinary circumstances, the growth of the share of government expenditures follows the slow growth of productivity.

Revenue from Taxation

The foregoing observations on government expenditures become more valid when they are related to tax revenues. Although tax revenues are not a necessary condition for expenditure activities, they

constitute a major constraint. The question as to
what extent expenditures are or should be met by
taxation is not a theoretical exercise, for it has
considerable practical significance. Most, if not
all, of the less-developed countries are undergoing
a stage of structure formation demanding huge capital outlays which are not immediately output-creating,
so that they tend to be inflationary. The government sector traditionally has been assigned a very
active role in this regard.

The paucity of voluntary savings, caused either
by the people's myopic outlook about the future or
simply by an utterly underdeveloped institutional
framework, has sent governments groping for the best
means of finance. Borrowing from the banking system
is easy, except that the fear of inflation and its
concomitant distortion of business expectations pose
a serious restraint. Borrowing from private savers
is of minor significance because of the lack of appropriate institutions, such as a securities market.
Foreign borrowing is of limited use as a continuous
mode of financing, since it may impose severe balance-
of-payments difficulties, especially if such borrowing is of the short-term type. Hence, tax finance
provides a vital alternative of generating savings
and possesses the advantage of being recognizably
noninflationary.

Government Tax Revenues
and National Income

If the logic of relying mainly on taxation to
finance government activities is accepted, the questions arise: how much, from whom, and how? These
questions involve a number of issues relevant to
less-developed economies. For instance, how much of
a country's income can be directed toward the public
sector in terms of taxes without hampering the economy? There seems to be no absolute rule in this respect, although historically it is almost patent
that developed economies can shoulder a much greater
percentage than the less-developed economies could,
such ratio being observed to range from 20 to 30 per

cent. In Table 33, the ratio of tax revenue ranges
from 5 per cent in India to 28 per cent in Ceylon.
With the possible exception of Ceylon, Malaysia, and
Burma, the unweighted average for all the countries
hovers at a low ratio of around 10 per cent. The
three are, for all intents and purposes, considered
to be less-developed countries, but they have surprisingly high ratios.

Considering expenditures and revenues together,
it seems, as indicated in Table 33, that under normal conditions, the share of government expenditures
and revenue varies directly with the level of productivity and, hence, with the stage of development.
Similarly, with the possible exception of Burma, the
ratio of expenditure to national income always exceeds the corresponding ratio of revenue to national
income, with the difference being conspicuous in
South Korea, Indonesia, and India.

There is no absolute optimum ratio of tax revenues to national income, for this depends on a country's political ideology, its patterns of production
and income distribution, and many other indigenous
factors. An approximate guide is that the flow of
tax revenues should follow as much as possible the
historical drift of expenditures toward increasing
demands for a more active role on the part of the
government. In many less-developed countries, post-
war government has become virtually a fetish. This
provides to a certain extent a valid justification
for an increased government draft on private resources. Also, a higher ratio of taxes to national
income is warranted if national income increases ap-
preciably. This means that the tax system should be
responsive to increases in income. In less-
developed economies this increase usually occurs
in the upper 10 per cent of income recipients.

Direct Versus Indirect Taxes[2]

The issue of responsiveness leads to consideration of the structure of the tax system. Public finance literature in less-developed economies is
literally cluttered with the now pervasive notion

that the lagging responsiveness of the tax system to
increases in income is due to the large dependence
on indirect taxes.

It is also the fad among some western authors
to frown upon attempts to increase the relative dependence on direct sources as sheer social and economic luxury, beyond the wildest dreams of these
struggling countries. This pessimistic outlook is
not wholly unjustifiable, since not only are incomes
"underdeveloped," but also the administrative machinery, degree of voluntary compliance, and political maturity. But carried to its extreme, it becomes as deplorable as the situation it seeks to de-
scribe. It is believed that there is wide scope for
increasing reliance on direct taxation.

The comparative dependence of selected countries on direct and indirect tax sources is shown in
Table 34. The underlying pattern confirms the commonly held belief that advanced countries derive a
relatively greater percentage of tax revenue from
direct sources than do the less-developed countries.
The median ratios for the high-, medium-, and low-
income countries are 43, 29, and 20 per cent, respectively. Some countries like Sweden, Denmark,
France, Norway, and West Germany rely more heavily
on indirect sources. Venezuela is an unexpected
member of the high-income group, with a ratio of 63
per cent coming from direct sources. This is probably due to the ubiquity of foreign investments.
The ratio for the Philippines is even below the median of 20 per cent for the low-income group.

The greater reliance on indirect taxes explains
why the incidence of direct taxation in less-developed countries is considered regressive. This means
that the main sources of tax revenue are what Kaldor
terms "articles of mass consumption." As a general
rule, the percentage of income spent on such articles drops as one moves up the income scale, imply-
ing that the wealthier classes are taxed proportionately less.

TABLE 34

High-, Medium-, and Low-Income Countries: Direct
Tax Revenue as Percentage of Total Central
Government Revenue, 1959

High-Income Countries (above $500 per capita per annum)		Medium-Income Countries ($200-$500 per capita per annum)		Low-Income Countries (below $200 per capita per annum)	
United States	80	South Africa	50	Syrian Arab Republic	33
Venezuela	63	Japan	47	Turkey	27
Netherlands	61	Colombia	42	Burma	25
Australia	59	Spain	40	Pakistan	24
Canada	56	Mexico	35	Peru	23
United Kingdom	51	Brazil	34	Korea	22
New Zealand	51	Chile	32	Honduras	21
Sweden	49	Portugal	31	Thailand	21
Denmark	43	Ireland	26	Ceylon	20
Belgium	40	Panama	25	United Arab Republic	20
Israel	35	Argentina	23	Indonesia	18
Austria	33	Italy	22	India	17
France	29	Greece	20	Ecuador	16
Switzerland	27	Lebanon	18	Philippines	13
Norway	27	Costa Rica	17	El Salvador	12
Finland	23	Malaysia	15	Iraq	10
Germany	20			Ghana	10
				Haiti	8
				Guatemala	7
Median	43	Median	29	Median	20

Source: U Tun Wai, "Taxation Problems and Policies
of Underdeveloped Countries," IMF Staff
Papers, IX (November, 1962), 428-48.

294

TABLE 35

Average Effective Rates of Philippine Taxes by Income Class, 1960

Income Class	Number of Families (thousands)	Total Taxes (per cent)	Taxes on Income and Property (per cent)	Taxes on Production and Sales (per cent)
All income classes (including SSS contributions)	4,751	100%	20.2	14.6	5.5
All income classes (excluding SSS contributions)	4,751	100%	19.1	14.2	4.8
Less than ₱ 500	1,206	25.0	23.0	21.3	1.8
₱ 500 - ₱ 999	1,471	31.0	18.7	16.7	2.0
₱ 1,000 - ₱1,499	770	16.2	17.0	14.1	2.9
₱ 1,500 - ₱1,999	502	10.6	17.3	14.4	2.9
₱ 2,000 - ₱2,999	372	7.8	18.6	15.5	3.1
₱ 3,000 - ₱3,999	153	3.2	18.2	15.0	3.2
₱ 4,000 - ₱4,999	98	2.1	16.9	13.9	3.0
₱ 5,000 - ₱5,999	47	1.0	15.7	12.8	2.9
₱ 6,000 - ₱6,999	34	0.7	13.1	10.5	2.7
₱ 7,000 - ₱7,999	20	0.4	14.2	11.4	2.8
₱ 8,000 - ₱8,999	15	0.3	15.7	10.7	5.0
₱ 9,000 - ₱9,999	10	0.2	17.9	12.7	5.2
₱10,000 - and over	53	1.1	33.5	12.2	21.3

Source: A Study of Tax Burden by Income Classes in the Philippines. Joint Legislative-Executive Tax Commission, 1964.

In the case of the Philippines, an observation
of the International Bank for Reconstruction and Development in a survey of the Philippine economy made
in 1960 is relevant:

> The over-all structure of taxation is
> such that revenue receipts are not re-
> sponsive to increases in income. As
> already noted, revenue receipts at ex-
> isting rates may fail to keep pace with
> G.N.P. (gross national product) between
> fiscal years 1960 and 1967. If no new
> taxes are enacted, the Philippine Gov-
> ernment will have to be content with
> playing a receding role in economic ac-
> tivity. Given the needs for public
> expenditures and capital transfers al-
> ready outlined, this outcome would lead
> to a most serious weakening of the eco-
> nomic and social base of the economy.
> If the Philippine Government wants to
> follow purposive economic policies, tax
> revenues must be raised significantly.

THE PHILIPPINE CASE: SOME OBSERVATIONS

As already indicated, the Philippines derives
the bulk of its tax revenues from indirect sources.
Table 36 shows that of total tax collections, an
average of 67 per cent comes from taxes on production and sales. Of this figure, specific taxes,
sales taxes, and import duties occupy the top position.

The big chunk coming from import duties and
fees is due to heavy importations, the average share
of which is 16 per cent over the eight-year period.
The boosting effect of the margin levy (the collection of which was suspended on January 21, 1962) is
shown by the rather sharp increase from 1960 on,
compared to the previous years. Imports are admit-
tedly a major source of revenue in less-developed
countries, because there is a high propensity to

import goods vital to development efforts. Similarly, high tariff rates can be imposed on goods with a high-income elasticity of demand that enter the country either because local production cannot meet the demand, or because "demonstration effects" have created a taste for foreign-manufactured articles. In any case, the percentage of imports to national income is much higher in less-developed countries than in the more advanced ones. For instance, the average ratio for the Philippines from 1955-62 is 12.6 per cent, but it ranges from a low 10.4 per cent to a high 17.5 per cent, compared to a corresponding average ratio (1960-62) of only about 3 per cent for the United States.

Direct taxes constitute an average of about 28.8 per cent, with taxes on corporate and personal incomes (15.5 and 8 per cent, respectively) heading the list.

Tax Incidence

The pattern described above accounts in large part for the view that the tax system of the country is regressive in nature. The Tax Commission, in a recent survey of tax incidence[3] in the Philippines for 1960, confirms this observation. Among the highlights of the study,[4] as gleaned from Table 36, are the following:

1. All income classes, numbering 4,751 thousand families, paid a total tax (including their social security contributions) of 20.1 per cent for every peso earned, or 20 centavos.

2. Of the 20 centavos total taxes paid, 14.5 centavos went to taxes on production and sales, and 5.5 centavos, to taxes on income and property.

3. Families earning between ₱500 and ₱999 a year paid total taxes of 18.7 centavos for every peso earned; 16.7 centavos went to taxes on production and sales, and 2 centavos, to taxes on income and property.

TABLE 36

Tax Collections by Type of Tax, FY 1956-62 (Thousand Pesos)

	1962	%	1961	%	1960*	%	1959	%
Total tax collection	1,293,833	100.0	1,125,929	100.0	1,348,562	100.0	868,309	100.0
Taxes on production and sales	857,212	66.2	759,232	67.4	997,484	73.0	604,561	69.6
Specific taxes	279,723	21.6	260,894	23.2	276,191	20.5	260,768	30.0
Fixed taxes on business and occupations	11,105	0.9	25,754	2.3	9,727	0.7	9,261	1.1
Sales taxes and per- centage taxes	270,060[a]	20.9	217,306[a]	19.3	207,270	15.4	149,515	17.2
Import duties and fees	242,484[a]	18.7	208,322[a]	18.5	457,007[a]	33.9	144,065	16.6
Licenses and fees	53,840	4.2	46,959	4.2	47,289	3.5	41,042	4.7
Taxes on income and property	404,237	31.2	363,328	32.3	337,850	25.1	261,087	30.1
Corporate income tax	204,650	15.8	173,065	15.4	160,766	12.0	117,563	13.5
Personal income tax	106,420	8.2	105,164	9.3	104,769	7.8	66,005	7.6
Motor vehicle tax (private use)	18,431	1.4	17,393	1.5	15,035	1.1	14,312	1.6
Real property tax (private use)	61,564	4.8	56,849	5.0	47,279	3.5	51,021	5.9
Residence taxes	6,980	0.5	5,557	0.5	5,366	0.4	5,655	0.7
Transfer taxes	6,192	0.5	5,300	0.5	4,645	0.3	6,532	0.8
Other taxes	32,384	2.5	3,369	0.3	13,228	1.0	2,571	0.3

	1958	%	1957	%	1956	%	Average %
Total tax collection	840,464	100.0	873,652	100.0	718,903	100.0	100.0
Taxes on production and sales	597,305	71.1	642,935	73.6	507,144	70.6	62.4
Specific taxes	242,180	28.8	237,238	27.2	208,888	29.1	25.8
Fixed taxes on business and occupations	9,035	1.1	14,460	1.7	9,055	1.3	1.3
Sales taxes and percentage taxes	156,749	18.7	177,173	20.3	148,698	20.7	13.0
Import duties and fees	154,029	18.3	181,006	20.7	108,928	15.2	16.3
Licenses and fees	35,312	4.2	33,058	3.8	31,575	4.4	14.7
Taxes on income and property	240,393	29.6	221,669	25.4	209,271	29.1	28.8
Corporate income tax	92,917	11.1	95,523	10.9	83,190	11.6	15.6
Personal income tax	75,122	8.9	58,312	6.7	58,782	8.2	8.1
Motor vehicle tax (private use)	12,508	1.5	11,833	1.4	13,302	1.9	1.5
Real property tax (private use)	48,124	5.7	46,021	5.3	43,729	6.1	5.2
Residence taxes	4,861	0.6	4,478	0.5	3,837	0.5	0.5
Transfer taxes	6,862	0.8	5,502	0.6	6,435	0.9	0.6
Other taxes	2,765	0.3	9,048	1.0	2,488	0.3	0.8

*Calendar year.

aIncludes margin levy.

Sources: Bureau of Internal Revenue, Bureau of Customs, Motor Vehicles Office, and Central Bank of the Philippines.

4. Families earning between ₱5,000 and ₱5,999
paid 15.7 centavos for every peso earned (12.8 centavos went to taxes on production and sales and 2.9
centavos, to taxes on income and property).

5. Families earning between ₱9,000 and ₱9,999
paid 17.9 centavos for every peso earned (12.7 centavos went to taxes on production and sales, and 5.2
centavos, to taxes on income and property).

6. As the income class moves up from the income bracket earning less than ₱500 per annum to the
₱6,999 income bracket, the tax burden declines from
23 centavos to 13 centavos for every peso earned;
from income bracket ₱7,000 to bracket ₱10,000 and
over, the tax burden rises from 14 centavos to 33.5
centavos.

7. The tax burden attributed to taxes on production and sales decreases as income of the families increases (21.3 centavos for every peso earned
by those earning less than ₱500, declining to 10.5
centavos for those in the ₱6,000 bracket, and then
rising to 12.2 centavos for those earning ₱10,000
and over).

8. The tax burden attributed to taxes on income and property increases as the income of the
families increases (1.8 centavos for every peso
earned by those earning less than ₱500, rising to
2.7 centavos for those in the ₱6,000 bracket, and
rising further to 21.3 centavos for those earning
₱10,000 and over).

On the whole, the survey findings indicate that
the burden of the low-income classes is regressive;
the incidence of taxes on production and sales is
regressive; and the incidence of taxes on income and
property is progressive, but not sufficiently to
offset the over-all regressive nature of the entire
tax structure. As pointed out in the same study,
given the distribution of income, if only income and
property taxes were imposed, such taxes would im-
pinge more on the higher-income group than on the
lower-income group, and would therefore be desirable

from a welfare standpoint, i.e., in forcing a more
equitable distribution of income. On the other
hand, if taxes on production and sales alone were
imposed, income inequality would be aggravated.

The Case for Direct Taxes

It is not obvious from the preceding discussion what type of tax should be relied on. The
question is one of political ideology--whether the
tax system should be used as an instrument of welfare or to accelerate economic development. Policy
prescriptions pointing toward the injection of more
progressive elements in the tax system involve more
than a question of improving the distribution of
income through rate adjustment. The broader aspects, such as the effect on work and investment incentives, are of vital consideration, especially at
a stage of development where such incentives need to
flourish.

This does not mean that there is no scope left
for increasing the progressive nature of the tax
system. For one thing, the ratio of direct taxes to
total government revenue is relatively low when
placed in juxtaposition with those of other less-
developed countries, such as India, Thailand, Burma,
Indonesia, Ceylon, and others (see Table 34). Furthermore, as revealed by the above-cited survey,
the upper 10 per cent (₱3,000 and over) of the families surveyed accounts for about two-fifths of total income. Any move to increase the progressive
aspects of the tax system should consider this income group. However, this group also constitutes
the investing class, and extreme care must be taken
to avoid the possibility of dampening incentives.

CONCLUSION

Except for some distortions in the relative
shares of the functional categories of expenditures,
the over-all distribution appears to be in the right
direction. Expenditures for social and economic development feature prominently; however, it seems

likely that expenditures for general administration, particularly national defense and general government, could be reduced without impairing efficient housekeeping operations. It also appears that the historical drift of aggregate expenditures is toward an increase, both in the absolute sense and as a percentage of national income.

With respect to tax revenues, the Philippines' case may well be taken as typical of the less-developed countries, insofar as the lagging response of tax receipts to increases in productivity is concerned. It is also typical of the classic dependence on indirect sources of revenue. The tax system is also generally regressive, which follows the general pattern of less-developed countries.

Taxation is a logical source of finance in the face of rising government expenditures, and in the light of attempts to reconcile the goals of economic growth and stability. On the whole, there is need for more tax revenues. Whether this can be done through greater dependence on direct taxation is a matter for policy to determine. However, it appears that there is scope for increasing the progressive nature of the tax system, subject to careful consideration of work and investment incentives.

There remains a basic problem which deserves more than the cursory attention of policy: This is the matter of improving the efficiency of the tax-collection machinery. From a basic standpoint, tax consciousness in the country is utterly lacking. The Tax Commission survey on tax consciousness in 1960 revealed this fact. Not only is awareness of taxes lacking, but voluntary compliance is deplorably low.

These findings underline the critical need for a comprehensive tax-education program. Beyond this, the responsibility devolves on the government tax machinery. There is as much need for tax education in this area of public administration as there is among taxpayers. The creation of a tax-collection group that is both efficient and beyond moral reproach is imperative. Otherwise, no amount of education for the taxpayers will suffice to bring about the optimum level of tax collection.

Notes to Chapter 12

1. See Joint Legislative-Executive Tax Commission, <u>Third Annual Report, 1961</u> (Manila: Bureau of Printing, 1962), pp. 56-63.

2. The terms "direct" and "indirect" taxes are here taken in their approximate sense to distinguish between those that cannot be and those that can be "shifted." The Tax Commission in its survey relating to the tax burden in the Philippines has used "taxes on income and wealth," and "taxes on production and sales" to avoid terminological problems.

3. The study defined incidence in the narrow Seligman case of determining the ultimate burden of taxation.

4. See Joint Legislative-Executive Tax Commission, <u>Fifth Annual Report, 1963</u> (Manila: Bureau of Printing, 1963), pp. 14-22.

CHAPTER **13** PERSONAL INCOME
TAX STRUCTURE OF
THE PHILIPPINES

INTRODUCTION

The Philippines is among the least-taxed countries in the world. Since 1960, its average tax cut
from the national income was only 10 per cent, compared to more than 20 per cent in Burma, Ceylon, and
Taiwan. A low taxation level is desirable and perhaps ideal if total tax proceeds can meet the needs
of a rapidly expanding population. But the Philippines has yet to provide the basic requirements for
orderly and stable economic development: The revenue from taxation has always been inadequate to cope
with current operating expenses and normal capital
outlays in the national budget. On the average,
taxes were able to finance no more than 80 per cent
of the national budget.

The Marcos Administration has programmed the
allocation of ₱3.4 billion for investment out of the
proposed ₱20.3 billion outlay for 1967-70. This
allocation is earmarked for the financing of infra-
structural and other basic facilities, such as highways, irrigation, water supply, and power development. This level of expenditures for public services
is expected to generate from the private sector an
additional investment of about ₱16.9 billion along
the lines suggested in the program.[1] To partly
finance the government's share, tax revenue will be
increased by ₱115 million annually. The remaining
₱735 million annually will have to come from savings
from current operations, depreciation, reparation,
bond issues, and foreign loans.[2]

There is no other choice but to rely on an efficient tax system and administration if the government is to spearhead and give the necessary push for the realization of the national economic goals. With this situation, three courses of action may be taken: to intensify tax collection; to raise some existing tax rates, and to introduce new taxes. Of course, an intensified tax-collection program is a sine qua non to an effective tax system and the hiking of some existing rates and the introduction of new taxes should be judiciously resorted to.

It has often been said that the burden of the total tax weighs heavily on the low-income earners. Supporting this contention is the fact that 82.3 per cent of total revenue comes from indirect taxes (sales, customs, excise, and other business taxes). Table 37 below shows how the Philippines compares with other countries with respect to direct and indirect tax collections. While the Tax Code establishes some degree of progressivity in the indirect tax structure by imposing heavier sales tax rates on luxury and nonessential items which are generally consumed by persons in the higher-income bracket, the bulk of the taxes nevertheless comes from levies on basic consumer goods predominantly purchased by the low-income group. To bring about a general proportionate increase in sales tax rates without considering the effect of the tax burden on the different income classes would only aggravate the regressivity of the tax system.

HISTORY OF INCOME TAXATION
IN THE PHILIPPINES

Income taxation was introduced in the Philippines by accident, not as a matter of fiscal necessity. It was instituted in the country in 1913 on the authority of the U.S. Revenue Act of 1913, when the country was a territorial possession of the United States. The U.S. Revenue Act of 1918 empowered the Philippine Legislature to modify the various revenue laws applicable in the Philippines to

TABLE 37

Revenue from Taxation of Selected Countries Classified
as to Direct and Indirect Taxes, 1960
(In Million Units of Respective Currency)

Country	Currency	Revenue from Taxation	Direct Taxes		Indirect Taxes	
			Amount	Per Cent Distribution	Amount	Per Cent Distribution
Thailand	Bahts	4,992	640	12.8	4,352	87.2
Philippines	Pesos	1,311	232	17.7	1,079	82.3
Malaya[a]	Malayan dollars	629	132	21.0	497	79.0
Pakistan	Rupees	1,619	362	22.4	1,317	77.6
Burma	Kyats	968	299	30.9	669	69.1
Mexico	Pesos	8,427	3,110	36.9	5,317	63.1
Indonesia[a]	Rupiah[b]	13,020	5,510	42.3	7,510	57.7
Japan	Yen[b]	1,373	682	49.7	691	50.3
Sweden	Kronors	12,280	6,375	51.9	5,905	48.1
Australia	Pound	1,243	742	59.7	501	40.3
Canada	Dollars	4,752	2,871	60.4	1,881	39.6
United States	Dollars	110,514	67,797	61.3	42,717	38.7

[a]Data are for 1959.   [b]In billion.

Sources: U.N. Statistical Yearbook, 1961; Report of the Auditor General to the
President and Congress of the Philippines on Local Governments, 1961.

make them suitable to local conditions. As a result, Public Act No. 2833 was passed by the Philippine Legislature. This act set the rates of 3 per
cent on net income below ₱10,000 earned beginning
January 1, 1920, and provided for graduated rates up
to 23 per cent on net income above ₱5 million. Upon
the recommendation of the first Tax Commission, Commonwealth Act No. 466, otherwise known as the National Internal Revenue Code, was enacted on July 1,
1939, and is still in force. Title II of this act
established a graduated tax on income earned at the
rate of 1 per cent on net income not exceeding
₱2,000 up to 45 per cent on net income in excess of
₱2 million. Soon after World War II, Republic Act
No. 82 was passed on October 29, 1946, increasing to
3 per cent the rate on the lowest net income bracket
not exceeding ₱2,000 and up to 60 per cent on the
highest-income bracket over ₱2 million. These rates
were operative in the years 1946-49, 1953, and 1956-
58. In 1950 Republic Act No. 590 brought about a
significant change in the Philippine personal income
tax law by further increasing the tax rates to 5 per
cent on net income not exceeding ₱2,000 and up to 60
per cent on net income exceeding ₱500,000. Another
change is the authority granted to the government to
withhold taxes due on income.

    The years 1950 through 1959 were characterized
by frequent changes in income tax rates. In 1954
Republic Act No. 1094 again changed the rates on the
net income bracket over ₱6,000 but not exceeding
₱10,000. This was divided into two income classes
of ₱6,000-₱8,000 with a tax rate of 17.0 per cent
and ₱8,000-₱10,000 with a tax rate of 20.0 per cent.
The latest revision in the personal income tax law
was effected by Republic Act No. 2343 on June 20,
1959. The rate on the lowest net income bracket not
exceeding ₱2,000 was reverted from 5 to 3 per cent.
While the applicable rate on the lower net income
bracket has been changed several times since 1950,
the tax rates on the higher brackets were more or
less stable during the same period. Another basic
change introduced by Republic Act No. 2343 is the
"self-assessment" and "pay-as-you-file" system. To

TABLE 38

Income Tax Rates Applicable in the Philippines, 1920-63

TAXABLE INCOME		REVENUE ACT — INCOME YEAR					
Over	Below	Public Act No. 2833 1920-38	Comm. Act No. 466 1939-40	R.A. No. 82 1946-49 1953 1956-58	R.A. No. 590 1950-52	R.A. No. 1094 1954-55	R.A. No. 2343 1959 Present
	(Thousand Pesos)						
—	2						
2	4	} 3	1	3	5	5	3
4	6		2	6	8	8	6
6	8		3	9	12	12	9
8	10		4	} 13	18	17	16
10	20	3½	5	17	24	20	20
20	30	4	6	22	30	24	24
30	40	4½	7	26	36	30	30
40	50	5	8	28	40	36	36
50	60	5½	9	30	42	40	40
60	70	6	10	32	44	42	42
70	80	6½	11	34	46	44	44
80	90	7	12	36	48	46	46
90	100	7½	13	38	50	48	48
100	110	} 8	} 14	} 40	} 52	50	50
110	120					} 52	} 52
120	130	} 8½	} 15		} 53		
130	140					} 53	} 53
140	150	} 9	} 17		} 54		
150	160					} 54	} 54
160	170	} 9½	} 19	} 42	} 55		
170	180					} 55	} 55

		56	56	56		23	10			
220	210				44	25		56	56	56
225	220	57	57	57		27	11	57	57	57
230	225					29				
240	230	58	58	58	46	31	12	58	58	58
250	240					33				
260	250	59	59	59	48	35	13	59	59	59
270	260					37				
275	270	60	60	60	50	39	14	60	60	60
280	275					40				
290	280				52	41	15			
300	290					42	16			
350	300				55	43	17			
400	350					44	18			
450	400				60	45	19			
500	450						20			
600	500						21			
700	600						22			
800	700						23			
900	800									
1,000	900									
1,200	1,000									
1,500	1,200									
2,000	1,500									
2,500	2,000									
3,000	2,500									
4,000	3,000									
5,000	4,000									
	5,000									

Source: Internal Revenue Code

309

effect these, the personal income tax form was simplified so that the taxpayer himself is able to compute the tax due on his income or the refund due him
as a result of excess withholding tax payments.
Table 38 shows the rates by income bracket set by
the different income tax laws from 1920 to the present.

THE CONCEPT OF PERSONAL INCOME TAXATION

Purposes

Classical and neoclassical works on income taxation and writings of twentieth-century economists
distinguish three important purposes of income taxation.

1. Like any other tax, the personal income tax
is a source of revenue. The importance of this
function depends upon the degree of economic development of a given country. The proportion of the
personal income tax to total revenue in more advanced countries is significantly higher than that
in the developing economies. Through the proper
handling of policies on personal income taxation,
the government can have a very effective tool for
increasing revenue and at the same time for promoting the general economic well-being. Through careful selection of the tax base and the right progression of tax rates, the government can maximize revenue collections from the personal income tax. It is
also axiomatic that as the economy progresses, a re-
examination of the personal income tax base and tax
rates could place both the economy and the taxpayers
at maximum advantage.

2. The personal income tax is the best means
for effecting a more equitable distribution of income. A more equitable distribution of income is
vital for economic growth and welfare. Especially
in the developing countries, where the number of income earners tends to concentrate in the low-income
group, carefully calculated progressive income tax

rates could effectively curtail the excessive purchasing power of the high-income class. The taxes
that would accrue to the government, if intelligent-
ly spent for social overhead, could in turn increase
the purchasing power of those who are in the low-
income group. Another merit of the income tax lies
in its "built-in flexibility." It is a self-
adjusting mechanism which can temper purchasing
power in times of inflation and boost it in times
of depression. By means of graduated tax rates, the
individual will be subjected to higher taxes during
periods of prosperity, which will thus reduce his
demand and possibly arrest the creeping inflation.
Conversely, taxable income would slide down to a
lower bracket in times of depression, thereby paving
the way for economic recovery.

3.   Finally, the income tax is a useful tool
for business expansion. In the United States and
other advanced Western European countries where tax
rates are generally high, tax cuts are usually considered to be a means of promoting business expansion. It is argued that cutting the degree of progression or proportionately reducing the graduated
tax rates would bolster the savings capacity of the
income earner-investor group. Such savings could be
channeled either to increase consumption or investment. In either case, business stands to benefit.

However, in most developing countries it is
doubtful whether a policy of tax reduction would be
an incentive for savings and, consequently, investment. Because of the predominance of the low-income
group covered by the income tax law and the prevailing high cost of living in these places, it is likely that most of the additional income that would be
made available to the taxpayer as a result of tax
cuts would be channeled mainly to consumption.

The Harvard Business School has done a series
of intensive studies on the effects of progressive
income taxes on business and investors' incentives
and decisions. The study has shown that an increase
in progressivity does not necessarily restrict

business incentives but only limits, to a certain
extent, the financial capacities of key groups in
the economy, for there are many nonfinancial incentives that drive business management to expand or
improve their current operations. Among these are
the desire to do a good job, the desire for the
power and prestige accompanying responsibility, and
dedication to an organization and its objectives.

However, the same findings may not apply to
countries whose income tax rates are generally low.
Because of the low rate of taxes, both incentives
and financial capacities may not be impaired by a
slight manipulation of tax rates.[3]

Tax Base in Personal Income Taxation

Although amount of income is widely used as a
basis for assessing income tax, economists still
disagree about a concept of "income" that would be
in consonance with the principle of justice in taxation. However, they are agreed on the requisites
as gleaned from a definition advanced by Henry C.
Simons: "Income must be conceived as something
quantitative and objective. It must be measurable;
indeed, definition must indicate or clearly imply an
actual procedure of measuring."[4] Within the context
of these requisites, he states that income should be
defined as the sum total of an individual's consumption and the change in his equity within a given
period as measured in terms of the market price.[5]
This represents the net income which the individual
allocates between consumption and increase in the
earner's wealth. It does not include that portion
of an individual's gross receipts which does not
form part of consumption or wealth accumulation.

The totality of income received by taxpayers,
"gross income," consists of compensation in any form
for services rendered, proprietary income, and production for own use. In spite of the seemingly
clear-cut definition of the scope of gross income,
certain ambiguities which remain make quantification
difficult. It is not clear, for example, whether or

not all economic activities that enhance income
should be included. The poorest families might be
shown to have larger incomes if a value were placed
on their housekeeping work and the yields from their
gardens were included in estimating their income.

Equally difficult to ascertain is net income or
that portion of the individual's gross income allocated for consumption and wealth accumulation. This
requires a clear delineation between consumption and
expense, or "allowable deductions." Individuals'
expenditures might be considered as business expense in one case and as consumption in another.
There are many such types of household expenditures,
such as an automobile that is used for both business
and pleasure.

These divergent concepts point to the necessity
of setting arbitrary decisions in the treatment of
the scope and limitation of income for purposes of
taxation.

Principle of Ability to Pay

The overriding consideration in formulating an
income tax measure is an appropriate basis for setting an optimum set of graduated rates that would
effect equal sacrifices among the various groups of
taxpayers.

There exist divergent views as to the best process of allocating the tax burden. One theory is
that the allocation should follow the "cost" and
"benefit" theory. On this theory, the cost of government incurred to benefit particular individuals
should be borne by the direct beneficiaries of such
government services. This approach is not practicable because of the difficulty of measuring the
cost in terms of benefit enjoyed by an individual,
but its fundamental defect is that it would not allow for the government to undertake services where
the cost or benefit cannot be recovered, as, for
example, relief services.

The other approach is the application of the
"ability-to-pay" principle. "Ability-to-pay" refers
to the relative real sacrifices involved in the payment of taxes. For instance, a person who can give
up a peso from his income with the least personal
sacrifice is the one with the greatest "ability to
pay" the next peso in taxes. This is a case of the
economic law of diminishing utility. This principle
implies a tax base capable of measurement and suggests a schedule of rates which would achieve equal-
ization of the tax burden.[6] The only way the government can maximize collection of the least useful
pesos of society is to have a knowledge of these aggregate amounts, which could be approximated using
the net income as basis. Even so, the use of net
income as a tax base has drawbacks: Two persons
with the same net income but with different numbers
of dependents, financial commitments, consumption
taste, and habits may have a different need for the
extra peso of their net income. However, among several theories, the "ability-to-pay" principle is the
most objective basis in measuring the tax burden
since it avoids moral judgments of each individual's
choices.

Rate of Taxation

Having established the appropriate tax base
from which the tax policy-maker can set the rates,
the next problem is to determine the desirable rates
based on ability to pay. There are three categories
of rate schedules. First, a progressive tax structure, in which the average rate of tax (tax liability as a percentage of income) rises if the income
scale is raised. Second, a proportional tax structure, in which the average rate of tax remains constant as the tax base increases. Third, a regressive
tax structure, in which the average rate falls with
a rise in income.[7] Schedules of income tax rates
are generally progressive, though in varying degrees.

To a large extent, policy objectives dictate
the nature of progression of income tax rates.
Where the intention is to increase revenue (assuming

that all taxpayers are properly discharging their
obligations), the policy-maker resorts to an increase of the tax base or an upward general revision
of the degree of progressivity. However, where the
policy of the tax authority is redistributing income, the shift in the degree of progression, using
a convenient middle-income group as pivot, would be
to effect a reduction in the tax rates on the lower
net taxable income bracket and an increase on the
higher-income group. If the intent is to provide
business incentive or more savings, then a reduction
of progressivity from the middle-income class to the
higher-income class might be effected. Ideally, the
degree of progression should be so constructed as to
provide maximum advantage to society.

Several minor lines of justification buttress
the case for progression. Realizing the government's
intensive and extensive participation in economic activities which need heavy financing from taxation
(public borrowing is presently being utilized to fill
the gap), progression would yield greater revenue
without concomitant undesirable effects on the country. Another positive case for progression is that
it compensates for the regressivity of the indirect
taxes. This argument is valid for developing countries, because any progression of income taxation is
nullified by the regressivity of excise and other
indirect taxes.

Computation of Gross and Net Income
in the Philippines

The gross income of an individual in the Philippines represents his receipts in money and in kind
during the year. These consist of wages, salaries,
interest, dividends, rents, royalties, and profits.
For example, improvements made by a lessee on a les-
sor's property and the rental value of living quar-
ters and meals provided by employers to employees
are included in gross income. Capital gains and
profits from sales or exchanges of capital assets
are also included. For tax purposes, benefit payments received from life insurance, annuities, and

endowments are not part of gross income, for these are not income, any more than are withdrawals from one's own deposit. Gifts and bequests received are also excluded, but the income from such properties is included in gross income. Also excluded are interests on government bonds, compensation for injuries or sickness, income expressly exempt under treaty obligations or by domestic laws, income of foreign governments received from their investments in the Philippines, and income from any public utility accruing to the government or to any of its political subdivisions.[8]

To arrive at net income, certain allowable deductions are authorized. When the gross income is realized from business operations, business expenses, such as wages, cost of materials, interest, and depreciation, are considered allowable deductions. If gross income is derived from sources other than business operations, as, for example, salaries or wages, certain comparable deductions are also allowed, such as interest paid on personal indebtedness. Also deductible are losses from fire, theft, storms, and shipwreck and bad debts, since these items represent impairment of the capital position of the taxpayer, the items lost having been previously purchased with income already subjected to tax. All taxes paid within the year, except income, estate, inheritance and gift taxes, and special assessment, are deductible. Reasonable allowance for depreciation of property and machinery used in the taxpayer's business is also allowed. Finally, contributions to recognized organized charities duly receipted can be deducted from gross income. All these deductions are allowed since they are expenses involved in earning the net income, unusual expenses, and charitable contributions.[9] Personal expenses, outlay for new buildings or improvements, maintenance, premiums on life insurance policies, and losses from sales or exchanges of property between closely related individuals are not deductible.[10]

Exemptions on Net Income

Exemptions are arbitrary amounts necessary to maintain a certain standard of living for the taxpayer which may be deducted from net income. The resulting balance is the net taxable income. Such types of exemptions are allowed to citizens, resident aliens, and nonresidents under certain situations. The personal and living exemptions are: (1) for single persons or married person separated from his or her spouse, ₱1,800; (2) for married couples, ₱3,000; (3) for single persons who are heads of families (single persons with dependent parents, brothers, sisters, legitimate or recognized natural or adopted children), ₱3,000 and (4) for heads of families, an additional exemption of ₱1,000 for each legitimate, recognized natural or adopted child not more than twenty-three years of age who is wholly dependent, unmarried, and not gainfully employed or incapable of self-support because mentally or physically defective.[11]

The distribution of the tax burden is based on "ability to pay." In other words, the government is allowed to share, in varying percentages, with the income of the individual after the cost of producing the income and the cost of minimum livelihood have been deducted. The rates have been set at 3 per cent for net income not exceeding ₱2,000 and increasing to 60 per cent for net income exceeding ₱500,000. For the detailed rates, refer to Table 38.

BRIEF ANALYSIS OF THE PERSONAL INCOME TAX IN THE PHILIPPINES

The survey on tax consciousness conducted by the Joint Legislative-Executive Tax Commission in 1961 showed that there are about 4,388,000 income earners. Income, in the context of the survey, included earnings in cash and in kind, which is consistent with the concept of income in the Tax Code. Of the 4,388,000 income earners, about 56.4 per cent had incomes below ₱1,000; 39.8 per cent earned about

₱1,000 but less than ₱5,000; and an insignificant
3.8 per cent reported incomes about ₱5,000 (Table
39).

TABLE 39

Distribution of Income Earners
by Income Class, 1960

Gross Income Class (pesos)		Number (thousand)	Per Cent Distribution
Total		4,388	100.0
Under	1,000	2,473	56.4
1,000	1,999	1,175	26.8
2,000	3,999	484	11.0
4,000	4,999	91	2.0
5,000	7,999	93	2.1
8,000	15,999	35	0.8
16,000	35,999	18	0.4
36,000	69,999	8	0.2
70,000	119,999	5	0.1
120,000	299,999	4	0.1
300,000	499,999	1	0.1
500,000	Over	1	

Source: Family Income Expenditure Survey 1960, conducted by the Joint Legislative-Executive
Tax Commission.

A married couple with two dependent children
has to earn a gross income of at least ₱5,575 to be
encompassed by the income tax law. However, the
average size of a Philippine family is six. On this
basis, the head of family must have a gross income
of at least ₱8,000 to make him liable to income tax.

It is clear that only about 3.8 per cent of the income earners have taxable income, mainly because of the low income level and the significantly uneven distribution of income earners among the various income classes, conditions that are characteristic of countries in the early stages of economic development. This unequal income distribution suggests the urgent necessity of redistributing income in a manner consonant with the requirements of population growth and economic stability. It should be emphasized that whatever policies the government may adopt to revise the personal income tax system must not, in any way, hurt the low-income earners (those with incomes below ₱5,000) who constitute 96.2 per cent of the total number of income earners in the country.

Another reason for the small percentage of taxable income earners in the Philippines is the high exemptions allowed to taxpayers. A comparison of exemption levels among a few selected industrialized and developing countries shows that the Philippine exemptions rank among the highest (Table 40). The exemption ratio of the Philippines, 62.5 per cent, is slightly lower than those of Australia (68.2 per cent), Japan (65.8 per cent), and Canada (66.7 per cent), but significantly higher than those of the United States (48.0 per cent), Indonesia (48.0 per cent), Pakistan (57.1 per cent), Sweden (31.8 per cent), and Thailand (5.8 per cent). This means that for every unit currency earned by a Filipino taxpayer, a good portion is set aside for family exemptions before the graduated tax rates are imposed. This is one of the reasons for the insignificant number of taxable income earners in this country. An examination of Philippine personal income tax exemptions conducted by Professor Frank H. Golay confirms this. He noted that

> The rates of the Philippine personal
> income tax are moderately progressive,
> with a maximum of 60 per cent on net
> income in excess of ₱500,000. The per-
> sonal exemptions of ₱3,000 and ₱1,800
> plus ₱600 (now ₱1,000) for minor

TABLE 40

Ratio of Personal Exemption to Gross
Income in Selected Countries
(For Family of Four Members)

Country	Currency	Gross Income	Exemption	Ratio of Exemption to Gross Income
Australia	Pound	400	273	68.2
Canada	Dollar	4,500	3,000	66.7
Japan	Yen	380,000	250,000	65.8
Philippines	Peso	8,000	5,000	62.5
Pakistan	Rupee	3,500	2,000	57.1
Indonesia	Rupiah	5,000	2,400	48.0
United States	Dollar	5,000	2,400	48.0
Sweden	Kronor	11,800	3,760	31.8
Thailand	Baht	108,000	6,300	5.8

Sources: Harvard Law School International Program
in Taxation, Taxation in Australia
(Boston: Little, Brown & Company, 1958);
Harvard Law School International Program
in Taxation, Taxation in Mexico (Boston:
Little, Brown & Company, 1957); Harvard
Law School International Program in
Taxation, Taxation in Sweden (Boston:
Little, Brown & Company, 1958); J. Harvey
Peny, Taxation in Canada (3rd ed.; Canada:
University of Toronto Press, 1961);
Douglas S. Paauw, Financing Economic De-
velopment--The Indonesian Case (Glencoe,
Illinois: Free Press, 1960).

dependent are excessively liberal. Such
exemptions are more than seven times the
average per capita income for married
persons who are heads of families and
somewhat more than four times the average per capita income for single persons. Moreover, the rate in the first
income bracket is quite low, 3.0 per
cent. The Philippine rate does not
match the minimum U.S. rate until net
income exceeds ₱10,000. Personal income taxation is excessively liberal
whether appraised in terms of welfare
standards or revenue needs.[12]

During the Second World War, Britain withdrew some
personal exemptions in order to raise more income
"to win the war." This move expanded the number of
taxable persons. However, the exemptions that were
withdrawn were never restored after the war ended.

Another equally important reason for the small
proportion of income taxpayers in the Philippines is
poor tax compliance. Table 39 indicates that in
1960 only 213,000 income earners reported an income
above ₱5,000. Moreover, the records of the Bureau
of Internal Revenue show that only 103,000 persons
paid taxes on their income. This leaves some 110,000
persons who should have filed, most of whom should
have paid income taxes. Of this number, the Tax Commission noted with much concern that more than half
(69,000) of the nonfilers were persons residing in
Metropolitan Manila and surrounding provinces. It
was estimated that had these 110,000 persons paid
their income tax, the government would have realized
a sizable amount in revenue.[13]

In most countries, the income tax plays an important role as a source of revenue. The average
ratio of personal income tax collections to total
tax collection in the developed countries is about
35.0 per cent. In the less-developed countries, the
average ratio stands at about 18.0 per cent. The
ratio in the Philippines is 6.9 per cent (Table 41).

Obviously, the low proportion of revenue from the
personal income tax stems principally from the high
initial tax base, ₱2,000, which is subjected to relatively low tax rates (Table 42).

TABLE 41

Ratio of Personal Income Tax to Total
Tax Collection in Selected
Countries, 1960

Countries	Currency (in mil- lions)	Total Tax Collection	Personal Income Tax	Ratio
Netherlands	guilder	9,546	3,847	40.3
United States	dollar	110,514	43,178	39.1
Canada	dollar	4,752	1,567	33.0
Germany	mark	49,422	14,248	28.8
Japan	yen	1,373	391	28.5
Indonesia*	rupiah	13,020	2,313	17.8
Peru*	soles	4,776	798	16.7
Pakistan	rupee	2,393	338	14.1
Philippines	pesos	1,311	91	6.9

*For fiscal year 1959.

Source: United Nations Statistical Yearbook, 1961.

TABLE 42

Lowest Net Taxable Income and Lowest Rate
of Tax of Selected Countries, 1960

Countries	Currency	Gross Income	Lowest Net Taxable Income	Ratio	Lowest Rate of Tax
Sweden	kronor	13,000	8,000	61.5	11.0
Indonesia	rupiah	5,000	3,000	60.0	3.0
Thailand	baht	19,000	10,000	52.6	10.0
United States	dollar	5,000	2,000	40.0	20.0
Japan	yen	500,000	150,000	30.0	10.0
Pakistan	rupee	3,500	1,000	28.6	25.0
Philippines	peso	8,000	2,000	25.0	5.0
Australia	pound	400	100	25.0	0.42
Canada	dollar	4,500	1,000	22.2	11.0

Source: Harvard Law School   International Program in
Taxation, World Tax Series (Boston: Little,
Brown & Co.).

The lowest taxable income of the Philippines is significantly lower than those of her neighboring countries. The comparison is clearest when the tax base
is expressed as a ratio to gross income: The Philippine ratio stands at only 25.0 per cent compared to
those of Indonesia (60.0 per cent), Japan (30.0 per
cent), Pakistan (28.6 per cent), and Thailand (52.6
per cent).

The effective rates of the Philippine income tax
are also lower than those of other countries with a
similar level of economic development (Table 43).
This means that the proportion of tax cut to net taxable income of the Philippines is among the lowest.
This observation is significant since, as noted in
Table 40, our allowance for exemptions is comparatively liberal. On the lowest-income bracket, the
Philippine effective rate at 3 per cent is significantly lower than those of Thailand (10 per cent),
Pakistan (25 per cent), Japan (10 per cent), and
Canada (11 per cent). Similarly, on the highest-income bracket, the Philippine effective rate is 53
per cent, which is also lower than those of Australia
(56.6 per cent), Canada (67 per cent), Indonesia
(74.5 per cent), Japan (57 per cent), and the United
States (67 per cent).

Despite the fact that the majority of income
earners are in the lower-income brackets the bulk
of total income tax assessment comes from the high-
income groups (Table 44). Expressed in quantitative
terms, in 1960 almost two-thirds (64.1 per cent) of
those who paid income tax had gross incomes below
₱8,000 or a net taxable income of below ₱2,000.
Their average tax burden was only ₱22. In relation
to gross income, this average shows that these taxpayers pay a tax of only one-third of a centavo for
every peso earned (the "effective rate of the tax").
This group comprises 63.5 per cent of all taxpayers
in the country. On the other hand, persons with net
taxable incomes reaching ₱100,000 paid an average
tax of ₱34,127 (on gross receipts of about ₱116,000),
or about twenty-nine centavos per peso gross income;
those with taxable incomes exceeding ₱400,000 but not
more than ₱500,000 paid a per capita tax of about
₱239,000 or 42.7 centavos per peso gross earning;
and those with net taxable incomes beyond ₱500,000
paid ninety-six centavos per peso earned. Only 305,
or less than 1 per cent of the total number of taxpayers, had taxable incomes in excess of ₱100,000.

TABLE 43

Exemptions, Tax Base, and Effective Rates of Tax of Selected Countries

Country	Currency	Exemptions		Tax Base		Effective Rate	
		Head of Family	Each Dependent	Lowest Net Taxable Income	Highest Net Taxable Income	Lowest (per cent)	Highest (per cent)
Australia	pound	143	65	100	16,000	0.42*	52.6
Canada	dollar	2,000	500	1,000	400,000	11	67
Indonesia	rupiah	*	600	3,000	10,000,000	3	74.5
Japan*	yen	200,000	50,000	150,000	50,000,000	10	57
Mexico	peso	*	*	300	50,000	1.5	27
Pakistan	rupees	2,000	a	1,000	70,000	25	47
Philippines	peso	3,000	1,000[a]	2,000	500,000	3	53
Sweden	kronor	3,760[b]	*	8,000	150,000	11	48
Thailand	baht	6,000	1,000	10,000	400,000	10	28
United States	dollar	1,200	600	2,000	400,000	20	67

* No exemptions allowed.

[a] No exemptions allowed; however, exemption on investment allowance and accrued income relief are granted.

[b] Average exemption only.

Sources: Harvard Law School International Program in Taxation: Taxation in Australia (Boston: Little, Brown & Company, 1958); Taxation in Mexico (Boston: Little, Brown & Company, 1957); Taxation in Sweden (Boston: Little, Brown & Company, 1958); J. Harvey Peny, Taxation in Canada (3rd ed.; Canada: University of Toronto Press, 1961); Douglas S. Paauw, Financing Economic Development--The Indonesian Case (Glencoe, Illinois: Free Press, 1960).

TABLE 44

Tax Burden and Effective Rates of Income in the Philippines,
by Income Class, 1960

Gross Income* (pesos)	Net Taxable Income	Number of Taxpayers	Tax Assessed (thousand pesos)	Average Tax Burden (pesos)	Average Effective Rate (per cent)
Below 8,000	2,000	65,578	1,407	22	0.3
10,000	4,000	15,905	1,906	120	1.2
12,000	6,000	7,122	2,333	328	2.7
14,000	8,000	3,883	2,310	595	4.3
17,000	10,000	2,465	2,515	1,020	6.0
28,000	20,000	4,482	9,140	2,039	7.3
38,000	30,000	1,618	7,955	4,917	12.9
50,000	40,000	749	5,602	7,479	15.0
60,000	50,000	440	5,614	12,759	21.3
71,000	60,000	272	4,386	16,125	22.7
82,000	70,000	145	3,086	21,283	26.0
94,000	80,000	95	2,464	25,937	27.6
105,000	90,000	66	1,956	29,636	28.3
116,000	100,000	63	2,150	34,127	29.4
138,000	120,000	80	3,361	42,013	30.4
149,000	140,000	51	2,643	51,823	34.8

172,000	160,000	27	1,721	63,741	37.1
227,000	200,000	38	3,002	79,000	34.8
283,000	250,000	18	1,958	108,778	38.4
338,000	300,000	13	1,886	145,077	42.9
450,000	400,000	8	1,437	179,625	39.9
560,000	500,000	7	1,673	239,000	42.7
Over 560,000	Over 500,000	2	6,454	537,833	96.0
Nonresident aliens		200	178	890	

*Computed on the assumption that income earners are heads of family with two dependent children, to allow for the fact that some taxpayers are unmarried.

Source: Bureau of Internal Revenue.

CONCLUDING COMMENTS

In theory and practice, the Philippine personal
income tax follows the basic tenets of a good personal income tax system. However, certain problems
in policy formulation and implementation need to be
dealt with.

There is a need for a more intensified tax collection, a re-examination of the income tax base,
and a revision of the tax rates to effect a desirable progressivity that is more in consonance with
the ability to pay principle.

Intensification of tax collection is imperative
so that income tax may become a significant source
of revenue. It was pointed out earlier that about
110,000 income earners with gross incomes of at least
₱5,000 did not file or pay taxes on their income.
A similar study of the Joint Legislative-Executive
Tax Commission[14] showed that out of the estimated
202,000 businessmen and professionals, only 20.4 per
cent of the former and 46.4 per cent of the latter
paid income taxes. Of course it is possible that
many of these persons might not have been subject to
payment due to exemptions and deductions allowed.
Nevertheless, remedial measures should be applied to
improve tax compliance. The incidence of tax evasion could be diminished significantly by removing
loopholes and strengthening tax administration and
enforcement. A great number of evaders could be
ferreted out if a complete tax register were to be
set up. As a long-run measure to improve tax compliance, a program to increase tax consciousness
should be undertaken through education and the mass
media.

If the resulting improvements in the tax-collection machinery are still not sufficient to meet the
expanding needs of the government, the personal income tax could be made to yield more by decreasing
the amount of allowable exemptions. For example, if
the exemption for a head of a family is reduced to
₱2,000 and for every dependent to ₱600, the tax base

of all taxpayers would be raised to the next taxable
income bracket. This would mean an added 480,000
taxpayers in addition to the 303,000 persons now
liable. Also, the exemption ratio would decrease
from 62.5 per cent to 53.3 per cent, which is still
high in comparison to those of other countries.

A third recourse involves the relatively low
effective rates in both the lowest and highest net
taxable income brackets which could provide the tax
policy-makers a wide latitude of action in manipu-
lating the tax rates to the fullest advantage of the
government and the taxpayers. Three courses of action could be followed to alter the present tax rates
and achieve progressivity. First, a reasonable rate,
perhaps 5 per cent, might be levied on the lowest
taxable income bracket (whose average gross income
is now about ₱5,000) with the rates rising in a de-
gressive manner up to a bracket of ₱10,000. This
action would certainly raise the revenue since it
would affect 92.1 per cent of the present taxpayers.
Alternatively, the tax policy-makers could maintain
the initial 3 per cent rate, but at the same time reduce the initial taxable bracket from ₱2,000 to
₱1,000. Second, the current rates on taxable income
not exceeding ₱10,000 could be maintained, and progressive but degressively increasing tax rates could
be applied from the bracket of ₱10,000 and over. In
addition to increased collections, further income redistribution could be achieved, but this step would
have the concomitant result of restricting the savings and investment capacity of the higher-income
groups. Third, a proportional increase in the tax
rates on all taxable brackets might be resorted to.
This action would not only restrict the savings capacity of all income groups but also maintain the
present inequitable distribution of income. The
only sector that would be benefited would be the government. Any attempt on the part of tax policy-
makers to revise the allowable exemptions and the
tax rates and their progressivity should not necessarily be viewed as detrimental to the low-income
group. Insofar as income taxation is concerned,
only the upper 15.6 per cent, at most, of the total

income earners would be affected by such revisions.
Under the present law, only 3.8 per cent of all income earners is affected by the income tax.

What should be of paramount consideration in
the process of tax revision are the effects on the
taxpayers. Before any revision is attempted, the
loopholes in the law should first be plugged; otherwise, the progressive adjustment of rates would only
aggravate waste and inefficiency in the economy. So
long as these defects in the income tax law persist,
increased progressivity past a given point would
only drive more taxpayers to use all the loopholes
to avoid payment of taxes.

Notes to Chapter 13

1. National Economic Council, Republic of the
Philippines, Four-Year Economic Program for the Philippines, Fiscal Years 1967-1970, pp. 11-13, 54-59.

2. Ibid., pp. 26-27.

3. J. Keith Butters, "Taxation, Incentives,
and Financial Capacity," in A. E. A. Readings in Fiscal Policy (Homewood, Illinois: Irwin, Inc., 1955),
pp. 502-18.

4. Henry C. Simons, Personal Income Taxation
(Chicago: The University of Chicago Press, 1938),
p. 42.

5. Ibid., pp. 49-51.

6. Philip E. Taylor, The Economics of Public
Finance (New York: The Macmillan Co., 1955), p. 247.

7. R. A. Musgrave and Tun Thin, "Income Tax
Progression, 1929-48," The Journal of Political
Economy, LVI (December, 1948), 498-514.

8. _National Internal Revenue Code_, Sections
29, 37.

9. _Ibid._, Section 30.

10. _Ibid._, Section 31.

11. _Ibid._, Section 23.

12. Frank H. Golay, _The Philippines: Public
Policy and National Economic Development_ (Ithaca,
New York: Cornell University Press, 1961), p. 189.

13. _Fourth Annual Report_, Joint Legislative-
Executive Tax Commission, p. 30.

14. _Survey on Tax Consciousness in the Philip-
pines_, Joint Legislative-Executive Tax Commission,
1962, p. 17.

CHAPTER **14** TAX BURDEN AND
INCOME DISTRIBUTION
IN THE PHILIPPINES

INTRODUCTION

Taxation is not always borne by the statutory taxpayer, for the tax burden can be transferred or "shifted." "Shifting" refers to the movement of the tax burden from the statutory taxpayer ("impact" or "legal incidence") to the ultimate taxpayer. The shifting may be backward or forward, partial or total, depending upon the kind of tax, cost conditions, demand-and-supply elasticities, the market structure, and other exogenous factors.[1] The individual effects of these factors on shifting and incidence are difficult to quantify. The various factors are so closely interrelated that no one can be conceptually isolated from the others without distortion. Nonetheless, incidence studies in a partial equilibrium setting can provide some useful approximations.

From a policy standpoint, the importance of determining or approximating the tax burden cannot be overstated, for any policy prescription requires it. Knowledge of tax-burden distribution is necessary in order to evaluate such fiscal actions as increasing existing tax rates, enacting new revenue measures, and repealing or revising old ones, and it is necessary in order to appraise the probable effects of such measures on revenue yield, incentives, and the rate of capital formation. Realizing these needs, the Joint Legislative-Executive Tax Commission, a bi-partisan research body created in 1959, undertook a pioneering study on tax burden by income class in the Philippines.

ASSUMPTIONS AND METHODOLOGY

The Commission's study is based on their 1961
survey of distribution of family income by income
class and expenditures on selected commodities. It
is also based on data on tax collections compiled
from reports of the Bureau of Internal Revenue, the
Bureau of Customs, the Budget Commission, the General Auditing Office, and other government agencies.

To facilitate the allocation of taxes among
households in different income classes, various assumptions were made. The total households (each consisting of six members) were classified into thirteen income classes, ranging from less than ₱500 to
₱10,000 and over. Family households with income of
less than ₱2,000 were regarded as the low-income
group; those with income of ₱2,000 but less than
₱10,000, the middle-income group; and those with income of ₱10,000 or more, the high-income group.

The various taxes were classified into two
broad groups: (1) taxes on production and sales,
and (2) taxes on income and property. This classification was designed to avoid the difficulties in
terminology that arise with respect to the distinction between direct and indirect taxes.

After these classifications were made, the problem was to apportion the tax burden among the various households belonging to the different income
classes. ("Tax burden" here was taken to mean the
money burden arising from the payment of a tax.)
On income and property, the burden was apportioned
among the various income classes according to the
pattern of income earned or the property owned; on
production and sales, the burden was allocated among
the households according to their patterns of expenditures. As far as possible, the various factors
affecting shifting, such as market structure and
elasticities, were taken into account.

Two ratios were estimated: the average money
burden[2] and the effective rate.[3] The average money
burden is the tax burden per unit of household,

while the effective rate of tax or effective tax burden is the ratio of total taxes paid to gross income.
A tax is regressive if the effective rate decreases
as income increases, proportional if the effective
rate is constant as income increases, and progressive
if the effective rate increases as income increases.

MAJOR FINDINGS OF THE STUDY

Among the significant findings revealed by the
study are the following:

1. The average tax contribution of family
households (4.8 million), including social security,
is ₱297 out of an annual average income of ₱1,474
(Chart 11). Excluding social security contributions
(which are not strictly taxes), the average money
burden is estimated at ₱281.

The money burden per household in the low-
income group is ₱154; the middle-income group, ₱608;
and the high-income group, ₱6,598. If this money
burden were to be allocated between the two broad
groups of taxes, the burden of taxes on production
and sales is ₱133 for the low-income group, ₱495 for
the middle-income group, and ₱2,407 for the high-
income group. The burden of income and property
taxes is ₱21 for the low-income group, ₱113 for the
middle-income group, and ₱4,191 for the high-income
group.

2. The over-all effective tax rate is 20.2 per
cent. This means that for every peso income of a
family household, ₱0.20 go to taxes. Of this amount,
₱0.15 are in the form of production and sales taxes
and about ₱0.05 represent taxes on income and property. If social security contributions were excluded,
the effective rate would be 19.0 per cent or ₱0.19
out of every peso income.

As an individual moves up the income scale, the
effective rate decreases from 19.5 per cent in the
low-income group to 17.7 per cent in the middle-
income group. However, it moves up steeply to 33.2

CHART 11

COMPOSITION OF THE TAX BURDEN OF THE FILIPINO HOUSEHOLD
(Per Peso Income)

* Household average tax burden, ₱ 297; divided into

    production and sales taxes, ₱ 215

    income and property taxes, ₱ 82

* Average tax burden of low-income household, ₱ 154
* Average tax burden of middle-income household, ₱ 608
* Average tax burden of high-income household, ₱ 6,598

LEGEND: ☐ Income and Property Taxes

      ▨ Production and Sales Taxes

AVERAGE HOUSEHOLD

5 ctvs

15 ctvs

HIGH-INCOME HOUSEHOLD

21 ctvs

12 ctvs

MIDDLE-INCOME HOUSEHOLD

3 ctvs

15 ctvs

LOW-INCOME HOUSEHOLD

2 ctvs

17 ctvs

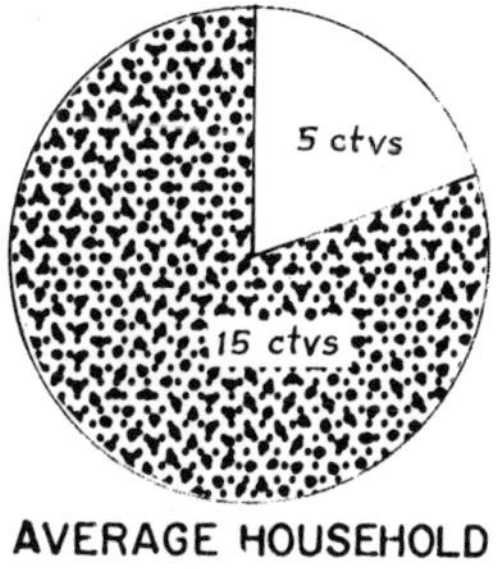

per cent in the high-income group. The effective
rates of taxes on production and sales for the broad
income groups are 17.3, 14.5, and 12.2, respectively;
with respect to taxes on income and property, the
corresponding effective rates are 2.2, 3.1, and 21.3
per cent, respectively.

On the whole, the tax structure is generally regressive, despite the steep movement of the effective
rate from 17.7 per cent in the middle-income group to
33.2 per cent in the high-income group, largely because taxes on production and sales are the predominant source of government revenue. Similarly, the
bulk of households and expenditures is concentrated
in the middle- and low-income groups. Chart 13
shows, at greater portions of the curves, the regressive character of the tax system. The portion of the
curves with a clearly progressive character covers
only about 2.4 per cent of total households and is
brought about largely by the steep portion of the
effective rate curve of taxes on income and property.

Compared with the effective rates in other countries, that of the Philippines is considerably lower.
In the United States the effective tax rate including social insurance is 27.6 per cent. In the United
Kingdom the effective tax rate is 32.1 per cent; in
Germany, 32.6 per cent; in France, 30.5 per cent;
and in Italy, 26.7 per cent.[4]

3. Revenue from taxation in 1960 totaled
₱1,426.1 million. Of this amount, about ₱1,024.3
million, or 71.9 per cent, represent collections
from taxes on production and sales, and about ₱388.6
million, or 27.3 per cent, collections from taxes on
income and property. The breakdown of collection
from major taxes on production and sales is shown in
Table 45.

Collections from taxes on income and property
came from the sources shown in Table 46.

TABLE 45

Tax Revenue from Production and Sales

	Amount (million pesos)	Per Cent of Total Taxes
T O T A L	₱1,024.3	71.9
Import duties, fees and the margin levy	459.5	32.2
Specific taxes	276.2	19.3
Sales taxes and other percentage taxes	207.3	14.5
Other taxes, licenses, and fees	47.3	3.3
Social security contributions (employer)	26.8	1.9
Fixed taxes on business and occupation	9.7	0.7

TABLE 46

Tax Revenue from Income and Property

	Amount (million pesos)	Per Cent of Total Taxes
T O T A L	₱388.6	27.3
Corporate income tax	160.8	11.3
Personal income tax	104.8	7.4
Social security contributions (public and private employees)	50.7	3.6
Real property taxes (personal use)	47.3	3.3
Motor vehicle tax (registration fees and drivers licenses	15.0	1.0
Residence tax	5.4	0.4
Transfer taxes	4.6	0.3

Of the fifty-seven different types of taxes, only ten are principal revenue sources, for they accounted for ₱1,196.6 million or 83.9 per cent of total tax collections in 1960 (Chart 12). Six are classified as taxes on production and sales. These are the margin levy[5] which totaled ₱216.1 million; special import tax,[6] ₱165.7 million; specific tax on tobacco (including tobacco inspection fees), ₱150.2 million; sales taxes, ₱121.1 million; taxes on fuel and oils, ₱91.1 million; and customs duties, fees and charges, ₱75.3 million. These taxes accounted for ₱820.9 million or 68.5 per cent of ₱1,196.6 million. The other four are taxes on income and property. These include the corporate income tax which yielded ₱160.8 million; personal income tax, ₱104.8 million; social security contributions of both public and private employees, ₱50.7 million; and real property tax, ₱47.3 million. Collections from these four taxes amounted to ₱376.4 million or 31.5 per cent of the total collections from the ten major revenue sources.

These figures indicate that of the total revenue from taxation, about 72 per cent was derived from taxes on production and sales and about 28 per cent from taxes on income and property. The ratio of direct tax collections to total revenue from taxation is relatively low compared with those of countries in a similar stage of economic development.[7] In Indonesia the ratio of direct taxes to total tax collections is 42.5 per cent; South Korea, 33.7 per cent; Laos, 42.5 per cent; and Singapore, 33.6 per cent. It is relatively higher, however, than those in Thailand and Cambodia, which are 9.2 per cent and 7.9 per cent, respectively.

4. The survey on household income and expenditures[8] indicates that in 1960 there were around 4,751,000 family households, of which 83.1 per cent belong to the low-income group, 15.8 per cent to the middle-income group, and 1.1 per cent to the high-income group (Chart 13). Of those belonging to the low-income group, about 1,206,000 family households or 25.6 per cent had incomes of less than ₱500 and another 1,471,000 family households or 31.0 per cent

CHART 12

REVENUE FROM TAXATION, 1960
(In Millions)

10 MAJOR SOURCES OF REVENUE

* MARGIN LEVY
* SPECIAL IMPORT TAX
* CORPORATE INCOME TAX
* SPECIFIC TAX ON TOBACCO (including inspection fees)
* SALES TAX
* PERSONAL INCOME TAX
* SPECIFIC TAX ON FUELS AND OILS
* CUSTOMS DUTIES, FEES AND CHARGES
* REAL PROPERTY TAX
* SOCIAL SECURITY CONTRIBUTIONS (public and private employees)

LEGEND:

Revenue from 47 other types of taxes

Revenue from 10 major types of taxes

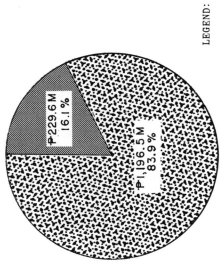

₱229.6 M
16.1%

₱1,196.5 M
83.9%

TOTAL REVENUE = ₱1,426.1 M

CHART 13

NUMBER OF FAMILY HOUSEHOLDS BY INCOME CLASS, 1960
(In Millions)

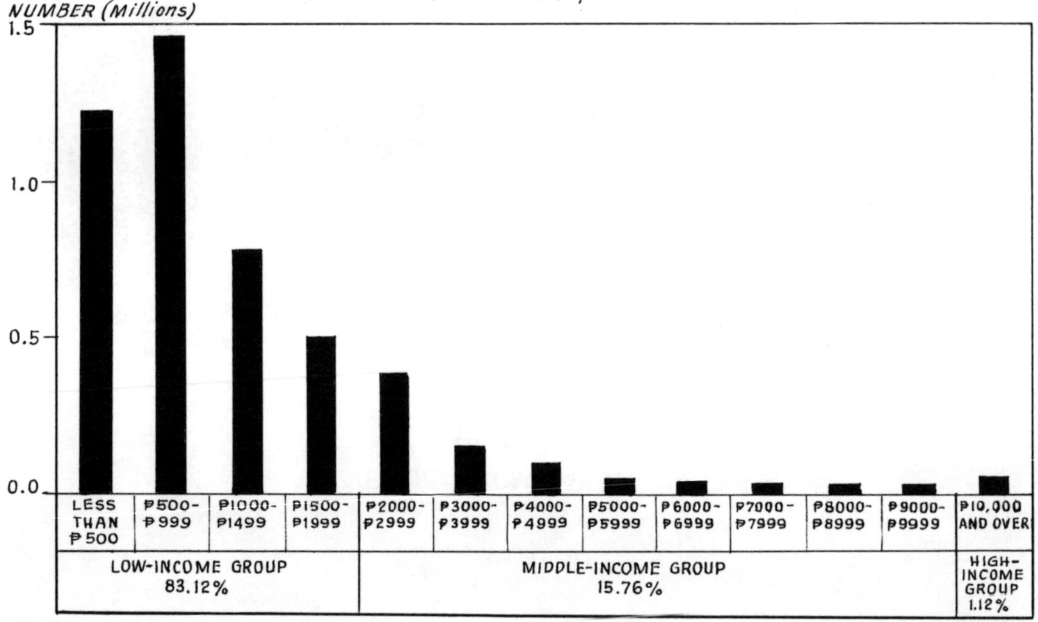

cf all family households had incomes of more than
₱500 but less than ₱1,000. These figures indicate
that a very large portion of the population is concentrated in the low-income strata.

The significant inequality in the distribution
of income in the Philippines is confirmed in Table 47.

TABLE 47

Distribution of Income in the Philippines

Cumulative Percentage of House- holds	Cumulative Percentage of Income			
	Before All Taxes	After All Taxes	After Taxes on Income and Property	After Taxes on Production and Sales
Lower 20	4.2	4.6	4.9	3.9
Lower 50	17.3	17.9	18.2	16.7
Lower 90	57.8	59.7	60.2	57.2
Upper 10	42.2	40.3	39.8	42.8

The lower 20.0 per cent of the total households in
the Philippines own only about 4.2 per cent of total
income. The cumulative 50.0 per cent of households
share about 17.3 per cent of total income. The proportion of total income owned by the cumulative 90.0
per cent of households from the lowest-income group
is about 57.8 per cent. This means that about 42.2
per cent of total income is owned by only 10.0 per
cent of the total households.

It was further revealed that the total income
of households amounted to ₱7,004.0 million. The average income per household is about ₱1,474. For all
households, the income in cash amounted to ₱5,443
million or 77.7 per cent of total income, while income in kind was valued at ₱1,561 million or 22.3
per cent. The smaller the income of households,

the greater is the relative proportion of income in
kind to total income. For the low-income group, income in kind constitutes 30.4 per cent of total income, while it is only 16.9 per cent of total income
for the middle-income group. For the high-income
group, income in kind constitutes only 12.4 per cent
(Table 48).

5. Of total expenditures of family households,
about 50 per cent is for food and about 21.5 per cent
is for household furnishings and equipment (Chart 14).
Miscellaneous expenses, including those for services
and transportation, comprise about 10.5 per cent.
Outlays for clothing and footwear represent about 8.5
per cent of aggregate family household expenditures.
Expenditures for luxuries, alcoholic beverages, and
tobacco products constitute about 3.1 per cent and
6.4 per cent, respectively. On the whole, about 80
per cent of aggregate expenditures, or ₱0.80 out of
every peso spent, goes to basic necessities and
about 20 per cent, or ₱0.20, goes to luxury items
(Table 49).

OBSERVATIONS AND ANALYSIS

These findings bring into focus two striking
facts about the Philippine tax system: The over-all
tax structure is mainly regressive and revenue productivity is low.

Although taxes on income and property are essentially progressive, they have done very little to
offset the regressivity of taxes on production and
sales (Chart 15). Heavy dependence on taxes on production and sales contributes significantly to the
regressivity of the whole tax system. This is so
because households in the low-income group shoulder
a relatively heavier burden with respect to production and sales taxes because 99 per cent of their
spending money goes for basic necessities, while the
middle-income and high-income groups spend only
about 70 per cent. This means that about 30 per
cent is spent on luxury goods by the latter groups.
In other words, the tax yield from taxes on production

TABLE 48

Family Income by Income Class, 1960

Income Class	Number of Family Households		Income (thousand pesos)			Average Income (pesos)
	Total (thousand)	Per Cent Distribution	Total	Cash	In Kind	
ALL INCOME CLASSES	4,751	100.00	7,004,047	5,442,604	1,561,443	1,474
Less than ₱500	1,206	25.38	422,100	227,512	194,588	350
₱ 500 - ₱ 999	1,471	30.96	1,082,656	708,057	374,599	736
₱1,000 - ₱1,499	770	16.21	939,400	684,823	254,577	1,220
₱1,500 - ₱1,999	502	10.57	855,910	677,025	178,885	1,705
₱2,000 - ₱2,999	372	7.83	878,292	715,808	162,484	2,361
₱3,000 - ₱3,999	153	3.22	516,069	439,691	76,378	3,373
₱4,000 - ₱4,999	98	2.06	433,552	378,057	55,495	4,424
₱5,000 - ₱5,999	47	0.99	255,163	228,371	26,792	5,429
₱6,000 - ₱6,999	34	0.71	216,444	179,865	36,579	6,366
₱7,000 - ₱7,999	20	0.42	140,120	111,395	28,725	7,006
₱8,000 - ₱8,999	15	0.32	127,980	105,328	22,652	8,532
₱9,000 - ₱9,999	10	0.21	92,420	72,180	20,240	9,242
₱10,000 and over	53	1.12	1,043,941	914,492	129,449	19,697

Source: A Study of Tax Burden by Income Class in the Philippines, Joint Legislative-Executive Tax Commission, 1964.

CHART 14

PROPORTIONATE EXPENDITURES FOR CONSUMPTION ITEMS
AT DIFFERENT INCOME LEVELS, 1960

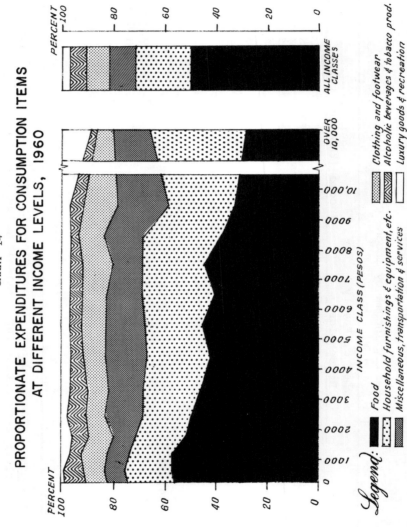

Legend:
Food
Household furnishings & equipment, etc.
Miscellaneous, transportation & services
Clothing and footwear
Alcoholic beverages & tobacco prod.
Luxury goods & recreation

344

TABLE 49

Per Cent Distribution of Family Expenditure by Major Category
of Expenditure by Income Class, 1960

Income Class	Total Expenditures (thousand pesos)	Per Cent of Total Expenditure by Income Class					
		Food	Alcoholic Beverages & Tobacco Products	Clothing and Footwear	Household Furnishings and Services	Luxury Goods and Recreation	Miscellaneous
ALL INCOME CLASSES	8,120,203	49.98	6.41	8.54	21.47	3.14	10.46
Less than ₱500	801,990	55.85	8.72	8.23	18.75	2.01	6.44
₱ 500 - ₱ 999	1,628,397	56.62	7.66	8.76	18.07	1.94	6.95
₱1,000 - ₱1,499	1,164,240	56.84	7.07	8.85	17.80	2.17	7.26
₱1,500 - ₱1,999	1,049,682	52.54	6.24	8.72	19.05	4.64	8.80
₱2,000 - ₱2,999	1,092,192	49.78	5.31	8.07	19.65	2.16	15.02
₱3,000 - ₱3,999	600,066	44.26	6.79	8.27	24.76	2.14	13.78
₱4,000 - ₱4,999	483,630	42.00	4.80	8.25	25.38	3.43	16.17
₱5,000 - ₱5,999	249,288	45.57	6.30	9.18	22.82	2.61	13.52
₱6,000 - ₱6,999	188,190	40.08	4.22	9.72	28.89	2.84	14.25
₱7,000 - ₱7,999	118,140	44.19	5.82	9.13	25.27	2.89	12.70
₱8,000 - ₱8,999	111,270	38.45	4.56	8.58	30.82	2.21	15.37
₱9,000 - ₱9,999	91,140	32.56	4.49	12.66	25.25	3.18	21.86
₱10,000 and over	541,978	27.47	3.13	7.28	38.20	10.92	12.99

Source: A Study of Tax Burden by Income Class, op. cit.

345

CHART 15

TAX BURDEN AS A PERCENTAGE OF INCOME, 1960

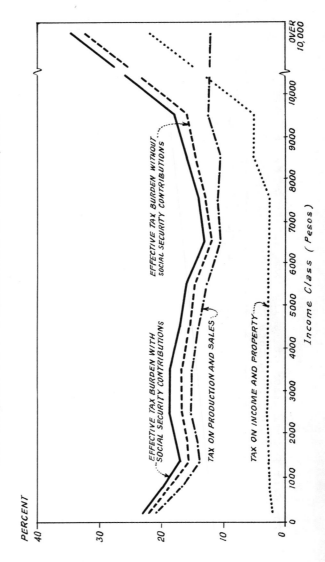

and sales is greater in proportion to income of those
in the low-income group than of those in the high-
income group. However, greater reliance on taxes on
production and sales than on taxes on income and
property is common in developing economies, for these
indirect taxes are more politically feasible.

The inability of the tax system to produce
enough revenues to meet expenditure requirements is
due largely to its low revenue productivity. From
1955-62, the total revenue as a percentage of national income averaged 9.0 per cent. Compared with those
of other countries in Asia for the same period, this
ratio is relatively low. In Thailand the ratio of
total revenue from taxation to national income is 13
per cent; in Ceylon, 21 per cent; in Malaysia, 18
per cent; in Burma, 26 per cent; and in Japan, 14
per cent (Table 50). This condition has often been
ascribed to several factors. First, the Philippines'
tax rates are comparatively low. For instance, the
rate on the first bracket of individual income tax
is lower than those of neighboring Asian countries,
some of which are in the same stage of development
as the Philippines, such as Thailand, 10 per cent;
South Korea, 7 per cent; Japan, 8 per cent; and
Malaysia, 6 per cent.[9]

Another factor is the narrowed-down tax base.
A case in point is the income tax law which allows
liberal deductions and exemptions. The ratio of exemptions and deductions to gross income of a married
taxpayer with six child dependents is higher in the
Philippines than in neighboring countries.[10] The
narrowing of the over-all tax base can be further
attributed to the grant of numerous tax exemptions.
From 1946 to 1963, forty-seven laws granting tax-
exemption privileges to various industries, entities,
and individuals were enacted by Congress, measures
that have deprived the government of a sizable amount
of revenue.[11]

While remedial measures have been taken to improve collection, certain deficiencies in the administrative machinery still remain. In-service training of internal revenue and customs personnel has

TABLE 50

Comparative Ratio of Tax Revenues to National Income of Selected
Asian Countries, 1955-62 (Per Cent)

Country	1955	1956	1957	1958	1959	1960	1961	1962	Average
Burma	28	23	25	28	28	26	24	29	26
Ceylon	-	21	21	20	19	20	21	22	21
India	-	-	4	6	4	-	5	6	5
Indonesia	8	9	8	8	12	18	16	-	11
Japan	-	13	13	15	15	14	15	15	14
Malaysia	18	19	17	16	18	20	17	-	18
South Korea	7	11	9	11	16	15	11	12	11
Thailand	11	12	13	19	13	13	14	14	13
Philippines	8	8	9	8	9	9	8	9	9

Source: Chapter 12.

been instituted with the establishment of the Finance
Academy in December, 1964. However, the people's attitude toward taxes has contributed in no small
measure to the low productivity of the tax system.
The "Survey on Tax Consciousness," another study by
the Tax Commission conducted in 1961, reveals a relatively low voluntary tax compliance. The study reports that of the 611,000 individuals with incomes
of ₱1,800 and over who were required to file returns,
about 478,000 individuals, or about 78 per cent, complied. The same survey revealed that of about 1.9
million taxpayers, only 1.4 million, or 75.6 per
cent, complied.

There is a compelling need to revise the Philippine tax system and structure. A good tax system
should not only meet the financial requirements of
government, but it must also help to attain a fundamental fiscal policy goal--a more equitable distribution of income.

In revising the tax system, the possibility of
introducing the element of progressivity should be
explored. One alternative is to infuse elements of
progressivity in taxes on production and sales.
This could be achieved by reclassifying consumer
goods and services to take into account income and
price elasticities. For instance, by imposing higher rates on items with high-income elasticities,
such as luxury articles, and lower rates on those
with relatively low-income elasticities, such as essential commodities and services, a relatively favorable tax-burden structure could be effected for
those on the less-favored income scale. The rationale for this is the fact that people in different income classes change their consumption habits as their
income changes.

Even if progressivity can be injected into production and sales taxes, taxes on income and property would still be more effective in redistributing
income because their effect on purchasing power is
immediate. By introducing more progressivity
through an adjustment of the rate structure, the
marked regressivity of the tax system would stand to
be mitigated.

Enhancement of equity is an attendant result of a progressive scheme of taxation based on ability to pay. Inasmuch as some sectors in the economy are not bearing their proportionate share of the cost of government, increasing their share and tapping those sectors which do not presently contribute their share would bring about a fairer distribution of the tax load.

Basically, revenue productivity depends on an economy's taxable capacity. The more taxable capacity is enhanced, the greater is the potential yield of the tax system. Since national income is generally a measure of taxable capacity, the yield of the tax system is directly proportional to the size of the national income. While the rate of growth of the national income has been quite low, the rate of population growth, which is estimated at 3.2 per cent, is showing signs of a further increase.

A broadened middle class is an essential attribute of a stable and enduring democracy. It follows that the tax system should contribute toward the building up of a broad middle class. This in turn would lead to the enhancement of the tax base. If a tax system is viewed from the perspective of revenue productivity alone, a broadened middle-income class would have a substantial impact on the tax yield.

This can be seen by considering a hypothetical situation in which the composition of the middle-income group is increased from the actual 16 per cent it was in 1960 to 30 per cent. Total revenue collection in 1960 was 1.3 billion, excluding social security contributions. After such a change, total revenue would have amounted to ₱1.9 billion, an increase in revenue of about half a billion pesos or 46 per cent. If it is further assumed that after five years, in 1965, a redistribution of family households among the three income groups were to have been effected, such that 50 per cent of the households are in the low-income group, 40 per cent in the middle-income group, and 10 per cent in the high-income group, the total tax yield, excluding social security, would have reached an estimated ₱4.5 billion, an increase of ₱2.6 billion or 137 per cent as a result of the broadened middle class.[12]

CONCLUSION

The study on tax burden has indicated the major weaknesses of the tax system--its regressivity and its low revenue productivity. It has also shown that a great disparity in the distribution of income exists. In view of this, there is urgent need to revise and update the present tax system to make it a more effective instrument of economic policy. This would call for the lowering of some tax rates, the increase of others, especially those established during prewar times, the abolition of obsolete taxes, the enactment of new ones in line with current economic conditions and trends, and the assessment of sectors in the economy that are not contributing their share to the cost of government.

An effective tax-revision program calls for the infusion of a greater degree of progressivity, particularly in the middle- and high-income groups. Such a program should take into account such equally worthwhile objectives as capital accumulation and business incentives, and should be buttressed with an efficient and effective tax-collection machinery.

On account of increasing population which calls for the expansion of government activities and desire to accelerate economic growth, there is need for more tax revenues. The Five-year Integrated Socio-Economic Development Program calls for an additional ₱1.5 billion in revenue from taxation to bridge the gap between available resources and the proposed expenditure of ₱12.9 billion during the program period (1963-67).[13]

No substantial success can be achieved through tax-revision efforts without an improvement in the attitude of the taxpaying public. A cooperative citizenry, with definite awareness of their tax obligations, can help to attain an effective tax system, a system that compares with those of modern nations.

Notes to Chapter 14

1. For a brief summary of these factors, see _A Study of Tax Burden by Income Class in the Philippines_, Joint Legislative-Executive Tax Commission (1964), pp. 2-7.

2. The average money burden at the hth income class is:

$$a = (100) \; \frac{t_{ijh}}{n_h}$$

Where t_{ijh} = imputed taxes paid by families from the ith tax on the jth commodity at the hth income class;

n_h = number of households at h^{th} income class

Generalizing, average money burden for all households can be ascertained:

$$A = (100) \; \frac{\sum_h t_{ijh}}{\sum_h n_h} = \frac{T_{ij}}{N}$$

Where N = Total number of households

3. The effective rate for each income class:

$$Y_{ijh} = (100) \; \frac{t_{ijh}}{Y_h}$$

Where t_{ijh} = the imputed taxes paid by families from the ith tax on the jth item at the hth income class;

Y_h = total gross income of families at the hth income class.

Generalizing, effective rate for all income classes can be ascertained:

$$R_{ijh} = (100) \frac{h \quad t_{ijh}}{h \quad Y_h} = \frac{T_{ijh}}{Y}$$

Where T_{ijh} = Total tax collection from the $i\underline{th}$ tax on the $j\underline{th}$ taxable item.

Y = Total gross income.

4. Data for the United States are as of 1958, and for the United Kingdom, Germany, France, and Italy, as of 1960.

5. The margin levy expired January, 1962.

6. The special import tax terminated on December 31, 1965; it was 6.8 per cent in 1960 and 1.7 per cent in 1965.

7. Caution in making comparisons should be taken due to discrepancies in classification.

8. Previous surveys on income distribution in the Philippines were made under the Bell Report in 1950, the MacMillan-Rivera Report in 1952, the Central Bank Household Survey Report in 1954, and the Philippine Statistical Survey of Households in 1957. These studies show that there has been no substantial change in the pattern of income distribution in the Philippines.

9. See Chapter 2.

10. The proportion of personal exemptions of married taxpayers with six child dependents to gross income is 81.82 per cent. In the Republic of China, it is 48.98 per cent; in Thailand, 53.27 per cent; in India, 64.28 per cent; in Malaysia, 68.15 per cent; in Singapore, 78.72 per cent; and in Japan, 80.95 per cent. Ibid., p. 139.

11. To the forty-six firms exempted from paying special import tax, customs duties, and the compensating tax under the Basic Industries Act (Republic Act No. 3127), the government has lost a total of ₱149.5 million from February, 1963,to September,

1964. For the same period, revenue foregone attributed to the textile industry (Republic Act No. 4086)
was ₱27.7 million.

12. Compared to the present revenue estimate
of about ₱1.5 billion, there would have been a difference of about ₱3 billion representing the amount
by which revenue could have increased by the broadened middle class. This amount would have been
greater had the 3 per cent annual increase in the
number of households been taken into account.

13. See Appendix II to The Five-Year Integrated
Socio-Economic Program for the Philippines, pp. 65-
66.

CHAPTER **15** THE PHILIPPINE
BUDGET SYSTEM*

GOVERNMENT BUDGETING--ITS RATIONALE
AND SIGNIFICANCE

The purpose of budgeting is the effective allocation of scarce resources to attain established objectives. For a government responsible for a wide
and complex array of functions, the budget is an effective device, particularly when financial resources
are limited. With a multitude of competing claims
exerting a heavy strain on the public coffers, a systematic pattern in public spending is needed.

There are hardly any governmental activities
that do not require financial sustenance. The national budget charts the magnitude and direction of
public expenditure and thereby constitutes the very
mold for the formulation of basic policy decisions.
It serves to integrate the ramified aspects of governmental administration and it functions for the judi-
cious apportionment of government funds so as to maximize the benefits derived from public disbursements.

Economy and efficiency considerations should
guide public expenditure decisions. Toward these
ends, the budgetary device serves to minimize unnecessary expenditures. In a government in which many

---

*This chapter was coauthored by Angel Q. Yoingco
and Avelino B. Lim, Associate Lecturer, Graduate
School of Public Administration, University of the
Philippines.

public service requirements are continually brought
to bear on an already overburdened treasury, expenditure proposals must be subjected to intensive review at successive echelons, initially within the
agency, by the Budget Commissioner, and then by
Congress and the Chief Executive.

In the Philippines the significance of the national budget has recently been accentuated by the
country's effort to accelerate economic development.
The progressively widening scope of governmental concern has occasioned a burgeoning bureaucracy undertaking new projects designed to enhance economic
growth. Considering that all such projects need to
be financed, it is imperative that a methodic approach be adopted in planning, authorizing, and im-
plementing them.

BUDGETING AND ECONOMIC DEVELOPMENT

Economic development is the process whereby economic resources in underdeveloped areas are utilized
with a view to achieving desirable levels of prices,
consumption, income, and employment. The optimum
utilization of developmental expenditures is vital
to this process. The government budget can contribute to effect a dynamic pattern of resource allocation consistent with the requirements of accelerated
economic growth.

The extent of government involvement and influence in the developmental process would vary depending on its economic setting. In an economy which is
principally private-enterprise oriented, the non-
government sector largely determines the method, as
well as the timing, of utilizing economic resources.
This does not eclipse the role that government may
assume in providing an atmosphere conducive to increased activity in the private sector through well-
conceived and properly implemented policies integrated
in an effective resource-utilization scheme.

In the Philippines the government provides social
overhead in the fields of health, education, and

welfare. It brings its influence to bear on investment decisions in the private sector, paving the way
for a pattern of resource allocation calculated to
serve developmental objectives. Thus tax exemptions
have been granted to basic and certain selected industries to stimulate private entrepreneurial activities.[1] The government has also pioneered in capital-
intensive undertakings and in essential productive
areas where private enterprise is reluctant to venture. Similarly, through its expenditure policies,
public investment resources may be concentrated on
such "impulse sectors" as power, irrigation, and public works construction.

There has been an increasing reliance on the
national budget as an instrument for economic development. Aside from reflecting financial authorizations for carrying out governmental functions, the
budgetary process is relied upon to implement the
nation's economic program. A more potent device for
the formulation and execution of public programs can
hardly be conceived, especially when the level of
total public spending in relation to gross national
product is considered.

TABLE 51

Public Spending in Relation to Gross
National Product, FY 1961-64

Year	Level of Public Spending (million pesos)	Gross National Product (current prices and in million pesos)	Spending as Per Cent of GNP
1961	2,044	12,779	15.99
1962	2,072	14,202	14.59
1963	2,490	16,059	15.51
1964	2,977	17,923	16.61

Note: GNP in fiscal year was arrived at by adding
       the two succeeding calendar years and divid-
       ing by two.

DEVELOPMENT OF BUDGETING IN
THE PHILIPPINES

Budgeting in a rudimentary form already existed when the country was under Spanish colonial domination. The system remained unaltered when America was sovereign over the Philippines at the turn of the twentieth century. Thus, the colonial administration hardly provided an atmosphere conducive to the development of an effective budgetary system.

Prior to the advent of fiscal reform in the early 1950's, budgeting was considered a ministrant function requiring little technical expertise. The lag in development of public fiscal management, particularly in the field of budgeting, can be ascribed to several factors. Certain stimuli that could have triggered improvements in Philippine fiscal administration were absent. Since revenues were sufficient for governmental functions, the need for effective allocation of public funds was not exigent. From this perspective, it is understandable that the appropriation process was unsystematic, with each department vying with others for as big a portion of the budget as it could wangle.

Efforts to improve Philippine budgeting stemmed primarily from the need for a more systematic pattern of allocating available funds among competing public expenditure requirements. The budget, accounting, and auditing modernization project was launched and a contract entered into by the Philippine Government and the U.S. management consulting firm of Booz, Allen, and Hamilton in July, 1954. Project costs were underwritten jointly by the United States and Philippine governments.[2] Like other reform projects implemented under the broad United States technical assistance program in the Philippines, budgetary improvement represented an attempt to initiate requisite changes in an area relatively neglected in the past. However, it differed from other programs in that it involved a technique that was untested in other jurisdictions: performance budgeting.

The budget-modernization project succeeded in

focusing attention on the significance of governmental budgeting. Organizational additions to the Budget Commission--the Fiscal Policy Staff, the Budget Planning Staff, and the Management Service--were established. The clientele form of organization in the examination of agency budget requests was adopted. Concrete steps were taken to usher in budgeting innovations. A budget-operations manual was issued.

A performance budget format was devised and put into experiment in twelve offices in 1956. An attempt was made to devise a measurement for units of work on which to base agency financial requirements. With program and work commitments established as the focal points of agency management, appraisal of status of operations has been facilitated. This was buttressed by a program audit system on which is plotted a more effective spending pattern consonant with agency fiscal needs. Determination of the staffing pattern and other operating requirements is now undertaken systematically, for administrators at all levels have become cognizant that the "rule of thumb" is ineffective in formulating agency decisions. Cost accounting was installed in a number of operating entities. Also, an economic-functional classification of expenditures has been integrated into the budget procedure.

These significant changes can be ascribed principally to the institution of performance budgeting as a result of the enactment of Republic Act No. 992.[3]

ORGANIZATION FOR BUDGETING

The Philippine Government adheres to an executive type of budget; the Chief Executive initiates the programs and projects which are generally financed for one fiscal year. As the principal staff arm of the President, the Budget Commission coordinates the phases of the budget process antecedent to legislative authorization, in addition to handling budget execution and control once the appropriations act has been enacted by Congress.

The Budget Commission is headed by a Budget Commissioner assisted by a Deputy Budget Commissioner. As a result of the budget-modernization project, certain organizational innovations were made in 1955. Thus the Budget Commission has a Fiscal Policy Staff that advises the Budget Commissioner on the economic implications of budget expenditures, a Budget Planning Staff that aids in the planning function, and the Management Service, which is concerned with the employment of sound management techniques.

The task of assisting agencies in the formulation of their budgets and conducting a review of agency expenditure proposals is done by the Budget Operations Service. Within the Service are five constituent units organized on a clientele basis. Each unit is responsible for determining financial requirements of a particular government department, including the examination of its annual expenditure proposals, as well as other aspects of budgetary operations.

At the departmental level, budget officers assist agency executives in formulating their respective blueprints of action for a fiscal year.

The financial operations of government-owned or -controlled corporations are outside the sphere of the regular budgetary process. The Office of Economic Coordination under the President determines the financial requirements of these entities.[4] While this system detracts from the comprehensiveness of the national budget, it serves the need for flexibility and autonomy in the operation of these concerns.

STAGES IN PHILIPPINE BUDGETING

Budget Formulation

Budget formulation is a process based initially on the expenditure estimates arrived at by the lower levels of the agency hierarchy; the estimates are consolidated and reviewed at successive higher echelons, with the aim of arriving at an integrated financial plan.

Agency expenditure estimates are submitted to the Budget Commission in late October or early November.[5] Allowing only two months for the preparation of such estimates, each agency has to forecast its financial requirements for twenty-two months in advance. Consequently, estimates can be made erroneous by adventitious circumstances that could occur during the fiscal year in which they are to apply.

There are other considerations relevant to agency budget formulation. First, administrators are prone to overemphasize the importance of their respective functions. This accounts for inflated expenditure programs that transcend actual agency needs. Also, the relative facility with which support of proposed programs can be drawn up and the subjective nature of executive and legislative budget review can result in deviations from a sound, systematic fiscal spending pattern. The extent of political support which can be mustered by the proponents of expenditure programs must be reckoned with. All these make it difficult to assess agency programs solely on merit.

In the budget-formulation phase, agency administrators are enjoined to develop the best possible program by giving due attention to the optimum linkage between program balance and emphasis, availability of revenues, efficiency of operations and the over-all economic and social impact of budget proposals. In addition, they have to conform to certain fiscal guides, such as target amounts, ceiling by fund, and specific budgetary instructions.[6]

The Budget Commission's present practice is to group national budgetary requirements into two distinct categories: programmed and unprogrammed expenditures,[7] the latter being conditional to the existence of a revenue surplus.

Legislative Authorization of the Budget

The appropriation of funds to finance governmental operations is solely a legislative prerogative,

and no discretion is left to the Treasury.[8] Consequently, the legislative imprimatur is necessary before government projects and programs can be carried
out. Congress possesses a potent vehicle of control
in this "power of the purse." Administrators have to
justify the operations of their respective departments
annually before Congress, which acts through the legislative finance committees--the House Committee on
Appropriations and the Senate Committee on Finance
and Economy. These hearings probe into issues relating to the stewardship of appropriated moneys by
government agencies and the judiciousness of financial requirements embodied in the Budget. In this
regard, the budget serves as the catalyst to executive action and contributes to the attainment of a
responsive and responsible bureaucracy. The extent
of the budgetary slashes effected by Congress for
the last three preceding fiscal years is indicated
below.

TABLE 52

Budgetary Requests vs. Appropriations of
the National Government (All Funds)
FY 1963, 1964, and 1965
(In Million Pesos)

Fiscal Year	Budgetary Requests (1)	Approved by Congress (2)	Difference (3) = (1) - (2)
1963	1,421.4	1,383.0	38.4
1964	2,159.8	1,972.1	187.7
1965	2,455.7	2,102.4	353.3

Source: Budgets for FY 1963, 1964, and 1965 and
RA 3845, RA 4164, and RA 3500.

The nature of legislative review can change in accordance with the way this prerogative is exercised. Conducted well, it can further the cause of effective administration, for legislative authorization of the budget underscores the role of Congress in the surveillance of executive action. Yet, legislative control through the budget can be used to cow administrators into submission, or the budget may be viewed by some legislators as a device to further partisan interests and reward protégés and constituents.

The Philippine fundamental law enjoins the President to submit within fifteen days of the opening of each regular Congressional session a budget of receipts and expenditures which become the basis of the general appropriation bill.[9] Congress cannot increase the appropriations that the President recommends for government operations as specified in the budget, except appropriations for Congress and the judiciary.[10]

Once the printed budget is submitted by the President, Congress, through the Committee on Appropriations of the House of Representatives, conducts budget hearings wherein department secretaries, bureau directors, and other ranking administrators defend their proposals. After this, the budget is opened to discussion and amendment. Following deliberations in the House of Representatives, the budget is transmitted to the Senate Committee on Finance and Economy which would then study it prior to floor amendments and enactments by the Senate. The conference committee composed of senators and congressmen serves to resolve basic disagreements about the budget between the two legislative chambers. After the appropriations bill is enacted, it is transmitted to the President who then acts on it. In the process, he may exercise his veto power.[11]

Budget Execution and Control

After the enactment of the appropriations act, certain mechanisms are instituted to ensure that

public funds are spent only for the specific purposes
for which they are appropriated. Budget execution
and control is that particular phase of the budget
process which uses these devices. Through budget
execution, plans for the use of appropriated funds
are adopted and budgetary controls put in force.[12]

The main objectives of a system of budget execution are: (1) preserving legislative intent, (2) ob-
serving financial limitations, and (3) maintaining
flexibility in governmental operations.[13] In the
Philippines the principal budget execution and control techniques are: the release of allotments to
governmental agencies, the institution of positive
retrenchment measures (including the outright slash-
ing of appropriations in the event that actual revenues do not come up to anticipated levels), the man-
datory setting up of reserves, and the institution
of accounting and auditing requirements in public
spending.

The allotment system compels agencies to adhere
to planned levels of work, and thereby averts a situation where agency appropriations are depleted before the end of the fiscal year. It provides a corre-
lation between revenues realized and national spending.[14] It conduces to proper programming in agency
management by requiring agency heads to submit to
the Budget Commissioner a request for quarterly allotment of funds showing the estimated amounts of
funds needed for each purpose for which the funds
are to be expended during the applicable allotment
period.[15] Agency requests for allotment are reviewed
by the Budget Commissioner to ascertain whether the
amounts and purposes of the estimates are within the
terms of the appropriations, having due regard for
the probable future needs of the Bureau, office, or
agency for the remainder of the fiscal year. Funds
are alloted for each project in terms of three major
classifications of expenditures: personal services,
maintenance, and other operating expenses and equipment. The power to modify or amend allotments previously made is vested in the Budget Commissioner.[16]
Thus, if revenues fail to reach expected levels, budget cuts may be effected. Such retrenchment measures

were utilized in the course of the fiscal year
1963-64.[17]

Agencies are also required to establish budgetary reserves against appropriations to provide for
contingencies and emergencies which may arise later
in the fiscal year to avoid a deficiency appropriation.[18] Such reserves must not be less than 5 per
cent of the total appropriated amounts programmed
for release for each bureau or office.[19]

There is also a legal injunction against any
agency disbursing funds without the certification of
the Chief Accountant as to the availability of funds
and the allotment against which the expenditure or
obligation may be charged.[20] There is also a prohibition against incurrence of overdrafts.[21]

Information about the progress of agency spending is secured by a government-wide system of financial reporting. To keep the central budget agency
informed, agencies are required to prepare monthly
reports on agency projects, work and obligation
levels, and deviations from established plans.[22]

Governmental accounting adheres to a decentralized pattern, with agencies recording appropriations
and obligations against such appropriations,[23] subject to standards prescribed by the National Accounting Service of the Budget Commission.

Auditing, under the General Auditing Office,[24]
determines whether governmental fiscal transactions
have been carried out in an accurate manner. Constant surveillance is thus maintained on the legal
aspects of transactions involving receipt and expenditure of public funds.

Performance Budgeting

Performance budgeting emphasizes accomplishments
of government rather than the means for carrying out
particular public functions. Because expenditure requirements are presented in terms of services,

activities, and work projects, the system is useful
for review and decision-making at and above the agency level. In addition, it serves as an effective
management tool, capable of effecting substantial
savings in governmental operations.

At its inception, performance budgeting was pic-
tured by some of its overzealous advocates as a
panacea. Consequently, the disillusionment caused by
unrefined performance classifications and spurious
agency accomplishment reports which are occasioned by
the target-setting requirement is readily understandable. The installation of performance budgeting furnishes a striking illustration of how a reform measure, applied in a tour de force manner, can be
thwarted. The Philippine experience with performance
budgeting supports the veracity of a statement made
by an American political historian, Professor Charles
A. Beard, almost half a century ago: "Whoever ex-
pects, therefore, to rush a 'budget bill' through the
coming legislature and to see an immediate revolution
in finances is designed to be disappointed."[25]

Performance budgeting in the Philippines had to
contend with a number of obstacles, the foremost of
which relates to lack of sustained support by Congress. Aside from the fact that legislators are not
prone to have their control over detailed items
diluted by a budget presentation which highlights
"functions, activities and projects," there is justification for the criticism that the performance-bud-
get document is replete with project characteriza-
tions which are not significant from the standpoint
of policy-making. The preoccupation with activity
costs and the imprecise work-measurement unit adopted
also explain why the performance budget is a maze of
data which render blurred project-agency objectives
and programs.

Although performance budgeting now constitutes
an integral feature of the country's governmental
process,[26] performance budgeting in the Philippines
has yet to gain unqualified acceptance. The legal
prescription for the system is not rigorously observed. Twelve years have elapsed since the enact-

ment of the Revised Budget Act. While the Budget
Commission has for years been presenting the budget
on a performance basis, legislators insist on authorizing the budget on a line-item scheme. Disenchant-
ment with performance budgeting culminated in the
introduction of a bill in the 1963 regular session
of Congress which sought to abolish the system. The
reasons adduced in support of the bill relate to the
complicated form of the performance budget, the time
required for its preparation, and its costly printing requirements.[27] This legislative opposition constitutes an impediment, for so long as it persists,
performance budgeting will remain just a decorative
feature in which the legislative branch has no faith.

CONCLUDING COMMENTS

In an era with a crucial need for an extended
base on which to plot further socio-economic developmental gains, budgeting in the Philippines has assumed a more significant role in the past decade. No
longer is budgeting conceived of as a ministerial
function requiring only a modicum of skills, but more
and more its utility in integrating the projects and
programs leading to national advancement is being
realized. One of the recent developments is performance budgeting. While this novel type of budget
classification has yet to gain unqualified acceptance, by refining performance classification and
measurement techniques, the Philippine Government
can still use it to full advantage.

As gains are made in the budgetary field, the
feasibility of adopting other innovations should be
explored. The consolidated cash budget, for example,
appears to be useful in the analysis of government-
public monetary flows. In governmental budgeting,
it is vital to keep pace with the cross-currents of
development. If progress in this direction is to be
attained, the basic framework for the expenditure of
public funds must be characterized by efficiency and
effectiveness.

Notes to Chapter 15

1. See Chapter 9.

2. Dollar assistance for the project, which terminated in 1957, amounted to $1,352,971.25. Peso support came up to ₱2,316,484.64.

3. Approved June 4, 1954.

4. The Congress of the Philippines has made several attempts to control the budgetary operations of government corporations. In 1950 H. B. No. 462, designed to attain such control, was passed by the legislature but was vetoed by the President. The following year H. B. No. 1565 was passed, but this measure was also thwarted by the Chief Executive's veto. Since then, a number of legislative proposals have been introduced in Congress to effect controls on the budget systems of these concerns.

5. Budget Commission, Budget Circulars, 141, 154, and 171, September 3, 1962; October 31, 1963; and August 21, 1964, respectively. Under Sec. 8 of R. A. No. 992, the Bureau of Treasury is required to submit balanced statements of the condition of the Treasury at the end of the fiscal year in progress, as well as the estimated condition of the Treasury at the end of the ensuing fiscal year (if the financial proposals contained in the Budget are adopted) showing the unencumbered and unobligated cash resources.

6. Budget Commission, Budget Circular, 171, August 21, 1964.

7. The former practice, which began with fiscal year 1956, Budget "B" but the Philippine Senate has been averse to this particular budgeting scheme because this widens the discretion of the President in the matter of public expenditures.

8. Article VI. Sec. 23(2) of the Constitution of the Philippines states that "no money shall be paid out of the Treasury except in pursuance of an appropriation made by law."

9. Constitution of the Philippines, Article
VI, Sec. 19(1).

10. Ibid.

11. "The President shall have the power to
veto any particular item or items of an appropriation bill, but the veto shall not affect the item or
items to which he does not object." Constitution of
the Philippines, Sec. 20(2).

12. Budget Commission, Budget Operations Manual
(Manila: Bureau of Printing, 1957), p. 371.

13. Jesse V. Burkhead, Government Budgeting
(New York: John Wiley & Sons, 1956), pp. 342-48.

14. The initial measure which provided for
budgetary control was Administrative Order No. 178
issued on February 6, 1952. Under this order, agencies were required to make quarterly allotments of
each appropriation item to prevent overdrafts and to
render quarterly reports on expenditures incurred.
In the event that expenditures exceed the allotment
by more than 10 per cent, agencies were required to
submit a statement enumerating the steps taken to
correct the situation.

15. Republic Act No. 992, Sec. 15(a).

16. Republic Act No. 992, Sec. 15(e) provides
that in case the Budget Commissioner "shall find at
any time that the probable receipts from taxes or
other sources for any fund will be less than were
anticipated and that as a consequence the amount
available for the remainder of the term of the appropriations, or for any allotment period will be less
than the amount estimated or alloted therefor, he
shall, with the approval of the President, and after
notice to the department or agency concerned, reduce
the amount or amounts to be alloted so as to prevent
deficits."

17. On July 15, 1963, only fourteen days after
the beginning of the fiscal year, upon instructions

of the President, the Budget Commissioner revised the program of expenditures and initiated the first round of cuts, reducing the gap between proposed expenditures and estimated income from ₱1,958.2 million to ₱375.7 million. The second round of cuts, on September 27, involved ₱73.3 million, thus reducing the gap to ₱302.4 million. The third round of cuts, on December 5, involved ₱94.6 million, thus reducing the gap to ₱207.8 million. Senate Committee on Finance and Economy constituted as A Special Committee to Study and Investigate the Financial Affairs of the Government and Instrumentalities Thereof. Transcript of hearings, February 24, 1964, pp. 4-5.

18. Republic Act No. 992, Sec. 16.

19. Budget Commission, Budget Circular 38, June 7, 1956.

20. Republic Act No. 992, Sec. 17.

21. Ibid., Sec. 20.

22. Budget Operations Manual, op. cit., p. 457.

23. "Before funds are disbursed, and expenditures or obligations chargeable against authorized allotments are authorized, a certification of availability of funds issued by the agency chief accountant is required." Republic Act No. 992, Sec. 17.

24. Under Article XI, Section 2 of the fundamental law, the General Auditing Office is charged with the auditing of all expenditures of funds or property pertaining to the Government. The Auditor General is likewise required to bring to the attention of the proper administrative officer expenditure of funds or property which, in his opinion, are irregular, unnecessary, excessive, or extravagant.

25. René Stourm, The Budget, trans. by Thaddeus Plazinski (New York: Appleton and Co., 1917), p. xiii.

26.   Section 2 of <u>Republic Act No. 992</u>, which
constitutes the legal foundation of performance budgeting in the Philippines, states that the whole
budgetary concept of the government is based on
"functions, activities, and projects," in terms of
expected results. Immediately after the enactment
of this basic law in 1954, twelve agencies, representing ten executive departments, were required to
adopt the performance budget.

27.   House Bill No. 4704 introduced in the
second session, Fifth Congress of the Republic of
the Philippines.

APPENDIXES

APPENDIX I

Appendix to Chapter 2

Income Tax Schedules of Selected Asian Countries
(In Their Respective Currencies)

Republic of China			India				
Income Brackets (NT$)		Tax Rates (per cent)	Income Brackets (Rupees)		Tax Rates (per cent)	Super Tax (per cent)	Surcharge (per cent of total tax)
Exceeding	Not Exceeding		Exceeding	Not Exceeding			
0	50,000	3	0	3,000	Free		
50,000	100,000	5	3,000	5,000	3		
100,000	150,000	7	5,000	7,500	7		5
150,000	200,000	9	7,500	10,000	10		5
200,000	250,000	12	10,000	12,500	12		5
250,000	300,000	15	12,500	15,000	15		5
300,000	400,000	18	15,000	17,500	20		5
400,000	500,000	22	17,500	20,000	23		5
500,000	650,000	26	20,000	25,000	25	8	5
650,000	800,000	30	25,000	30,000	25	18	5
800,000	1,000,000	35	30,000	40,000	25	22	5
1,000,000	—	40	40,000	50,000	25	32	5
			50,000	60,000	25	40	5
			60,000	70,000	25	45	5
			70,000	—	25	47.5	5

Income Tax Structure of Indonesia, 1964

Taxable Bracket	Absolute Tax
Below Rp 6,000	Exempt
Rp 6,000	3%
Over 6,000– 11,999	Rp 180 + 5 Rp for every Rp 100 in excess of Rp 6,000
12,000– 17,999	Rp 480 + 7 Rp for every Rp 100 in excess of Rp 12,000
18,000– 23,999	Rp 900 + 9 Rp for every Rp 100 in excess of Rp 18,000
24,000– 29,999	Rp 1,440 + 11 Rp for every Rp 100 in excess of Rp 24,000
30,000– 35,999	Rp 2,100 + 13 Rp for every Rp 100 in excess of Rp 30,000
36,000– 41,999	Rp 2,880 + 15 Rp for every Rp 100 in excess of Rp 36,000
42,000– 47,999	Rp 3,780 + 17 Rp for every Rp 100 in excess of Rp 42,000
48,000– 59,999	Rp 4,800 + 20 Rp for every Rp 100 in excess of Rp 48,000
60,000– 74,999	Rp 7,200 + 23 Rp for every Rp 100 in excess of Rp 60,000
75,000– 89,999	Rp 10,650 + 26 Rp for every Rp 100 in excess of Rp 75,000
90,000– 104,999	Rp 14,550 + 30 Rp for every Rp 100 in excess of Rp 90,000
105,000– 149,999	Rp 19,050 + 35 Rp for every Rp 100 in excess of Rp 105,000
150,000– 224,999	Rp 34,800 + 40 Rp for every Rp 100 in excess of Rp 150,000
225,000– 299,999	Rp 64,800 + 45 Rp for every Rp 100 in excess of Rp 225,000
300,000– 419,999	Rp 98,550 + 50 Rp for every Rp 100 in excess of Rp 300,000
420,000– 539,999	Rp 158,550 + 55 Rp for every Rp 100 in excess of Rp 420,000
540,000– 749,999	Rp 224,550 + 60 Rp for every Rp 100 in excess of Rp 540,000
750,000–1,199,999	Rp 350,000 + 65 Rp for every Rp 100 in excess of Rp 750,000
1,200,000–1,799,999	Rp 643,050 + 70 Rp for every Rp 100 in excess of Rp 1,200,000
Over 1,200,000	Rp 1,063,050 + 75 Rp for every Rp 100 in excess of Rp 1,800,000

Source: Asian Taxation, 1964.

Japan			Malaysia		
Income Brackets (Yen)		Tax Rates (per cent)	Income Brackets (Malaysian $)		Tax Rates (per cent)
Exceeding	Not Exceeding		Exceeding	Not Exceeding	
	100,000	8	0	2,500	6
100,000	200,000	10	2,500	5,000	8
200,000	500,000	15	5,000	7,500	10
500,000	800,000	20	7,500	10,000	12
800,000	1,200,000	25	10,000	15,000	15
1,200,000	1,800,000	30	15,000	20,000	18
1,800,000	2,500,000	35	20,000	25,000	20
2,500,000	4,000,000	40	25,000	30,000	22
4,000,000	6,000,000	45	30,000	35,000	25
6,000,000	10,000,000	50	35,000	40,000	30
10,000,000	20,000,000	55	40,000	45,000	35
20,000,000	30,000,000	60	45,000	55,000	40
30,000,000	45,000,000	65	55,000	-	45
45,000,000	60,000,000	70			
60,000,000	-	75			

Philippines Income Brackets (Pesos)			Singapore Income Brackets (Malaysian $)		
Exceeding	Not Exceeding	Tax Rates (per cent)	Exceeding	Not Exceeding	Tax Rates (per cent)
0	2,000	3	0	1,500	5
2,000	4,000	6	1,500	2,000	6
4,000	6,000	9	2,000	3,000	7
6,000	8,000	16	3,000	4,000	8
8,000	10,000	20	4,000	5,000	10
10,000	20,000	24	5,000	7,000	12
20,000	30,000	30	7,000	10,000	15
30,000	40,000	36	10,000	15,000	18
40,000	50,000	40	15,000	25,000	25
50,000	60,000	42	25,000	35,000	30
60,000	70,000	44	35,000	50,000	40
70,000	80,000	46	50,000	100,000	50
80,000	90,000	48	100,000	-	55
90,000	100,000	50			
100,000	120,000	52			
120,000	140,000	53			
140,000	160,000	54			
160,000	200,000	55			
200,000	250,000	56			
250,000	300,000	57			
300,000	400,000	58			
400,000	500,000	59			
500,000	-	60			

| Type of Income | Income Brackets (Won) | | Tax Rates (per cent) |
	Exceeding	Not Exceeding	
A. Real estate income, net	0	60,000	15)
	540,000	-	45) Progressive*
B. Dividend and interest income, gross			
1. Paid within the country or by domestic corporation			12) (Flat Rate)
2. Others			12) (Flat Rate)
3. Interest accruing from nonbusiness loan			15) (Flat Rate)
C. Business income, net	0	60,000	15)
	540,000	-	45) Progressive*
D. Wages and salaries, gross			
1. Wages and salaries earned from sources other than (2) below	0	20,000	7)
	20,000	50,000	15) Progressive**
	50,000	60,000	25)
	60,000	-	35)
2. Daily and hourly wages of persons not employed by any definite employer			7) (Flat Rate)
3. Compensation received from UN forces, US forces, and foreign mission in Korea, or withholding obligor failing to fulfill his obligation or whose location is uncertain	0	60,000	7)
	180,000	-	35) Progressive*
E. Other incomes, gross	0	20,000	7)
	20,000	50,000	15) Progressive**
	50,000	60,000	25)
	60,000	-	35)

*The taxable brackets and the tax rates available are only the minimum and the maximum.

**The two middle-income brackets and tax rates were taken from the 14th Series of Laws and Regulations of Supreme Council of National Reconstruction (Korea, 1962), pp. 102, 103. For lack of source materials, it is assumed that the maximum bracket and tax rate in the condensed report submitted in the Tokyo Tax Seminar in April, 1963, is an addition to the three income brackets and tax rates contained in the 14th Series of 1962. The maximum level contained in the report is not found in the Series of 1962.

	South Vietnam			Thailand		
	Income Brackets (Piasters)		Tax Rates (per cent)	Income Brackets (Baht)		Tax Rates (per cent)
	Exceeding	Not Exceeding		Exceeding	Not Exceeding	
A. Tax on profits of individuals			16	0	10,000	10
B. Income tax on salaries and wages:	0	50,000	1	10,000	50,000	13
	50,000	100,000	2	50,000	100,000	16
	100,000	500,000	5	100,000	150,000	20
	500,000	1,000,000	10	150,000	200,000	25
	1,000,000	-	16	200,000	250,000	30
				250,000	300,000	35
				300,000	350,000	40
				350,000	400,000	45
				400,000	-	50
C. General income tax (levied on all income subject to the income tax on salaries and wages and on profits realized by individuals):	0	10,000	1			
	10,000	20,000	2			
	20,000	30,000	3			
	30,000	40,000	4			
	40,000	50,000	5			
	50,000	60,000	6			
	60,000	70,000	7			
	70,000	80,000	8			
	80,000	90,000	9			
	90,000	100,000	10			
	100,000	200,000	15			
	200,000	300,000	20			
	300,000	400,000	25			
	400,000	500,000	30			
	500,000	600,000	35			
	600,000	700,000	40			
	700,000	800,000	45			
	800,000	-	50			

Appendix to Chapter 2

Personal Exemptions Allowed in Selected Asian Countries
(In Their Respective Currencies)

Republic of China	India
1. For the taxpayer, married or unmarried NT$ 6,000	1. For unmarried person Rs 1,000
2. For spouse 6,000	2. For married person a. Whose total income does not exceed Rs 20,000 3,000
3. For dependents a. Any parent or grandparent of the taxpayer or his spouse, who is over 60 years of age, dependent on the taxpayer, and unable to support himself 6,000	b. Whose total income exceeds Rs 20,000 (after allowing this exemption, the next Rs 4,000, instead of Rs 2,000, will be subject to 3% tax rate) 1,000
b. Any brother or sister of the taxpayer under 20 years of age, or over 20 years old who is in school or disabled and incapable of self-support 6,000	3. Children a. For the first child only 300
c. Any other dependents who are regarded as relatives pursuant to Article 1114 or 1123 of the Civil Code who are either under 20 or over 60 years old and are unable to support themselves 6,000	b. For two or more child dependents, a total of 600

J a p a n		M a l a y s i a	
1. For the taxpayer	¥ 110,000	1. For the taxpayer, married or unmarried	M$ 2,000
2. For the spouse living with the taxpayer whose income does not exceed 50,000 yen	105,000	2. For the spouse	1,000
3. For dependents (relatives, ex-cluding the spouse, supported by a taxpayer in one household and having an income of not more than 5,000 yen)		3. For the children:	
		a. For the first child	750
a. Where an exemption is allowed for the spouse		b. Each for the next two children	500
1) For each dependent at least 15 years of age	50,000	c. Each for the fourth and fifth child	300
2) For each dependent less than 15 years of age	35,000		
b. Where no exemption is allowed for the spouse		NOTE: When the child is maintained and educated outside Malaysia, the deduction may be increased to the total amount spent for the child up to twice the appropriate deduction.	
1) For the first dependent 15 years of age or over	70,000		
2) For each of the other dependents 15 years of age and over	50,000		
3) For each of the other dependents less than 15 years of age	35,000		

Philippines	Singapore
1. For unmarried taxpayer or married person who is legally separated from his or her spouse ₱ 1,800	1. For the taxpayer M$ 2,000
2. For married taxpayer or head of family 3,000	2. For the spouse 1,000
3. For dependents: For each child dependent less than 23 years of age, unmarried, and un- employed or incapable of self-support due to mental or physical de- fects 1,000	3. For child dependents: a. First child 750 b. Each for the second and third child 500 c. Each for the fourth and fifth child 300 d. Each for the sixth, seventh, eighth, and ninth child 200
	NOTE: When the child is maintained and educated outside Singapore, the deduction may be increased to the total amount spent for the child up to twice the appropriate de- duction.

Thailand

	Baht
1. For the taxpayer	4,000
2. For the spouse	2,000
3. For dependents	900

Each lawful or adopted child under 25 years old and studying in a university (or other educational institution on a university level), or who is a minor, or who is adjudged incompetent or quasi-incompetent

South Vietnam

	VN$
1. Single person and head of household	30,000
2. Spouse whose income does not exceed VN$ 15,000	15,000

3. Children:
   For each child under 21 years of age supported by the taxpayer and having no income or under 25 years of age who is either studying in a university or physically handicapped, regardless of age — 5,000

4. Other dependents:
   For each parent or grandparent over 60 years of age supported by the taxpayer or under 60 years who is ill and incapable of self-support — 3,000

5. Family allowances:

	Employees in Private Sector		Government Employees
	Europeans & Foreign Residents	Vietnamese and Asian Residents	
	VN$	VN$	VN$
As married person	8,604	5,544	8,400
Additional for:			
1st child	5,601.60	2,217.60	7,200
2nd child	6,681.60	2,217.60	7,200
3rd child	8,301.60	2,217.60	7,200
4th child	8,301.60	2,217.60	7,200
5th child	8,301.60	2,217.60	7,200
After the 5th child a deduction each of	1,108.80	1,108.80	3,000

APPENDIX III

Appendix to Chapter 3

CORPORATE TAX

REPUBLIC OF CHINA   (NT$)

A. Domestic corporation

   1. Income included   income from sources both
      for tax purposes   within and outside the
                             Republic of China

   2. Tax rates

Income Bracket		Tax Rate
Over	Not over	
0	10,000	0
10,000	50,000	6
50,000	100,000	12
100,000	–	18

B. Foreign corporations
carrying on business
in the Republic of
China

   1. Income included   income derived only from
      for tax purposes   domestic sources

   2. Tax rates   same rates applied to
                            domestic corporations

   3. Deductions   deductions for expenses in-
                            curred in producing income

C. Foreign corporations
having no fixed place
of business or an
agency in the Repub-
lic of China

   1. Income included   dividends, interest, rent,
      for tax purposes   royalties, etc.

   2. Tax rates   15% withholding tax

   3. Deductions   no deduction allowed

INDIA (Rupees)

A. Resident corporation

   1. The flat income tax rate of 25% applies to total income.

   2. In addition to the above tax, the corporation pays the following supertaxes:

Rate of Supertax

	Companies in which the public is substantially interested and whose total income does not exceed Rs 25,000*	Other Companies
a) On dividends received from:		
1. A subsidiary Indian Company** formed and registered before January 4, 1961.	5	5

---

   *A corporation is one in which the public is substantially interested if: (1) 40 per cent or more of its stock is held by the central government or a state government or, (2) it is not a "private company" for purposes of the general corporate law and in addition shall meet certain conditions.

   **The Income Tax Laws do not define a subsidiary. Section 4(1) of the Companies Act of 1956 provides that a corporation shall be deemed a subsidiary of any other corporation which controls the company or its board of directors or holds more than half of the nominal value of its equity share capital. A corporation which is the subsidiary of a second corporation is also a subsidiary of a third corporation of which the second is a subsidiary.

    2. An Indian Company,
not being a subsidiary, formed
and registered on or after
January 4, 1959.   5   10

    3. Any other Indian
company formed and registered
on or before January 4, 1959.   5   20

  b) On all other income   20   25

      In the case of a company in which the public
is not substantially interested and which distributes
dividends less than 60 per cent of its distributable
income, an additional tax (supertax) is levied on
the remaining part of such income. This percentage,
in the case of certain companies engaged in manufacturing and mining industries or in the production of
electricity or power, is fixed at 45 per cent. The
distributable income is computed after deducting
from the total income of the company the taxes paid
by it, sums paid to charitable institutions or funds,
income arising outside India in a country whose laws
prohibit or restrict the remittance of money to India, and, in the case of a banking company, the
amount transferred to certain Reserve Funds. The
additional tax is levied at the rate of 35 per cent
on the distributable income as reduced by the amount
of dividends actually distributed and certain other
expenses which, though incurred by a company, have
not been allowed as a deduction in the computation
of its total income.

B. Nonresident foreign corporations

    1. Nonresident corporations are taxed only on in-
       come received or deemed to be received in India
       and on income that accrues to the company in
       India.

    2. Nonresident corporations which have made the
       prescribed arrangements for declaration and
       distribution of dividends within India are
       treated at par with resident corporations;
       that is, they are taxed at 25 per cent and

subject to the different surtaxes imposed on resident companies.

If the nonresident companies have not made the arrangements prescribed, they are usually taxed at 63 per cent.

INDONESIA (Rupiah)

A. Domestic and Resident Corporations

   1. Income included for tax purposes
      Income from all sources

   2. Tax Rates:

Income Brackets		Tax Rates
Over	Not Over	
0	500,000	40
500,000	1,000,000	42 1/2
1,000,000	1,500,000	45
1,500,000	2,000,000	47 1/2
2,000,000	2,500,000	50
2,500,000	-	52 1/2

B. Nonresident foreign corporations are taxed at the same rates imposed on domestic and resident corporations on income derived from sources in Indonesia, regardless of whether they are engaged in business.

JAPAN (Yen)

A. Domestic corporations

   1. Scope of Income   entire income received from within and outside Japan

   2. Tax rates
      a) Ordinary company

Taxable Income	Tax Rate
Distributed income:	
For the first ¥2,000,000	24
In excess of ¥2,000,000	28

                              Undistributed Income:
                              For the first
                                  ¥2,000,000   33
                              In excess of
                                  ¥2,000,000   38

    b) Family corporation
          If the amount retained from earnings is
    in excess of 15 per cent of the total earnings
    of ¥1,000,000, whichever is greater, the cor-
    poration is subject to the following additional
    tax:

Excess Amount	Tax Rate
Not more than ¥3,000,000	10
Over ¥3,000,000	15
Over ¥10,000,000	20

B. Foreign corporations

    1. Engaged in trade or business
        a) Scope of income   income derived from
                                  sources in Japan
        b) Tax rates   same rates of tax im-
                                  posed on domestic cor-
                                  porations
        c) Deductions and
           allowances   expenses incurred in
                                  Japan

    2. Not engaged in trade or business
        a) Scope of income   income derived in Japan
        b) Tax rate   20 per cent of gross re-
                                  ceipts
        c) Deductions and
           allowances   none allowed

SOUTH KOREA (Won)

A. Domestic corporations

    1. Scope of income   entire income wherever
                                  received

2. Tax rates | Taxable Income | Tax Rate |
| --- | --- |
| Not more than 1,000,000 won | 20 |
| More than 1,000,000 won | 25 |

B. Foreign corporations engaged in trade or business

1. Scope of income   income derived from sources within South Korea
2. Tax rates   same rates imposed on domestic corporations
3. Deductions   same deductions allowed to domestic corporations

MALAYSIA (M$)

A. Resident corporations

1. Scope of income   income received in Malaysia from any source
2. Tax rate   40 per cent
3. Deductions   losses and expenditures incurred in the production of income

B. Nonresident corporations

1. Scope of income   income received from Malaysia
2. Tax rate   40 per cent
3. Deductions   losses and expenditures incurred in the production of income

PHILIPPINES (Pesos)

A. Domestic corporations

1. Scope of income   entire income from any source, wherever received
2. Tax rates   22 per cent on the first ₱100,000 taxable income
33 per cent on the excess over ₱100,000 taxable income

B. Foreign corporations

    1. Engaged in trade
       or business   income received from any
                          source within the Philip-
                          pines
        a) Tax rates   same rates applicable to
                          domestic corporations
        b) Deductions   deductions allowed to domes-
                          tic corporations but limited
                          to those incurred in the
                          Philippines

    2. Not engaged in
       trade or business

        a) Scope of income   income received from the
                          Philippines
        b) Tax rate   30 per cent of gross in-
                          come
        c) Deductions   no deductions allowed

SINGAPORE (Malaysian Dollar)

A. Resident corporations

    1. Scope of income   income received in Singa-
                          pore from any source
    2. Tax rate   40 per cent
    3. Deductions   losses and expenditures
                          incurred in the production
                          of income

B. Nonresident corporations

    1. Scope of income   income received from
                          Singapore
    2. Tax rate   40 per cent
    3. Deductions   losses and expenditures
                          incurred in the production
                          of income

THAILAND (Baht)

A. Domestic corporations

    1. Scope of income   income from sources derived within and outside Thailand

    2. Tax rates

Taxable Income	Tax Rate
on the first 500,000 baht	15%
on the next 500,000 baht	20%
on the excess of 1,000,000 baht	25%

B. Foreign corporations

    1. Scope of income   income from sources within Thailand

    2. Tax rates   same rates imposed on domestic corporations

    3. Deductions   same deductions allowed to domestic corporations so long as they are incurred in Thailand in producing income.

APPENDIX IV

Appendix to Chapter 5

INDIA

1. Rates of Gift Tax

Taxable Gifts		Tax on	Rate on Excess over
Lower Limit	Upper Limit	Lower Limit	Lower Limit
Rs 0	50,000	Rs 0	4%
50,000	100,000	2,000	6
100,000	150,000	5,000	8
150,000	200,000	9,000	10
200,000	300,000	14,000	12
300,000	500,000	26,000	15
500,000	1,000,000	56,000	20
1,000,000	2,000,000	156,000	25
2,000,000	3,000,000	406,000	30
3,000,000	5,000,000	706,000	35
5,000,000		1,406,000	40

2. Rates of Estate Tax

Aggregate Estate		Tax on	Rate on Excess over
Lower Limit	Upper Limit	Lower Limit	Lower Limit*
Rs 0	50,000	Rs 0	0%
50,000	100,000	0	4
100,000	150,000	2,000	6
150,000	200,000	5,000	10
200,000	300,000	10,000	12
500,000	1,000,000	52,000	20
1,000,000	2,000,000	152,000	25
2,000,000	3,000,000	402,000	30
3,000,000	5,000,000	702,000	35
5,000,000		1,402,000	40

*Estate Duty Act Amendment, 1958.

3. Rates of Wealth Tax

Net Wealth		Amount of Tax on Lower Limit	Rate on Excess over Lower Limit
Lower Limit	Upper Limit		
Individuals			
Rs 0	200,000	Rs 0	0%
200,000	1,200,000	0	1.0
1,200,000	2,200,000	10,000	1.5
2,200,000		25,000	2.0
Hindu Undivided Families			
Rs 0	400,000	Rs 0	0%
400,000	1,300,000	0	1.0
1,300,000	2,300,000	9,000	1.5
2,300,000		24,000	2.0
Corporations			
Rs 0	500,000	Rs 0	0%
500,000		0	0.5

4. Rates of Expenditure Tax

Taxable Expenditure Less Adjustments		Tax on Lower Limit	Rate on Excess over Lower Limit
Lower Limit	Upper Limit		
Rs 0	10,000	Rs 0	10%
10,000	20,000	1,000	20
20,000	30,000	3,000	40
30,000	40,000	7,000	60
40,000	50,000	13,000	80
50,000		21,000	100

Source: Taxation in India, op. cit.

APPENDIX V

Appendix to Chapter 5

SINGAPORE

Scale of Estate Duty Payable on Estates of
Persons Dying on or after November 9, 1955

Principal Value of the Estate	Rate of Duty
For every dollar of the first $ 10,000	Nil
" " " " " next $ 15,000	5 per cent
" " " " " " $ 25,000	$7\frac{1}{2}$ " "
" " " " " " $ 25,000	10 " "
" " " " " " $ 25,000	$12\frac{1}{2}$ " "
" " " " " " $ 50,000	15 " "
" " " " " " $ 50,000	20 " "
" " " " " " $ 100,000	25 " "
" " " " " " $ 100,000	30 " "
" " " " " " $ 100,000	35 " "
" " " " " " $ 250,000	40 " "
" " " " " " $ 250,000	45 " "
" " " " " " $1,000,000	50 " "
" " " " " " $2,000,000	55 " "
" " " exceeding $4,000,000	60 " "

Source: <u>Reports of the Estate Duty Office and the
Stamp Office for the Years 1955-56</u>.

APPENDIX V-A

New Estate Tax Rates of Malaysia since January 1, 1965 (Malaysia and Singapore)

First M$ 25,000 of value of estate		Nil
Next 25,000 " " " "		50%
" 50,000 " " " "		7½%
" 50,000 " " " "		10%
" 50,000 " " " "		12½%
" 100,000 " " " "		15%
" 100,000 " " " "		20%
" 200,000 " " " "		25%
" 200,000 " " " "		30%
" 200,000 " " " "		35%
" 500,000 " " " "		40%
" 500,000 " " " "		45%
M$2,000,000		
Remainder of value of estate		50%

Source: <u>Tax Changes within Malaysia</u>, Budget Speech of the Minister of Finance, Malaysia

APPENDIX VI

Appendix to Chapter 5

JAPAN

1. Rates of Inheritance Tax

Taxable Amount Over	But Not Over	Tax Liability
¥	¥ 300,000	
¥ 300,000	¥ 700,000	¥ 30,000 plus 15% of amount over ¥ 300,000
¥ 700,000	¥ 1,500,000	¥ 90,000 plus 20% of amount over ¥ 700,000
¥ 1,500,000	¥ 3,000,000	¥ 250,000 plus 25% of amount over ¥ 1,500,000
¥ 3,000,000	¥ 5,000,000	¥ 625,000 plus 30% of amount over ¥ 3,000,000
¥ 5,000,000	¥ 7,000,000	¥ 1,225,000 plus 35% of amount over ¥ 5,000,000
¥ 7,000,000	¥ 10,000,000	¥ 1,925,000 plus 40% of amount over ¥ 7,000,000
¥ 10,000,000	¥ 20,000,000	¥ 3,125,000 plus 45% of amount over ¥ 10,000,000
¥ 20,000,000	¥ 30,000,000	¥ 7,625,000 plus 50% of amount over ¥ 20,000,000
¥ 30,000,000	¥ 50,000,000	¥12,625,000 plus 55% of amount over ¥ 30,000,000
¥ 50,000,000	¥ 70,000,000	¥23,625,000 plus 60% of amount over ¥ 50,000,000
¥ 70,000,000	¥100,000,000	¥35,625,000 plus 65% of amount over ¥ 70,000,000
¥100,000,000		¥55,125,000 plus 70% of amount over ¥100,000,000

2. Rates of Gift Tax

Taxable Amount		Tax Liability
Over	But Not Over	
	¥ 300,000	15%
¥ 300,000	¥ 500,000	¥ 45,000 plus 20% of amount over 300,000
¥ 500,000	¥ 700,000	¥ 85,000 plus 25% of amount over 500,000
¥ 700,000	¥ 1,000,000	¥ 135,000 plus 30% of amount over 700,000
¥ 1,000,000	¥ 1,500,000	¥ 225,000 plus 35% of amount over 1,000,000
¥ 1,500,000	¥ 2,000,000	¥ 400,000 plus 40% of amount over 1,500,000
¥ 2,000,000	¥ 3,000,000	¥ 600,000 plus 45% of amount over 2,000,000
¥ 3,000,000	¥ 5,000,000	¥ 1,050,000 plus 50% of amount over 3,000,000
¥ 5,000,000	¥ 7,000,000	¥ 2,050,000 plus 55% of amount over 5,000,000
¥ 7,000,000	¥10,000,000	¥ 3,150,000 plus 60% of amount over 7,000,000
¥10,000,000	¥30,000,000	¥ 4,950,000 plus 65% of amount over 10,000,000
¥30,000,000		¥17,950,000 plus 70% of amount over 30,000,000

Source: An Outline of Japanese Taxes, 1964.

Appendix to Chapter 5

PHILIPPINES

1. Rates of Inheritance Tax

Net Estate		Rate (%)	Payment of Tax
Over	But Not Over		
₱	₱ 12,000.00	2	The inheritance taxes are due and
12,000.00	30,000.00	4	payable within twelve months after the
30,000.00	50,000.00	6	decedent's death and are paid by the
50,000.00	70,000.00	8	executor, administrator, or the heirs,
70,000.00	100,000.00	12	as the case may be, to the Commissioner
100,000.00	150,000.00	14	of Internal Revenue or to the treasurer
150,000.00	250,000.00	16	of the province, city or municipality in
250,000.00	500,000.00	18	which the decedent was domiciled at the
500,000.00	1,000,000.00	20	time of his death.
1,000,000.00	up	22	

2. Rates of Estate Tax

Net Estate		Rate	Payment of Tax
Over	But Not Over	(%)	
₱	₱ 5,000.00	exempt	The estate taxes are due and payable
5,000.00	12,000.00	1	within nine months after the decedent's
12,000.00	30,000.00	2	death and are paid by the executor, ad-
30,000.00	50,000.00	2.5	ministrator, or the heirs, as the case
50,000.00	70,000.00	3.0	may be, to the Commissioner of Internal
70,000.00	100,000.00	5.0	Revenue or to the treasurer of the
100,000.00	150,000.00	7.0	province, city, or municipality in which
150,000.00	250,000.00	9.0	the decedent was domiciled at the time
250,000.00	500,000.00	11.00	of his death.
500,000.00	1,000,000.00	13.00	
1,000,000.00	up	15.00	

3. Gift Taxes

A. Rates of Tax Payable by Donor

Net Gifts		Rate (%)
Exceed	But Do Not Exceed	
₱	₱ 5,000.00	exempt
5,000.00	12,000.00	1
12,000.00	30,000.00	2
30,000.00	50,000.00	3
50,000.00	70,000.00	4
70,000.00	100,000.00	5
100,000.00	150,000.00	7
150,000.00	250,000.00	9
250,000.00	500,000.00	11
500,000.00	1,000,000.00	13
1,000,000.00	up	15

B. Rates of Tax Payable by Donee

Net Gifts		Rate (%)
Exceed	But Do Not Exceed	
₱	₱ 12,000.00	2
12,000.00	30,000.00	4
30,000.00	50,000.00	6
50,000.00	70,000.00	8
70,000.00	100,000.00	12
100,000.00	150,000.00	14
150,000.00	250,000.00	16
250,000.00	500,000.00	18
500,000.00	1,000,000.00	20
1,000,000.00	up	22

Payment of Tax

The gift taxes are payable on or before the fifteenth day of May following the close of the calendar year and are paid by the donor or donee, as the case may be, to the Commissioner of Internal Revenue or to the treasurer of the province, city, or municipality of which the donor or the donee is a resident.

4. Residence Tax

   A. Individuals
      (1) Class A - ₱0.50 annually
      (2) Class B - (additional tax)
         (a) For every ₱5,000 worth of real property in the Philippines, in excess of ₱10,000 - ₱2.00
         (b) For every ₱5,000 of gross receipts or earnings, in excess of ₱10,000 derived by such person from business in the Philippines - ₱2.00
         (c) For every ₱1,000 of salaries or gross receipts or earnings derived by such person from the exercise of any profession in the Philippines - ₱1.00.

   B. Corporations
      (1) Class C - ₱5.00 annually
      (2) Class C-1 - (additional tax)
         (a) For every ₱5,000 worth of real property in the Philippines - ₱2.00
         (b) For every ₱5,000 of gross receipts or earnings, derived by it from its business in the Philippines - ₱2.00.

   C. Exempt Class
      (1) Class D - ₱0.20 for every head of family or individual not falling in any one of the above classes.

Source: National Internal Revenue Code.

APPENDIX VIII

Appendix to Chapter 5

REPUBLIC OF CHINA

Estate Tax Rates

Taxable Amount		Tax Rate
Exceeds	But Does Not Exceed	
20,000 Yuan	40,000 Yuan	4%
40,000 "	60,000 "	5%
60,000 "	80,000 "	6%
80,000 "	100,000 "	7%
100,000 "	120,000 "	9%
120,000 "	140,000 "	11%
140,000 "	160,000 "	13%
160,000 "	180,000 "	15%
180,000 "	200,000 "	17%
200,000 "	250,000 "	20%
250,000 "	300,000 "	23%
300,000 "	350,000 "	26%
350,000 "	400,000 "	29%
400,000 "	450,000 "	32%
450,000 "	500,000 "	35%
500,000 "	600,000 "	39%
600,000 "	700,000 "	43%
700,000 "	800,000 "	47%
800,000 "	900,000 "	51%
900,000 "	1,000,000 "	55%
1,000,000 "	1,500,000 "	60%
1,500,000 "	2,000,000 "	65%
2,000,000 "		70%

Source: Laws of the Republic of China (Taiwan: The Republic of China, Oct., 1962), pp. 554-55.

403

Appendix to Chapter 5

THE LAND LAW OF THE REPUBLIC OF CHINA

A. Land Value Tax

Art. 169. The basic rate of the land value tax shall be 1.5 per cent of the statutory land price.

Art. 170. Where the total price of all the lands owned by any landowner does not exceed the initial point of land price subject to progressive rates, the land value tax on his lands shall be levied according to the basic rate prescribed in the preceding articles. Where the total price of all the lands owned by any landowner exceeds the initial point of land price subject to progressive rates, the land value tax on that part of the total price of his lands which exceeds the said initial point shall be levied according to the following progressive rates:

1. Where the total land price exceeds the said initial point by not more than 500 per cent, a rate of 0.2 per cent in addition to the basic rate shall be levied on that part of the total land price which exceeds the initial point;

2. Where the total land price exceeds the said initial point by not more than 1,000 per cent, another rate of 0.3 per cent in addition to the rates prescribed in the preceding sub-paragraph shall be levied on that part of the total land price which exceeds the initial point by more than 500 per cent;

3. Where the total land price exceeds the said initial point by not more than 1,500 per cent, still another rate of 0.5 per cent in addition to the rates prescribed in the preceding sub-paragraph shall be levied on that part of the total land price which exceeds the initial point by more than 1,000 per cent. Thereafter, another rate of 0.5 per cent in addition

to all the preceding rates shall be levied on every additional 500 per cent increase in the total land price, until the total cumulative rate has reached the maximum limit of five per cent.

B. Land Value Increment Tax

Art. 181. The land value increment tax shall be levied at the following rates:

1. Where the net increment of the price of any land is not more than 100 per cent of the original price of such land, the rate shall be 20 per cent of the net increment;

2. Where the net increment of the price of any land is not more than 200 per cent of the original price of such land, the rate shall be 40 per cent of that part of the net increment which exceeds the original price by more than 100 per cent, aside from the rate prescribed in the preceding sub-paragraph;

3. Where the net increment of the price of any land is not more than 300 per cent of the original price of such land, the rate shall be 60 per cent of that part of the net increment which exceeds the original price by more than 200 per cent, aside from the rates prescribed in the preceding sub-paragraph;

4. Where the net increment of the price of any land is over 300 per cent of the original price of such land, the rate shall be 80 per cent of that part of the net increment which exceeds the original price by more than 300 per cent, aside from the rates prescribed in the preceding sub-paragraph.

Source: Laws of the Republic of China, op. cit.

Appendix to Chapter 6

Revenue from Taxation and Taxes on Production and Sales of Some Selected
Asian Countries, 1962 and 1963 (Amount in Million Currency)

Country and Year	Unit Currency	Total Revenue from Taxation	Taxes on Production and Sales		Import and Export Taxes		
			Amount	Per cent to Revenue from Taxation	Amount	Per Cent to Total Revenue from Taxation	Per Cent to Taxes on Prod. and Sales
1962							
Ceylon	rupee	1,309	933	71.3	704	53.8	75.5
India	rupee	8,230	6,044	73.4	1,996	24.3	33.0
Indonesia	rupiah	74,018	24,707	33.4	6,706	9.1	27.1
Japan[a]	yen	2,366	972	41.1	144	6.1	14.8
Malaysia	Malaysian $	880	621	70.6	550[b]	62.5	88.6
Philippines	pesos	1,293	889	68.8	242[c]	18.7	27.2
Singapore	Malaysian $	277	152	54.9	103	37.2	67.8
Thailand	baht	7,455	6,691	89.8	3,105	41.6	46.4
South Korea	won	28,690	22,000	76.7	3,060	10.7	13.9
1963							
Ceylon	rupee	1,280	960	75.0	677	52.9	70.5
India	rupee	13,101	9,077	69.3	3,200	24.4	35.3
Indonesia	rupiah	162,129	55,820	34.4	14,267	8.8	25.6
Japan[a]	yen	2,512	927	36.9	186	7.4	20.1
Malaysia	Malaysian $	891	640	71.8	569[b]	63.9	88.9
Philippines	pesos	1,483	1,017	68.6	273[d]	18.4	26.8
Singapore	Malaysian $	299	165	55.2	–	–	–
Thailand	baht	7,812	3,486	44.6	3,105	39.7	89.1
South Korea	won	31,078	18,184	58.5	6,350	20.4	34.9

Note: For the year 1962, collections for sales taxes included special excise
tax in some countries. Discrepancies in figures on total revenue,
revenues from production and sales taxes and revenue from taxes on income and property with those of the other chapters are due to differences in classifications utilized.

n.a.:   Not available.

a   in thousand million yen.
b   includes excise tax.
c   includes margin levy but excludes export tax.
d   import tax only.

Sources: Asian Taxation, 1963; Economic Research Journal, XI, No. 3, Dec., 1964;
United Nations, Economic Survey for Asia and the Far East, 1962.

	Sales Taxes			Special Excise Taxes			Licenses & Other Bus. Taxes	
Amount	Per Cent to Total Revenue from Taxation	Per Cent to Taxes on Prod. and Sales	Amount	Per Cent to Total Revenue from Taxation	Per Cent to Taxes on Prod. and Sales	Amount	Per Cent to Total Revenue from Taxation	Per Cent to Taxes on Prod. and Sales
166	12.7	17.8	–	–	–	63	4.8	6.8
n.a.	–	–	–	–	–	4,048	49.2	66.9
4,940	6.7	20.0	10,845	14.7	43.9	2,216	3.0	9.0
722	30.5	74.3	–	–	–	106	4.5	10.9
n.a.	–	–	–	–	–	71	8.1	11.4
270	20.9	30.4	280	21.7	31.5	97	7.5	10.9
26	9.4	17.1	–	–	–	23	8.3	15.1
2,451	32.9	36.6	–	–	–	1,135	15.2	17.0
11,190	39.0	50.9	–	–	–	7,750	27.0	35.2
n.a.	–	–	211	16.5	22.0	72	5.6	7.5
88	0.7	1.0	5,675	43.3	62.5	114	0.9	1.3
9,624	5.9	17.2	27,164	16.8	48.7	4,765	2.9	8.5
124	4.9	13.3	535	21.3	57.7	82	3.3	8.8
n.a.	–	–	n.a.	–	–	71	8.0	10.1
349	23.5	34.3	321	21.6	31.6	74	5.0	7.3
n.a.	–	–	112	37.5	67.9	53	17.7	32.1
n.a.	–	–	278	3.6	8.0	103	1.3	29.5
3,775	12.1	20.8	5,038	16.2	27.7	3,022	9.7	16.6

Appendix to Chapter 6

Revenue from Taxation and Taxes on Production and Sales of Selected Asian Countries, 1962 and 1963 (Amount in Million Currency)

Country and Year	Unit Currency	Total Revenue from Taxation	Taxes on Income and Property		Taxes on Production and Sales	
			Amount	Per Cent to Revenue from Taxation	Amount	Per Cent to Revenue from Taxation
1962						
Ceylon	rupee	1,309	376	28.7	933	71.3
India	rupee	8,230	2,186	26.6	6,044	73.4
Indonesia	rupiah	74,018	49,311	66.6	24,707	33.4
Japan[a]	yen	2,366	1,394	58.9	972	41.1
Malaysia	Malaysian $	880	259	29.4	621	70.6
Philippines	pesos	1,293	404	31.2	889	68.8
Singapore	Malaysian $	277	125	45.1	152	54.9
Thailand	baht	7,455	764	10.2	6,691	89.8
South Korea	won	28,690	6,690	23.3	22,000	76.7

Ceylon	rupee	1,280	320	25.0	960	75.0
India	rupee	13,101	4,024	30.7	9,077	69.3
Indonesia	rupiah	162,129	106,309	65.6	55,820	34.4
Japan[a]	yen	2,512	1,585	63.1	927	36.9
Malaysia	Malaysian $	891	251	28.2	640	71.8
Philippines	pesos	1,483	466	31.4	1,017	68.6
Singapore	Malaysian $	299	134	44.8	165	55.2
Thailand	baht	7,812	4,326	55.4	3,486	44.6
South Korea	won	31,078	12,894	41.5	18,184	58.5

Note: For the year 1962, collections for sales taxes included special excise tax in some countries. Discrepancies in figures on total revenue, revenues from production and sales taxes, and revenue from taxes on income and property with those of the other chapters are due to differences in classifications utilized.

[a] In thousand million yen.

Source: Asian Taxation, 1963; Economic Research Journal, XI, No. 3 (December, 1964); United Nations, Economic Survey for Asia and the Far East, 1962.

APPENDIX XII

Appendix to Chapter 9

THE REPUBLIC OF PHILIPPINES INVESTMENT
INCENTIVES ACT (Republic Act No. 5186)

The Philippines has formulated several development programs designed to attain a faster rate of
economic development. In these blueprints, investment requirements are invariably higher than what
the economy is actually investing. Hence, such programs need to be accompanied by various actions
which will not only increase the level of domestic
investment, but also encourage the inflow of foreign
resources because domestic savings cannot fully
cover the programmed level of investment.

As far back as 1954 attempts were made to establish a definite policy concerning foreign investments in the Philippines. Among the issues to be
settled have been the appropriate incentives afforded
to foreign investors, the areas to be opened up, the
employment of foreign nationals, and those issues relating to foreign-exchange matters with respect to
repatriation of capital and remittances of profits.
Another problem has faced the economy: Despite the
various incentives afforded domestic investments,
there has been no appreciable redirection of domestic
resources from the consumption sector to the investment sector. The Investment Incentives Act, passed
in 1967, has been so structured as to effectively
deal with these problems. Tax and nontax incentives
are given to (i) investors in a registered enterprise, (ii) Philippine nationals investing in pioneer
enterprises, (iii) registered enterprises, (iv) pioneer industries, and (v) registered enterprises engaged in export.

A "registered enterprise" is defined as a corporation (1) incorporated, organized, and existing
under Philippine laws, (2) owned as follows: except

410

as otherwise provided in the Act, at least 60 per
cent of the capital stock outstanding and entitled
to vote is owned and held by Philippine nationals,
and at least 60 per cent of the members of the Board
of Directors are citizens of the Philippines, (3) engaged in a preferred area of investment, and (4) duly
registered with the Board of Investments. The term
specifically excludes corporations engaged in banking, financing, distribution, and services.

"Pioneer enterprise" is defined as a registered
enterprise (1) engaged in the manufacture, processing
or production, and not merely in the assembly or
packaging, of goods, products, commodities, or raw materials that have not been or are not being produced
in the Philippines on a commercial scale, or (2) using
a design, formula, scheme, method, process, or system
of production or transformation of any element, sub-
stance, or raw material into another raw material or
finished good that is new and untried in the Philippines.

The act does not list specific preferred and pioneer areas of investment, but several criteria are
enumerated which will serve as guidelines in desig-
nating such areas. This makes the act flexible: Industries can be added to or deleted from the preferred areas as changing conditions demand, thus
avoiding the delay occasioned by legislative amendments. The preferred and pioneer areas of investment relate to those areas of investment which best
accomplish the policy declared in the act. Possible
areas of investment include those which will produce
substitutes for goods presently being imported in
large quantities and especially those areas which
will process further agricultural, mining, and timber products already being produced for export or
which will develop new products that can be sold com-
petitively in export markets. A preferred area of
investment is any area where an enterprise (1) is engaged in the exportation of finished products completely processed and manufactured in the Philippines
with at least 70 per cent of the peso value of its
total raw material content being Philippine raw

material; (2) is exporting more than 50 per cent of its total production; and (3) does not enjoy any preferential treatment arising from any agreement or arrangement between the Philippine Government and the importing country.

The following criteria shall similarly be taken into account:

(1) The gaps between prospective demand and existing supply for specific products, commodities, and services, and the additional production capacities that must be induced where such gaps exist;

(2) The potential of such areas of investments for creating new markets, both domestic and foreign, for domestic suppliers of raw materials and/or intermediate goods, or new resources of supply for domestic consumers of the products;

(3) The potential of such areas of investment for creating productive employment, considering the necessity for the dispersal of industries in the country on a planned and balanced basis to the extent that is economically feasible and practicable;

(4) The extent to which investment in such areas will integrate existing production facilities;

(5) The amounts of import substitution or of new exports such areas of investment will promote;

(6) The amount of capital normally needed thereby;

(7) The nature of the risk, commercial or otherwise, which may be entailed;

(8) The proportion of the required capital, raw material, and labor inputs of indigenous origin;

(9) The rate of profitability;

(10) The rate of return to the economy;

(11) The maintenance of competition; and

(12) Such other criteria as the Board of Investments may adopt.

The following are the tax incentives afforded:

(1) Investors in a Registered Enterprise. An exemption from income tax is allowed on that portion of the gains realized from the sale, disposition, or transfer of capital assets that correspond to the portion of the proceeds of the sale that is invested in new issues of capital stock of a registered enterprise, subject to certain administrative provisions.

(2) Philippine Nationals Investing in Pioneer Industries. (a) An investment allowance is granted to the extent of the investment and shall be allowed as a deduction from taxable income but not to exceed 10 per cent thereof, subject to some given conditions; (b) An exemption from income tax on capital gains, similar to that of the above is granted; and (c) An exemption is allowed from income tax on all gains realized from the sale, disposition, or transfer of stock dividends from a pioneer enterprise.

(3) Registered Enterprises. A registered enterprise, to the extent of engagement in a preferred area of investment, is granted the following incentives, subject to some conditions: (a) All capitalized organizational and preoperating expenses attributable to the establishment of a registered enterprise may be deducted from its taxable income over a period of not more than ten years beginning with the month the enterprise begins operation; (b) At the option of the taxpayer, fixed assets may be depreciated to the extent of not more than twice as fast as normal rate of depreciation or depreciated at normal rate of depreciation if expected life is ten years or less, or depreciated over any number of years between five years and expected life if the latter is more than ten years; (c) A net operating loss incurred in any of the first ten years of operations may be carried over as a deduction from taxable income for the

six years immediately following the year of loss;
(d) Within seven years from the date of registration
of the enterprise, importation of machinery and equipment, and spare parts shipped with such machinery and
equipment shall not be subject to tariff duties and
compensating tax; (e) A tax credit equivalent to 100
per cent of the value of the compensating tax and
customs duties that would have been paid on the machinery, equipment, and spare parts had these items
been imported shall be given to the registered enterprise which purchases such domestically; (f) A tax
credit for taxes withheld or interest payments on
foreign loans; (g) When a registered enterprise re-
invests its undistributed profit or surplus, the
amount so reinvested shall be allowed as a deduction
from its taxable income in the year in which such reinvestment was made; and (h) The banning for a limited period the importation of goods or commodities
which unfairly or unnecessarily compete with those
produced by registered enterprises.

(4) Pioneer Industries. In addition to those
incentives granted to registered enterprises, the
following are given: (a) Exemption from all taxes
under the National Internal Revenue Code, except income tax, to the following extent: 100 per cent up
to December, 1972; 75 per cent up to December, 1975;
50 per cent up to December, 1977; 25 per cent up to
December, 1979; and 10 per cent up to December, 1981;
and (b) Post-operative tariff protection to an extent
not exceeding 50 per cent of the dutiable value of
imported items similar to those being manufactured
or produced by a pioneer enterprise.

(5) Registered Enterprises Engaged in Exports.
(a) A deduction from taxable income twice the amount
of the ordinary and necessary expenses incurred for
the purpose of promoting the sale of these products
abroad; (b) A deduction from taxable income twice
the amount of shipping freight incurred in connection with the export of these products; and (c) A
tax credit equivalent to 7 per cent of the total
cost of the raw materials and supplies purchased by
registered enterprises or an amount equivalent to

the taxes actually paid by registered enterprises on
said raw materials, whichever is higher, to the extent used in manufacturing exported products and commodities.

Besides the various tax concessions, registered
and pioneer industries are accorded nontax incentives.
In the case of foreign investments, repatriation of
investments, remittance of earnings, and foreign-
exchange requirements arising from foreign loans and
contracts are guaranteed. The guarantees of freedom
from expropriation and requisition of investment,
except for public use or in the interest of national
welfare and defense, as provided by the Philippine
Constitution, are specifically included as basic
rights of and guarantees to foreign investment. The
protection of patents and other proprietary rights
is similarly granted. Restrictions on the employment of foreign nationals are relaxed so that production does not suffer from the lack of technical
personnel.

A significant nontax incentive relates to the
protection from government competition. Except for
certain situations, no agency or instrumentality
of the government shall import, or allow the importation of, tax and duty-free, products or items that
are being produced by registered enterprises. It
has been the experience of some industries that although they are given tax concessions, such concessions are negated by the heavy importation of their
finished products (and its subsequent sale at subsidized prices) by a government agency. With respect to financing, government financial institutions, such as the Development Bank of the Philippines and the Government Service Insurance System,
subject to their respective charters, are required
to accord high priority to applications for financial assistance submitted by registered enterprises.
Restrictions on the investment portfolio of insurance companies are lifted so that they can invest
in new issues of stock of registered enterprises.

To carry out the purposes of the act, a Board
of Investments has been created to establish and
execute a national investment plan. The Board, besides determining the economic activities eligible
to receive the various incentives enumerated above,
is granted the exercise of all the powers necessary
or incidental to attain the purposes of the act.
The presence of a continuing and full-time body
would insure that the national investment plan keeps
in step with changing economic conditions.

APPENDIX XIII

Appendix to Chapter 11

National Income of Selected Asian Countries (At Current Factor Cost)

Country	1958	1959	1960	1961	1962	Average Annual Rate of Growth 1958-62 (Per Cent)
Cambodia[1] (million riels)	14,307	14,689	15,658*	16,691*	17,576*	5.3
Ceylon (million rupees)	5,308.2	5,602.3	5,738.1	5,850.4	6,043.4	3.3
China (million new Taiwan dollars)	32,827	38,513	48,008	53,531	58,731	15.8
India[2] (thousand million rupees)	126	130	142	146	147	4.3
Indonesia (thousand million rupiah)	174.2	202.9	213.3	239.1*	267.8*	12.0
Japan (thousand million yen)	8,359	9,666	11,504	13,730	15,421	16.6
Malaysia (million Malaysian dollars)	3,903	4,232	4,535	4,712*	5,013*	6.4
Philippines (million pesos)	9,436	10,008	10,604	11,746	12,862	8.1
South Korea (thousand million won)	150.7	157.3	178.5	212.7	241.7	12.6
Thailand (million bahts)	37,109	40,909	46,336	50,026	53,700	9.7

[1]Gross domestic product at 1956 prices.

[2]Accounts are reckoned on a fiscal year basis which begins on April 1.

Notes:
1. No data available for Singapore and South Vietnam.
2. Accounts with asterisk are estimates based on the respective average annual growth rate of national income from 1955.

Sources: United Nations, Yearbook of National Accounts Statistics 1962; United Nations, Economic Survey of Asia and the Far East 1962; and United Nations, Monthly Bulletin of Statistics, February, 1964.

Appendix to Chapter 11

Government Revenue and Expenditure of Selected Asian Countries
(In Millions of Their Respective Currencies)
FY 1958-62

Item	Cambodia (riels)					Ceylon (rupees)				
	1958	1959	1960	1961	1962	1957/58	1958/59	1959/60	1960/61	1961/62
Total Revenue	2,649	3,120	3,300	3,658	3,600	1,171	1,214	1,282	1,390	1,478
Nontax revenue	594	917	772	799	880	127	139	142	147	169
Tax revenue	2,055	2,203	2,528	2,859	2,720	1,044	1,075	1,140	1,243	1,309
Tax on income and wealth	240	260	332	435	...	279	218	214	314	376
Land tax	14	15	13	13	...	-	-	-	8	12
Customs duties	716	650	1,041	1,082	...	617	696	734	739	704
On import	636	638	923	969	...	292	367	407	435	426
On export	78	112	118	113	...	325	329	327	304	278
Transaction and cons. taxes	822	886	915	932	...	93	108	135	136	166
Licenses, stamps, etc.	124	132	196	368	...	19	25	25	26	32
Other tax revenue	141	160	31	29	...	36	28	32	20	19
Total Expenditure	2,650	3,908	4,420	4,887	5,300	1,444	1,656	1,741	1,881	2,090
Defense	602	1,515	1,494	1,609	1,373	64	72	70	74	77
Subsidies	-	-	-	-	-	112	146	193	248	171
Economic services	151	179	185	217	247	149	173	185	189	210
Social services	809	956	1,048	1,124	1,193	360	421	459	459	497
Cont'r to prov. and loc. gov't.	...	...	...	...	...	32	35	36	36	37
Other current expenditure	674	722	1,461	1,650	2,152	249	348	329	375	384
Investment	414	536	232	287	335	465	405	412	439	644
Loans and advances (net)	...	...	...	...	...	13	56	57	61	70
Balance	(1)	(788)	(1,120)	(1,229)	(1,700)	(273)	(442)	(459)	(491)	(612)

Item	India (rupees)					Indonesia (rupiah)				
	1957/58	1958/59	1959/60	1960/61	1961/62	1958	1959	1960	1961	1962
Total Revenue	9,219	9,645	10,778	12,291	14,114	23,273	30,571	50,318	62,759	
Nontax revenue	3,465	4,114	4,354	4,990	5,884	9,346	6,606	12,085	23,363	
Tax revenue	5,754	5,531	6,424	7,301	8,230	13,927	23,965	38,233	39,396	
Tax on income and wealth	1,588	1,627	1,905	2,013	2,186	3,989	5,536	8,579	11,876	
Land tax	-	-	-	-	-	11	12	13	14	
Customs duties	1,800	1,383	1,561	1,700	1,996	1,854	2,174	4,307	8,122	
On import	1,509	1,165	1,358	1,494	1,806	1,669	1,858	2,848	5,055	
On export	291	218	203	206	190	185	316	1,459	3,067	
Transaction and cons. taxes	...	...	...	...	...	7,595	15,741	24,543	)	
Licenses, stamps, etc.	...	...	...	...	...	147	137	215	19,384)	
Other tax revenue	2,416	2,521	2,958	3,583	4,228	334	365	576	)	
Total Expenditure	16,032	17,053	17,388	18,850	22,164	35,313	44,350	58,336	79,624	
Defense	2,828	2,787	2,670	2,809	3,275	11,085	14,071	22,431	31,732	
Subsidies	258	235	184	263	287	...	...	...	...	
Economic services	...	...	...	...	...	1,404	1,927	3,036	6,218	
Social services	...	...	...	...	...	2,884	3,124	5,083	6,945	
Cont'r to prov. and loc. gov't.	1,009	1,241	1,546	1,946	1,889	...	...	...	...	
Other current expenditure	3,047	3,467	4,026	4,368	4,992	18,646	23,279	23,962	27,678	
Investment	5,219	5,453	4,482	4,595	5,582	1,294	1,949	3,824	7,051	
Loans and advances (net)	3,671	3,870	4,478	4,869	6,139	...	...	...	...	
Balance	(6,813)	(7,403)	(6,610)	(6,559)	(8,050)	(12,040)	(13,779)	(8,018)	(16,865)	
Saving	2,077	1,920	2,350	2,905	3,671	(10,746)	(11,830)	(4,194)	(9,814)	

Appendix XIV to Chapter 11, continued

Item	Japan (thousand million yen)					South Korea (thousand million won)				
	1957/58	1958/59	1959/60	1960/61	1961/62	1958	1959	1960	1961	1962
Total Revenue	1,332	1,503	1,746	2,238	2,529	19.87	26.20	31.44	30.05	37.02
Nontax revenue	83	86	131	137	163	2.99	1.76	3.87	5.96	8.33
Tax revenue	1,249	1,417	1,615	2,101	2,366	16.88	24.44	27.57	24.09	28.69
Tax on income and wealth	628	770	897	1,243	1,394	3.22	4.36	4.47	4.59	6.69
Land tax	-	-	-	-	-	2.03	1.93	1.53	1.21	-
Customs duties	51	52	82	111	144	2.96	3.55	5.14	4.85	3.06
On import	...	...	...	...	...	...	...	...	...	...
On export	...	...	...	...	...	...	...	...	...	...
Transaction and cons. taxes	570	476	519	602	722	4.12	5.29	6.54	8.03	11.19
Licenses, stamps, etc.	-	36	43	51	60	0.48	0.75	0.64	0.78	0.97
Other tax revenue	-	83	74	94	46	4.08	8.56	9.19	4.63	6.78
Total Expenditure	1,221	1,484	1,693	2,012	2,460	40.62	40.54	42.79	62.33	81.41
Defense	176	154	161	164	185	12.78	13.97	14.76	16.70	19.42
Subsidies	32	...	...	...	...	1.63	0.61	0.26	2.51	1.15
Economic services	...	36	39	37	50	0.98	1.15	1.14	1.86	1.87
Social services	408	289	333	400	504	5.51	6.52	7.76	9.91	11.89
Cont'r to prov. and loc. gov't.	233	376	421	521	614	1.51	2.60	2.51	2.10	1.58
Other current expenditure	198	302	349	380	503	4.38	5.54	6.41	9.23	9.87
Investment	170	322	385	504	598	4.24	4.10	3.95	6.76	11.45
Loans and advances (net)	4	5	5	6	6	9.59	6.05	6.00	13.26	24.18
Balance	111	19	53	226	69	(20.75)	(14.34)	(11.35)	(32.28)	(44.39)
Saving	285	346	443	736	663	(6.92)	(4.19)	(1.40)	(12.26)	(8.76)

Appendix XIV to Chapter 11, continued

Item	Malaysia (Malaysian dollars)					Philippines (pesos)				
	1958	1959	1960	1961	1962	1957/58	1958/59	1959/60	1960/61	1961/62
Total Revenue	816	953	1,111	1,040		1,015	1,051	1,265	1,379	1,514
Nontax revenue	187	200	212	222		203	221	203	268	211
Tax revenue	629	753	899	818		812	830	1,062	1,111	1,303
Tax on income and wealth	126	132	193	204		162	184	236	278	323
Land tax	-	-	-	-		-	-	-	-	-
Customs duties	419	528	604	506		262	243	328	325	345
On import	282	301	347	339		262	243	328	325	345
On export	137	227	257	167		-	-	-	-	-
Transaction and cons. taxes	26	26	25	25		170	186	188	195	201
Licenses, stamps, etc.	50	56	67	71		180	172	210	258	320
Other tax revenue	8	11	10	12		38	45	100	55	114
Total Expenditure	1,043	1,062	1,139	1,463		1,086	1,045	1,233	1,494	1,551
Defense	166	142	136	119		181	184	190	197	196
Subsidies	-	-	-	-		...	...	...	32	36
Economic services	46	45	59	59		147	149	200	232	236
Social services	216	231	266	289		315	337	377	441	495
Cont'r to prov. and loc. gov't.	-	-	-	-		74	64	88	116	118
Other current expenditure	361	383	407	455		134	134	165	150	195
Investment	254)	261)	271)	541)		235	177	213	287	245
Loans and advances (net)						...	...	...	39	30
Balance	(227)	(109)	(28)	(423)		(71)	6	32	(115)	(37)
Saving	27	152	243	118		164	183	245	211	238

421

Appendix XIV to Chapter 11, continued

Item	Singapore (Malaysian dollars)					Thailand (baht)				
	1958	1959	1960	1961	1962	1958	1959	1960	1961/62	1962/63
Total Revenue	271	274	311	345	386	5,602	6,037	6,777	7,378	8,323
Nontax revenue	76	72	104	92	109	568	715	690	583	868
Tax revenue	195	202	217	253	277	5,034	5,322	6,087	6,795	7,455
Tax on income and wealth	70	80	80	101	125	405	428	640	657	764
Land tax	-	-	-	-	-	-	-	-	-	-
Customs duties	91	88	96	94	103	1,915	2,215	2,550	2,932	3,105
On import	91	88	96	94	103	1,622	1,806	2,061	2,537	2,734
On export	-	-	-	-	-	293	409	489	895	371
Transaction and cons. taxes	20	21	24	27	26	1,518	1,519	1,681	2,100	2,451
Licenses, stamps, etc.	8	8	13	27	20	198	186	259	146	148
Other tax revenue	6	5	4	4	3	998	974	957	980	987
Total Expenditure	291	250	255	386	561	6,013	6,442	6,710	8,345	9,588
Defense	11	8	7	7	10	1,390	1,420	1,378	1,586	1,631
Subsidies	-	-	-	-	-	-	22	20	9	8
Economic services	18	15	22	26	32	304	552	501	796	1,022
Social services	100	104	108	146	181	1,497	1,547	1,698	2,027	2,278
Cont'r to prov. and loc. gov't.	-	-	-	-	-	47	109	118	150	150
Other current expenditure	90	93	76	86	113	1,813	1,617	1,803	2,178	2,399
Investment	72	30	42	121	225	962	1,175	1,190	1,599	1,989
Loans and advances (net)	...	...	...	...	...	-	-	2	-	111
Balance	(20)	24	56	(41)	(175)	(411)	(405)	67	(967)	(1,265)
Saving	52	54	98	80	50	551	770	1,259	632	835

Appendix XIV to Chapter 11, continued

Item	South Vietnam (piastres)					Republic of China (New Taiwan dollars)				
	1958	1959	1960	1961	1962	1957/58	1958/59	1959/60	1960/61	1961/62
Total Revenue	9,083	9,791	9,435	12,062	13,889	5,454	6,275	...	6,742	6,954
Nontax revenue	954	1,614	1,085	3,652	4,431					
Tax revenue	8,129	8,177	8,350	8,410	9,458					
Tax on income and wealth	569	627	672	700	784					
Land Tax	140	142	148	160	317					
Customs duties	2,614	2,762	2,524	2,316	3,750					
On import	2,536	2,650	2,401	2,160	3,400					
On export	78	112	123	156	350					
Transaction and cons. taxes	3,916	4,002	4,253	4,494	3,104					
Licenses, stamps, etc.	648	516	600	600	635					
Other tax revenue	242	128	153	140	866					
Total Expenditure	14,314	15,276	19,038	20,382	29,210	5,408	7,019	...	7,885	8,714
Defense	6,017	6,173	7,303	8,082	11,000					
Subsidies	-	-	-	-	-					
Economic services	...	...	...	...	...					
Social services	...	...	...	...	...					
Cont'r to prov. and loc. gov't.	...	...	...	...	...					
Other current expenditure	5,197	5,429	7,890	8,518	12,471					
Investment	2,920	3,674	3,845	3,782	5,739					
Loans and advances (net)	...	...	...	...	...					
Balance	(5,051)	(5,485)	(9,603)	(8,320)	(15,321)	46	(744)	...	(1,145)	(1,760)
Saving	(2,131)	(1,811)	(5,758)	(4,538)	(9,582)					

Appendix XIV to Chapter 11, continued

Country	Fiscal Year	Type of Account				
		1958	1959	1960	1961	1962
Cambodia	January to December	E	E	E	E	E
Ceylon	October to September	A	A	A	A	RE
China, Republic of	July to June	A	A	...	A	A
India	April to March	A	A	A	A	RE
Indonesia	January to December	PR	PR	PR	PR	...
Japan	April to March	A	A	A	A	RE
Malaysia	January to December	A	A	AE	DE	...
Philippines	July to June	A	A	A	A	DE
Singapore	January to December	A	A	A	AE	DE
South Korea	January to December	A	A	A	RE	DE
South Vietnam	January to December	A	DE	A	RE	DE
Thailand[1]	October to September	A	A	A	DE[2]	DE[2]

A - accounts   AE - approved estimates
PR - provisional results   DE - draft estimates
RE - revised estimates

[1]Thailand had a fiscal year extending from January to December from 1941 to 1960; January to September, 1961; October to September from 1961/62.

[2]For fiscal years 1961/62 and 1962/63, respectively.

General Notes to Appendix XIV, Chapter 11

... - not available
-   - nil or negligible
( ) - negative amount

    Figures relate to central governments.

    In general, only the net results of public enter-
prises and fiscal monopolies are included; positive
balances are shown under revenue and negative balances
under expenditure. Currency and mint transactions are
excluded. Interest charges to public enterprises and
entities are included in revenue and not deducted from
interest payments on the expenditure side.

Revenue:
    Total revenue: excluding proceeds from loans,
other forms of borrowing, grants and aid, transfers
from reserve funds, and counterpart funds.

    Transaction and consumption taxes: excise duties,
turnover taxes, sales taxes, and entertainment duties.

Expenditure:
    Total expenditure: including current expenditure,
capital outlays, and loans and advances (net) granted
by the government but excludes debt redemption, contributions to sinking funds, and transfers to reserve funds.

    Defense: including defense capital outlay. Expen-
diture on military pensions is included in "other current expenditure."

    Economic services: including current expenditure
on agriculture, forests, industrial development, scientific and technical research, irrigation, public works,
ports, lighthouses, commerce, planning, etc.

    Social services: including current expenditure on
education, health, social welfare, relief, etc.

    Contributions to provincial and local governments:
including contributions towards meeting current expenditures.

    Investment: covers capital outlays of public works
department, including maintenance, and of government
enterprises and other departments and grants to provinces and local authorities for the same purposes.

    Loans and advances (net): mainly granted to prov-
inces, local authorities, public and private undertakings for capital outlay.

Source: United Nations, Economic Survey of Asia and
         the Far East 1962.

APPENDIX XV

Appendix to Chapter 11

U.S. Aid to Southeast Asia (U.S. $ Million)

Country	Economic Aid		Military Aid		Total Aid	
	1962	1946-62	1962	1946-62	1962	1946-62
Cambodia	31.2	250.7	8.7	84.9	39.9	335.6
Ceylon	5.7	79.4	-	-	5.7	79.4
India	775.1	3,867.0	-	-	775.1	3,867.0
Indonesia	82.9	681.5	-	-	82.9	681.5
Japan	67.8	2,660.2	74.0	1,022.0	141.8	3,682.2
Malaysia	0.9	23.2	-	-	0.9	23.2
Philippines	49.9	1,334.1	21.5	402.9	71.4	1,737.0
South Korea	194.4	3,425.2	136.9	1,843.9	331.3	5,269.1
South Vietnam	143.2	1,687.5	144.0	759.5	287.2	2,447.0
Taiwan	76.0	2,044.6	84.4	2,305.3	160.4	4,349.9
Thailand	47.7	338.1	39.1	428.6	86.8	766.7

(To Foreign Assistance Act countries: obligations and loan authorizations, cumulative July, 1945–June, 1962 and Fiscal Year 1962 (July, 1961–June, 1962.)

Source: Dick Wilson (ed.), Far Eastern Economic Review 1964 Yearbook, p. 28.

APPENDIX XVI

A Brief Description of the
Selected Asian Countries

CAMBODIA

Cambodia is a Buddhist constitutional monarchy
in the Indo-Chinese Peninsula, bounded on the south
and east by South Vietnam, on the north by Laos and
Thailand, on the west by Thailand, and on the southwest by the gulf of Siam. Its land area is 66,607
square miles, supporting a population of 5,700,000.
The population is 76 per cent Cambodian, 5 per cent
Annamese, and 4 per cent Chinese.

The territory consists chiefly of a sandy plain
surrounded by heavily forested mountain ranges. The
Mekong River lies to the east. Lake Tonle Sap, a
natural storage basin of the Keong, is in the center
of the plain. Substantial deposits of iron ore,
limestone, and phosphate have been only slightly
tapped.

The principal cities are Phnompenh, the political capital, and Battambang.

The Cambodian economy is basically agricultural.
Rice, the chief crop, is grown principally in the
Battambang area. Other major crops are rubber, tobacco, cotton, kapok, maize, and pepper. Native industries include silk and cotton weaving, rice milling, and fish salting. In addition to rice and rubber, the country's leading exports are wool, hides,
and other animal products.

The Cambodian currency is the riel, equivalent
to U.S. $0.029.

The political life of Cambodia has been domin-
ated by Prince Norodom Sihanouk, who abdicated the
throne in order to play a more active political role
in the country. The Popular Socialist Community,

427

which he organized, has controlled the government
since 1955. Under the strong leadership of its
former monarch, Cambodia has pursued a policy of
nonalignment in world politics.

CEYLON

Ceylon is a self-governing island-dominion of
the British Commonwealth of Nations, located in the
Indian Ocean off the southern tip of India. Having
an area of 25,323 square miles, the island is composed of flat coastal lands and central mountainous
regions. Its population of ten million has two predominant linguistic and cultural groups: about 70
per cent are Sinhalese, most of them Buddhists, and
21 per cent Tamils, who are predominantly Hindus.

The Ceylonese economy relies principally upon
the export of tea, rubber, and coconuts. The proceeds from these exports are used to finance the
country's food imports. Other products include rice,
cinnamon, cacao, iron, ilmenite, zircon, monazie,
and quartz. Ceylon's industries produce plywood,
paper, glassware, ceramics, cement, and acetic acid.

The Ceylonese currency is the rupee, equivalent
to U.S. $0.21.

Colombo, the political capital, is also the
chief port. The Colombo Plan, a cooperative economic-
development effort among Western countries (led by
Great Britain and Australia) and Asian nations, was
born in this city.

The government is parliamentary, with the Prime
Minister chosen from among the popularly elected rep-
resentatives of political constituencies in the
National Legislature.

THE REPUBLIC OF CHINA (TAIWAN)

Taiwan, the seat of the Chinese Nationalist Government, is an island with an area of 13,952 square niles, separated from mainland China to the west by the Formosa straits, and lying north of the Philippines and south of Japan. Most of the island's population of 11,300,000 are of Chinese descent. Only about one-fourth of the total land area is arable.

Basically an agricultural economy, Taiwan is able to produce almost all the basic foods for its population. The major crops are sugar and rice. The island is a leading source of camphor, and the government has a monopoly over camphor production. Livestock, especially cattle and water buffalo, are raised on a commercial scale. The major exports are sugar, rice, tea, citronella oil, cement, coal, salt, bananas, canned pineapples, and cotton piece goods.

Taiwan has become one of the most industrialized countries in the Far East. Its industrial potential was bolstered by effective planning consonant with the principles of a free-enterprise economy. The chief industries are food processing and textile manufacturing. Light industries have been developed to the extent that Taiwan is now in a position to engage in exporting light machineries and equipment.

The unit of currency of the Republic of China is the NT dollar, exchanged at the rate of NT$ 40.03 per U.S. $1.

The political capital of Taiwan is Taipei, a city of about 900,000. Other principal cities are Kachsuing, a seaport and major industrial center, and Tainan, noted for agricultural products.

The government of the Republic of China is basically parliamentary. The president is elected for a seven-year term and may be re-elected. The Prime Minister is usually the head of the ruling party in the Legislative Yuan.

REPUBLIC OF INDIA

The Republic of India, located in the Indian subcontinent, is bounded on the north by East and West Pakistan, Tibet, Nepal, Bhutan, and Sikhim; on the south by Ceylon and the Indian Ocean; on the east by the Arabian Sea; and on the west by the Bay of Bengal. India has an area of 1,261,416 square miles and a population of approximately 440 million (including Jammu and Kashmir). Roughly 85 per cent of the population are Hindus, 9.9 per cent Moslems, 2.3 per cent Christians, and 1.7 per cent Sikhs.

India still retains membership in the British Commonwealth of Nations, and is considered a leader of the so-called middle-of-the-road countries.

India gained its political independence from the British on August 15, 1947. Its Constitution, adopted by the Constituent Assembly on November 26, 1949, provides for a parliamentary form of government. The constitutional head of state is the president, elected every five years. He is advised by a prime minister and a cabinet. The cabinet, which is based on a majority of the bicameral legislature, consists of the Council of State, representing the constituent units of the Republic, and a House of the People (Lok Sabha), elected every five years by universal adult (over twenty-one) suffrage.

The leading export products are tea, jute, cotton products, yarn fabrics, hides, skins, leather, and leather goods.

The Indian unit of currency is the rupee, valued at U.S. $0.22.

New Delhi, the political capital, is also one of the main trade centers. The Bombay and Calcutta areas have the main concentrations of industrial population. India's principal industries are textile manufacturing, engineering, and chemical industries. Madras and Hyderabad are the other trading centers.

INDONESIA

The world's largest archipelago, Indonesia lies
along the equator with the Asian mainland and the
Philippines on the north and Australia on the south.
Of its population of about 105 million (the fifth
largest in the world), more than one-half is concentrated in the island of Java, where the capital,
Jakarta, is located.

Indonesia has a total land area of nearly 576,000
square miles (excluding West New Guinea) composed of
approximately 2,000 islands, the biggest ones being
Sumatra, Java, Celebes, and Borneo (except Brunei,
Sarawak, and Malaysian North Borneo). The western
half of New Guinea has recently been added to the
territory of this island-nation.

On August 17, 1945, Indonesia proclaimed its
political independence from the Dutch; the Nether-
lands formally recognized its independence on December 27, 1949.

The government has changed from a federal to a
unitary system, from a parliamentary to a presidential form, from a popular democracy to the "Guided
Democracy" of President Sukarno, and, finally, to a
military regime under Acting President General Suharto.

A country rich in oil and minerals, Indonesia's
major products are oil, tin, rice, corn, cassava,
ground nuts, soy beans, tobacco, coffee, rubber, coconut, and sugar. Most of these items are exported in
their raw or unprocessed forms, with the exception of
oil. Several refineries have been established by
foreign corporations, and were subsequently national-
ized by the government as part of its political-
economic campaign of nationalism.

The monetary unit of Indonesia is the rupiah,
equivalent to U.S. two cents.

JAPAN

Japan, perhaps the only truly industrialized country in the Far East, is composed of a group of islands whose total area is 142,726 square miles south of the Kamchatka Peninsula and north of the Republic of China (Formosa), with the Pacific Ocean bounding it from the east and the Sea of Japan from the west. The largest islands of the Japanese archipelago are Honshu, Hokkaido, Kyushu, and Shikoku. Japan has a population of approximately 96 million. Buddhism and Shintoism are the major religions in the country.

Tokyo, the capital, has the largest population of any city in the world. Other large cities are Yokohama, Nagoya, Osaka, and Kyoto.

Heavy industries figure heavily in the Japanese economy. In shipbuilding Japan ranks first in the world in terms of tonnage of new ships constructed yearly, with Great Britain and West Germany following behind. Japan is also a leader in electronics and light industry products. Industries like textile, chemical, agriculture, wood, fertilizer, ceramics, and machinery also contribute significantly to the national income. Exports are chiefly industrial finished products, while agricultural and mineral raw materials constitute the bulk of imports.

The Japanese monetary unit, the yen, is equivalent to U.S. $0.2673.

The government is parliamentary, and the various local political constituencies are represented in the National Diet. The political party to which the majority of the elected representatives belong is considered the ruling party. The head of the victorious party, who is an elected member of the Diet, is appointed Prime Minister by the Emperor and functions as the head of the government.

Japan's Constitution, promulgated in November, 1946, superseded the Meiji Constitution of 1889.

REPUBLIC OF KOREA

The Republic of Korea comprises the southern half of the mountainous Korean peninsula, which
projects approximately 500 miles out from the north-
eastern part of the Asian continent. Bounded on the
north by the thirty-eighth parallel, on the east by
the Eastern Sea, on the west by the Yellow Sea, and
on the south by the comparatively narrow Korean
Strait, "The Land of the Morning Calm" has an area
of 37,427 square miles and a population of 27.3 million. Buddhism, Confucianism, and Christianity are
the principal religions.

The principal cities are Seoul, the capital,
Pusan, and Taegu.

The Republic of Korea was formed immediately
upon partition of the peninsula-country after the
Korean War. The portion lying north of the thirty-
eighth parallel became known as "The People's Republic of Korea" and adheres to the Communist ideology,
while the other portion (south of the thirty-eighth
parallel), the Republic of Korea, adopted the democratic system of government, with a popularly elected
President as head of state and a legislative assembly
composed of members elected from among the different
constituencies throughout the country.

South Korea, like other typical Asian states,
has an agricultural economy. The major products are
rice, barley, wheat, and tobacco. The country also
has gold and silver mines. Some of its fast-develop-
ing industries are cotton spinning and weaving, silk-
worm culture, flour mining, woolen textiles, cement
production, and shipbuilding.

The South Korean monetary unit, the won, is
exchanged at the rate of 130 won to the U.S. $1.

MALAYSIA

On August 31, 1957, the Union of Malaya became
the Federation of Malaya, a sovereign state within
the British Commonwealth of Nations. On September
16, 1963, the Federation of Malaya joined with British North Borneo, Singapore, and Sarawak to form the
Federation of Malaysia. Singapore seceded after two
years on August 9, 1965. With Kuala Lumpur as its
capital, the country occupies the Malay Peninsula,
bounded on the north by Burma and Thailand, on the
east and south by the China Sea, with Singapore at
its southern tip, and on the southwest and west by
the Straits of Malacca and the Bay of Bengal. It
has an area of 50,690 square miles, about 75 per
cent of which is dense jungle, swamps, and mountains.

Malaysia has a mixed population of about 7 million, which is approximately 50 per cent Malay, 37.5
per cent Chinese, 11 per cent Indian, and the rest
Pakistani and others. The population is predominantly Muslim.

Malaysia has a limited constitutional monarch,
known as the "Yang di Pertuan Agong" (Paramount
Ruler), who wields no real power but performs cere-
monial duties. The head of government is the Prime
Minister, who is directly responsible to the one
hundred members of the Legislative Assembly. Each
member of the Assembly serves for five years. The
Senate (the Dewan Negara), has thirty-eight members,
twenty-two of them elected and sixteen nominated,
with six-year terms.

Malaysia is the chief world producer of rubber
and tin. Together with Indonesia, Malaysia supplies
the world with 90 per cent of its rubber. About one-
third of the world's total tin production comes from
the Kinta Valley in Perak. After rubber and tin, the
chief agricultural products are rice, coconuts,
tapioca, sugar, pepper, copra, camphor, nepah, and
palmoil.

In terms of per capita income, Malaysia ranks
third in the Far East.

The monetary unit is the Malaysian dollar, equivalent to U.S. $0.36.

REPUBLIC OF THE PHILIPPINES

The Philippine Republic, "The Pearl of the Orient," consists of a group of 7,100 islands, strategically located in southeast Asia. With the island of Formosa lying ninety miles north of the northernmost island, Borneo, and less than fifty miles south of the Sulu Archipelago, the Philippines has a total land area of 115,707 square miles, with a coastline longer than that of the United States. The largest islands are Luzon, in which Quezon City, the capital, and Manila, the leading commercial and political centers, are located; Mindanao, where the country's Moslem population is concentrated; Samar; and Leyte.

The population of 32 million is increasing at the rate of 3.2 per cent each year. Most are Malaysians, but a minority are of Hispanic-American descent. Chinese influence is highly evident in Filipino cultural, social, and commercial life. The long period of Spanish colonization is reflected by the fact that about 85 per cent of the people are Catholic.

Eighty-seven dialects are spoken, but Filipino (or Tagalog) is the official national language, and English and Spanish the other official languages.

The Philippines became a republic on June 12, 1898, after more than three centuries of Spanish rule, with Emilio Aguinaldo as the first President. The country once again reverted to a colonial status in 1899--this time under American rule. After forty-seven years of American control, the country regained its independence on July 4, 1946, barely a year after the end of World War II.

The Philippines has a unitary form of government. The three branches of government--the executive, the legislative, and the judiciary--are coequal.

The major exports are sugar, copra, logs and lumber, coconut oil, abaca, copper concentrate, desiccated coconut, plywood, canned pineapple, and chromite ore. The chief imports are machinery, base metals, transport equipment, mineral fuels and oils, cereals, dairy products, and textile fibers.

Since World War II, the Philippines has made significant progress toward industrialization under its various long-range economic programs.

The monetary unit is the peso, which, since the adoption of decontrol in 1960, has reached its free market value of U.S. $0.26.

SINGAPORE

The State of Singapore consists of the island of Singapore off the southern tip of the Malay Peninsula and adjacent islets. The total area of Singapore and the surrounding islets is 224.5 square miles. The population of about 1.7 million is predominantly Chinese.

The Singapore economy is based mainly on commerce. Buying, selling, shipping, and other activities arising from the country's strategic importance make it one of the busiest trading centers in the world. The entrepôt trading business in Singapore is estimated to be valued at about M$7,000 million each year. Singapore is not only an important seaport, but is also the focal point of air communication in southeast Asia.

Singapore acts as the exporter for Malaysia and Indonesia, which produce such raw materials as rubber, tin, copra, palm oil, pineapple, and petroleum products.

The currency of Singapore is the Malaysian dollar, valued at U.S. $0.36.

After a long colonial period under the British, Singapore became a member of the Federation of

Malaysia on September 16, 1963, together with the
Federation of Malaya, Sarawak, and the former British North Borneo (Sabah). On August 9, 1965, however, Singapore seceded from the Federation to become a sovereign state.

Singapore is closely linked historically, geo-
graphically, and economically, with Malaysia. This
affinity is reflected in Singapore's tax system,
which is strikingly similar to that of Malaysia.

REPUBLIC OF SOUTH VIETNAM

The Republic of South Vietnam occupies the part
of the former state of Vietnam lying south of the
seventeenth parallel. North of the seventeenth
parallel lies the Democratic Republic of North Vietnam. South Vietnam includes the former states of
Cochin-China and the southern part of Annam. It has
an area of 65,948 square miles and a population
of about 15 million. Buddhism and Christianity
are the predominant religions. Saigon, the capital,
is also the chief port. Other principal cities are
Tourane, Danang, and Hue.

Since the 1954 partition of the former state of
Vietnam into two independent states, the Republic of
South Vietnam has constantly been under Communist
pressure, particularly the all-out insurgency of the
Viet Cong, a military organization that is under the
command of the Hanoi Government (North Vietnam).
The unsettled political conditions arising from the
subversive activities of the Communists, along with
other social and cultural problems, have contributed
to the frequent changes of government and to the
country's economic instability. However, South Vietnam continues to be a surplus producer of rice,
which other southeast Asian countries buy.

Other products of South Vietnam are tea, coffee,
rubber, coal, fish, lumber, pepper, cattle and hides,
corn, zinc, and tin. South Vietnam is considered to
have a lighter industrial potential than North Vietnam because most industrial complexes established

during the French colonial period were located in
the northern part of the State of Vietnam.

The piastre, the monetary unit of South Vietnam, is valued at U.S. $.015 in the foreign-exchange
market.

THAILAND

Thailand ("Free Nation," formerly known as
"Siam") is a constitutional monarchy that lies in
southeastern Asia, bordered by Burma, Cambodia, Laos,
and the Gulf of Thailand (which is part of the China
Sea). With a population of 25.5 million, it has an
area of 200,148 square miles. Its capital is Bangkok,
one of the busiest political, cultural, and commercial centers of southeast Asia. Of the total land
area, 12 per cent is devoted to rice culture, and 91
per cent of the population is engaged in agriculture.

Thailand is the only country in southeast Asia
that has never been subjugated by any foreign power.

On October 20, 1958, after successfully staging
a coup d'état, Field Marshal Srisdi Djanarajata suspended the 1952 Constitution and Assembly to combat
the inroads of Communist elements. On January 28,
1959, the King proclaimed an interim constitution
and appointed Field Marshal Djanarajata Prime Minister.

Rice, the staple food and chief export, accounts
for 50 per cent of Thailand's total foreign-exchange
earnings. Other major exports are tin, teak, and
tungsten. Also produced in quantity are coconut,
pepper, tobacco, cotton, jute, and tapioca flour.
Coal, iron, manganese, antimony, and mercury serve
to bring into the country much-needed foreign exchange.

The Thai currency is the baht, equivalent to
U.S. $0.04.

BIBLIOGRAPHY

BIBLIOGRAPHY

Books and Pamphlets

Alpert, Paul. Economic Development: Objectives and
Methods. New York: Free Press of Glencoe, 1963.
308 pp.

Bird, Richard, and Oldman, Oliver (eds.). Readings
on Taxation in Developing Countries. Baltimore:
The Johns Hopkins Press, 1964. 536 pp.

Burkhead, Jesse V. Government Budgeting. New York:
John Wiley and Sons, 1956. 498 pp.

Butters, J. Keith. "Taxation, Incentives, and Financial Capacity," Readings in Fiscal Policy, pp.
502-18. Vol. VII of The Series of Republished
Articles on Economics, edited by a Committee of
the American Economic Association. Homewood,
Illinois: Richard D. Irwin, 1955.

Cole, David. "Tax Exemption for New Investments in
Vietnam." Michigan State University Vietnam Advisory Group, 1960. (Mimeographed.)

Dalton, Hugh. Principles of Public Finance. 4th ed.
London: Routledge and Kegan Paul, 1954. 255 pp.

Davies, S. Gethyn (ed.). Central Banking in South
and East Asia. Aberdeen: Hongkong University
Press, 1960. 194 pp.

Due, John F. Government Finance: An Economic Analysis.
3rd ed. Homewood, Illinois: Richard D. Irwin,
1963. 627 pp.

Golay, Frank H. The Philippines: Public Policy and
National Economic Development. Ithaca, New
York: Cornell University Press, 1961. 455 pp.

Groves, Harold M. _Financing Government_. 4th ed.
New York: Henry Holt and Company, 1955. 618 pp.

Harvard Law School International Program in Taxation. _Taxation in Australia_. Boston: Little,
Brown and Company, 1958. 826 pp.

_____. _Taxation in the Federal Republic of Germany_.
Chicago: Commerce Clearing House, 1963. 932 pp.

_____. _Taxation in India_. Boston: Little, Brown
and Company, 1960. 555 pp.

_____. _Taxation in Sweden_. Boston: Little, Brown
and Company, 1959. 723 pp.

_____. _Taxation in the United Kingdom_. Boston:
Little, Brown and Company, 1957. 534 pp.

Heller, Jack, and Kauffman, K. M. _Tax Incentives
for Industry in Less Developed Countries_. Cambridge: Law School of Harvard University, 1963.
288 pp.

India Investment Center. _Investing in India_. New
Delhi: India Investment Center, 1962.

International Bank for Reconstruction and Development. _A Public Development Program for Thailand_.
Baltimore: Johns Hopkins Press, 1959. 301 pp.

International Chamber of Commerce. _Taxation and Developing Nations_. Paris: International Chamber
of Commerce, 1959.

Japan Tax Association. _Asian Taxation 1964_. Tokyo:
Japan Tax Association, 1965. 138 pp.

_____. _Asian Taxation 1965_. Tokyo: Japan Tax
Association, 1966. 148 pp.

_____. _Proceedings of the Special Meeting on Tax
System and Administration in Asian Countries,
April 8th to 16th, 1963_. Tokyo: Japan Tax
Association, 1964. 274 pp.

Kendrick, M. Slade. Public Finance: Principles and Problems. Boston: Houghton Mifflin Company, 1951. 708 pp.

Lutz, Harley L. "Tax Administration," Encyclopaedia of the Social Sciences, XIV, 526-28. New York: The Macmillan Company, 1935.

Maxwell, James. Tax Credits and Intergovernmental Fiscal Relations. Washington, D.C.: The Brookings Institution, 1962. 202 pp.

Nevin, Edward. Capital Funds in Underdeveloped Countries. London: The Macmillan Company, 1961. 111 pp.

Shultz, William J., and Harriss, C. Lowell. American Public Finance. 7th ed. Englewood Cliffs, New Jersey: Prentice-Hall, 1959. 631 pp.

Simons, Henry C. Personal Income Taxation. Chicago: The University of Chicago Press, 1938. 238 pp.

Sloan, Harold S., and Zurcher, John A. Dictionary of Economics. New York: Barnes and Noble, 1957. 356 pp.

Smith, Dan Throop. Federal Tax Reform. New York: McGraw-Hill Book Company, 1961. 328 pp.

_____, and Butters, J. Keith. Taxable and Business Income. New York: National Bureau of Economic Research, Inc., 1949. 342 pp.

Stourm, René. The Budget. Translated by Thaddeus Plazinski. New York: D. Appleton-Century, 1917.

Tax Changes Within Malaysia. Kuala Lumpur: Jabatan Chetak Kerajaan, 1964.

Taylor, Milton. Taxes of Vietnam. Michigan State University Vietnam Advisory Group, 1960.

Taylor, Philip E. The Economics of Public Finance.
    3rd ed. New York: The Macmillan Company, 1961.
    588 pp.

Periodical Articles

Abayasekara, H. E. R. "Plans to Boost Exports,"
    Far Eastern Economic Review, XL (April 11, 1963),
    61.

"Another Batch of Reforms," Far Eastern Economic Re-
    view, XL (June 6, 1963), 526.

Bank of Thailand Monthly Report. April, 1963.

Bok, Han Nae. "Can Korea Hold the Line?" Far East-
    ern Economic Review, XLI (September 19, 1963),
    737–42.

Cohen, Leo. "An Empirical Measurement of the Built-
    in Flexibility of the Individual Income Tax,"
    American Economic Review, XLIX (May, 1959).

"Economic Development and Planning," Economic Bulle-
    tin for Asia and the Far East, XIV (December,
    1963).

"The Economic Function of Credit Insurance," U.N.
    Trade Promotion News (March, 1956), 5–7.

"Foreign Trade Aspects of the Economic Development
    Plans of ECAFE Countries," Economic Bulletin
    for Asia and the Far East, XIV (June, 1963), 12.

Goode, Richard. "New System for Direct Taxation in
    Ceylon," National Tax Journal, XIII (December,
    1960), 374–85.

Gulati, I. S. "A Note on the Capital Gains Tax in
    India," Public Finance, XVIII (1963), 101–7.

"Indonesia's May 27 Reform," Far Eastern Economic
    Review, XL (June 13, 1963), 600-603.

Kauffman, Kenneth M.   "Income Tax Exemption and Eco-
    nomic Development," National Tax Journal, XIII
    (September, 1960), 263.

"Korea Invites Foreign Capital," Korean Report, II
    (March, 1962), 6-7.

Musgrave, R. A., and Tun Thin.   "Income Tax Progres-
    sion, 1929-1948," The Journal of Political
    Economy, LVI (December, 1948), 498-514.

"New Trade Measures in Indonesia," Far Eastern Eco-
    nomic Review, XXXV (November, 1960), 256-58.

"Problems of Industrialization in Relation to Eco-
    nomic Development in the Countries of Asia and
    the Far East," Economic Bulletin for Asia and
    the Far East, IX (December, 1958), 23-24.

"Relationship Between Agricultural and Industrial
    Development: A Case Study on Taiwan, China,
    1953-1960," Economic Bulletin for Asia and the
    Far East, XIV (June, 1963), 53.

Rothwell, Kenneth J.   "Taxes on Exports in Under-
    developed Countries," Public Finance, XVIII
    (September-December, 1963), 310-25.

"Six-Year Economic Development Plan," Thai Chamber
    of Commerce Journal, XIV (November, 1960), 79-80.

"State Trading by Underdeveloped Countries," Law and
    Contemporary Problems, XLV (Summer, 1959), 476.

Surrey, Stanley S.   "Tax Administration in Underde-
    veloped Countries," University of Miami Law
    Review, XII (Winter, 1958).

Takita, Kazuo.   "New Steps to Boost Exports," Far
    Eastern Economic Review, XL (June 6, 1963).

Thiem, Tan That.   "Economic Development in South
    Vietnam," The Malayan Economic Review, VI
    (April, 1961), 55-70.

Tran-Ngoc-Liem. "The Growth of Agricultural Credit and Cooperatives in Vietnam," (Speech . . . before the American Friends of Vietnam Conference, October 24, 1959). Reprinted in Commissariate General for Cooperatives and Agricultural Credit, 1960.

Trinidad, Ruben F. "National Income Accounts with Special Reference to the Philippines," Economic Research Journal (University of the East, Manila), VIII (June, 1961), 39.

U.N. Economic Survey of Asia and the Far East, 1961.

United Nations Finance Commission. "Special Features of Corporate Taxation in Underdeveloped Countries," Corporate Tax Problems (E/CN 8/66, Nov. 25, 1962), Chapter 6, 57-75. (Mimeographed.)

"World Tax Review," Bulletin for International Fiscal Documentation, XVIII (March, 1964), 113-15.

Yoingco, Angel Q. "Tax Commission: Its Role in Tax Policy Formulation," Economic Research Journal (University of the East, Manila), VIII (December, 1961), 139.

Government Publications

China (Republic). Income Tax Law of the Republic of China.

_____. Laws of the Republic of China. Taipei: October, 1962.

_____. Foreign Exchange and Trade Control Commission. Foreign Exchange and Trade Handbook, 1961. Taipei: Foreign Exchange and Trade Control Commission, 1961.

_____. Laws, Statutes, etc. Investment Laws of the Republic of China. September, 1960.

_____. Ministry of Economic Affairs. Industrial
    Planning and Coordination Group. The Industrial
    and Mining Program under Taiwan's Third Four-
    Year Plan. December, 1961. 150 pp.

Davis, Ray E. Progress Report on Accomplishments in
    1962 including Work Program for 1963 and Recom-
    mendations of Vietnam Directorate General of
    Taxation. Saigon: United States Operations
    Mission-AID.

India (Republic). Ministry of Finance. Report,
    1961-1962.

Japan Tax Bureau. An Outline of Japanese Tax 1963.
    Tokyo: Tax Bureau, Ministry of Finance, 1963.
    253 pp.

_____. An Outline of Japanese Taxes 1964. Tokyo:
    Tax Bureau, Ministry of Finance, 1965. 252 pp.

_____. An Outline of Japanese Taxes 1965. Tokyo:
    Tax Bureau, Ministry of Finance, 1966. 265 pp.

Korea (Republic). Bureau of Taxation. Yearbook of
    Tax Statistics, 1961.

_____. Economic Bureau. Trade and Investment Guide
    to Korea. Seoul: Ministry of Foreign Affairs,
    1963.

Korean Reconstruction Bank. A Guide to Investment
    in Korea--Basic Information for Foreign Busi-
    nessmen. Seoul: Korean Reconstruction Bank,
    1962.

Malaya. Income Tax Ordinance, 1947, Sec. 46.

_____. Department of Inland Revenue. Annual Report
    1961.

Philippines (Republic). Department of Finance. A
    Study on Establishing a Finance Academy. Manila:
    1964. v.p. (Mimeographed.)

_____. General Auditing Office. <u>Report of the Auditor General to the President and the Congress of the Philippines on Local Government and Provincial Hospitals for the Fiscal Year ended June 30, 1960</u>; 1961; 1962.

_____. Joint Legislative-Executive Tax Commission. <u>Annual Report</u>. Manila. Third, 1961; Fourth, 1962; Fifth, 1963.

_____. Joint Legislative-Executive Tax Commission. <u>Handbook on Philippine Taxes</u>. Manila: Joint Legislative-Executive Tax Commission, 1963. 39 pp.

_____. Joint Legislative-Executive Tax Commission. <u>A Study of Tax Burden by Income Class in the Philippines</u>. Manila: Joint Legislative-Executive Tax Commission, 1964. 122 pp.

_____. Joint Legislative-Executive Tax Commission. <u>A Survey of Tax Consciousness in the Philippines</u>. Manila: Joint Legislative-Executive Tax Commission, 1962. 74 pp.

_____. Laws, Statutes, etc. <u>National Internal Revenue Code, C.A. No. 466 as amended up to August 1963</u>. Manila: Bureau of Printing, 1964. 449 pp.

_____. Laws, Statutes, etc. <u>Tariff and Customs Code</u>. Manila: Bureau of Printing, 1957. 382 pp.

_____. President, 1961-65. Macapagal, Diosdado. <u>Five-Year Integrated Socio-Economic Program for the Philippines</u>. Manila: Bureau of Printing, 1962. v.p.

_____. Presidential Economic Staff. <u>Four-Year Economic Program for the Philippines, Fiscal Years 1967-1970</u>. Manila: 1966. vi, 77 pp.

Singapore. Estate Duty Office and Stamp Office. <u>Reports for the Year 1955-1956</u>. Singapore: Government Printing Office, 1957.

Thailand. Laws, Statutes, etc. <u>Promotion of Invest-</u>
<u>ment Industrial Act, B.E. 2505</u>. Bangkok: 1962.

_____. Revenue Department. <u>The Revenue Code</u>. Com-
piled and translated by Sanan Kettudat and Vid
Tantayakul. Bangkok: Revenue Department, 1961.

U.S. Department of Commerce. <u>Investment in Indo-</u>
<u>nesia, Basic Information for United States</u>
<u>Businessmen</u>. Washington, D.C.: Government
Printing Office, 1956.

ABOUT THE AUTHORS

Angel Q. Yoingco has been Executive Director of the Joint Legislative-Executive Tax Commission of the Philippines since 1960. Until 1964 he was Managing Editor of the Economic Research Journal, published by the University of the East, Manila. His research on budgeting, taxation, and economic development has appeared in leading professional journals in the Philippines and Japan. Mr. Yoingco has attended numerous international economic conferences as a delegate from the Philippines. He was an Associate Professor at the Graduate School of the University of the East and is now Professor of Economics at the Lyceum of the Philippines.

Ruben F. Trinidad is Chief of the Research and Statistics Branch of the Joint Legislative-Executive Tax Commission of the Philippines. Before joining the Tax Commission, he was a statistician with the National Economic Council of the Philippines. In 1963 he served as Assistant to the Philippine Representative to a special meeting on taxation of thirteen Asian countries sponsored by the Japan Tax Association. He is an Associate Professor in the Graduate Schools of the University of the East and Far Eastern University.